Lecture Notes in Computer Science 12341

More information about this series at http://www.springer.com/series/7409

Yuhua Luo (Ed.)

Cooperative Design, Visualization, and Engineering

17th International Conference, CDVE 2020
Bangkok, Thailand, October 25–28, 2020
Proceedings

 Springer

Editor
Yuhua Luo (iD)
University of the Balearic Islands
Palma, Mallorca, Spain

ISSN 0302-9743   ISSN 1611-3349 (electronic)
Lecture Notes in Computer Science
ISBN 978-3-030-60815-6   ISBN 978-3-030-60816-3 (eBook)
https://doi.org/10.1007/978-3-030-60816-3

LNCS Sublibrary: SL3 – Information Systems and Applications, incl. Internet/Web, and HCI

This Springer imprint is published by the registered company Springer Nature Switzerland AG
The registered company address is: Gewerbestrasse 11, 6330 Cham, Switzerland

Preface

This year, the 17th International Conference on Cooperative Design, Visualization and Engineering (CDVE 2020), which was planned to take place in Bangkok, Thailand, during October 25–28, was held virtually and online due to the unprecedented COVID-19 pandemic. It was a fresh experience for the conference organizers and the participants. The papers presented in this proceedings book is a collection of the accepted papers for CDVE 2020.

From the papers of this volume, we can see new concepts, new applications, new angles of view in the development of cooperative design, visualization, and engineering technology. The papers cover a very broad range of application areas. The areas involved are health care, industrial design, banking IT systems, cultural activities support, operational maritime cybersecurity assurance, emotion communication, and social network data analytics, etc.

Among applying the CDVE technology to the new applications, a paper describes the ongoing work of a Finnish national project to increase the maritime cybersecurity. Small and medium sized ports for cargo traffic are in a highly real-time cooperative environment. Security awareness and visualizing operational cybersecurity situations for them involve a great variety of devices in completely different networks. The system being developed can help the users to identify perceived threats and risks to port assets and provide collaborative responses to emerging cybersecurity attacks.

Another active area is health care. A paper reports the development of a collaborative home-based patient-therapist system for stroke patient rehabilitation. The prototype system is designed for home-based rehabilitation exercises matched with the status of the patient. Direct communication is provided to allow the physicians to be better informed for timely clinical decisions based on the progress of the patient.

From the papers about cooperative applications, we can see that the researchers are raising the cooperative design to a higher level. Not only manual cooperative design is supported, but the automation of the cooperative design is under development. An automated toolkit for aerospace power controllers is being developed to generate correct-by-design flight hardware from high-level requirements with a minimum of manual engineering effort.

In the area of cooperative support system for enterprises, such as banking IT applications, big data processing and analytics can play an important role in boosting the business. The work reported in a paper shows that clustering the bank customers and predicting their behavior can help marketing decision making, forecasting the customer deposits in the near future, etc.

We notice that there are a couple of new concepts being studied in this volume. For example, the concept of a "service internet system" is described in a paper as a complex, networked, and comprehensive service system, formed by a large number of service units in different networks through a highly cooperative relationship. The paper tries to form an overall evolution model for these kinds of systems based on their similarity to the natural ecosystem. They perform some theoretical analysis of its life cycle and evolution path, similar to a new species entering the ecosystem. The authors use real-world electronic technology industry cluster data to verify the proposed model, which seems to better reflect and predict the evolution trend of the service internet system.

To view and solve traditional problems with new angle of view is an inspiration for new technology development. In the cloud storage optimization, particularly for big data storage optimization, a paper treats the topic using a fuzzy logic view for tiering the storage to be different categories. From the view angle of fuzzy logic and automatic machine learning, the paper shows a new appearance of the cloud data storage problem which seems to be easier to deal with.

In this special and difficult time of a pandemic in the human history, our authors showed their persistent effort in research and development in our field. I am honored to have the opportunity to express my sincere thanks to all the authors for submitting their papers to the CDVE 2020 conference. I would also like to thank all our volunteer reviewers, Program Committee members, and Organization Committee members for their contribution. The success of this year's conference would not have been possible without their support.

October 2020   Yuhua Luo

Organization

Conference Chair

Yuhua Luo   University of Balearic Islands, Spain

International Program Committee

Program Chair

Thomas Tamisier   Luxembourg Institute of Science and Technology
                                   (LIST), Luxembourg

Members

Conrad Boton   Université du Québec, Canada
Jose Alfredo Costa   Federal University of Rio Grande do Norte, Brazil
Philipp M. Fischer   German Aerospace Center, Germany
Sebastia Galmes   University of Balearic Islands, Spain
Halin Gilles   School of Architecture of Nancy, France
Figen Gül   Istanbul Technical University, Turkey
Shuangxi Huang   Tsinghua University, China
Tony Huang   University of Technology Sydney, Australia
Claudia-Lavinia Ignat   INRIA, France
Ursula Kirschner   Leuphana University of Lüneburg, Germany
Jean-Christophe Lapayre   Centre National de la Recherche Scientifique, France
Pierre Leclercq   University of Liege, Belgium
Jang Ho Lee   Hongik University, South Korea
Jaime Lloret   Polytechnic University of Valencia, Spain
Kwan-Liu Ma   University of California, Davis, USA
Manuel Ortega   University of Castilla-La Mancha, Spain
Juan Carlos Preciado   University of Extremadura, Spain
Niko Salonen   Rolls-Royce Oy Ab, Finland
Chengzheng Sun   Nanyang Technological University, Singapore
Nobuyoshi Yabuki   Osaka University, Japan
Xinwei Yao   Zhejian University of Technology, China

Organization Committee

Chair

Chakkrit Snae Namahoot   Naresuan University, Thailand

Co-chair

Sebastia Galmes   University of Balearic Islands, Spain

Members

Michael Brückner	Naresuan University, Thailand
Kanokkarn Snae Namahoot	Naresuan University, Thailand
Sanya Khruahong	Naresuan University, Thailand
Chayan Nuntawong	Nakhon Sawan Rajabhat University, Thailand
Kitkawin Aramrun	Division Office of Atoms for Peace, Thailand
Sakesan Sivilai	Pibulsongkram Rajabhat University, Thailand
Naruepon Panawong	Nakhon Sawan Rajabhat University, Thailand
Takayuki Fujimoto	Toyo University, Japan
Alex Garcia	University of Balaric Islands, Spain
Guofeng Qin	Tongji University, China
Linan Zhu	Zhejiang University of Technology, China

Reviewers

Conrad Boton
Bryden Cho
Jose Alfredo Costa
Hongfei Fan
Philipp M. Fischer
Takayuki Fujimoto
Pilar Fuster-Parra
Sebastia Galmes
Halin Gilles
Figen Gül
Shuangxi Huang
Tony Huang
Claudia-Lavinia Ignat
Alexandre Kabil

Maksym Kholiavchenko
Ursula Kirschner
Manoj Kumar Patra
Paweł Kwiatoń
Jean-Christophe Lapayre
Pierre Leclercq
Jang Ho Lee
Jaime Lloret
Manuel Ortega
Juan Carlos Preciado
Niko Salonen
Chengzheng Sun
Thomas Tamisier
Nobuyoshi Yabuki

Contents

A Home-Based Adaptive Collaborative System for Stroke Patient Rehabilitation

Paul Craig[1]([⊠]), Yanhao Jin[1], and Jie Sun[2]

[1] School of Advanced Technology, Xi'an Jiaotong Liverpool University,
Suzhou, China
p.craig@xjtlu.edu.cn

[2] Department of Industrial Design, Xi'an Jiaotong Liverpool University,
Suzhou, China
jie.sun@xjtlu.edu.cn

Abstract. This paper describes research into the development of a collaborative home-based patient-therapist system for stroke patient rehabilitation. Our prototype system is designed so that home-based rehabilitation exercises are interactive and adapt to the progress of the patient. This way patients are encouraged to do the exercises most appropriate for their stage in the recovery process and can make the most of the time spent working on their rehabilitation. The system also keeps a record of patient progress that is communicated to the patient and medical professionals via mobile or personal-computer interfaces so they can work together towards a more effective overall plan for rehabilitation. This allows the physician to be better informed to make clinical decisions based on the progress of the patient. Results of early evaluations demonstrate the utility of our prototype system to provide users with a stimulating interactive experience as well as the systems potential to support medical experts to make more informed decisions relating to patient treatment. Results also indicate that patients feel more involved in their rehabilitation and that general communication between the medical experts and patients is improved.

Keywords: Human-computer interaction · Healthcare · Stroke rehabilitation

1 Introduction

Strokes are a leading cause of serious long term disability that affect approximately three percent of the global adult population during the course of their lifetime. The effects of a stroke are major debilitation of the sufferers cognitive and physical capabilities which can have a catastrophic effect quality of life [17].

Stroke victims can however recover through effectively administered programmes of rehabilitation. These have the potential to help most stroke patients to regain all, or at least some, of their pre-stroke cognitive and physical abilities. With proper treatment, 10 percent of people who have a stroke will recover

© Springer Nature Switzerland AG 2020
Y. Luo (Ed.): CDVE 2020, LNCS 12341, pp. 1–10, 2020.
https://doi.org/10.1007/978-3-030-60816-3_1

almost completely and 25% recover with just some minor impairments [1]. These programmes of rehabilitation can however be expensive and inconvenient for patients who have to attend regular appointments at a medical facility before they can be fully recovered. Hence, this project looks at how more of the patient's rehabilitation can be done in a home-environment using a stroke exercise system that adapts to the patients progress and records data to be shared with medical experts at a remote location.

In most cases, the recovery and rehabilitation of stroke patients can be accelerated with the aid of task-based exercises to improve manual dexterity. These are initially prescribed in a medical institution under the supervision of a qualified therapist and continued at home by the patient using simple mechanical devices. The problem is that the exercises can become tedious for the patient and medical professionals have limited capacity to track the patients progress or their engagement with the programme of treatment. Specialised apparatus used in the hospital is designed to be more stimulating and can be used to provide a snapshot of the patients abilities at any given time [3,4]. However, for many patients, regular visits to the hospital are not practical or convenient. Moreover, medical professionals feel that they would benefit from a more continuous record of the patient's progress while providing the patient with more stimulating rehabilitation apparatus that can be used in the patient's own home environment.

The motivation of the research presented in this paper is to look at how we can design an effective system that improves the quality of stroke rehabilitation exercises using interfaces that facilitate better patient-therapist collaboration. This focuses on the development of an intelligent interface with real-time monitoring for customized healthcare for stroke patients at home.

2   Related Work

Over the past decade research into systems to support stroke patient recovery has largely focused on systems that monitor daily activities rather than rehabilitation exercises. For example, Escuderdo et al. [6] look at different dimensions for home-based stroke rehabilitation. Other research has focused on hospital based monitoring systems including the application of sensor-based restoration via robotic assistance [3], and a real-time clinical dashboard and health-data retrieval to evaluate the quality of collaboration between patients and caregivers [2,5,7,15].

mHealth [7] is an example of a web-based collaborative system that supports rehabilitation. This is a project for the home-based healthcare of chronic diseases survivors, which includes an innovative model for cooperation between patients and caregivers. Patients can update their health status on a mobile app with data shared using a cloud server. The mHealth app can also be used to provide medical advice to the patient. A limitation of this type of system is that self-reporting can be a burden on the patient and they do not always feel inclined or have the ability to accurately report their condition.

Home Rehab Master [2] is a virtual interaction based system for home rehabilitation. To use the system patients wear a measuring device and a posture sensor which record information related to the patients mobility. Operation then involves a training stage and an assessment stage. In the training stage the patient is asked to perform different activities that exercise their arms and hands. These include a fishing game, a parkour game and virtual walks in the countryside. In the assessment stage, the system applies the Fugl-Meyer model [8,9] to evaluate the quality of the patient's activity.

Virtual activities, such as those used in the Home Rehab Master system and other similar systems [12], are shown to encourage patients' motivation to do recovery exercise [2]. Data recording and analysis can also effectively evaluate the patient's recovery progress [2]. However, these types of system are limited in that the style of interaction is based on virtual interaction rather than real actions. Patients engaged in virtual activities need to focus on a TV screen which may not feel natural for groups such as elderly people. Indeed nearly half of elderly people state that they would be hesitant about engaging in such virtual activities [11]. Moreover, there is no resistance from contact with solid objects and this type of tactile feedback is seen as particularly important for rehab exercises [13,14]. Hence there is a need for systems with proper tactile feedback (similar to the mechanical devices used in traditional rehab exercises) that can also be used to record activity data and feed this back to medical professionals.

3   System Design

In order to investigate the feasibility effective home-based patient-therapist collaborative for stroke patient rehabilitation, we developed our own system which accommodates three principal stages of user activity. These are the tabletop arm exercise stage which uses a tangible embedded device, the performance evaluation which employs an algorithm based on the a Fugl-Meyer scale [8,9], and the representation stage which relies on our web-based and mobile user interfaces.

We also identified two principal user groups for our system. These are patients who have suffered from a stroke and need to do rehabilitation exercises at home, and therapists who provide care. The former group of individuals use the tangible embedded device to develop their upper limb exercise and undergo rehabilitation with the support of the interface. The latter group use the dashboard to monitor the patient's motor ability and the status of recovery. This can be done remotely or with the user in a rehab center.

To further facilitate home-based rehabilitation, the system also supports an assessment stage and a customization stage. The performance of exercise can be evaluated via an algorithm implementing Fugl-Meyer specific action assessment scheme [8] and the parameters of the exercise are adjusted accordingly.

The healthcare data of the patient can also be shared with therapists via a cloud server. Here, the dashboard can represent and visualize motion data of the patient's upper limb together with some analysis and assessment results. To further encourage the patient and give them some control over the process of exercise we also provide them with a WeChat Mini Program whereby they can view their progress together with the therapists recommendations. This aims to motivate patients by giving them more of a sense of involvement with their rehabilitation.

3.1 Tabletop Arm Reaching Exercise Tool

In the course of post-stroke rehabilitation therapy reaching exercises are important to prevent muscle contraction and re-stimulate nerves [18]. These require patients to glide a wooden or plastic reaching tool to target point (see Fig. 1a). With conventional therapy patients need to repeat the exercise with a series of instructions given by caregivers. In our system a tangible interactive interface replaces the conventional reaching tool.

Our new interactive tool is constructed using a Raspberry Pi, an RGB colour sensor, a speaker and an LED light strip. The Raspberry Pi serves as the central controller in the tangible embedded device. It controls the process of training, and collects and pre-processes the data. The LED strip and speaker provide visual and audio instruction and feedback for patients during the exercise. The RGB sensor and MPU6050 Six-Axis Gyroscope and accelerometer gather motion information from the patient's upper limb (Fig. 1b). A motion map is generated using a piano keyboard printed mat which has one initial point and four different target points with different colours and associated musical notes. The primary mechanism of interaction is that patients move towards the target with the specific colour area on the map when the light changes according to a random generated colour pattern with the speaker playing the corresponding musical note (Fig. 1c). The RGB sensor detects the colour directly below the device and senses when the device reaches the correct point on the mat for each step of the exercise to be completed.

In addition, there are three different modes of upper limb reaching exercise designed for patients. These are tutorial Mode, single exercise mode and composite exercise mode. The exercise in tutorial mode can teach patient how to use the device to conduct the tabletop upper limb reaching training. To start with, a patient should hold the handle of exercise device and place the device at the starting point. When LED light in the handle turns on with random colour and corresponding musical note, the patient is expected to glide the device towards the correct spot on the map (Fig. 1d). Once an individual reaches the target spot, which means that RGB sensor is detecting the correct colour, the light turns white to indicate that it is time to move back to the starting point. Otherwise, if the device detects any other colour (which means the device is over the wrong spot), the speaker attached to device gives an appropriate instruction for the user to correct their action. The single exercise mode is the same as tutorial mode except that patients have control over the number of movements. The composite exercise mode is more difficult than single mode and tests the user's memory as well as their motor skills. Here the led and speaker play a sequence of musical notes with their corresponding colours and the user is expected to remember and repeat the previous sequence in the same order.

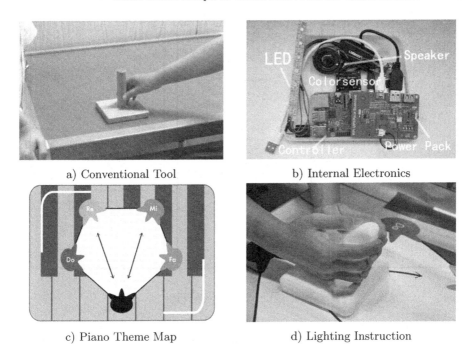

a) Conventional Tool   b) Internal Electronics

c) Piano Theme Map   d) Lighting Instruction

Fig. 1. Tabletop arm reaching exercises

3.2 Performance Assessment and Training Customization

In the conventional home-based rehabilitation exercise, the stroke patients' training cannot be observed and it may lead the exercise to be ineffective. In order to remedy this, a performance assessment method and training customization algorithm are used to evaluate the patients progress and adjust the difficulty of the games accordingly. In order to adapt the difficulty of the tasks to the users progress, first, data generated from the patient's movement is preprocessed to characterise their ability. Data preprocessing also involves recording, saving and uploading the data to a server. According to previous researchers' work, a general motor ability index is given for quantifying the patient's motor ability in executing the assigned motor task without assistance [4]. The parameters used in the performance assessment are the speed of patient's upper limb movement, the speed of their reaction to visual instructions, the patient's reaching distance (i.e. the distance that a patient's upper limb moves for each exercise and the movement accuracy which is the rate at which patients can reach correct points without error.

   These parameter values are saved to the memory of the Raspberry Pi and uploaded to a remote server. As it is essential to ensure the security of data and the privacy of the patient, the data is scrambled with a private key before transmission and unscrambled at the sever after it is uploaded. The process of evaluating the patients progress is to read the data, compare the data with scale data, calculate each index, then calculate the patient's score based on the index.

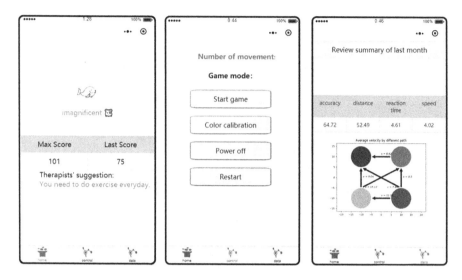

Fig. 2. Patient mobile app

In the process of stroke patients' rehabilitation, customisation and adaptation are an essential aspect that can serve to remedy a patient's own individual motor weaknesses. This means the state of the system changes to suit the patient as the patient's rehabilitation progresses [3]. These changes are based on the data generated by the user themselves so that, for example, when the user becomes more capable exercise become harder or if the patient relapses they become a little easier.

The method of customization we use is based on statistical analysis of the data generated. The program of customization is called after each sixty exercise sessions to read the data and apply the algorithm. The data is then classified by different motions on the map. As a result, if a patient shows weaker motor ability in one path, such as the slow speed of movement and low recognition rate, the algorithm will give individual more chance to exercise in this path. Finally, the device will adjust the strategy of exercise according to recent results. This process of customization is to read the data, calculate the mean value, sort the path by average, then adjust the difficulty based on the output value.

Patients can also use a mobile app to interact with the exercise device. This is operated using a WeChat [19] mobile app. The main functions of our system are divided into three principle components that are mapped onto the three default wechat app tabs in the patients' mobile app. These allow the user to review a summary of activities, start the exercise and check the results of an exercise (see Fig. 2).

Therapists can also use a PC control-panel type interface to monitor and guide the process of patient rehabilitation and send suggestions on how to modify their exercises to the patient. The main functions of the PC interface are to allow the therapists to review the patient's information, explore the exercise data and send feedback and advice to the patient (see Fig. 3).

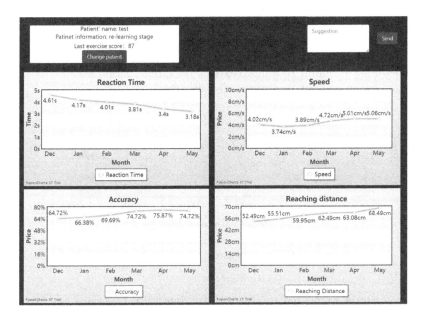

Fig. 3. Therapist web app

4 System Evaluation

The objective of our pilot user testing is to discover if the system can satisfy our patients' and therapists' requirements and be effective in a real-world environment. User testing was conducted in 2 medical centers with ten patients in the senior relearning motor rehabilitation stage.

Our test group for evaluation comprised of eight males and two females between 50 and 70 years old. Firstly, patients were encouraged to try and use the exercise device with instructions and little assistance. Patients and patients' families were then allowed to operate the mobile app on the smartphone to check the summary of performance related to the previous exercise. This session was also supervised by professional therapists who evaluated the patients' motor ability. The main positive result of our evaluation was that in the process of user testing, most patients could use the device to do upper limb reaching exercise successfully without assistance.

4.1 Questionnaire

The experience of rehabilitation is known to have strong positive effect on both rehabilitation and the confidence of patients [10]. In order to gauge the effect of our system, its impact on patients and therapists was evaluated according to the following criteria.

1. Ease of understanding and operation
2. Increased interest in rehabilitation
3. Improvement in upper limb movement
4. Willingness to commit to a more extended exercise period
5. Willingness to commit to more regular exercise

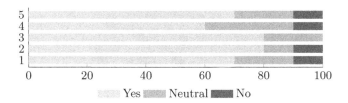

Fig. 4. Result of patients' questionnaire

These criteria were used to generate the interview questions and patients' interview responses at the medical centers to evaluate the system. From the results of this questionnaire (see Fig. 4), we can see that most patients believe the product can better facilitate their rehabilitation. In particular, almost all of the patients considered that the tangible embedded device with various modes of exercise and visual or audio feedback could increase their interest in rehabilitation exercises.

A second set of interviews were conducted at the medical centers to gauge the therapists' satisfaction with the design of rehabilitation system. The questions used in this set of interviews are listed below with the results shown in Fig. 5.

1. Does the system effectively support multi-user application?
2. Does the system record rehabilitation session?
3. Does it adapt appropriately patients' rehabilitation progress?
4. Is the system motivate the patients to do exercise?
5. Can the system be adequately customized for home rehabilitation?
6. Is the variety of games sufficient?

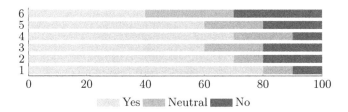

Fig. 5. Result of therapists' questionnaire

From the results of our second set of interviews, we can see most of therapists were convinced that the product could effectively facilitate the rehabilitation of their patients. The majority of therapists also considered that the information generated by the system was helpful. They did however also consider that the system would benefit from including more data and, specifically, data related to muscle tissue activity such as EMG data.

5 Conclusion and Future Work

The intelligent interface for stroke patients is a computer-based system which facilitates collaboration between patients and therapists to support home-based post-stroke rehabilitation. The interface uses an interactive tool for tabletop arm reaching exercises. The tool also adapts to the users progress and allows therapists to gain an insight into the user's progress so they can adjust the rehabilitation programme accordingly.

Hospital pilot trial results show that the system may increase patients' motivation in engaging upper limb exercise. Therapists also consider that the tool can help them to make a decision for patients' recovery and improve the quality of feedback provided to the patient. Both these types of users consider it is easy to interact with the personal-computer and mobile interfaces to access the information they need to work together towards the recovery of the patient.

For future work, we plan to improve the design of prototype to enrich the game experience to further motivate patients and improve the physical interface so it can incorporate a greater range of exercises [16]. This research will focus on how to integrate several different types of exercise into one universal system or framework. We also plan to continue long-term user testing and focus on finding out how patients use this type of system in their home environment so we decide on better ways to integrate rehabilitation exercises into the patient's daily routine.

Acknowledgments. The authors are thankful for the support provided by the therapists and patients in the branch of rehabilitation in Suzhou BenQ Medical Center and the First Affiliated Hospital of Soochow University for participating in the user testing stage and evaluation of this project. This work is supported by XJTLU Key Program Special Fund KSF-E-10 and Research Development Fund RDF-14-03-22.

References

1. Adamson, J., Beswick, A., Ebrahim, S.: Is stroke the most common cause of disability? J. Stroke Cerebrovasc. Dis. **13**(4), 171–177 (2004)
2. Bai, J., Song, A.: Development of a novel home based multi-scene upper limb rehabilitation training and evaluation system for post-stroke patients. IEEE Access **7**, 9667–9677 (2019)
3. Caimmi, M., Malosio, M., Pedrocchi, N., Vicentini, F., Tosatti, L.M., Molteni, F., et al.: Upper limb robotic rehabilitation: Treatment customization. Gait Posture **37**, S13–S14 (2013)

4. Colombo, R., et al.: Robotic techniques for upper limb evaluation and rehabilitation of stroke patients. IEEE Trans. Neural Syst. Rehabil. Eng. **13**(3), 311–324 (2005)
5. De Capua, C., Meduri, A., Morello, R.: A smart ECG measurement system based on web-service-oriented architecture for telemedicine applications. IEEE Trans. Instrum. Meas. **59**(10), 2530–2538 (2010)
6. Escudero, D.A., Marqués, L.A., Taboada, F.C.: Up-date in spontaneous cerebral hemorrhage. Med. Intensiva **32**(6), 282–295 (2008)
7. Estrin, D., Sim, I.: Open mHealth architecture: an engine for health care innovation. Science **330**(6005), 759–760 (2010)
8. Fugl-Meyer, A.R., Jääskö, L., Leyman, I., Olsson, S., Steglind, S.: The post-stroke hemiplegic patient. 1. a method for evaluation of physical performance. Scand. J. Rehabil. Med. **7**(1), 13–31 (1975)
9. Gladstone, D.J., Danells, C.J., Black, S.E.: The fugl-meyer assessment of motor recovery after stroke: a critical review of its measurement properties. Neurorehabilitation Neural Repair **16**(3), 232–240 (2002)
10. Hecimovich, M.D., Volet, S.E.: Importance of building confidence in patient communication and clinical skills among chiropractic students. J. Chiropractic Educ. **23**(2), 151–164 (2009)
11. Huygelier, H., Schraepen, B., van Ee, R., Abeele, V.V., Gillebert, C.R.: Acceptance of immersive head-mounted virtual reality in older adults. Sci. Rep. **9**(1), 4519 (2019)
12. Kang, Y.J., et al.: Development and clinical trial of virtual reality-based cognitive assessment in people with stroke: preliminary study. CyberPsychology Behav. **11**(3), 329–339 (2008)
13. Party, I.S.W., et al.: National Clinical Guideline for Stroke, vol. 20083. Citeseer, Princeton (2012)
14. Prevention, S.: Guidelines for medical treatment for stroke prevention. Ann. Intern. Med. **121**, 54–55 (1994)
15. Ruiz-Zafra, A., Noguera, M., Benghazi, K., Ochoa, S.F.: A cloud collaborative approach for managing patients wellness. In: 2015 IEEE 19th International Conference on Computer Supported Cooperative Work in Design (CSCWD), pp. 637–642. IEEE (2015)
16. Saunders, D.H., Greig, C.A., Mead, G.E.: Physical activity and exercise after stroke: review of multiple meaningful benefits. Stroke **45**(12), 3742–3747 (2014)
17. Suzman, R., Beard, J.: Global health and aging. NIH Publ. **1**(4), 273–277 (2011)
18. Thrasher, T.A., Zivanovic, V., McIlroy, W., Popovic, M.R.: Rehabilitation of reaching and grasping function in severe hemiplegic patients using functional electrical stimulation therapy. Neurorehabilitation Neural Repair **22**(6), 706–714 (2008)
19. Wu, J.: How WeChat, the most popular social network in china, cultivates wellbeing (2014)

User Comfort Achievement by Fuzzy Preferences Through an Emotion Communication System

Pilar Fuster-Parra[1,2]([✉]) [iD] and Sebastià Galmés[1,2] [iD]

[1] Universitat de les Illes Balears, Cra. de Valldemossa km. 7.5,
07122 Palma de Mallorca, Spain
{pilar.fuster,sebastia.galmes}@uib.es
[2] Institut d' Investigació Sanitària de les Illes Balears (IdISBa), Hospital Son
Espases, 07120 Palma de Mallorca, Spain

Abstract. An emotion communication system based on linearly ordered fuzzy preferences is proposed, whose objective is to determine the appropriate actions on the environment in order to enhance user comfort. Once a subset of elementary preferences is obtained via basic human-machine interactions, the rest of preference relations are determined in such a way that the consistency of the system is guaranteed. For this purpose, the Łukasiewicz t-conorm is applied as a rule for aggregation.

Keywords: Emotion communication · Decision making · Human-robot interaction · Fuzzy preference relations

1 Introduction

Several research results based on emotion communication systems have appeared in the last years [5, 11] with the objective of avoiding the limitation of traditional human machine interaction (HMI) systems. As a result, there is currently a wide variety of methods and technology for human emotion identification and human robot interaction [12]. However, emotion identification entails a high computational overhead, so that robots rely on the cloud platform, which inputs user data for emotion analysis and outputs emotions.

In our approach, an emotion communication system is used in order to achieve user comfort. As the process requires some decision making technique to take the appropriated action until user's comfort state is reached, the use of a type of binary relation, the fuzzy preference relation [1,3], is chosen because it represents the user preference in a natural way; fuzzy preference relations are among the most commonly used preference models in decision making. Of course, the set of preference relations is determined in such a way that the preferences guarantee the consistency of the system [1, 2, 4, 6, 13, 14].

The rest of the paper is organized as follows. In Sect. 2, the concept of preference relation is revised, as it is the basis of the proposed approach. In Sect. 3, the

© Springer Nature Switzerland AG 2020
Y. Luo (Ed.): CDVE 2020, LNCS 12341, pp. 11–18, 2020.
https://doi.org/10.1007/978-3-030-60816-3_2

emotion communication system under consideration is described and the problem to be solved is formulated. In Sect. 4, an application example is presented via the notion of fuzzy preferences. Finally, Sect. 5 concludes the paper and exposes pending research activity.

2   Preference Relations

In decision making under uncertainty, the construction of appropriate models to represent the preferences of decision makers is frequently adopted. Among the most prominent existing methodologies concerning multicriteria decision making, it could be notably mentioned AHP (Analytic Hierarchy Process) developed by Saaty in the 1970s (see [14], and MACBETH (Measuring Attractiveness by a Categorical Based Evaluation Technique) (see [7]).

Let us recall that a binary relation R on a given set S is a subset of the cartesian product $S \times S$. If (s_1, s_2) belongs to R, then both the notations $(s_1, s_2) \in R$ or $s_1 R s_2$ are used indifferently. The binary relation R on S can also be defined as a function $R : S \times S \rightarrow \{0, 1\}$.

A preference relation P is a binary relation P on a set of alternatives S (xPy means x is preferred to y, and $yP^c x$ means y is not preferred to x), $P \subset S \times S$, which is a strict weak order if and only if the following conditions hold for all $x, y, z \in S$ [1]: 1) xPy implies $yP^c x$ (asymmetry), 2) xPy and yPz imply xPz (transitivity), 3) xPy and any $z \in A$ imply xPz or zPy (negative transitivity).

On the other hand, the indifference relation I is a binary relation I on a set of alternatives S (xIy means x is indifferent to y, i.e., $xP^c y$ and $yP^c x$), I is an equivalence relation: 1) I is reflexive (xIx), 2) symmetric (xIy and yIx) and 3) transitive xIy and yIz imply xIz.

Associated to P there is a linearly ordered partition of S: $(S/I, >)$, such that given $S_i = [s_i], S_j = [s_j] \in S/I$ then $[s_i] > [s_j]$ if and only if $s_i P s_j$. In S/I there is a complete order: $S_1 > S_2 > \ldots > S_n$, with $n \leq k$, i.e, a ranking between classes of alternatives from the best to the worst.

In [1], it is proved that there exists a bijection between the set of strict weak orders on S and the set of linearly ordered partitions (or rankings) of S.

The degree of preference between consecutive clases of alternatives is adequately represented by means of the preference relation.

Definition 1. *A preference relation P on a set of classes of alternatives S/I is characterized by a function $\mu_P : S/I \times S/I \rightarrow D$, where D denotes the domain of representation of preference degrees.*

The preference relation may be conveniently represented by an $n \times n$ matrix $P = (p_{ij})$ (also called matrix of preferences), where $p_{ij} = \mu_P(S_i, S_j) \quad \forall i, j \in \{1, \ldots, n\}$, which is interpreted as the preference degree or intensity of the class of alternatives S_i over the class of alternatives S_j measured as a value in D.

In this work the methodology adopted to obtain the preference degrees consists of building differences of attractiveness from the ones for consecutive classes of indifferent alternatives by using either smooth t-conorms as aggregator [1] or other more general aggregation functions considered in [3]. Therefore, only these differences of attractiveness between consecutive classes (S_i and S_{i+1} for instance) are required, since the whole set of differences of attractiveness is automatically obtained from them, i.e. only p_{ii+1} are required, which are also called *elementary preferences* [3]. In case the class S_i is preferred to class S_j then $p_{ij} > 0$.

3   Emotion Communication System

An emotional communication system [5] is understood as a cognitive system that collects human's emotion data, understands human emotions and achieves emotion interaction. Here, emotion is conceived as a kind of information that is similar to multimedia, which means that emotions can be elaborated, produced, stored, shared and transmitted. A representation of an emotion communication system is given in Fig. 1.

The specific emotional communication system has to be able to carry out the following tasks:

- Collect the data that can express emotion.
- Establish communication between the different components, that is, user and robot, robot and cloud, cloud feedback to robot and robot feedback to user.
- Cloud analytics, where data is treated in order to obtain a model of user emotions.
- Emotional feedback for the robot to execute some action to improve current user comfort.

Data may be collected through different emotion recognition methods. In this case we assume a HMI system based on audio or visual information through machine learning algorithms, and/or on physiological signals like body temperature, heart rate, blood pressure, etc. In order to achieve a model of emotion analysis, some technique of decision making has to be considered in order to select the appropriate actions towards user comfort improvement. In this sense, the use of fuzzy preferences is adopted [1,3,4,6,8].

Looking for maximum user comfort [11], let us consider $V = \{v_1, v_2, \ldots, v_m\}$ the set of variables that determine user comfort, and $L_i = \{l_{i_1}, l_{i_2}, \ldots, l_{i_q}\}$ for $i = 1, \ldots, m$, the set of possible levels for these variables. The set of all possible states $S = \{s_1, \ldots, s_k\}$ constitutes a set of alternatives for the user, where each s_i is an ordered m-tupla representing the label value of each variable.

In this set we consider the binary relations P of preference and I of indifference in such a way that $s_i P s_j$ if and only if the decision maker through the *Emotion Communication System* prefers s_i to s_j, whereas $s_i I s_j$ if and only if $s_i P^c s_j$ and $s_j P^c s_i$ (I is then an equivalency relation).

In order to establish preferences between different states, usually a questioning procedure is adopted [2,13,14], which has to be implemented through emotion communication by the *Emotion Communication System*. Associated to P there is a linearly ordered partition of S, $(S/I, >)$, such that, given $S_i = [s_i], S_j = [s_j] \in S/I$, then $[s_i] > [s_j]$ if and only if $s_i P s_j$. In S/I there is a complete order: $S_1 > S_2 > \ldots > S_n$, with $n \leq k$.

Let us consider E the set of possible emotions. Each class state has an associated emotion, in such a way that there is a bijection between the set of emotions E and S/I, i.e., there exists $f : S/I \to E$. For simplicity, with no loss of generality, we can assume $f(S_i) = E_i$ for all $i = 1, \ldots, n$.

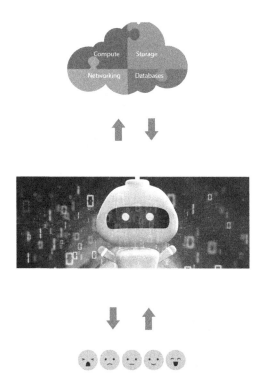

Fig. 1. Architecture of an emotion communication system.

The complete order between classes of states $S_1 > S_2 > \ldots > S_n$ has associated degrees of preferences between consecutive classes, which can be obtained through the use of machine learning algorithms [9,10]. These elementary preferences can then be used to obtain the whole set of preferences by appropriate aggregation functions as pointed out in [1,3]. The result is a matrix of preferences:

$$\hat{P} = \begin{array}{cc} & \begin{array}{cccccc} E_1 & E_2 & E_3 & \cdots & & E_n \\ S_1 & S_2 & S_3 & \cdots & & S_n \end{array} \\ \begin{array}{cc} E_1 & S_1 \\ E_2 & S_2 \\ \vdots & \vdots \\ E_{n-1} & S_{n-} \\ E_n & S_n \end{array} & \left(\begin{array}{cccccc} 0 & p_{12} & p_{13} & \cdots & & p_{1n} \\ 0 & 0 & p_{23} & \cdots & & p_{2n} \\ \vdots & \vdots & \vdots & \cdots & & \vdots \\ 0 & 0 & 0 & \cdots & p_{(n-1)n} \\ 0 & 0 & 0 & \cdots & & 0 \end{array} \right) \end{array} \quad (1)$$

Here, p_{ij} denotes the degree of preference of class S_i to class S_j, with $p_{ij} \in (0,1]$ whenever $i < j$, and $p_{ij} = 0$ whenever $i \geq j$, $1 \leq i, j \leq 9$. The class S_i is preferred to class S_j in case $p_{ij} > 0$.

Whenever the current emotional state is E_k with $k > 1$, the system will take an action A_k to drive the user to state E_1, which is associated to the class of states S_1. This class may be composed by different states, and so the emotional state system will select the most appropriate one according to energy efficiency and health conditions.

4   Application Example

Let us assume that the variables that determine user comfort are, for instance, room temperature (T), room humidity (H), room luminosity (L), and noise level (N). More formally, let $V = \{v_1 = T, v_2 = H, v_3 = L, v_4 = N\}$ be the set of variables controlled by the robot, and, for simplicity, let us assume that all such variables are categorized according to the same levels as *low (l)*, *moderate (m)*, *high (h)*, or simply $\{l, m, h\}$. Also, let us define S as the set of all possible states $s_i = (s_i^1, s_i^2, s_i^3, s_i^4)$, with s_i^j denoting the value at state i of variable v_j, with $j = 1, 2, 3, 4$. Obviously, S contains a total of 3^4 states, namely $S = \{s_1 = (l, l, l, l), s_2 = (l, l, l, m), s_3 = (l, l, l, h), s_4 = (l, l, m, l), s_5 = (l, l, m, m), s_6 = (l, l, m, h), \ldots, s_{79} = (l, h, h, h), s_{80} = (m, h, h, h), s_{81} = (h, h, h, h)\}$.

S constitutes a set of alternatives for the user, and on this set we consider the binary relations P of preference and I of indifference introduced in the previous section. $s_i P s_j$ if and only if the decision maker through the *Emotion Communication System* prefers s_i to s_j, equivalently $s_i I s_j$ if and only if $s_i P^c s_j$ and $s_j P^c s_i$, I is a equivalency relation.

Through the *Emotion Communication System* is possible to established a linearly ordered partition of S: $(S/I, >)$. Let us assume for simplicity that $n = 9$, and so the complete order in S/I is given by $S_1 > S_2 > \ldots > S_9$. Let us also assume that the degrees of preference of each class S_i to the next one S_{i+1}, namely $p_{i,i+1}$ (elementary preferences), are given for all $i = 1, \ldots, 8$, i.e.,

$$
\hat{P} = \begin{array}{c}
\\
S_1 \\
S_2 \\
S_3 \\
S_4 \\
S_5 \\
S_6 \\
S_7 \\
S_8 \\
S_9
\end{array}
\begin{array}{c}
\begin{array}{ccccccccc}
S_1 & S_2 & S_3 & S_4 & S_5 & S_6 & S_7 & S_8 & S_9
\end{array} \\
\left(\begin{array}{ccccccccc}
0 & 0.1 & p_{13} & p_{14} & 15 & p_{16} & p_{17} & p_{18} & p_{19} \\
0 & 0 & 0.2 & p_{24} & p_{25} & p_{26} & p_{27} & p_{28} & p_{29} \\
0 & 0 & 0 & 0.1 & p_{35} & p_{36} & p_{37} & p_{38} & p_{39} \\
0 & 0 & 0 & 0 & 0.2 & p_{46} & p_{47} & p_{48} & p_{49} \\
0 & 0 & 0 & 0 & 0 & 0.4 & p_{57} & p_{58} & p_{59} \\
0 & 0 & 0 & 0 & 0 & 0 & 0.1 & p_{68} & p_{69} \\
0 & 0 & 0 & 0 & 0 & 0 & 0 & 0.3 & p_{69} \\
0 & 0 & 0 & 0 & 0 & 0 & 0 & 0 & 0.1 \\
0 & 0 & 0 & 0 & 0 & 0 & 0 & 0 & 0
\end{array}\right)
\end{array}
\tag{2}
$$

where p_{ij} denotes the degree of preference of class S_i to class S_j, with $p_{ij} \in (0,1]$ whenever $i < j$, and $p_{ij} = 0$ whenever $i \geq j$, $1 \leq i, j \leq 9$. Once the elementary preferences are determined, any preference $p_{i,j}$ $(i < j)$ can be obtained as

$$
p_{i,j} = F(p_{i,i+1}, p_{i+1,i+2}, \ldots, p_{j-1,j}),
\tag{3}
$$

where F is a function that allows consistency in the set of preferences as indicated in [3]. Let us consider, for instance, $F = S_L(x, y) = \min(x+y, 1)$ (the Lukasiewicz t-conorm). In this case we obtain the following matrix of preferences:

$$
\hat{P} = \begin{array}{c}
\\
S_1 \\
S_2 \\
S_3 \\
S_4 \\
S_5 \\
S_6 \\
S_7 \\
S_8 \\
S_9
\end{array}
\begin{array}{c}
\begin{array}{ccccccccc}
S_1 & S_2 & S_3 & S_4 & S_5 & S_6 & S_7 & S_8 & S_9
\end{array} \\
\left(\begin{array}{ccccccccc}
0 & 0.1 & 0.3 & 0.4 & 0.6 & 1 & 1 & 1 & 1 \\
0 & 0 & 0.2 & 0.3 & 0.5 & 0.9 & 1 & 1 & 1 \\
0 & 0 & 0 & 0.1 & 0.3 & 0.7 & 0.8 & 1 & 1 \\
0 & 0 & 0 & 0 & 0.2 & 0.6 & 0.7 & 1 & 1 \\
0 & 0 & 0 & 0 & 0 & 0.4 & 0.5 & 0.8 & 0.9 \\
0 & 0 & 0 & 0 & 0 & 0 & 0.1 & 0.4 & 0.5 \\
0 & 0 & 0 & 0 & 0 & 0 & 0 & 0.3 & 0.4 \\
0 & 0 & 0 & 0 & 0 & 0 & 0 & 0 & 0.1 \\
0 & 0 & 0 & 0 & 0 & 0 & 0 & 0 & 0
\end{array}\right)
\end{array}
\tag{4}
$$

For instance, if the user is in state S_8 and feels uncomfortable, the system will drive him/her towards any state S_1, S_2, S_3 and S_4, which are all preferred over state S_8 with maximum degree of preference:

$$\hat{P} = \begin{array}{c} \\ S_1 \\ S_2 \\ S_3 \\ S_4 \\ S_5 \\ S_6 \\ S_7 \\ S_8 \\ S_9 \end{array} \begin{array}{ccccccccc} S_1 & S_2 & S_3 & S_4 & S_5 & S_6 & S_7 & \overset{\downarrow}{S_8} & S_9 \\ 0 & 0.1 & 0.3 & 0.4 & 0.6 & 1 & 1 & \boxed{1} & 1 \\ 0 & 0 & 0.2 & 0.3 & 0.5 & 0.9 & 1 & \boxed{1} & 1 \\ 0 & 0 & 0 & 0.1 & 0.3 & 0.7 & 0.8 & \boxed{1} & 1 \\ 0 & 0 & 0 & 0 & 0.2 & 0.6 & 0.7 & \boxed{1} & 1 \\ 0 & 0 & 0 & 0 & 0 & 0.4 & 0.5 & 0.8 & 0.9 \\ 0 & 0 & 0 & 0 & 0 & 0 & 0.1 & 0.4 & 0.5 \\ 0 & 0 & 0 & 0 & 0 & 0 & 0 & 0.3 & 0.4 \\ 0 & 0 & 0 & 0 & 0 & 0 & 0 & 0 & 0.1 \\ 0 & 0 & 0 & 0 & 0 & 0 & 0 & 0 & 0 \end{array} \qquad (5)$$

Note that although S_1 is the most preferred state, the activated action A_8 will select the more appropriate alternative according to energy efficiency and health conditions in addition to user preference.

5   Conclusions

In this paper, we have proposed an emotion communication system that relies on the paradigm of user preferences to determine the most appropriate action to be performed on the user environment. The ultimate goal of this system is to achieve the conditions for maximum user comfort. In essence, an ambient intelligence system is being developed, where the environment cooperates with the user in order to optimize his/her subjective experience of comfortability. Further work is oriented to characterize the responsiveness of the proposed system.

Acknowledgement. The authors acknowledge financial support from FEDER/ Ministerio de Ciencia, Innovación y Universidades-Agencia Estatal de Investigación_Proyecto PGC2018-095709-B-C21, and by Spanish Ministry of Economy and Competitiveness under contract DPI2017-86372-C3-3-R (AEI, FEDER, UE).

References

1. Aguiló, I., Calvo, T., Fuster-Parra, P., Martín, J., Mayor, G., Suñer, J.: Preference structures: qualitative judgements based on smooth t-conorms. Inf. Sci. **366**, 165–176 (2016). https://doi.org/10.1016/j.ins.2016.05.014
2. Bana, C.A., Costa, E., De Corte, J.M., Vansnick, J.C.: MACBETH. Int. J. Info. Tech. Decis. Mak. **11**(2), 359–387 (2012)
3. Calvo, T., Fuster-Parra, P., Martín, J., Mayor, G.: On aggregation for linearly ordered fuzzy preference relations based on consistency (2020, submitted)
4. Capuano, N., Chiclana, F., Herrera-Viedma, E.: Fuzzy rankings for preferences modeling in group decision making. Int. J. Intell. Syst. **33**, 1555–1570 (2018). https://doi.org/10.1002/int.21997

5. Chen, M., Zhou, P., Fortino, G.: Emotion communication system. IEEE Access **5** (2017). https://doi.org/10.1109/ACCESS.2016.2641480
6. Chiclana, F., Herrera, F., Herrera-Viedma, E.: Integrating three representation models in fuzzy multipurpose decision making based on fuzzy preference relations. Fuzzy Sets Syst. **97**, 33–38 (1998). https://doi.org/10.1016/S0165-0114(96)00339-9
7. Bana e Costa, C.A., Vansnick, J.C.: MACBETH - an interactive path towards the construction of cardinal value functions. Int. Trans. Oper. Res. **1**, 489–500 (1994)
8. Fodor, J., Roubens, M.: Fuzzy Preference Modelling and Multi-criteria Decision Aid. Kluwer, Dordrecht (1994)
9. Fuster-Parra, P., García-Mas, A., Cantallops, J., Ponseti, F.J.: Cooperative team work analysis and modeling: a Bayesian network approach. In: Luo, Y. (ed.) CDVE 2015. LNCS, vol. 9320, pp. 1–10. Springer, Cham (2015). https://doi.org/10.1007/978-3-319-24132-6_1
10. Fuster-Parra, P., García-Mas, A., Cantallops, J., Ponseti, F.J., Luo, Y.: Ranking features on psychological dynamics of cooperative team work through Bayesian networks. Symmetry **8**, 34 (2016). https://doi.org/10.3390/sym8050034
11. Galmés, S.: Expected time for comfort achievement in human-robot emotion communications. In: Luo, Y. (ed.) CDVE 2018. LNCS, vol. 11151, pp. 134–137. Springer, Cham (2018). https://doi.org/10.1007/978-3-030-00560-3_18
12. Goodrich, M.A., Schultz, A.C.: Human-robot interaction: a survey. Found. Trends Hum.-Comput. Interact. **1**(3), 203–275 (2007)
13. Roberts, S.: Measurement Theory. Addison Wesley, London (1979)
14. Saaty, T.L.: Relative measurement and its generalization in decision making: why pairwise comparisons are central in mathematics for the measurement of intangible factors - the analytic hierarchy/network process. Rev. R. Acad. Exact Phys. Nat. Sci. Ser. A **102**(2), 251–318 (2008)

A Personalized Food Recommendation Chatbot System for Diabetes Patients

Phupat Thongyoo[(⊠)], Phuttipong Anantapanya[(⊠)],
Pornsuree Jamsri[(⊠)], and Supannada Chotipant[(⊠)]

Faculty of Information Technology, King Mongkut's Institute of Technology
Ladkrabang, Bangkok, Thailand
{590700135,59070122,pornsuree,
supannada}@it.kmitl.ac.th

Abstract. Diabetes is a disorder of the body that is unable to produce enough insulin. Diabetes causes the body to improperly burn sugar, which affects the blood sugar level leaving a sugar residue. Diabetes is related to genes, body weight, lack of exercise and aging. When patients with diabetes neglect good nutrition this can cause many health problems. This research, therefore, develops a chatbot named "Waan-Noy" to recommend a diet suitable for individuals with diabetes and build a cooperative health society. Our chatbot recommends personalized eating. It is suitable for use by diabetes patients as indicated by their evaluations. Through use of nutrition therapy controls, Waan-Noy recommends specific foods. The user's evaluation is divided into 3 areas: content, design, and implementation to determine user degree of satisfaction with Waan-Noy.

Keywords: Diabetes · Cooperative health society · Health chatbot · Nutrition therapy · Food recommendation

1 Introduction

Patients with diabetes are often unaware they have it because the disease does not show obvious symptoms. Lack of food knowledge, especially of sugar in the diet led the researcher to conduct a preliminary survey on food choices among diabetic patients. The researcher used a questionnaire with a sample groups of 16 patients. With a scale between 1 and 5 from low to high, the results showed a difficulty to evaluate food nutrition ranging between middle to upper middle. The survey revealed factors of food selection. It was found that 56.3% of patients choose to eat food by reviewing raw materials, 37.5% choose on the advice of doctors or nutrition experts and 6.3% use the search method from the Google website.

Diabetes can alleviate symptoms or prevent the disease entirely by adopting nutrition therapy principles. Eating the right foods according to beneficial nutrition principles will meet the body's sufficient need for proper nutrition. Each person's body has different nutrient requirements depending on personalized factors, such as gender, age, weight, and height, etc. It is a vital to build a cooperative health society between experts (doctors and nutritionists) and patients (diabetics) through popular technology

© Springer Nature Switzerland AG 2020
Y. Luo (Ed.): CDVE 2020, LNCS 12341, pp. 19–28, 2020.
https://doi.org/10.1007/978-3-030-60816-3_3

to disseminate diet for patients with diabetes. They can exchange diabetics information. Currently, difficulties in choosing nutritious food are often overlooked due to our fast-paced lifestyle and other social conditions [1]. Some popular health chatbots, however, are available including Tuinui bot [2], Jubjai bot [2], Dr. Meaw bot [2], kBot, and SWITCHes. Still, a diabetes chatbot specific to nutritional choices is lacking. This research, thus, introduces chatbot "Waan-Noy" to meet the need of diabetic individuals.

Dialogflow technology assists computers to understand human language, from text. Waan-Noy utilizes Dialogflow. The chatbot's five features are 1) Food Recommendation; 2) Data Collection; 3) Nutrition Information; 4) Advice 5); Reports It can be used in both Android and iOS systems on mobile devices. This research paper has 7 parts: 1) introduction; 2) related work; 3) system structure; 4) intent design; 5) development and prototype; 6) results and discussion; 7) conclusions and future research.

2   Related Work

2.1   Diabetics Situation in Thailand

From the statistical data of diabetes from the International Diabetes Federation, Diabetes in Western Pacific (2017), Thailand has 4,426,959 people with diabetes (ages 18 to 99), representing 8.2 percent of the population. Thailand has the fourth largest number of diabetics after China, India, and Japan. There were 51,052 deaths from diabetes and related complications in 2017, accounting for 11.5 percent of the Thai population with diabetes [3].

2.2   Main Reasons of Diabetes

The main cause of diabetes is the occurrence of obesity. This cause reflects a lack of knowledge in choosing the correct diet including amount of healthy food. There is a need for sources of information to determine the nutritional value of foods appropriate for health. As discussed in the next section. technology can assist this issue [4].

2.3   Sample Health Chatbots

Thai Chatbots Samples. "Tuinui bot" is the health chatbot developed by Zwiz.AI with the primary purpose of providing calorie information. Its target group is people who want to lose weight. Its menu items include BMI and BMR values and various exercise styles. Tuinui bot's disadvantage is that it cannot recommend a diet [2]. Jubjai bot screens for depressive disorders. It includes automatic assessment of symptoms to help individuals understand their depression. Persons at risk of depression is its target group. Its disadvantage is that it takes a long time to talk into and evaluate the condition [2]. Dr. Meaw bot can advise and discuss health problems, including advice on basic primary care. Its target group is any person with a health problem. It is not possible to inquire about food nutrition information [2].

Other Chatbots Samples. "kBot" deals with preliminary asthma assessments. Its focus is to provide information about the disease and medicines for its target group of asthmatic patients. "SWITCHes" is for health counseling, using real time advice from health-based clinics in Taiwan. Its target group is any person with a health problem [6].

3 System Structure

The system structure is divided into 2 main parts: 1) user interface and 2) the back end as shown in Fig. 1.

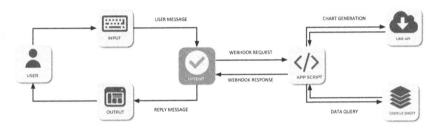

Fig. 1. System structure of chatbot

The system starts with receiving initial user information. Dialogflow analyzes the sentences in accordance with the intent that the researcher specified. It sends the data to the Google App Script for processing. This allows Google API and Google Sheet to work, send the response information to Dialogflow and output to the user.

User Interface. This part is where users can interact with the system of the chatbot. It is the part where users type messages in queries with chatbot. This section shows results from chatbot for users to see displayed output.

Back-End. This illustrates the way the system completes various processes as the developer has specified. The system structure diagram includes Natural Language Processing (NLP), intent, code, and database. This will make connections with other operations with the following components. Dialogflow combines NLP and intent. Google App Script are the central part of the connection between the chatbot together with the LINE API database. This is the LINE chatbot control section. This part starts creating chatbots. Google Sheet is the storage section of chatbots. It uses Google Sheet as the system database that stores data in the form of cells.

4 Intent Design

This section called intent needs to be defined for any specified chatbot. Previously, Dialogflow, an intent-based chatbot, relied on each intent. Within each intent, there is a sequence of conversations based on the purpose of 4 main intents.

Food Recommendation. When a user enters the message "Suggest food", the system allows the user to choose a food type adds more user options. The recommendations is based on specified rules as in Fig. 2.

Data Collection. When a user enters "Fill in information", the system allows a user to specify the information used as a reference. Energy value displays that users receive per day as in Fig. 3.

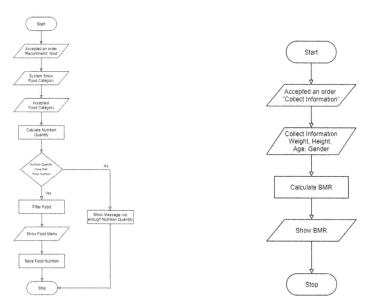

Fig. 2. Flow chart food recommendation   **Fig. 3.** Flow chart data collection

Nutrition Information. When a user enters the message "Nutrition" in the chat, the bot will ask the name of the food menu and retrieve it from the database by showing pictures, names, energy, carbohydrates, proteins, fats, sugar and the amount of food as in Fig. 4.

Report. When a user enters message "Nutrition Info" in the chat, the bot will create graphs based on user data received within that day. It shows the details of various nutrients that user has received that day as in Fig. 5.

Fig. 4. Flow chart food nutrition information   **Fig. 5.** Flow chart food report

5   Research Development and Prototype

This section explains creating a prototype of "Waan-Noy" LINE chatbot. It has been designed and developed to meet research scope and objectives to aid diabetes patients and others at risk from lack of healthy food nutrition. Waan-Noy is a chatbot for mobile devices that support Android and iOS operating systems.

Recommendation Concept. Basal Metabolic Rate (BMR), represents the required calories per day for each person. The Clinical Practice Guideline for Diabetes 2017 states that diabetic patients' requirements of daily nutrients for BMR are: Protein 20%; Carbohydrate 50%; Fat 30%; and Sugar 12 g [8]. Waan-Noy chatbot will calculate quantity in grams: Protein and Carbohydrate of 4 kcal = 1 g.; Fat of 9 kcal = 1 g.) It also uses this ratio to recommend food to help cure diabetes causes and effects.

$$BMR = 66 + (13.7 \times Weight(kg)) + (5 \times Height(meter)) - (6.8 \times Age) \quad (1)$$

A Persona Example:(Calculation of BMR and nutrition): The 49-year old male, weight 99 kg, and height 177 cm. has a BMR equal to 1,974 kcal. This calculates into Protein 98.7 g., Carbohydrate 246.75 g., Fat 65.8 g. and Sugar 12 g.

Back-End Process. Food recommendations start with user's data input for calculation. The remaining nutrients of each food's nutrition in the database is compared. Then, chatbot shows the main healthy menu the user can eat that day. In the initial development, the researcher pulled data from Google Sheet and used a "For loop" to search for results. However, the result initially was very slow processing data. Bots were not responding effectively as in the sample Pseudo Code in Fig. 6.

```
FoodRec1(user_id):
  get all user records -> user_arr
  for each user in user_arr:
    if (user == user_id):
      get all remaining nutrients -> nutrient_arr
  get all menu records -> menu_arr
  for each menu in menu_arr:
    if (nutrients in menu is less than or equals to nutrient_arr) :
      add menu into recommended_arr
  for each rec_menu in recommended_arr:
    transform rec_menu to json file
    send to DialogFlow
end FoodRec1
```

```
FoodRec2(user_id):

  get all user records -> user_arr

  get index of from user_arr -> user_nutrition

  get all menu records -> menu_arr

  filters menu by menu_nutrtion < user_nutrition

  map each menu with flex message form

  send to DialogFlow

end FoodRec2
```

Fig. 6. Pseudo code FoodRec1   **Fig. 7.** Pseudo code FoodRec2

After identifying the problem, the researcher adjusted the code by modifying the data extracting model of all data into 2D Array and using **indexOf** and **filter** methods to find the menus relevant to the user's remaining nutrition requirements. In addition, this change assists the bot to respond more quickly by gradually reducing unresponsiveness data as in the sample Pseudo Code in Fig. 7.

5.1 Prototype

Entering Information to Get Started. When using the chatbot for the first time, users must fill out demographic data including age, weight, height, and gender to calculate their BMR and to reference a specific dietary criterion.

By inputting the message or clicking the food recommendation menu, the chatbot can introduce food by division into main dishes, desserts, fruits and beverages. The results are displayed in the form of a carousel. Within a single dish food is also categorized into different types of cooking and preparing methods. The system calculates the food menu that a user can eat by referring to the personal information previously entered. It displays the menu and nutrient information in carousel format as in Fig. 8.

Fig. 8. Food Carousel

Fig. 9. Food card in nutrition information

Add Menu and Nutrition Information. The system can fill out the food menu followed by the amount that is eaten, such as "Tom Yum Kung 3 cups". The system will calculate the nutrients that users receive for that menu. It will also alert if the user has exceeded their nutrients' quota. This is displayed according to the excess nutrients list followed by the amount in grams as in Fig. 9.

Fig. 10. Daily graph

Daily and Weekly Report. The chatbot records daily nutrition received in a bar chart. A user can select the menu chart showing historical data. There are two data charts to choose either daily or weekly data. The daily chart data extracts data from the user database and creates graphs from Google App Script for display through chatbot. The system displays a graph of the nutrients the user chooses in a bar graph. The graph is displayed for the past 7 days (1 week) since the starting date the user executed the command in the chatbot. The graph shows historical data as in Fig. 10.

6   Results and Discussion

In this section, the researcher's discussion includes 2 parts: 1) evaluation results and 2) chatbot performance.

6.1   Evaluation Results

System satisfaction assessments were conducted in the form of online questionnaires for users with diabetes and users not having diabetes, aged between 14–72 years, with 11 males and 13 females for 45.8% and 54.2%, respectively. The assessment topics are divided into 3 main areas, namely, content, design and usage. The scale of satisfaction is from 1 as least satisfied to 5 as most satisfied. The total of 24 respondents, represents a total score of 120 points. Details of the satisfaction results in the 3 areas are as follows:

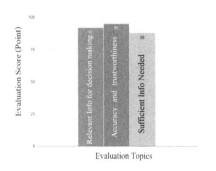

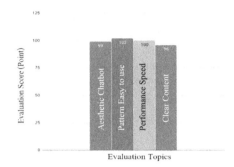

Fig. 11. A graph of content satisfaction   **Fig. 12.** A graph of design satisfaction

Content. The content satisfaction evaluation found that the average of satisfaction scores in all 3 topics is 91.66 points. The users are satisfied with the system in terms of accuracy, clarity and reliability as in Fig. 11.

Design. From the results of the design satisfaction assessment, it was found that the average of the satisfaction results is 99.25 points. The users are very satisfied with the easy-to-use formatting and the speed in which data displays as in Fig. 12.

Implementation. From the results of the satisfaction evaluation for implementation, it was found that the average of user satisfaction scores is 109 points. Users are very satisfied with the useful information for the users and for further usage as in Fig. 13.

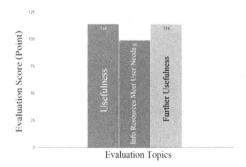

Fig. 13. A graph of implementation satisfaction

6.2 Chatbot Performance

As mentioned in Sect. 4, after modifying the performance of the bot, the researcher tested on processing time by comparing the old and new systems. The measurement of two features is for Food Recommendation and Nutrition Information. The comparison chart is created in the form of line graphs as in Fig. 14.

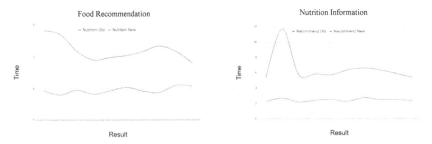

Fig. 14. A comparison graph between FoodRec1 (version1) and FoodRec2 (version2) (Color figure online)

In the graph, the red line represents the version 1 (old system) and the green line version 2 (new system). It can obviously be seen that the bots are faster and more stable. Both have clear features. Stable operation will affect the bot's response. This caused the new system to definitely have a better performance than the old system.

7 Conclusions and Future Research

7.1 Conclusions

Waan-Noy chatbot prototype was successfully developed with Google App Script and Google Sheet and available on iOS and Android. The main features would work for food recommendations and nutrition information for diabetics. This benefits the user in terms of ease of use to choose the menu to eat, gain health awareness and food recommendation based on an individual's nutritional needs profile.

From the evaluation of the satisfaction, it was found users are very satisfied with the system in each aspect. Especially the case of convenience and speed, ease of use, and useful health information. The developer has studied and asked about the needs of users through questionnaires to iterate the system from actual user's requirements. Combining the chatbot with LINE chatbot is a new approach to respond immediately for nutrition information. Easy to use with a LINE chatbot allows many features to satisfy user expectations and needs. However, there is also least satisfaction scores in some cases because the information is minimal and not yet utilized and a small amount of data in database. Since, every menu item has to contain the main nutrients that relate to diabetes. This can cause the limited requests in food database.

7.2 Future Research

This study gives an opportunity to develop the system to recommend food more precisely by taking other factors into calculation of nutrients and energy the body needs such as the amount of exercise. Another aspect is to use this food recommendation system for other groups of users with healthy diet needs related to a disease(s) in addition to diabetic patients. Thus, future research will benefit from this prototype and expand to cooperative chronic diseases society such as asthma and cancer.

References

1. Diabetes should not be overlooked. https://www.bangkokpattayahospital.com/th/healthcare-services/dm-and-endocrinology-center-th/diabetes-articles-th/item/1068-diabetes01-th.html
2. Tuinui bot, Jubjai bot, Dr. Meaw bot. https://www.zwiz.ai
3. International Diabetes Federation. https://diabetesatlas.org/resources/2017-atlas.html
4. Petcharat, K., Boonchan, W., Umaporn, U., Chalermsri, N.: Perceived risk, criteria-based risk to diabetes mellitus, and health-promoting lifestyles in the first degree relatives of persons with diabetes mellitus, pp. 178–180 (2010)
5. Huang, C., Yang, M., Huang, C., Chen, Y., Wu, M., Chen, K.: A chatbot-supported smart wireless interactive healthcare system for weight control and health promotion. In: 2018 IEEE International Conference on Industrial Engineering and Engineering Management (IEEM), Bangkok, pp. 1791–1795 (2018). https://doi.org/10.1109/IEEM.2018.8607399
6. Kadariya, D., Venkataramanan, R., Yip, H.Y., Kalra, M., Thirunarayanan, K., Sheth, A.: kBot: knowledge-enabled personalized chatbot for asthma self-management. In: 2019 IEEE International Conference on Smart Computing (SMARTCOMP), Washington, DC, USA, pp. 138–143 (2019). https://doi.org/10.1109/SMARTCOMP.2019.00043
7. Suksom, N., Buranarach, M., Thein, Y.M., Supnithi, T., Netisopakul, P.: A knowledge-based framework for the development of personalized food recommendation system. School of Information Technology, King Mongkut's Institute of Technology Ladkrabang, Bankok, Thailand (2010)
8. Clinical Practice Guideline for Diabetes (2017). https://www.dmthai.org/attachments/article/443/guideLINE-diabetes-care-2017.pdf

Collaborative Design Automation Toolkit for Power Controllers in Aerospace Applications

Janis Sebastian Häseker[(⊠)] and Niklas Aksteiner

Institute of Space Systems, German Aerospace Center (DLR),
28359 Bremen, Germany
janis.haeseker@dlr.de

Abstract. In this work we present the latest status on our rapid design process and automated toolkit for aerospace power controllers. The goal is to generate correct-by-design flight hardware from high level requirements with a minimum of manual engineering work. This is achieved by maintaining a database of readily usable design elements (circuit designs, PCB layouts, simulation models and documentation snippets). In this paper we focus on the different roles of human interaction with the toolkit and how we can streamline the process to final flight worthy hardware by parallelizing single design tasks.

Keywords: Design automation · Power systems · Aerospace

1 Introduction

The aerospace sector is known for its stringent requirements towards the reliability of avionic systems. Oftentimes this leads to the reuse of existing designs and heritage from previously deployed systems. This contradicts the path of the space industry to highly innovative, smaller and cheaper missions and ambitious project timelines. For these scenarios a design process is needed to provide bespoke avionics under mass and budget limits without sacrificing reliability.

This can only be achieved if the manual labor is supported by an automated design process. However not all manual engineering tasks can be automated, so it is advantageous to establish a process where this work can be done in a parallelized fashion.

All these factors are addressed by our design process and automation toolkit for aerospace power controllers. It supports the path from high level requirements of the power system, architecture definition, detailed design of circuits, the verification and testing, as well as the manufacturing and integration. This approach follows the philosophy of Platform Based Design, where the design process is understood as a series of refinement steps from the highest level of requirements to the final product using elements designed in bottom-up approach [1].

© Springer Nature Switzerland AG 2020
Y. Luo (Ed.): CDVE 2020, LNCS 12341, pp. 29–36, 2020.
https://doi.org/10.1007/978-3-030-60816-3_4

2   State of the Art

Today the design of avionic systems for aerospace applications is most of the time a labor intensive process. This is due to the massive amount of documentation combined with the use of a lot of different engineering tools that are not directly interconnected. In the case of spacecraft power systems the design starts with a set of requirements provided by the system engineering team. A preliminary architecture is defined that often depends heavily on the reuse of previously designed units. If the requirements cannot be fulfilled with existing designs single changes to the previous version are proposed. There is a strong focus to keep the design as close as possible to previously flown solutions to ensure that the new unit can most likely be reliable as the old one by means of similarity. This is called heritage in the space industry and oftentimes has a big impact on decisions which component to use, even if there are choices with higher performance or lower price. This slows down innovation massively. If innovative and new designs are used, extensive qualification campaigns are necessary. These are highly expensive and time consuming.

Additionally detailed information on the single avionic products can be included in system studies only late in the project, if these products are developed in parallel. If this is true for multiple products the system design cannot be optimal and the risk of late changes with high impact on cost and schedule arises.

We want to tackle these shortcomings in the traditional design process by redefining how heritage is handled in the design phase. The introduction of design automation techniques with an integrated design tool offers potential for a reliable and fast design of power controllers with a high level of maturity right from the start. In the following sections we introduce our collaborative design automation toolkit, its role in the design of aerospace power controllers and how it supports the collaboration of different engineering disciplines.

3   Proposed Design Process and Toolkit

3.1   Overview

The classical way to start the design of a new avionic product is to check if existing designs can satisfy the requirements. This step can be automated if the requirements and performance indicators are captured in a way that can be processed by machines. We split up the overall system into blocks that represent recurrent functions for power controller design. In this way we can not only check if an old design of the overall power controller can be used but also if a new combination of previously designed functions can fulfill the requirements. These building blocks are kept in a database that acts as the central part of our process. It contains pre-designed implementations of power system functions such as DC-DC converters or load switches. Each entry consists of a set of important performance parameters, simulation models with varying levels of fidelity, printed circuit board layouts and other production information, as well as snippets for the auto-generation of documentation and test plans.

To lower the barrier of using our system and ensure the most consistent user experience it was decided to build a web application. In this way we can ensure that no special requirements are enforced on the users working environment.

Our design automation toolkit consists of two components: A web based software solution called the design automation application and a rapid hardware prototyping solution called the PCDU modular breadboard. The software includes the necessary functions to perform subsystem level design task, contribute to system level design and interface to other domain specific tools. The PCDU modular breadboard allows a quick evaluation of PCDU designs in real hardware that can be compared to analysis and simulation results. This direct link between design, prototyping and validation tools ensures that solutions with a high quality can be reached in less time and with fewer resources compared to a classical design process.

3.2   Interaction of Engineering Roles with the Toolkit

In the following sections we will illustrate how the different engineering roles interact with this design information and how efficient collaboration is promoted.

Power System Engineer

The Power System Engineer has the role to ensure that the overall power system with means for power generation, storage and distribution satisfy the system requirements. From this the requirements of the power distribution unit are derived, especially the description of interfaces and their expected behavior. This is shown in Fig. 1.

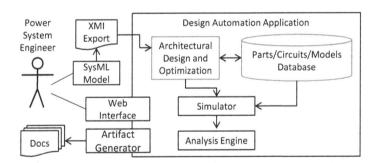

Fig. 1. Interaction of power system engineer with the design automation application

The information can be provided via the web interface, XMI exports from SysML system models or domain specific modeling solutions like Virtual Satellite [2]. With a set of requirements and the contents of the database the "Architectural Design and Optimization" (ADO) algorithm can choose and connect a subset of building blocks to provide a possible implementation for the needed power controller functionality. For all generated baseline solutions the system will perform simulations using SystemC-AMS models, and present the analysis results via auto-generated documentation.

By automating the step of design exploration a much broader design space can be studied and trade-offs between the solutions can be made. Additionally the Power

System Engineer gains deeper insight into the design parameters such as mass, volume and electrical efficiency.

Electronic Design Engineer

The Electronic Design Engineer has the role to maintain the database of circuits that can be used for the design as illustrated in Fig. 2. These entries can have different maturity levels: from a simple simulation model based on datasheet values over more sophisticated circuit simulations up to measurements of real hardware with full documentation and design files. In our application simulations are performed using SystemC-AMS. It allows the application of a wide range of abstraction levels from behavioral description of elements down to circuit level models.

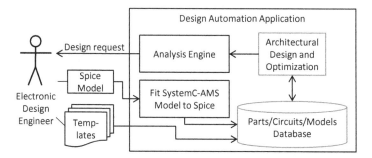

Fig. 2. Interaction of electronics design engineer with the design automation application

If the ADO process results in non-optimal results in terms of efficiency, mass or volume it is beneficial to manually design new elements for the database. For this Spice models of the circuits are developed that are automatically approximated by SystemC-AMS simulation models used in the application. The engineer also needs to provide documentation templates, to allow the application to produce artifacts like test plans for the newly added element.

Test Engineer

The role of the Test Engineer is to perform all verification steps on the designed hardware as shown in Fig. 3. For every element in the database there exists an evaluation board that can be used to rapidly assemble a whole power unit using our rapid prototyping solution: the PCDU modular breadboard [3]. It interconnects all the single circuit boards and provides control and telemetry interfaces to provide a fully functional PCDU. The configuration and test plans for this are auto-generated. Measurements from the setup are directly transferred to the database via the Modular Breadboard interface. Additional information of the test performance can be provided via the web interface. This setup not only allows to test the hardware design itself, but also to validate the test procedures that can be later used for the flight models.

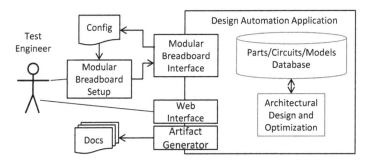

Fig. 3. Interaction of the test engineer with the design automation application

Production/Integration Engineer

In the final step the output is generated to manufacture, verify and use the power controller as illustrated in Fig. 4. This includes printed circuit board layout data, as well as CAD drawings for the enclosure. Also the documentation such as user manual, interface control documents and component lists are automatically generated from documentation snippets that are stored with the used building blocks in the database. In the aerospace sector a big part of the work is related to documentation that can be massively reduced by design automation tools.

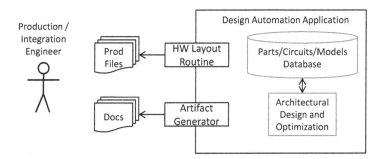

Fig. 4. Interaction of the production and integration engineer with the design automation application

3.3   Impact on the Engineering Roles

The overall working scheme promotes a single source of truth on subsystem (PCDU) level inside our web application that is connected to a system level SysML model. This ensures that it is clear where the data for each engineering task can be obtained. To ease the acceptance for our approach we have a strong focus on keeping the work processes that are present in the engineering roles before as similar as possible. The biggest impact can be recognized for the power system engineer. All input to the design tool can be provided via the SysML system model using appropriate attributes, but this model is often not available early in the project. It makes sense to replace previously used preliminary design tools in the form of Microsoft® Excel® sheets or Matlab® scripts [4] with the functionality provided by our web tool. In this way much more detailed information can be gathered in terms of first estimates for mass, volume and power losses for the PCDU while satisfying the power system requirements. This ensures a more optimal system design early on. For the electronic design engineer there is no change in the tools, but in the way to share the results of circuit design. Circuit simulations of DC-DC converters and load switches are performed in SPICE with predefined templates for the input and output circuit to ensure compatibility with the simulation engine of the web application. Lookup tables of the simulation results are uploaded to the database together with the original simulation model, performance parameters and documentation snippets. For testing of the different PCDU models the input is mainly auto-generated. This reduces the work load of the test engineer and ensures consistent execution of the verification procedures. Instead of providing written report, test documentation shall be performed inside the web tool. By having a direct connection to the test setup most of the data is gathered automatically. In the end the PCDU must be manufactured using existing supply chains. Here no special tools shall be enforced, especially in the case of external suppliers. We are in the process to collect all the essential data to also auto-generate the necessary design files and documentation which reduces the amount of manual labor to start the production of the final product.

3.4 Collaborating on Design Tasks

During the PCDU development there is a strong interaction between the roles of the power system, the electronics design und the test engineer. To keep the process of PCDU design well documented we push towards the sole exchange of information via our web application. In the following we will outline the how collaboration on the design will occur over the different project phases.

During preliminary design of the spacecraft power system the power system engineer needs to quickly iterate on different PCDU designs taking into account the changing system level requirements. Automatically generated PCDU architectures that interconnect functional blocks from the database are analyzed to assess their performance in terms of mass, volume and electrical efficiency. The system tracks if the different building blocks are used and how they perform in the current design. The database contains not only circuits that have been evaluated in hardware, but also mockup elements generated from datasheet values. If these elements are picked during the design process the system generates reports to indicate the need for further investigation towards the electronic design engineer. In this way it can be assured that the focus for the expansion of the catalog of functional blocks will be laid on the ones with the biggest impact for the different projects. This mechanism can be compared to issue tracking systems in software engineering where the most severe bugs are resolved before the work is started on minor problems. By closely tracking the parts chosen for different design trends for certain parameters, combinations can be identified and used for the selection of circuits to be investigated and qualified for use in space in the future.

When new circuits are designed, evaluation boards with standardized interfaces are manufactured. These can be used for functional and environmental (e.g. radiation, EMC) testing but also to assemble a fully functional model of the PCDU using our PCDU Modular Breadboard. We foresee to directly generate test plans on single circuit and PCDU unit level. With our application being the place where simulation and measurement results with the associated models and test plans are stored, a continuous automated check between simulation and hardware can be performed. This allows all parties to quickly react to deviations between high and low level design as well as measurements on hardware. We foresee that the application can directly connect to the hardware setups allowing test plans to be automatically executed and resulting measurements data to be acquired to ensure repeatability.

Because most verification and test strategies are developed using one tool it eases the communication and collaboration on these topics between the system side and the people that conduct the test activities. The documentation for external suppliers and the integration and verification team gets generated from the same dataset ensuring consistency. It still needs to be assessed how feedback of generated artifacts is handled most efficiently such that the information loop between all parties can be closed.

4 Conclusion and Future Work

In this work we presented our web based design tool for the partly automated design of aerospace power controllers. We illustrated how the different engineering roles interact with the application and how efficient collaboration during the design phases is promoted. The application as well as the PCDU development logic behind it is still under development, but there is first evidence showing that a lot of resources can be saved by applying it to our small satellite projects. By reducing the recurring work for the different engineering roles and try to blend in with established modes of work we ensured high acceptance of our tools.

At the moment the application covers the functionality needed for power system and electronic design engineering. In the upcoming time we will expand the application to cover the full development cycle as outlined in this paper. Especially the interface to our PCDU Modular Breadboard rapid prototyping setup will massively accelerate our design activities. We will deploy the system to be used in upcoming small satellite projects at DLR and use it for the development of PCDUs of different sizes and capabilities.

References

1. Sangiovanni-Vincentelli, A.: Quo Vadis, SLD? Reasoning about the trends and challenges of system level design. In: Proceedings of the IEEE 95-3, pp. 467–506 (2007)
2. Fischer, P.M., et al.: Spacecraft interface management in concurrent engineering sessions. In: Luo, Y. (ed.) CDVE 2019. LNCS, vol. 11792, pp. 54–63. Springer, Cham (2019). https://doi.org/10.1007/978-3-030-30949-7_7

3. Häseker, J., Strowik, C., Aksteiner, N., Dannemann, F.: Design process and modular breadboard for rapid development of mission specific power conditioning and distribution units. In: Poster SSC19-P1-16, Small Satellite Conference, Utah State University, Logan, UT, USA (2019)
4. Pedersen, J.: Power system for the Eu: CROPIS satellite - results from design trade-offs, analysis, simulation and testing. In: E3S Web of Conferences, vol. 16, p. 13010 (2017). https://doi.org/10.1051/e3sconf/20171613010

Collaborative Product Design for Product Customization: An Industrial Case of Fashion Product

Somlak Wannarumon Kielarova[(✉)] and Prapasson Pradujphongphet

ID3 - Industrial Design, Decision and Development Research Unit,
Faculty of Engineering, Naresuan University, Phitsanulok 65000, Thailand
somlakw@nu.ac.th

Abstract. This paper proposes a new platform of collaborative product design for product customization. The proposed platform of the collaborative product design process is scoped in internal enterprise level, which includes customers, designers, engineers, and technologists into a single platform. The platform can generate a design solution to the design objective. The collaborative design platform was developed in term of an interactive design on a Computer-Aided Design (CAD) software. In the platform, customer can input the design requirements, designer can monitor the shape generation and improve the resulting design, engineer can define the manufacturing conditions, and technologist can perform the optimization of design and process parameters. At the end of the collaborative design process, the design solution, therefore, is generated in terms of a three-dimensional (3D) model, which is directly integrated to the manufacturing process in line, until obtaining the physical product. This platform has been implemented in a jewelry product enterprise, and the result indicates that it can reduce time in design and manufacturing process approximately 66%.

Keywords: Collaborative design · Interactive genetic algorithm · Evolutionary design · Design optimization · Jewelry design

1 Introduction

Nowadays, most of enterprises are moving from mass production to mass customization to survive in both local and global competitions. In product design development process, a design team generally is overwhelmed with several activities such as conceptual design, detailed design, manufacturing analysis, prototype making, testing, etc. The challenges of mass customization are providing the product variety with the varied demands of customers at lower cost and short lead-time. Most of enterprises are hardly trying to reduce the lead time of each activity in the product development process to rapidly launch out new collection and customized product. Quick response to customer needs with high flexibility in product design is needed in this digital age. Product architecture, therefore, plays a key role in forming a common product structure and allowing a variety of the product.

© Springer Nature Switzerland AG 2020
Y. Luo (Ed.): CDVE 2020, LNCS 12341, pp. 37–46, 2020.
https://doi.org/10.1007/978-3-030-60816-3_5

Mass customization is a current key strategy in the fashion industry. Mass customization aims at satisfying the individual customer's requirements with the customized products, in a short lead time and at a cost closed to mass production.

This paper, therefore, aims to propose a collaborative product design platform for supporting the activities in the product customization strategy. An interactive collaborative design was developed on Computer-Aided Design (CAD) software. It focuses on the product design process in the internal enterprise level. CAD is a major tool that mostly used to model, increase the productivity of designers, improve the design quality, improve communications, as well as create design and manufacturing databases [1]. The proposed platform has integrated across customers, designers, engineers and technologists to collaborate along the product design process. Customer can customize their designs through the product structure, while designers can monitor the shape generation and improve the resulting designs. Engineers can analyze the manufacturing conditions and manufacturability. As well as technologist can perform the optimization of design and process parameters throughout the platform.

This paper is organized into five sections. The next section provides the related works include collaborative design and interactive genetic algorithm. Section 3 describes the platform of the computer supported in product design for product customization. The case study of designing a fashion product like as jewelry, as well as, the experimental results are described and discussed in Sect. 4. Finally, this research work and its future directions are summarized in Sect. 5.

2   Related Works

2.1   Collaborative Product Design and Development

Collaborative engineering is an approach in optimizing engineering processes. It aims to improve product quality, to shorten lead-time, to improve competitive cost and to obtain higher customer satisfaction [2]. The application of collaborative engineering to product design is generally called Computer Supported Collaborative Design (CSCD), which is also called Concurrent Design, Cooperative Design, or Interdisciplinary Design).

CSCD is the product design process with collaboration among shareholders such as designers, engineers and other related product developers for the entire product life cycle [2]. The functions in product design and development process cover from preliminary design, detailed design, prototyping, manufacturing, testing, quality control and other activities until the end of product life cycle.

In a collaborative design process, product structure and product model are the most important issues and related to the CAD system that enterprise used. With collaborative product development individual users and enterprises can manage, share and view the CAD projects.

The platform-based strategy and approach to support collaborative product development and customization was introduced in [3]. The approach can be used as guidelines for a product data management system to share product knowledge, to improve product quality, to shorten time-to-market, and to obtain customer satisfaction.

This paper considered the approach of [3] to be a guideline to develop product platform for developing collaborative product development.

2.2   Genetic Algorithm and Interactive Genetic Algorithm

Evolutionary art [4] and design systems [5] offer an effective approach to the creation of art forms. The evolutionary process in the evolutionary art and design systems works as a design parameter optimizer and a form generator. Using the advantages of this process, the designers or users can explore various design alternatives.

Genetic Algorithm (GA) is one family of Evolutionary Algorithm (EA) [6]. A typical GA requires a genetic representation of the solution domain and a fitness function to evaluate that solution domain. The major elements of a GA [5] are consisted of genotype, phenotype, genetic operators, fitness function and selection.

Genotype is a genetic representation. It is usually encoded in form of the string of chromosomes. It is considered as the basic units of evolution. More suitable chromosome structures and more suitable genotype representations are designed, easier genetic operators can be applied. Genotype is typically encoded either in binary or real numbers. During an evolutionary design process, before the quality of an individual will be evaluated, genotypes are mapped onto phenotypes. Phenotypes consist of sets of parameters that represent shape or form of the studied product. Phenotypes have been represented by various techniques depending on the objectives of the system. New offspring are typically reproduced by genetic operators: crossover and mutation. Crossover is an event where parts of the chromosomes of at least two selected parents are randomly recombined to create a new set of offspring. These offspring, therefore, inherit the characteristics of each parent. Mutation modifies an arbitrary part in a genetic sequence from its original state. Mutation is typically used to maintain the population diversity during evolution process.

Fitness function characterizes a heuristic evaluation of the solution quality. It is derived from the objective functions, to measure the qualities or the properties of phenotypes. The fitness is usually the value of the objective function in the optimization problem being solved. It is a key factor for leading the individuals' evolution. For every phenotype, its fitness must be evaluated by the fitness function. In an evolutionary design, the computational time mostly is spent in the evaluation process [5], which can take few minutes until several hours to evaluate a single solution. This process can be improved by reducing the number of evaluations during the evolutionary process. Population size is often less than ten individuals [5], which are then evaluated rapidly in each generation. Selection is a process of choosing suitable phenotypes according to their fitness. The selection scheme can determine the generating direction of the evolutionary process.

In GA a population of individuals or phenotypes is evolved toward better solutions as part of the optimization problem. [7]. The evolutionary process starts from a population of randomly generated individuals. It is an iterative process with the population. Each iteration called a generation. In each generation, the fitness of every individual in the population is evaluated. The more fit individuals are stochastically selected from the current population. Each individual is modified by crossover and mutation, to form a new generation. The new generation of candidate solutions is then used in the next iteration. GA typically terminates when either a maximum number of generations has been reached, or a satisfactory fitness level has been achieved for the population.

There have been several reports that applied GA and other types of EA in design applications and creations of artworks e.g. [8–20]. Some of them integrated EA with other techniques such as artificial neural network, fuzzy set, etc., depending on the problem domains.

In this paper, GA is used for shape optimization or form finding problem. Shape optimization or form finding is a technique, which has been applied successfully to various design problems, for example, product design, engineering structures [21], architecture design [22], etc.

Interactive Genetic Algorithm (IGA) is one type of Interactive Evolutionary Computation (IEC) for optimization problems based on subjective human evaluation [23]. Fitness function in IEC, therefore, is substituted by human evaluation. This method becomes popular in product design problems because designers are able to express their emotions or preferences onto the generated designs. In IGA, the genes of each chromosome describe a possible design [24]. The genes of each chromosome are transformed into the predefined design corresponding to that chromosome. It is presented to the user through a graphical user interface. The user serves as a fitness function, and gives scores to the candidate alternatives. Afterwards, selection and genetic operators are applied and a new generation is generated. This evolutionary process is iterated until the user reaches his/her preferred design [25]. Various applications in artistic and design applications using IGA are found in [10, 26–29].

3 Collaborative Product Design for Product Customization

This paper proposes a collaborative design support platform. The platform of the collaborative product design is scoped in the internal enterprise. The platform includes customers, designers, engineers, and technologists into a single platform, as shown in Fig. 1. The collaborative design platform was developed in term of an interactive design on Computer-Aided Design (CAD) software through web-based integration and collaboration. The mobile application was developed for inputting the design requirements by customer/user. Designer can monitor the shape generation and improve the resulting designs, and re-negotiate with customer via the mobile application. Database server was built to store and manage the databases of the design and manufacturing knowledges and the rule-based system. They were stored on the server and to provide data access for authorized designers, engineers and technologists. At the end of the collaborative design, the design solution, therefore, is generated in three-dimensional (3D) models, which is directly integrated to manufacturing process in line, until obtaining the physical product.

In the platform of collaborative product design, the designer developed the product structure and the product model for designing the product that can be customized in various design solutions associated to design parameters known as parametric design. The engineer developed the manufacturing databases, which contain the product data, the manufacturing conditions, and the manufacturability model. The technologist

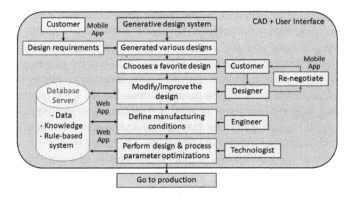

Fig. 1. The proposed collaborative product design platform.

developed the optimization model for optimizing the design parameters and the shape of the product.

4   An Industrial Case Study of Jewelry Halo Ring Design

The collaborative design support platform was applied for designing the mass customized product like as fashion product. During this research project, we collaborated with a jewelry entrepreneur in Thailand. An industrial case study of halo gemstone ring design was chosen as the showcase problem. The industrial case study undertaken in the course of this project was aimed to collaborate internally among customer, designer, engineer and technologist for automatically generating and customizing halo gemstone rings.

Jewelry halo gemstone ring is one of the most popular type of jewelry rings that enjoys a high demand in the jewelry market. Halo ring is a ring in which a center gemstone is surrounded with a set of halo stones (a set of round pave diamonds or faceted color gemstones). There are various product variety of halo gemstone ring that can be customized for customers. The designer set up the product model as show in Fig. 2.

Fig. 2. Illustration of an example of product model.

We have identified a bottleneck in the design process of halo ring, which is the setting of halo gemstones surrounding the center stone with suitable equal gaps. Changing of the gemstone size and/or changing the ring size requires rearrangement or re-setting of halo gemstones on the head of the ring to obtain the proper gaps between the halo gemstones to achieve desired aesthetics. This necessitates further metalsmith's work. The rearrangement of halo gemstones to optimize the gaps between them by manual approach with trial-and-error method is therefore relatively time-consuming.

In this study, the center gemstone cuts are limited to round cut and cushion cut, while only round cut is used for the halo gemstone. The center gemstone cut dominates the setting pattern of the halo setting, number of halo gems, and gap size between the halo gemstones.

In this research, IGA is used for optimizing the gaps between halo gemstone, that employed the mathematic model of the relationships between halo gemstone setting for round-cut center gemstone by surrounding it with one layer from Kielarova et al. [30].

The prototype system was developed using Grasshopper® in Rhinoceros® 5.0 on a computer workstation with Intel Xeon CPU Processor 1.8 GHz Dual and 4.0 GB of RAM, working on 64 bit. The framework of the collaborative design support platform is shown in Fig. 3.

The collaborative design platform was developed on Computer-Aided Design (CAD) software, named Rhinoceros® [31], with Grasshopper® plug-in [32].

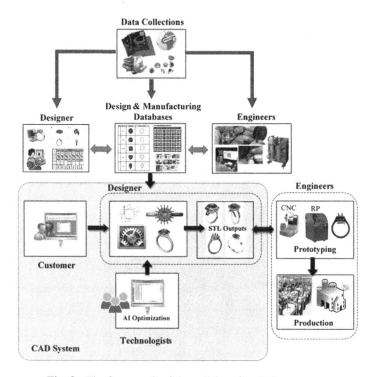

Fig. 3. The framework of the collaborative design support.

Galapagos® [33], a plug-in in Grasshopper® was employed to optimize design parameter in IGA integrated with the collaborative design support platform.

The collaborative design process starts with customer requirements. Customer inputs his requirements of two design parameters: size of center gemstone and size of the halo gemstones to the system via the mobile application (see Fig. 4).

The collaborative design support system then automatically works with the product model and generates the resulting 3D model. The designer, engineer and technologist

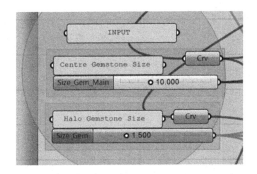

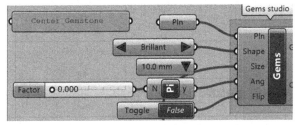

Fig. 4. Examples of customer user interfaces.

monitor the resulting 3D model, if not thing goes wrong, the model will be passed to the production process. Otherwise, the designer can interact with CAD platform to improve the 3D model and re-negotiate with the customer via the mobile application, the engineer can reject or give feedback for the model or enhance the manufacturability of the model, while technologist can adjust the optimization model through the platform.

Comparing the proposed collaborative design support platform to the traditional approach, it is able to reduce design and production time from 45 min to 15 min on the task, or about 66%. Moreover, the platform can support mass customization of the halo gemstone rings and can be easily extended to other product models (Fig. 5).

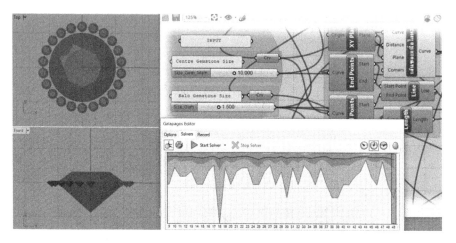

Fig. 5. An experimental result of the proposed collaborative design support platform.

5 Conclusions and Future Direction

A collaborative product design support platform was proposed for product cus-tomization applications. With the collaboration with a jewelry entrepreneur in Thai-land, an industrial case focused on designing halo gemstones rings to achieve an aesthetic appearance through the manufacturability was performed.

Based on the experimental results, the proposed platform is capable of automati-cally design the halo gemstones rings, which is set the center stone, and halo gemstones by using a set of inputs from customer. The inputs that the system requires are the size and cut of the center gemstone and the size of the halo gemstone. Those parameters are considered as a fitness function in the IGA-based collaborative design system. It was developed by using data and information about jewelry ring design from jewelry designers and a jewelry manufacturer. The system testing with the manufacturer showed that the proposed system can aid the CAD designers and reduce halo setting and arrangement time by about 66% in comparison with the standard manual method. In future, we plan to include other product models and product structures in our system.

Acknowledgments. This research has been conducted with the financial support of Faculty of Engineering, Naresuan University with the Project Contract No. R2562E009 and PhD scholar-ship. The author would like to gratefully thank all participants for their collaboration in this research.

References

1. Narayan, K.L., Rao, K.M., Sarcar, M.M.M.: Computer Aided Design and Manufacturing, 1st edn. Prentice Hall of India, New Delhi (2008)
2. Shen, W., Hao, Q., Li, W.: Computer supported collaborative design: retrospective and perspective. Comput. Ind. **59**, 855–862 (2008)
3. Zha X.F., Sriram, R.D.: Collaborative product development and customization: a platform-based strategy and implementation. In: 2004 ASME Design Engineering Technical Conference, Salt Lake City, Utah, USA, pp. 1–12 (2004)
4. Sims, K.: Artificial evolution for computer graphics. Comput. Graph. **25**, 319–328 (1991)
5. Bentley, P.: Evolutionary Design by Computers. Morgan Kaufmann, San Francisco (1999)
6. Bentley, P.J., Corne, D.W.: An introduction to creative evolutionary systems. In: Bentley, P. J., Corne, D.W. (ed.) Creative Evolutionary Systems. Morgan Kaufmann, San Francisco, pp. 1–75 (2002)
7. Whitley, D.: A genetic algorithm tutorial. Stat. Comput. **4**, 65–85 (1994). https://doi.org/10.1007/BF00175354
8. Lourenço, N., Assunção, F., Maçãs, C., Machado, P.: EvoFashion: customising fashion through evolution. In: Correia, J., Ciesielski, V., Liapis, A. (eds.) EvoMUSART 2017. LNCS, vol. 10198, pp. 176–189. Springer, Cham (2017). https://doi.org/10.1007/978-3-319-55750-2_12
9. Muehlbauer, M., Burry, J., Song, A.: Automated shape design by grammatical evolution. In: Correia, J., Ciesielski, V., Liapis, A. (eds.) EvoMUSART 2017. LNCS, vol. 10198, pp. 217–229. Springer, Cham (2017). https://doi.org/10.1007/978-3-319-55750-2_15
10. Tabatabaei Anaraki, N.A.: Fashion design aid system with application of interactive genetic algorithms. In: Correia, J., Ciesielski, V., Liapis, A. (eds.) EvoMUSART 2017. LNCS, vol. 10198, pp. 289–303. Springer, Cham (2017). https://doi.org/10.1007/978-3-319-55750-2_20
11. Cohen, M.W., Cherchiglia, L., Costa, R.: Evolving mondrian-style artworks. In: Correia, J., Ciesielski, V., Liapis, A. (eds.) EvoMUSART 2017. LNCS, vol. 10198, pp. 338–353. Springer, Cham (2017). https://doi.org/10.1007/978-3-319-55750-2_23
12. Rodriguez, L., Diago, L., Hagiwara, I.: Interactive genetic algorithm with fitness modeling for the development of a color simulation system based on customer's preference. Japan J. Ind. Appl. Math. **28**, 27–42 (2011). https://doi.org/10.1007/s13160-011-0032-2
13. Dou, R., Zong, C., Li, M.: An interactive genetic algorithm with the interval arithmetic based on hesitation and its application to achieve customer collaborative product configuration design. Appl. Soft Comput. **38**, 384–394 (2016)
14. Byrne, J., Cardiff, P., Brabazon, A., O'Neill, M.: Evolving parametric aircraft models for design exploration and optimisation. Neurocomputing **142**, 39–47 (2014)
15. Gong, D., Yuan, J., Sun, X.: Interactive genetic algorithms with individual's fuzzy fitness. Comput. Hum. Behav. **27**, 1482–1492 (2011)
16. Mok, P.Y., Xu, J., Wang, X.X., Fan, J.T., Kwok, Y.L., Xin, J.H.: An IGA-based design support system for realistic and practical fashion designs. Comput. Aided Des. **45**, 1442–1458 (2013)
17. Ono, S., Maeda, H., Sakimoto, K., Nakayama, S.: User-system cooperative evolutionary computation for both quantitative and qualitative objective optimization in image processing filter design. Appl. Soft Comput. **15**, 203–218 (2014)
18. Poirson, E., Dépincé, P., Petiot, J.-F.: User-centered design by genetic algorithms: application to brass musical instrument optimization. Eng. Appl. Artif. Intell. **20**, 511–518 (2006)

19. Tang, C.Y., Fung, K.Y., Lee, E.W.M., Ho, G.T.S., Siu, K.W.M., Mou, W.L.: Product form design using customer perception evaluation by a combined superellipse fitting and ANN approach. Adv. Eng. Inform. **27**, 386–394 (2013)
20. Wannarumon, S., Bohez, E.L.J., Annanon, K.: Aesthetic evolutionary algorithm for fractal-based user-centered jewelry design. Artif. Intell. Eng. Des. Anal. Manuf. **22**, 19–39 (2008)
21. Su, Y., Ohsaki, M., Wu, Y., Zhang, J.: A numerical method for form finding and shape optimization of reciprocal structures. Eng. Struct. **198**, 109510 (2019)
22. Agkathidis, A.: Generative Design: Form-finding Techniques in Architecture. Laurence King Publishing, London (2016)
23. Takagi, H.: Interactive evolutionary computation: fusion of the capabilities of EC optimization and human evaluation. Proc. IEEE **89**, 1275–1296 (2001)
24. Brintrup, A.M., Ramsden, J., Tiwari, A.: An interactive genetic algorithm-based framework for handling qualitative criteria in design optimization. Comput. Ind. **58**, 279–291 (2007)
25. Sheikhi Darani, Z., Kaedi, M.: Improving the interactive genetic algorithm for customer-centric product design by automatically scoring the unfavorable designs. Human-centric Comput. Inf. Sci. **7**, 38 (2017)
26. Kielarova, S.W., Sansri, S.: Shape optimization in product design using interactive genetic algorithm integrated with multi-objective optimization. In: Sombattheera, C., Stolzenburg, F., Lin, F., Nayak, A. (eds.) MIWAI 2016. LNCS (LNAI), vol. 10053, pp. 76–86. Springer, Cham (2016). https://doi.org/10.1007/978-3-319-49397-8_7
27. Brintrup, A.M., Ramsden, J., Takagi, H., Tiwari, A.: Ergonomic chair design by fusing qualitative and quantitative criteria using interactive genetic algorithms. IEEE Trans. Evol. Comput. **12**, 343–354 (2008)
28. Evolutionary principles applied to problem solving using galapagos (2017)
29. Hu, Z.-H., Ding, Y.-S., Zhang, W.-B., Yan, Q.: An interactive co-evolutionary CAD system for garment pattern design. Comput. Aided Des. **40**, 1094–1104 (2008)
30. Kielarova, S.W., Pradujphongphet, P., Nakmethee, C.: Development of computer-aided design module for automatic gemstone setting on halo ring. KKU Eng. J. **43**, 239–243 (2016)
31. McNeel, R.: Rhinoceros 3D Modelling Software (2020)
32. Davidson, S.: Grasshopper-algorithmic modeling for rhino (2020)
33. Rutten D: Galapagos evolutionary solver (2020)

Towards Automatic Generation of Storyline Aided by Collaborative Creative Design

Iwona Grabska-Gradzińska[1]($\boxtimes$) (iD), Ewa Grabska[3] (iD),
Leszek Nowak[2] (iD), and Wojciech Palacz[3] (iD)

[1] Department of Games Technology, Faculty of Physics, Astronomy
and Applied Computer Science, Jagiellonian University, Krakow, Poland
`iwona.grabska@uj.edu.pl`
[2] Department of Information Technologies, Faculty of Physics, Astronomy
and Applied Computer Science, Jagiellonian University, Krakow, Poland
`leszek.nowak@uj.edu.pl`
[3] Department of Design and Computer Graphics, Faculty of Physics, Astronomy
and Applied Computer Science, Jagiellonian University, Krakow, Poland
`{ewa.grabska,wojciech.palacz}@uj.edu.pl`

Abstract. This paper proposes a new collaborative design on an educational platform that supports automatic game generation based on graph rules. The platform enables computer game researchers to analyze and discuss students' needs and preferences. In this approach, the computer game is created on the basis of a layered graph representing the functional elements of the story, characters, locations, and objects. This layered graph is dynamic changed by graph rules whose sequence represents the player's actions. The goal of the cooperative work that took place at the Jagiellonian University in Poland was to create, prepare and implement the plot of the adventure game in such a way as to design a set of singular player actions. A player in any game can use prepared actions in any number of tasks, sequentially and repeatedly, to create their own way to achieve the goal. All student work was placed in a system implemented on the base of Godot Engine, enabling the creation graph structures and graph rules as well as automatic generation of animations. At the final stage of the project, students have the opportunity to evaluate the game and analyze the narrative sequences, their length and objects used in the context of the story. In the future, our research can be also treated as a study of the preferences of computer game players obtained thanks to the suggestions of a selected group of people without professional or specialized knowledge in the field of computer game design.

Keywords: Decision support · Collaborative design · Graph transformations · Procedural storytelling

1 Introduction

In the process of designing Role-Playing Games (RPGs) there is a need to use a formalized method of creating stories. This is dictated by the method of implementation of quest systems, dialog system, events and character interactions [1]. Each specific

© Springer Nature Switzerland AG 2020
Y. Luo (Ed.): CDVE 2020, LNCS 12341, pp. 47–56, 2020.
https://doi.org/10.1007/978-3-030-60816-3_6

implementation is unique and rarely published outside of the studios developing games. This paper proposes a new collaboration project on an educational platform that supports the automatic generation of gameplays based on graph rules. The platform enables computer game researchers to analyze and discuss students' needs and preferences. In the presented approach a story design tool is created with the use of the layered graph consisting with four layers whose nodes stand for: functional story elements, characters, locations, and items.

The collaboration described in this paper took place at the Faculty of Physics, Astronomy and Applied Computer Science of Jagiellonian University in Poland and lasted one semester. It was attended by 36 computer science students divided teams of three and four researchers.

In the proposed approach the outline of the plot and the goal of the game was presented by the researchers to the students. The aim of the cooperative work was to create, prepare and implement the plot of the adventure game. A set of singular player actions was created, represented by series of graph rules. In total 13 subsets were made, each representing unique quest designed by a team. However, the player playing the game can use any of the actions in any order in any number of tasks, sequentially and repeatedly, to create their own way to achieve the main objective of the game.

All student work was implemented in Godot Engine [2]. The work included creation of graph structures, productions, and animations. Animation sequence corresponds to one gameplay and can was generated automatically using shorter animations representing actions. Generated story enables testing the consistency of the game world and narrative elements. As the last step of the project, students have the options to evaluate the game and analyze the narration sequences, their length and utilized objects in the context of the story.

2   RPG Plot Design Process

The main idea of role-playing games is to discover the story described by the sequence of events, which leads the player to a certain conclusion during the game. By event we mean the smallest set of changes in the game world that create plot twists. The order of the sequence of events depends on the cause-and-effect relationship between the events. It is assumed that the stories presented in RPGs should be developed in many variants. The most common solution is to prepare consistent minor stories that can be played in a different order or selectively.

The game world is a set of all objects presented in the game together with specific relationships among them and their possible interactions. It can be seen that in existing role-playing games, these minor stories, usual "quests", lead the player to the assumed end of the game. The completed task is, as mentioned, a sequence of events. Identical or very similar events can occur in many different game quests. The significance of the narrative of the event is achieved taking into account the context. We can create an event typology that shows event similarity groups, e.g. actions of fight, conversations, sales, relocations, etc.

This paper deals with the conceptual stage of the design process related to RPGs. This stage of game design is based on the outline of the plot, start and the goal of the game, which is important for the game designer, however not comprehensible for the computer. Supporting the design process by the computer requires graph data structures integrating the representation of the designed objects and the process of generation of their models.

3 Graph Model

In order to formalize and (partially) automatize building the storyline, the method of describing a point within a story must be defined. To address this challenge, we are using a layered hierarchical graph to represent a state of the world (state graph). To influence the world, we are using actions and events, that are represented as graph rules, that can transform corresponding fragments of game state graph.

We have decided to use graph representation to aid the plot design process. The creative actions of the designers can be reported as the standard graph operations, easily compared and consolidated and sometimes automatized.

3.1   Initial Word State and Rules of Changing It

State of the World Representation. Game world is represented by a layered hierarchical graph hereafter referred to as the Game State Graph, as presented in Fig. 1. Every graph node stands for one object of the game world. All objects are divided into four categories, represented as graph layers. Dependencies between objects are represented by the graph edges (spatial relations, ownership, affiliation, etc. – narrative meaning depends on the layer it uses). Object properties are expressed by node attributes.

Formal definitions are shown below.

A **hierarchical graph** is a system

$$G = (V, E, s, t, ch, lab, atr),$$

where:

- V and E are finite disjoint sets of nodes and edges,
- $s: E \rightarrow V$ and $t: E \rightarrow V$ are edge source and edge target functions,
- $ch: V \cup E \rightarrow 2^{V \cup E}$ is a child nesting function such that $\forall x \in V \cup E: x \notin ch^+(x)$,
- $lab: V \cup E \rightarrow L$ is a labeling function,
- $atr: V \cup E \rightarrow 2^A$ is an attributing function.

This definition provides attributes, but does not determine what their values are. It can be said that nodes and edges in these graphs are generic.

Let us come back to the game. We can have a node which represents a sword, with attributes for damage dealt and its price in gold pieces, but it is an abstract sword – we do not know if it is a +50 sword of dragon slaying which costs ten thousand, or a worthless −1 rusty sword. A graph with concrete values assigned to its attributes is known as an instance.

A **graph instance** is defined as

$$I = (V, E, s, t, ch, lab, atr, val),$$

where:

- *(V, E, s, t, ch, lab, atr)* is a graph,
- *val: (V ∪ E)* × *A → D*, with $D = U_{a \in A} D_a$, is a partial function such that

  for all $x \in V \cup E$ and $a \in A$
  if $a \in atr(x)$ then $val(x, a) \in D_a$.

  Let us assume that L (the set of labels) consists of three disjoint subsets Σ_V, Σ_D, and Σ_U, which are used to label nodes, directed edges, and undirected edges. Further-more, let $Y = \{Y_1, Y_2, ... Y_n\}$ be a partition of Σ_V.

Graph G or instance I is layered if and only if

$$\text{for all } x \in V$$
$$lab(x) \in Y_i \text{ implies that } lab(V \cap ch^+(x)) \subset Y_i$$

(i.e., a node and all other nodes nested in it have labels from the same layer). In the specific case presented in this paper

$$Y = \{PLOT, CHAR, LOC, ITEM\}.$$

Summarizing, a gameplay graph is, formally speaking, a layered graph instance. Figure 4 shows an example of one layer of such a graph model. The more detailed description of layered graphs and their game application is in [3, 4].

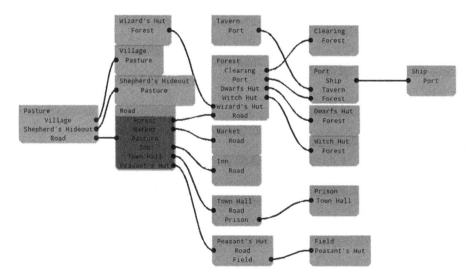

Fig. 1. Example of the Locations layer of Game State Graph.

Events Representation. As the Game State Graph represents the actual state of the game world, the natural way to represent actions taken by the player is to use graph rules, called productions. A production is a pair of graphs called left-hand side and right-hand side of the production. The application of the production to a given Game State Graph turns its subgraph representing the object(s) involved into action (show in Fig. 2.) into a new subgraph representing the consequences of the action (see Fig. 3).

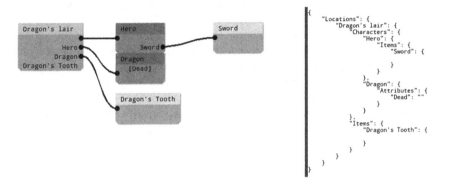

Fig. 2. Graph representation of left side of production with its associated JSON notation

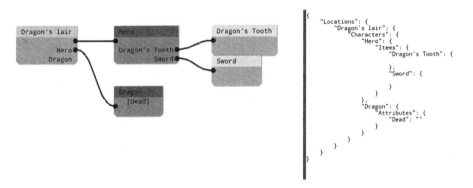

Fig. 3. Graph representation of right side of production with its associated JSON notation

As mentioned above, one production stands for the smallest set of changes in the game world, which can be regarded as purposeful. The exact decision on splitting the story into productions lays with story writers, but decision process is made easier by using the idea of generic productions.

3.2   Hierarchy of Graph Rules

The Game State Graph and the set of productions describes the game but are not very useful while describing the design process and ongoing evolution of the game from the rough concept to the final product. It is necessary to expand the proposed system with hierarchical structure of productions, in which productions defined as pair of subgraphs are the lowest element of the hierarchy, to use this system to coordinate and facilitate the process of collaborative design process. Let's then introduce the idea of generic production.

While analyzing the existing RPG narrations, we observed that lot of events are similar. For example, the same action taken by different characters using different objects in the same purpose (e.g. gunsmith selling the riffle to traveler, farmer selling chicken to traveler etc.), similarly actions of the same type but different narrative consequences (e.g. traveler buying the chicken, traveler stealing the chicken etc.). We can build the hierarchy of productions starting from the most generic interactions derived directly from the game mechanics. The production elements can use variables in place of any objects or any element of a specific layer. Such productions are called "generic productions". Generic productions can be refined and made more "specific" by adding context and restrictions. In this case some of the variables are replaced with specific nodes. The most detailed productions are made only of nodes found in Game State Graph with exact value of attributes, which can be directly applied on Game State Graph during the gameplay. We call them "detailed productions".

4   Graph Representation Using JSON Format in Godot

In our attempts to create suitable method that allows easy collaboration we have decided to use JSON (JavaScript Object Notation) format [5] to write productions. JSON format proved to be versatile and human readable [6, 7]. Example usage of JSON is presented in Fig. 2 and Fig. 3. For collaboration purpose the JSON notation is visualized using Godot Game Engine, free and opensource software designed for game development. Usage of the built-in graph system in Godot allowed us to create tool that allow for fast production browsing and visualization [8]. Furthermore, using the same system, we can display Game State Graph (see Fig. 1) as a location graph with option to examine each location. This is shown of Fig. 4, where detailed view of road node is shown. This approach allows us to observe changes made to the game world as the production are applied to Game State Graph. The tool allows for listing the productions that are applicable to the current world state, modifying JSON notation of productions.

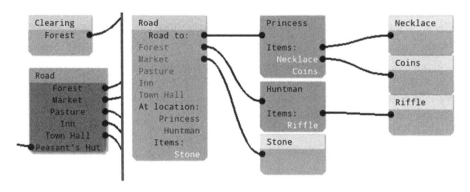

Fig. 4. Left: fragment of Game State Graph with selected Road node. Right: detailed view of the Road node.

Finally, we use Godot to create animation sequences using graphic assets that correspond to graph nodes used in productions. Such animations currently serve as visual hints for the story designers.

5   Collaboration Cycle

The system described above is invented to enable the group of designers to cooperate in order to create RPG. Three groups of coworkers were assumed: world designers, story writers and artists. The first role corresponds to defining the world assumptions, restrictions and world objects: locations, main characters and items. The second team prepares minor stories available within the limits of the world definition: quests, minor events, short stories and dialogs. Graphics designers works on visualizations of world elements and animating the storylines. To complete the cycle, the world designers add connections between the quests and add world events.

5.1   Creating Fundamentals of Game World

The first step of design process is to define objects types, essential characters and all possible generic actions and interactions character can take. This process is done by world designers. The graph representation for these elements are Game State Graph nodes and generic productions (PG). The world designers prepare the rough frame of the plot by creating the initial production (P_{in}) and the final production (P_{out}): the winning conditions or simply conclusion of the main story arc. These are the only detailed productions prepared by world designers. Those are shown in Fig. 2 part 1 and are marked with violet color.

5.2   Creating the Set of Possible Detail Productions for Every Generic One and Preparing Minor Stories

The next step in collaboration process, is to fill the frames of the plot with possible stories that leading the player through the world a conclusion. Writers create detail productions on the base of the generic productions provided by world designers. Created detailed productions use objects from the game world, add attributes to nodes, etc. (see part 2 in the Fig. 5). Each story writer prepares a set of detailed productions that represents a short minor story/quest in form of event chain starting form P_{in} to P_{out} (see part 3 in the Fig. 5). A this stage a story writer may introduce new objects to the world. If needed this will add locations, characters, items, etc.

5.3 Generation of Possible Storylines

When complete stories are ready it is possible to the advantages of the graph structure proposed in our system. The prepared graph productions can be applied to the Game State Graph in any order. This order can simulate a player trying to play a game in various ways. It is possible to rush to the story, go through any available quest, or simply randomly wander the game world. This stage allows us to see if it is possible complete the game differently than initially designed. With every added minor story, the diversity of possible gameplays rises distinctly. Having the option to simulate gameplays is crucial for game designing process.

Every generated sequence stands for one potential player gameplay (see part 4 in the Fig. 5). The story writers craft is to prepare detail productions in the way to avoid trivial conclusion or blocked paths. The generated gameplays can be reviewed to find such problems.

5.4 Creation of Art Assets

In parallel to designers and writers, the graphics designers can work on visual representation of the objects of game world. They prepare assets for every location, character and item and visual variants of these objects with some attributes if needed, e.g. dead character, broken glass (see part 4 in the Fig. 5).

5.5 Animations (After Step 3)

The final step of artists work is to create animations for every single detail production. (see part 5 in the Fig. 5). The animations of each productions are designed to be easily combined into a sequential animated film, showing how specific gameplay will play-out. The challenge here is to blend the animations to match each other in any configuration. The animations can be partially automated as standard action like, picking up an item or interacting with character can be animated by Godot script and will be mostly dependent on object locations within the scene.

5.6 The Game as a Final State of Design Process

The player can see picture based on the actual state of the GSG and list of all productions applicable in the current state of the GSG. It is presented as a list of dialogue and monologue options. Choosing the dialog option means applying production. After then the picture and the dialogue option list are updated. The most common player actions are available also as keyboard shortcuts (Fig. 6).

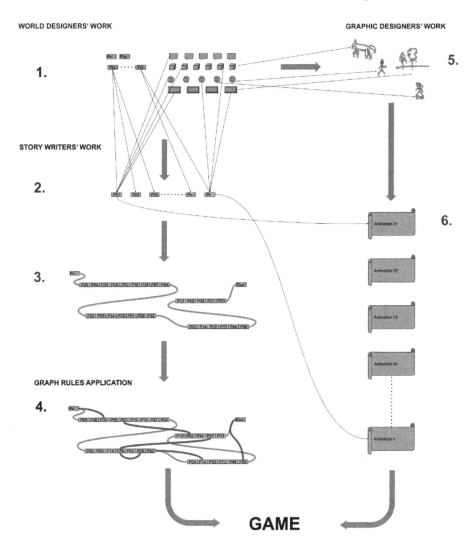

Fig. 5. A collaboration schema for users involved into design process. Elements created by world designers are violet, by story designers – blue and graphic designers – green. Narrow arrows show direct connections between elements from one group, wide arrows – between groups. (Color figure online)

Fig. 6. A collaboration schema legend.

6 Conclusion

In this paper a collaborative design system supporting automatic storyline generation has been proposed. The system can be easily converted to a format game, in which the player experiences the game thanks to the options available to him by the system. If we limited player to detailed productions, it can be considered as a classical visual novel style game. On the other hand, the player can choose mainly generic productions that would suit the form of standard adventure games. Future work with the system focused on making the writing process only dependent on graph representation within Godot Engine. This will eliminate the need for the writers to use JSON notation at all and will allow one to add more useful metadata to JSON files that are useful to the editor, e.g. the coordinates of each object in the scene.

References

1. Kjeldsen, J.L.B.: The Quest for the Custom Quest System, 18 August 2017, GameDev.net. https://www.gamedev.net/articles/game-design/game-design-and-theory/the-quest-for-the-custom-quest-system-r4728/
2. Linietsky, J., Manzur, A., et al.: Godot Engine Homepage. https://godotengine.org/. Accessed 04 Apr 2020
3. Grabska-Gradzińska, I., et al.: Graph-based data structures of computer games. In: Annual International Conference on Computer Games, Multimedia & Allied Technology, pp. 88–96 (2013)
4. Grabska-Gradzińska, I., et al.: Towards a graph-based model of computer games. In: Das, V. V., Ezendu, A. (eds.) Advances in Information Technologies and Communication 2012: proceedings of Joint International Conferences on ICT, CIT, PECS and EMIE - 2012. Computer Science Series, ISSN 2213-2805; 3. Amsterdam: ACEEE, pp. 34–39 (2012)
5. Grabska-Gradzińska, I., Nowak, L., Palacz, F., Grabska, E.: Collaborative Story Generation using JSON in Godot Engine as Decision Making Support Tool. IC on Cognitive Decision Support Systems & Technologies (2020)
6. Peng, D., Cao, L.-D., Xu, W.-J.: Using JSON for data exchanging in web service applications. J. Comput. Inf. Syst. 7(16), 5883–5890 (2011)
7. Wehner, P., Piberger, C., Göhringer, D.: Using JSON to manage communication between services in the Internet of Things. In: 2014 9th International Symposium on Reconfigurable and Communication-Centric Systems-on-Chip (ReCoSoC), Montpellier, pp. 1–4 (2014)
8. Manzur, A., Marques, G.: Godot Engine Game Development in 24 Hours, Sams Teach Yourself: The Official Guide to Godot 3.0 (2018)

Cooperative Design of an Interactive Museum Guide

Grażyna Ślusarczyk⬤, Barbara Strug$^{(\boxtimes)}$⬤, and Andrzej Kapanowski⬤

Institute of Applied Computer Science, Jagiellonian University,
Lojasiewicza 11, 30-348 Kraków, Poland
{grazyna.slusarczyk,barbara.strug,andrzej.kapanowski}@uj.edu.pl

Abstract. This paper deals with the problem of supporting museum
visitors in searching for interesting artworks and finding their visiting
routes compatible with personal preferences. The proposed application
uses knowledge related to museum building structure and topology, and
to substantive content of museum collections. Therefore the cooperation
between the designer of a museum guide with the museum curator, who
provides information about artworks and their assignment to exhibitions,
collections and rooms, is indispensable. All this data is stored in a graph,
where nodes represent building spaces, edges correspond to accessibility
relations between these spaces, while node attributes describe both geo-
metrical properties of spaces and semantic information related to art
pieces and collections. The user can specify artworks, exhibitions, collections he wants to visit together with personal preferences concerning
the visiting path (like using lifts). Then graph algorithms are used to
find the most appropriate route for the user. Moreover, the user can
define personalized collections and share them with other users of the
application.

Keywords: Graph structure · User interface design · Museum guide

1 Introduction

This paper deals with the problem of providing contextual information in a
museum guide, which would support the visitors in managing their personalized
ways of visiting and finding their way through complex museum halls. The proposed application offers intelligent knowledge-based navigation, which supports
moving around a museum, while taking into account not only artistic interests of
users but also their possible restrictions in mobility. Such applications improve
visitors' experience in a museum [1]. The existing applications dedicated for
museums in Warsaw allow for finding out in which museums and in which rooms
the interesting objects are, but do not allow for finding efficient routes leading through selected rooms and which additionally, for example, do not include
stairs. In contrast to other existing applications, where way-finding for museum
exploration is usually based on RFID technology or marker-based localization

© Springer Nature Switzerland AG 2020
Y. Luo (Ed.): CDVE 2020, LNCS 12341, pp. 57–66, 2020.
https://doi.org/10.1007/978-3-030-60816-3_7

systems [2,3], our approach does not require any sensors, tags or markers located inside buildings. Moreover the proposed application enables the user to define her/his personalized collections containing any pieces of art from the museum catalog and share them with other application users.

In order to find different types of routes in a museum building two types of knowledge are needed. The first type is related to the structure and topology of the building which is to be visited. The other one is related to semantics, i.e., substantive content of museum collections. Often museum visitors want to see only art belonging to selected collections (e.g. secession, foreign art, polish painting, sacred art, medieval art), created by selected artists, temporary exhibitions or only most famous works, in case of their first visit in a museum. Therefore the cooperation between the designer of the museum guide interface and the curator of the museum is indispensable.

The information about the building structure and topology is extracted from the building floorplan and stored in a graph [4,5]. Graph nodes represent building elements (spaces, rooms, stairs, lifts, ramps), while edges correspond to accessibility relations between these elements. Nodes are labelled by names of functions of building elements (e.g., a cloak room, coffee shop, toilet) or numbers of exhibition spaces. Attributes assigned to graph nodes encode properties of building elements, like their sizes or door specification. Attributes of graph edges represent costs of moving between spaces, which can depend on width of openings, existence of lifts, distances between spaces, and door types. The information about the substantive content of the museum collections is specified by the museum curator. She/he determines the assignment of art pieces to exhibition rooms together with descriptions and characteristics of these works. In addition, it is determined which rooms contain elements from selected collections as well as permanent and temporary exhibitions. This semantic information is stored in suitable attributes of graph nodes representing exhibition rooms. All this data together allows for performing any user-defined task related to path planning. The user can specify complex criteria for a museum tour path by indicating the galleries, collections, art pieces or groups of art pieces he wants to visit and selecting communication elements that should or should not be included in the path (stairs, lifts, escalators). Then the found path is shown on the screen on subsequent partial plans, on which the current place and the places, to which the user should go are marked.

The GUI of the proposed application is generated dynamically and therefore it is always compatible with information encoded in the graph and the semantic information introduced by the curator. It is self-adapting, which means that in case of any changes in the accessibility of museum rooms (i.e., a lift can be out of order, some rooms can be inaccessible due to the renovation) or in data concerning collections, the application will show the user appropriately modified information. The proposed application is useful for first-time visitors who want to find only famous art pieces in an unknown building, visitors who want to see only specific pieces, and for museum curators and maintenance operators who need support in their daily needs to move around the building.

2   A Graph Representation of Museum Floorplans

As the internal model of museum floorplans, attributed labelled graphs are used. They constitute semantically rich data structures, which encode both spatial and non-spatial information of different types, and on which several algorithms searching for shortest paths or algorithms solving the traveling salesman problem can be performed.

Graph nodes represent museum halls, rooms, cabinets, stairs, lifts, and ramps, while edges correspond to vertical (through openings or doors) or horizontal (through stairs, lifts or ramps) accessibility relations between these elements. A set of node labels contains numbers of exhibition halls and rooms, functional types of spaces and rooms (like a cloak room, coffee shop, toilet) and names of elements allowing for vertical and horizontal communication. Attributes assigned to graph nodes encode properties of building elements, like their sizes, openings and door specification. The positions and widths of openings as well as the door types and their opening directions are saved in attributes assigned to the node representing the considered space. For each space with more than one door or opening, costs of passing this space from any entry to any leaving point is stored in an attribute called a lookup table [5].

Attributes of graph edges represent costs of moving between and through spaces, which can depend on existence of lifts or ramps, distances between spaces, and door types. In cases when the cost of passing the same path but in different direction is not be the same, due to slopes of stairs and ramps, and unalike forces need for opening different types of doors, the directed graphs with two edges representing passing spaces in both directions are used.

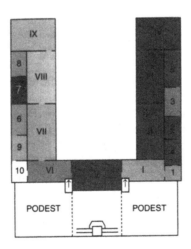

Fig. 1. A plan of the first floor of the of National Museum in Warsaw

A plan of the first floor of the building of the National Museum in Warsaw is depicted in Fig. 1. On this floor the Gallery of 19th Century Art is located. The

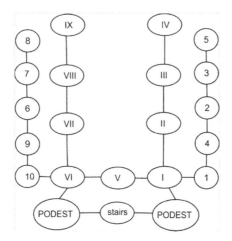

Fig. 2. A graph representing the accessibility between spaces of the first floor of the Museum

layout of the floor is composed of nine exhibition halls, ten cabinets and stairs with two landings connecting this floor with other storeys.

The space layout illustrated in Fig. 1 is represented by a graph shown in Fig. 2. Graph nodes labelled I–IX represent exhibition halls, nodes labelled 1–10 represent cabinets, and nodes labelled PODEST represent stair landings. Edges connecting nodes represent the accessibility relation between spaces. The costs assigned to them are equal to 0 as there are no doors to open between these spaces.

3   Museum Guide User Interface

In order to create an application supporting the museum visitor in finding routes in a building the information about the substantive content of the museum collections is needed. The assignment of art pieces to exhibition rooms together with their descriptions and characteristics, specification of rooms hosting permanent galleries, collections and temporary exhibitions is determined by the curator of the museum in the proposed application. The *Curator* functionality (see Fig. 3), which is available only for the museum's curator, is used for this purpose. All this information is stored in attributes assigned to graph nodes representing museum rooms. Therefore from each graph node the data about art pieces in the corresponding room and about collections to which this room is dedicated can be extracted.

As the potential visitor usually does not know in which room the interesting art pieces are, the interface provides different search criteria. The user can specify a collection (for example sacred art or foreign art) or a permanent gallery, all work pieces of the chosen artist, temporary exhibitions or the most famous artworks. In such cases one of the predefined routes through the museum is proposed by the application and presented in the interface. The visitor has also the possibility to specify selected artworks or groups of works he wants to visit and indicate elements, like stairs or lifts, that should be included or excluded from the path. In this case the application searches for the chosen art pieces in the graph attributes and the traveling salesman algorithm is used to find the best route to visit all the rooms in which the interesting works are. Then the found path is shown on the screen on subsequent partial plans, on which the current place and the places, to which the user should go are marked. If the places to be visited are located on different floors, then the path leads through rooms of each considered floor and then to stairs or lifts and continues on the other floor. The users initial position is by default assumed to be the entrance hall of the museum but if the visitor wants to start from a different place they may enter a room number in which they are. Such a way of locating a visitor has an additional advantage of being independent from any tracking device which often fail in providing reliable vertical positions. As the room numbers are unique within each museum this approach can work in any building without the need to adapt.

The main screen of the prototype application is shown in Fig. 3. After expanding the menu *Galleries* the user has the possibility to select permanent exhibitions, namely the Faras Gallery, Gallery of Medieval Art, Gallery of Old Masters, Gallery of 19th Century Art, Gallery of 20th and 21st Century Art, Gallery of Polish Design, or temporary exhibitions. The rooms in which the art pieces belonging to the chosen exhibition are placed, are highlighted on the floor plans. Similarly, when the menu *Collections* is developed the user can select Italian, Flemish, Dutch, French, religious painting, etc. and the appropriate rooms of the floorplans are highlighted. The tool bar gives also the possibility to select all pieces of a given artist or individual works of art.

Figure 3 presents the interface screen after selection of Wyspiański artworks. The cabinet number 7 on the first floor plan is highlighted as Wyspiański paintings are located there. In Fig. 4 menu windows allowing for selecting available galleries and famous paintings are shown.

After selecting the interesting art pieces the visitor can be guided to them by the application. *Route* menu enables the user to exclude stairs or lifts from his tour, and then searches for the shortest path leading to all selected elements. The found path is drawn on subsequent floor plans on which the current place and the places, to which the user should go are marked.

In Fig. 5 the shortest path leading through museums rooms on the first floor to the hall where the painting titled *The Battle of Grunwald* by the famous polish artist Jan Matejko can be seen, and then to the cabinet number 7, where paintings of Stanisław Wyspiański are exhibited, is shown.

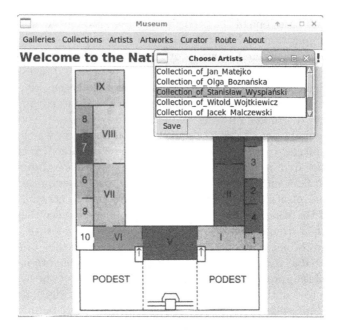

Fig. 3. The main screen of the prototype application

4   Creating Personal Collections and Sharing Information

The user interface described in Sect. 3 allows the museum curator or other administrative staff to add information about all pieces of art in a museum together with their attributes (like authors, type of art, period, material, country of origin) as well as the location within the museum space. This information is mostly permanent with only occasional updates when a new piece of art is acquired or a temporary exhibition is opened. In this regard, information sharing is possible, for example when a temporary exhibition is travelling from one museum to another all the information about its content may be shared between participating institutions.

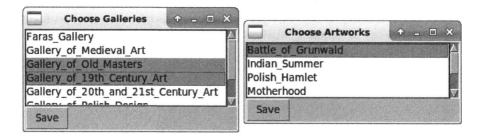

Fig. 4. Menu windows for selecting galleries and famous artworks

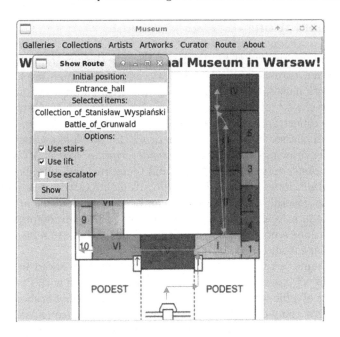

Fig. 5. The path leading to *The Battle of Grunwald* by Jan Matejko and paintings of Stanisław Wyspiański

The museum curator may also create special paths comprising specific thematically arranged artworks to make it easier for visitors to move through the museum. As no curator is able to predict all the visitors interests, the application allows the visitor to define his personalized collections (for example collections on the selected themes like paintings with horses). Such a collection is created by selecting any pieces of art from the museum catalog and can be either private or shared with other users of the application. The visitor can also create a personalized collection by extending or narrowing down any of the predefined collections. For example, the visitor can make public a collection containing all the 20th century paintings by Polish painters, but another visitor may create on the basis of this collection the one that contains only works by female painters.

In Fig. 6 the flow of such a cooperation is presented. The museum curator is responsible for building a museum database which contains all artworks. She/he also adds all required attributes including the location of each artwork within the museum by assigning to it a room number. The curator can also create public collections that contain permanent or temporary exhibitions as well as thematic collections. The visitors can create their personal collections that can be shared with other users. When a collection is accepted by the museum curator it is placed in the shared set of collections and can be accessed by other visitors in the same way as "official" collections added by museum employees. Moreover the visitors can cooperate on particular collections adding elements to them, thus creating specific, thematic or other collections.

5   Implementation

The application is implemented in Python 3 because this programming language has clean syntax, extensive standard library, and builtin high level data structures (lists, dictionaries, sets) [6]. The Graphical User Interface is built with the *tkinter* package, a set of wrappers that implement the *Tk* widgets as Python classes. It is a robust and platform independent windowing toolkit.

Three main classes were created: *Artwork* for art pieces such as paintings, sculptures, drawings (attributes: *name, description, room*); *MCollection* for museum collections, permanent galleries, and temporary exhibitions (attributes: *name, description, items*); *Room* for building elements (attributes: *name, available, items*). In general, many attributes can be used to describe artworks, collections or museum rooms, but we have determined the minimum set that can reflect the relations among base class instances. The attribute *name* serves as a unique identifier for all objects.

Data on rooms, artworks, and museum collections are saved in JSON files (JavaScript Object Notation) because this format plays well with Python classes [7]. A fragment of a file with data on artworks in JSON format is shown in Fig. 7. Python supports many other file formats for data persistence (XML, CSV) and data can be migrated from JSON to a better format in future.

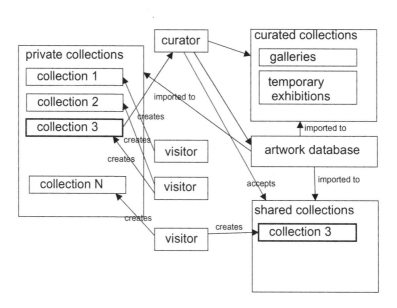

Fig. 6. The flow of the cooperation

```
[
  {
    "class": "Artwork",
    "name": "Battle_of_Grunwald",
    "description": "famous painting by Jan Matejko, 1878",
    "room": "roomIV"
  },
  {
    "class": "Artwork",
    "name": "Self-portrait_Bozna\u0144ska",
    "description": "painting by Olga Bozna\u0144ska, 1893",
    "room": "room8"
  },
  {
    "class": "Artwork",
    "name": "Motherhood",
    "description": "famous painting by Stanis\u0142aw Wyspia\u0144ski, 1905",
    "room": "room7"
  },
  {
    "class": "Artwork",
    "name": "Abduction_of_the_King's_Daughter",
    "description": "famous painting by Witold Wojtkiewicz",
    "room": "room9"
  },
```

Fig. 7. A fragment of a file with data on artworks in JSON format

6 Conclusions and Future Work

The proposed application supports museum visitors in searching for interesting artworks and finding their visiting routes compatible with personal preferences. The knowledge required for the museum route search consists of information about elements representing spaces, elements enabling both vertical and horizontal communication, and substantive content of museum collections. Therefore the cooperation between the designer of a museum guide with the museum curator is needed. The obtained data is stored in the graph representing both the topology of the building and information about artworks, their collections and location in museum rooms. The knowledge stored in the graph enables the user to specify interesting art pieces and personal preferences related to the way of communication. Then graph algorithms are used to find the best route which is drawn on floor layouts.

The current version of our guide allows the users to create personalized collections and apply for them to be accepted by the curator and placed in the shared collections set to be accessed by the public. In future we plan to extend the cooperative possibilities for groups of visitors to work on a single collection as well as allowing for updating already accepted collections in cooperation with the curator.

References

1. Jarrier, E., Bourgeon-Renault, D.: Impact of median devices on the museum visit experience and on visitors behavioral intentions. Int. J. Manag. **15**, 18–21 (2012)
2. Proctor, N.: Mobile Apps for Museums: The AAM Guide to Planning and Strategy. The American Association of Museums, Washington, D.C. (2011)
3. Emmanouilidis, C., Koutsiamanis, R., Tasidou, A.: Mobile guides: taxonomy of architectures, context awareness, technologies and applications. J. Netw. Comput. Appl. **36**, 103–125 (2013)
4. Ślusarczyk, G.: Graph-based representation of design properties in creating building floorplans. Comput. Aided Des. **95**, 24–39 (2018)
5. Strug, B., Ślusarczyk, G.: Reasoning about accessibility for disabled using building graph models based on BIM/IFC. Vis. Eng. **5**, 1–12 (2017)
6. Lutz, M.: Learning Python, 5th edn. O'Reilly Media, Newton (2013)
7. Standard ECMA-404. The JSON Data Interchange Syntax, 2nd edn. (2017). http:// www.ecma-international.org/publications/standards/Ecma-404.htm

A Hybrid Architecture for Tiered Storage with Fuzzy Logic and AutoML

Marwan Batrouni[✉]

University of Burgundy, Dijon, France
marwanbatrouni@gmail.com

Abstract. The explosion of storage needs pauses a multifaceted challenge for organizations, not only it exerts a large pressure on precious resources, but also creates a sub-optimal data environment where the noise level may overwhelm the actual signal. However, despite the economies of scale achieved by major cloud platforms, the fundamental issue of storage optimization did not go away.

The past few years witnessed a renewed interest in storage optimization strategies beyond the brute force of cloud scale, one of these strategies is storage tiering, which provides the capability of a dynamic and optimized matching between data and storage systems.

In this paper we propose an enhanced architecture that involves the synthesis of fuzzy logic and automated machine learning (AutoML) for an intelligent tierd storage system.

Keywords: Automated machine learning (AutoML) · Fuzzy Logic Controller · Storage tiering · Cloud storage

1 Introduction

At the time of this writing, the Covid-19 pandemic is raging across the planet, causing devastation and social upheaval. One of the consequences of the pandemic is the explosion of digital communication due to the work from home setup and other needs, a situation which promotes a huge amount of digital footprint such as Zoom meetings, Microsoft Teams... etc.

In this context, a good proportion of the communication files and logs may eventually be destined to a long term storage. Such increase of the digital footprint would potentially exacerbate the need for an optimized storage ecosystem.

Even before the pandemic, a study conducted by IDC [17] projected the size of data produced worldwide to increase at least five folds by 2025 to a massive 175 Zeta bytes. We can imagine this number to be a conservative estimate given the current events.

Despite the emergence of new tiering features proposed by popular cloud platforms (such as AWS), organizations should not be absolved from seeking storage optimization, mainly because it allows them the flexibility of selecting different storage providers and/or technologies, be it on-premise or cloud based.

© Springer Nature Switzerland AG 2020
Y. Luo (Ed.): CDVE 2020, LNCS 12341, pp. 67–74, 2020.
https://doi.org/10.1007/978-3-030-60816-3_8

For instance, it is conceivable that a storage system may persist data in S3, Azure, Google storage... etc., in addition to a local object storage, all simultaneously. Consequently, an independent tiering system capable of effective recommendation becomes a necessity.

Intelligence-driven tiering system is an active area of research. Several published papers, such as [12] proposed different ML driven strategies for tiering.

Our approach is to create a synthesis between AutoML and fuzzy logic to propose a high-performance architecture for a tiering system.

The first part of this paper provides a short synopsis around the domains involved. The second part describes our approach.

2 Overview of Foundational Concepts

In this section, we outline the key ingredients used in the architecture, namely Fuzzy Logic Controller (FLC) and AutoML.

2.1 Fuzzy Control Systems

The fuzzy logic theory was initiated by L. Zadeh in his 1965 seminal paper on Fuzzy sets [19], It is defined by [18] as: *Intended to model logical reasoning with vague or imprecise statements like "Petr is young (rich, tall, hungry, etc.)".* More formally [1] Let X is universal set. A fuzzy set A in X is defined by a membership function denoted by A; that is $A : X \to [0, 1]$.

One of the many applications of fuzzy logic is called Fuzzy Logic Controller (FLC) it originated from the work of E. H. Mamdani in the seventies [14], FLC is described as *Provides an algorithm which can convert the linguistic control strategy based on expert knowledge into an automatic control strategy* [13]. Typically, in the literature the FLC design pattern is shown as in Fig. 1. The general layout of the FLC architecture includes:

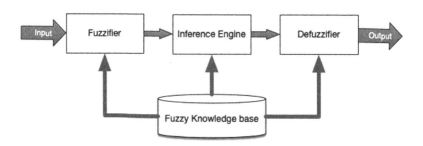

Fig. 1. Fuzzy Logic Controller (FLC) pattern.

1. A Fuzzification component: This is essentially an adapter that transforms a crisp input into a fuzzy value, for instance, a digit into something like (Small, Large, Extra Large...) enumeration.

2. Fuzzy rules: A set of **IF** <Condition> **THEN** <Consequent>, for instance, **IF** file read access average ≤100 per month **THEN** Past Access Frequency (PAF)=LOW
3. Inference system: This is the engine that interprets the fuzzy rules to reach a final outcome. It may be a rule engine such as DROOLS [9].
4. Defuzzification component: An adapter that takes in a fuzzy value and produces a crisp value, for instance, if the input of a file size is *SMALL* then the output may be something like 100 KB

The FLC pattern has been applied successfully in many domains [4] such as automobile manufacturing, cement processing, medical instruments, and academia to name just a few. In the next section, we visit the second main element in the architecture which is AutoML.

2.2   Automatic Machine Learning

The field of Machine learning, has a long and rich history [16], the fifties saw the creation of the artificial neuron called the *Perceptron* by Frank Rosenblatt, since then the field expanded exponentially, especially with the advent of big data and cloud computing.

Nonetheless, the richness and extreme diversity of algorithms and tools of ML created a challenge for the non-experts, not to mention the need to automatically adjust to the fast changing data patterns and business requirements even for experts. A challenge summed up by how to navigate through the maze and select the most optimal approach to use ML.

To address some of these challenges, the past few years saw the emergence of Automated machine learning (AutoML), which is a framework that *provides methods and processes to make Machine Learning available for non-Machine Learning experts* [3] it is conceived to be an automated construction of a machine-learning pipeline on a limited computational budget [11] One of its key features of interest to us is its ability to match an appropriate machine learning algorithm to a dataset. Many open source frameworks exist that implements AutoML such as Auto-SKLearn, Auto-Weka, TPOT among others, as benchmarked and surveyed in [5,10].

With this and the previous section outlines, now we have the two important ingredients to construct our tiered storage architecture, by creating a synthesis framework.

3   A Synthesis Architecture

In recent years, several major industry players adopted tiered storage [2], however, the inner workings of the different architectures remain largely proprietary. Few research papers described possible approaches [6,8,12], however, to the best of our knowledge the approach proposed in this paper incorporates improvements on the general intelligent tiering idea.

The main premise behind our architecture is that even with an ML or AutoML driven tiered storage, at some point the load put on the recommendation system may be overwhelming, especially in a cloud setting that deals with big data. Therefore, injecting a dose of fuzzification with FLC may help improve responsiveness and scalability by trading precision for performance.

This section lays out the high level conceptual architecture along with its dynamic aspects, represented by two key use cases, which are the creation of the tier recommendation model, and the tier recommendation request by a storage system.

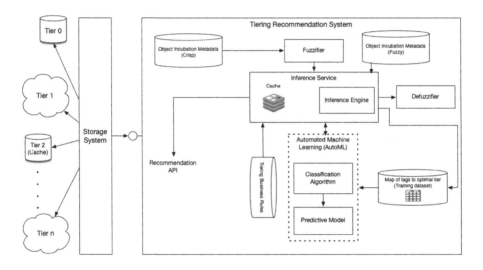

Fig. 2. A hybrid tiering system layout.

Figure 2 shows the conceptual layout of the architecture, the following is a description of the components shown in the diagram.

1. **Storage system:** Represents the front end of a storage system which can be either file or Object type, the system services call the tiering recommendation service API to obtain a storage tier recommendation.
2. **Tiering recommendation system:** The set of services responsible for producing a storage tier recommendation depending on the object characteristics and tags.
3. **Storage tier:** Any type of storage targets, such as cloud (S3, Dynamo Db, Azure blob... etc.) or local domain (SAN, NAS, Object, Redis cache... etc.)
4. **Tiering business rules:** A set of business rules which ultimately determine if a storage tier is eligible to host the object, these rules can be fuzzy and/or crisp rules.
5. **Object incubation metadata:** A set of object data points collected over a certain period of time (called an incubation phase). These data points (called tags), which can either be fuzzy or crisp variables and fall in two main types:

- *Native tags:* provided by the object sender and attached to the transaction metadata, for instance a tag indicating the importance level of the object (i.e Low importance, Medium importance, High importance, Very high importance)
- *Surrogate tags:* Assigned by the tiering system to the object, these tags may be calculated or deduced using transaction logs, for instance, the object Past Access Frequency (PAF).
   In addition to the tags types mentioned above, there exists a set of hyper-parameters specifying the tiering framework, for instance, how many tiers, the prices for storage or access per tier, the locations of these tiers... etc.

6. **Automated machine learning:** The component responsible for recommending a classification algorithm, this component would be a service wrapping and exposing a framework such as Auto-SKLearn, which will abstract the classification algorithm and the predictive model.
7. **Classification algorithm:** This is the AutoML framework selected classification algorithm, which can be any supervised ML such as ANN, Random forest... etc.
8. **Predictive model:** The trained classification model used to predict tag values.
9. **Cache:** A key value dictionary mapping a hash of combined object tags to a recommended tier.

Figure 3 captures the workflow use case for the predictive model creation, this is the model responsible for recommending an optimal tier given a set of object tags.

Following is a brief description of Fig. 3 steps:

1. For a predetermined period of time and for each object coming into the system, collect its tags and properties and save them in a database, this would become the incubation data.
2. Compile all incubation data by transforming crisp tags and properties (such as size, importance level... etc.) into fuzzy values using the fuzzifier.
3. Use the inference engine (rules interpreter) to select the eligible tiers (tiers that satisfy business criteria), for instance, there can be a rule stating: **No objects tagged with** *Highly-Important* **to be put in Tier-1.**
4. Defuzzify the incubation data tags to determine the optimal tier from among the eligible tiers determined in the previous step. Here to determine an optima tier including cost, heuristic algorithms such as simulate annealing [7] or Monte-Carlo [15] can be used.
5. Create a new table that maps the object tags to an optimal tier (determined in the previous step)
6. Use the table in the previous step as a training dataset into an AutoML framework (such as Auto-SKLearn) to create the predictive model.

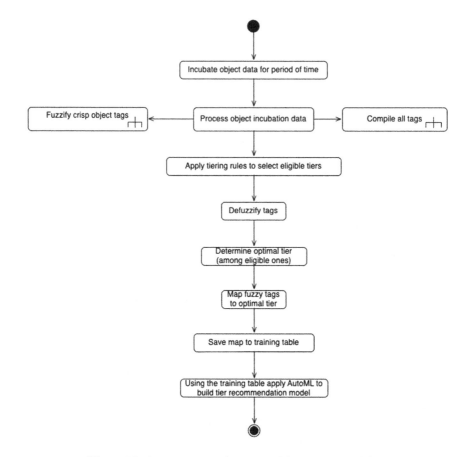

Fig. 3. Tiering recommendation model creation workflow.

Figure 4 captures the workflow use case for returning an optimal tier given an API call with an input of a set of object tags.

Following is a brief description of Fig. 4 steps:

1. Storage system calls the tiering system API with a set of object tags and characteristics.
2. Tiering system takes the API call arguments and fuzzifies all arguments.
3. Tiering system takes the input from the previous step and creates a hash key, for instance, this could be a concatenation of the object fuzzy tags.
4. Tiering System checks if the key is in cache.
5. If the key is in cache return recommended tier else call the predictive model with the object tags (from step 2) and return a tier recommendation.

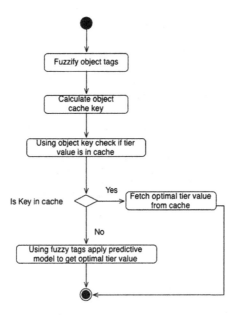

Fig. 4. Return tier recommendation workflow.

4 Conclusion

One of the most important pillars of cloud computing is the Platform As a Service (PAAS) paradigm, for which the goal is to make it as seamless and as easy as possible for users. In this context, adopting an enhanced tiered storage becomes a competitive advantage. In this paper, we proposed an approach for such enhancement, which also can be adapted by independent actors to leverage a hybrid and multi-provider landscape. Still, to our knowledge, there's no unified and public benchmark for measuring the performance of different tiered storage strategies. Providing an industry-wide benchmark may help take the tiered storage paradigm to the next level.

References

1. Bhargava, A.K.: Fuzzy Set Theory Fuzzy Logic and their Applications. S. Chand Publishing, New Delhi (2018). https://www.amazon.com/Fuzzy-Theory-Logic-their-Applications-ebook/dp/B06XKRWHW4
2. Ramakrishnan, R., et al.: Azure data lake store: a hyperscale distributed file service for big data analytics (2017). http://www.cs.ucf.edu/~kienhua/classes/COP5711/Papers/MSazure2017.pdf
3. AutoML. https://www.automl.org/
4. Bai, Y., Wang, D.: Fundamentals of fuzzy logic control – fuzzy sets, fuzzy rules and defuzzifications. In: Bai, Y., Zhuang, H., Wang, D. (eds.) Advanced Fuzzy Logic Technologies in Industrial Applications. AIC, pp. 17–36. Springer, London (2006). https://doi.org/10.1007/978-1-84628-469-4_2

5. Balaji, A., Allen, A.: Benchmarking automatic machine learning frameworks (2018). arXiv: 1808.06492
6. Batrouni, M., Finch, S., Wilson, S., Bertaux, A., Nicolle, C.: Intelligent cloud storage management for layered tiers. In: Luo, Y. (ed.) CDVE 2018. LNCS, vol. 11151, pp. 33–43. Springer, Cham (2018). https://doi.org/10.1007/978-3-030-00560-3_5
7. Bertsimas, D., Tsitsiklis, J.: Simulated annealing. In: Statistical Science (1993). http://www.mit.edu/~dbertsim/papers/Optimization/Simulatedannealing.pdf
8. Cheng, Y., et al.: CAST: tiering storage for data analytics in the cloud. In: HPDC15 (2017). https://cs.gmu.edu/~yuecheng/docs/hpdc15-cast.pdf
9. Drools-engine. https://www.drools.org/
10. Feurer, M., et al.: Practical automated machine learning for the AutoML challenge 2018. In: ICML 2018 AutoML Workshop (2018). http://www.tnt.uni-hannover.de/papers/data/1407/18-AUTOML-AutoChallenge.pdf
11. He, X., Zhao, K., Chu, X.: AutoML: a survey of the state-of-the-art. In: Knowledge-Based Systems (2019). https://arxiv.org/abs/1908.00709
12. Herodotou, H., Kakoulli, E.: Automating distributed tiered storage management in cluster computing. (2019). arXiv: 1907. 02394
13. Lee, C.C.: Fuzzy logic in control systems: fuzzy logic controller. I. IEEE Trans. Syst. Man Cybern. **20**(2), 404–418 (1990). https://ieeexplore.ieee.org/document/52551
14. Mamdani, E.H.: Application of fuzzy algorithms for control of simple dynamic plant. In: Proceedings of the Institution of Electrical Engineers, vol. 121, pp. 1585–1588 (1974). https://ieeexplore.ieee.org/document/5250910
15. Metropolis, N., Ulam, S.: The monte carlo method. J. Am. Stat. Assoc. **44**(247), 335–341 (1949). https://doi.org/10.1080/01621459.1949.10483310. https://www.tandfonline.com/doi/pdf/10.1080/01621459.1949.10483310
16. ML-BriefHistory. https://www.dataversity.net/a-brief-history-of-machine-learning/
17. Seagate-whitepaper. https://www.seagate.com/files/www-content/our-story/trends/files/idc-seagate-dataage-whitepaper.pd
18. Stan-encyclopedia. https://plato.stanford.edu/entries/logic-fuzzy/
19. Zadeh, L.A.: Fuzzy sets. In: Information and Control (1965). http://www.sciencedirect.com/science/article/pii/S001999586590241X

Textual Representation of Pushout Transformation Rules

Wojciech Palacz$^{(\boxtimes)}$ and Iwona Grabska-Gradzińska

The Faculty of Physics, Astronomy and Applied Computer Science,
Jagiellonian University, ul. Lojasiewicza 11, 30-348 Kraków, Poland
{wojciech.palacz,iwona.grabska}@uj.edu.pl

Abstract. This paper is concerned with representing graphs and graph transformation rules using ASCII text only. It proposes an approach based on the textual graph representation used in Cypher Query Language and PGQL. Replacing visual rule languages with a pure text-based language eliminates the need for specialized graphical rule editors. Instead, standard software engineering tools can be used to collaboratively develop a set of graph rules.

Keywords: Textual representation of graph rules · Single-pushout transformation rules · Cypher query language.

1   Graph Transformations

In software engineering, when designing a new computer application, one of the most important choices is the choice of its main data structures. They need to be able to represent a fragment of the real world that the application is concerned with, and they should do it in an efficient and straightforward way.

There are many well-known data types: records, arrays, trees, relational database tables, and so on. Graphs are among these types. They can be used to model nearly any structure which consists of objects and relations between these nodes, and therefore can be used in many different domains.

From the mathematical point of view a graph consists of a set of nodes, a set of edges, and several functions which specify their properties. The number of these functions depends on the type of a given graph. Directed graphs have functions which assign source and target nodes to edges, labelled graphs have a function which assigns labels to nodes, etc.

This formal idea of a graph can be easily implemented in an object-oriented programming language. Nodes correspond to objects, and edges to object references. For some languages, there are even libraries which provide graphs as a distinct data type.

A graph transformation rule is another mathematical idea, which encapsulates a set of changes that should be applied to a graph. For example, in a business management application, moving an employee to a new unit will probably require at least finding nodes representing this employee, its old unit and

Y. Luo (Ed.): CDVE 2020, LNCS 12341, pp. 75–80, 2020.
https://doi.org/10.1007/978-3-030-60816-3_9

its new unit, then deleting an edge representing an association with the old unit
and creating a new edge going to the new unit node.

Implementing rules by hand is time-consuming and error-prone. A developer
has to write a procedure which will find all required graph elements and modify
them one by one. It would be much more convenient if a rule could be specified
in a formal language designed specifically for representing graph rules.

Research done in the last quarter of the XX century has produced several graph transformation programming environments which use diagram-based
visual languages. Detailed discussion of those environments and their underlying
theory can be found, e.g., in [1,2]. Figure 1 displays a picture from [1], showing
three different types of diagrams.

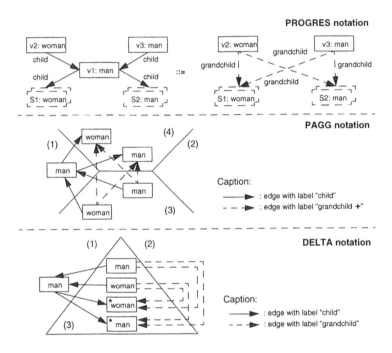

Fig. 1. A transformation rule in three different diagram languages (see [1] p. 524).

2   Graph Query Languages

An alternative avenue of research was started in the XXI century by people
connected to the database industry. By the start of this century it was obvious
that traditional SQL databases are not the best fit for areas in which data is not
homogeneous. Proposed alternatives, known collectively as NoSQL databases,
included also graph databases.

This led to creation of specialized graph query languages. Two of them, Cypher [3] and PGQL [4], are of special interest to this paper. They are purely textual, yet try to "draw" graphs by using ASCII-art. The results are quite intuitive, see the following examples:

- a graph with three nodes connected by two edges:

```
() <-- () --> ()
```

- two labelled nodes, one edge:

```
(:Poland) --> (:Thailand)
```

- three nodes with labels and identifiers, four labelled edges:

```
(a:Alice) -[:husband]-> (b:Bob) -[:wife]-> (a),
(c:Charlie) -[:mother]-> (a), (c) -[:father]-> (b)
```

The last example uses identifiers. The mathematical definition of a graph does not include them, but Cypher needs them to be able to "say" that two nodes in the ASCII-diagram are, in fact, the same node.

Other parts of the Cypher language are similar to SQL. For example, a query which returns all nodes representing grandfathers (both maternal and paternal) could be specified like this:

```
MATCH () -[:mother]-> () -[:father]-> (m)
RETURN m
UNION
MATCH () -[:father]-> () -[:father]-> (p)
RETURN p
```

Neither Cypher nor PGQL provide the concept of a graph rule. They have update queries which can modify a graph, but these queries require specifying step-by-step what needs to be done: match a part of the graph, then create a node, then create an edge which connects this new node to a specific node in the matched part, then create another edge, etc.

3   Textual Representation for Traditional Rules

This paper proposes to combine two approaches described above, preserving the concept of a transformation rule while replacing graphical, two-dimensional diagrams with linear ASCII-art diagrams.

The goal is to make application development easier. The traditional approach required a specialized editor to open and modify files with graph rules. It was an extra tool, which members of the development team had to learn to use. After the proposed change developers will be able to use any text editor to work with graph rules.

Even more important, graph rule files will be ordinary text files, and thus will be processable by source code repositories, change review systems, and other standard software engineering and collaborative tools. Teams wanting to use graph rules in their code will be able to start doing that without introducing new tools or changing their workflow.

The paper has an additional goal: to have rules which can be translated into corresponding Cypher queries. This will eliminate the need for a dedicated rule execution engine, as translated rules can be executed by any graph database which understands the Cypher language.

There are many different types of graph transformation rules. In order to check the general viability of the proposed approach we have chosen one of simpler types: single-pushout rules operating on directed, optionally node- and edge-labelled graphs. A rule of this type consists of two graphs (known as the left hand side and the right hand side) and a partial graph morphism between them. For the purposes of this paper, it is sufficient to know that a partial morphism is a pair of partial functions which map nodes to nodes and edges to edges.

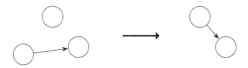

Fig. 2. A diagram representing a single-pushout rule.

Figure 2 displays a rule of this type. Nodes have no labels; only their positioning on the diagram implies which nodes on the left hand side correspond to which nodes on the right hand side. Since the node in the bottom-left corner is not mapped, it along with its attached edge will be removed when this rule is applied. The rule will also create one new edge.

Single-pushout rules are straightforward to convert to a textual form. The sides can represented by ASCII-diagrams; the morphism is represented by corresponding identifiers. Also, there must be some kind of separator between two ASCII-diagrams. The result of the conversion could look like this:

```
LEFT HAND SIDE
(a), (b) --> (c)
RIGHT HAND SIDE
(a) --> (c)
```

A single-pushout rule is applied to a given graph by matching the whole left hand side to a part of this graph, then adding new elements present only on the right side, and finally removing elements present only on the left side. It is a straightforward sequence of operations, which can be expressed as a Cypher query. The query derived from our graph rule would be constructed like this:

```
MATCH (a), (b) -[e]-> (c)
CREATE (a) --> (c)
DELETE e
DELETE b
```

Let us consider another example. It represents an action which can be executed by a hero in a computer game: picking an item lying on the ground. In this game, the state of the world is modelled by a graph. Nodes representing items have edges which connect them to either a place, or a character.

```
LEFT HAND SIDE
(h:Hero) --> (r:Road) <-- (s:Stone)
RIGHT HAND SIDE
(h:Hero) --> (r:Road), (s:Stone) --> (h)
```

4 Conclusion

This paper has proposed an outline of a new approach to representing graph transformation rules, which uses pure text instead of visual diagrams. It was shown that this textual notation can represent single-pushout rules; it is probable that more complex types of rules can be accommodated, too.

Being able to view and edit graph rules in a simple text editor eliminates the need for specialized graphical rule editors. It also allows for usage of other developer tools meant for working with and sharing of ordinary source code.

The paper has also shown the possibility of generating a Cypher update query corresponding to a given graph rule. This is a fact with remarkable practical consequences, as it means that graph rules can be used in any environment which provides a graph database and a Cypher execution engine.

Future work should investigate in the first place how to handle node attributes, as they are necessary in nearly all areas of potential practical application. In the second place, advanced rule formalism which have left hand sides with optional and forbidden parts should be examined.

Acknowledgments. This paper was inspired by a project described in [5]. Students taking part in a lecture on graph grammars were supposed to jointly develop a grammar describing a role-playing game (RPG). They have exchanged their partial rule sets, corresponding to different parts of the game, as JSON files structured according to the requirements of the game engine.

That project has demonstrated that representing graph transformation rules in a purely textual format is viable, at least for students of computer science. This led to a search for a more accessible rule representation format, based on a widely-known query language and potentially useful in other programming environments.

References

1. Rozenberg, G. (ed.): Handbook of Graph Grammars and Computing by Graph Transformation, vol. 1: Foundations. World Scientific, Singapore (1997)

2. Ehrig, H., et al. (eds.): Handbook of Graph Grammars and Computing by Graph Transformations. Applications, Languages and Tools, vol. 2. World Scientific, Singapore (1999)
3. Cypher query language. http://www.opencypher.org/. Accessed 1 May 2020
4. van Rest, O., et al.: PGQL: a property graph query language. In: Proceedings of the Fourth International Workshop on Graph Data Management Experiences and Systems (GRADES 2016), pp. 1–6. ACM, New York (2016). Article no. 7. https://doi.org/10.1145/2960414.2960421
5. Grabska-Gradzińska, I., et al.: Towards automatic generation of storyline aided by collaborative creative design. In: Proceedings of the 17$^\text{th}$ International Conference on Cooperative Design, Visualization and Engineering (CDVE 2020) (2020)

Blockchain vs GDPR in Collaborative Data Governance

Rahul Dutta[1], Arijit Das[2], Ayan Dey[1], and Sukriti Bhattacharya[3(✉)]

[1] University of Calcutta, Kolkata, India
rahul39dutta@gmail.com, adakc_rs@caluniv.ac.in
[2] Narula Institute of Technology, Kolkata, India
arijit1080@gmail.com
[3] Luxembourg Institute of Science and Technology, Esch-sur-Alzette, Luxembourg
sukriti.bhattacharya@list.lu

Abstract. Data Governance is the trending topic in today's security-privacy-concerned digital ecosystem. Blockchain technology is probably one of the most acclaimed evolutions in recent times. Blockchain technologies can be a game-changer for data governance in the areas of transparency and data provenance. As a distributed ledger technology (DLT), blockchain is being touted as a potentially transformational force in collaborative data governance. The General Data Protection Regulation (GDPR) entered into force on May 25, 2018. It is the latest in a series of European Union (EU) legislative measures designed to give EU citizens more control over their data. GDPR, which directs a centralized 'data controller' (GDPR Article 4) to manage user data, clashes with the blockchain's decentralized data storage and management process. The GDPR and the blockchain both have a common ideological ground, emphasizing the need for a change in managing personal data. While GDPR takes care of the policy side by setting up a standard, the blockchain helps enable the implementation side by providing a unique framework. In this paper, the authors analyze the clashes between the two and the potential solutions to those clashes for blockchain to comply with GDPR.

Keywords: Data governance · GDPR · Blockchain · Data protection

1 Introduction

Collaborative data governance is the future of data management practices in an organization to keep pace with the dynamic nature of today's business world. On the broad spectrum, it answers the following questions related to the data: the data owner, the data quality, how to manage the data, and the possible use cases for the data. The world became aware of blockchain technology in 2009 with the release of Bitcoin [1] by Satoshi Nakamoto, a digital currency that is independent of a central authority. Blockchain technology is versatile enough to handle any information that can be digitized beyond the cryptocurrency. Blockchain holds

Y. Luo (Ed.): CDVE 2020, LNCS 12341, pp. 81–92, 2020.
https://doi.org/10.1007/978-3-030-60816-3_10

built-in security and privacy. It offers trust, transparency, autonomy, and consensus. The collaborative data governance allots with the issues of availability, usability, security, data integrity, and analytics. Blockchain has suddenly surfaced as an elixir for these issues with a throng of facilities and benefits that enhance data governance and increase trust. Blockchain simplifies the management of trusted information over communication networks by enabling transparent interactions among different parties in a faster, safer, and more reliable way. Given that the blockchain is trustworthy, secure, and cannot be tampered with, it is seeping into corporate awareness. From what data governance needs and what blockchain provides, it's easy to see they are an excellent fit for each other.

In parallel, the General Data Protection Regulation, better known by its acronym, GDPR is a new framework for consumer data protection that came into effect in Europe from 25th May 2018. The implementation of the GDPR is fundamentally linked to a company's data governance program. It significantly empowers several rights where 'data subjects'[1] can demand companies to provide them with the whereabouts of their personal data and what processing is being done on them. The regulation addresses data protection rules for personal data export outside of the EU and enforces EU data protection laws to guide foreign organizations that process personal data about residents of the EU (GDPR Chapter 5)[2].

In some critical ways, blockchain shares many goals with the GDPR. However, there exist some real conflicts between GDPR and blockchain as well. In this paper, we discuss these issues from the collaborative data governance perspective. The rest of the paper is divided into three Sections - **GDPR against the Blockchain** (Sect. 3), **GDPR for the Blockchain** (Sect. 4) and **Conclusion** (Sect. 5).

2   Background

In this Section General Data Protection Regulation[3] and blockchain [1] is explained in brief.

2.1   General Data Protection Regulation (GDPR)

Ensuring the confidentiality of personal data of data subjects and giving them the option to impose access, erasure and rectification of the data are the primary goals of GDPR. The GDPR realizes four different roles : (a) Data Subject, the provider of the data to the controller (GDPR Article 4(1)), (b) Data Controller, the legal body who determines the purposes of data and the means of their processing (GDPR Article 4(7)), (c) Data Processor, the legal body that processes the data as determined by the data controller (GDPR Article 4(8))

---

[1] GDPR Article 4(1), https://gdpr-info.eu/article-4.

[2] GDPR Chapter 5, https://gdpr-info.eu/chapter-5/.

[3] GDPR, www.gdpr-info.eu/.

and (d) Third Parties, who are not the above three, but have the authority of data processing under the authority of the controller (GDPR Article 4(10)).

GDPR gives "privacy by design" significant importance. It calls for inclusion of data protection from the onset of designing systems, implementing appropriate technical and infrastructure measures (GDPR Article 25)[4]. Failing to adhere to the regulation will result in a fine of upto 20 million Euros or 4% (or 2%) of global turnover, whichever is higher[5].

2.2 Blockchain

A blockchain is a network that uses distributed ledger technology (DLT) where the data stored is decentralized, transparent and immutable. Data is stored in a list of blocks where each block, added in an append-only manner contains a hash of previous block, a time stamp, and a set of data as shown in Fig. 1.

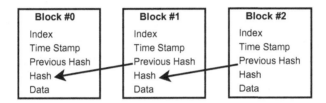

Fig. 1. Blocks in a blockchain

The key properties of blockchain in terms of the three types of blockchain are shown in Table 1.

Table 1. Types of blockchain and their properties

Properties	Public permissionless	Public permissioned	Private Permissioned
Data control	Decentralized	Decentralized	Decentralized
Network	Highly Decentralized	Semi-centralized	Highly centralized
Privacy	None	Low	High
Border	Cross-bordered	Cross-bordered	Bordered
Data immutability	Yes	Yes	Yes
Data persistency	Yes	Yes	Yes
Anonymity	High	Low	None

---

[4] GDPR Article 25, www.gdpr-info.eu/art-25-gdpr/.
[5] GDPR Fines/Penalties, https://gdpr-info.eu/issues/fines-penalties/.

3   GDPR Against Blockchain

In this section, we investigate the significant conflicts in the GDPR-blockchain relationship and the legal challenges for blockchain to comply with the regulation. The conflicts and challenges are discussed by answering the following five questions.

Q3.1: How does GDPR's right to be forgotten (Article 17) and right to rectification (Article 16) clashes with blockchain's immutable ledger?

☐ GDPR right to be forgotten, also called right to erasure directs that the data subjects (personal data subjects) shall have the "right to obtain from the controller the erasure of personal data concerning him or her without undue delay" as stated in GDPR Article 17 (1). The right is not absolute and applies only in certain circumstances such as if the personal data is no longer in use "for the purposes for which they were collected" (GDPR Article 17(1(a))) or the data subject withdraws consent to processing of the data (GDPR Article 6 and Article 9)[6] [7] and their is "no other legal ground for the processing" (GDPR Article 17(1(b))) or in circumstances where their is 'unlawful' processing of the personal data (GDPR Article 17(1(d))). If the controller has made the personal data public, "reasonable measures, including technical measures" must be taken taking into account available technology and the cost of implementing such measures (GDPR Article 17(2)). However, blockchain is fundamentally immutable. A typical transaction in a blockchain, consists of the sender, recipient and amount of asset transfered which are personal data and are stored permanently on the ledger. It is designed to retain its information indefinitely as a mechanism to eliminate any fraud and assures ownership of data in the ledger. Moreover, GDPR addresses data adjustability in right to rectification by mandating that the data subject can exercise their "right to obtain from the controller without undue delay the rectification of inaccurate personal data concerning him or her" (GDPR Article 16). Any modification of the data on the blockchain breaks the links between the blocks and therefore, the chain is broken and the entire blockchain is rendered useless. GDPR's demand for data minimization is also another blow to the blockchain's immutable nature. According to the regulation, the personal data must be "adequate, relevant and limited" to protect privacy so that only absolutely necessary facts about the data is shared (GDPR Article 5(1(c)))[8].

---

[6] GDPR Article 6, https://gdpr-info.eu/art-6-gdpr/.

[7] GDPR Article 9, https://gdpr-info.eu/art-9-gdpr/.

[8] GDPR Article 5, https://gdpr-info.eu/art-5-gdpr/.

Q3.2: How GDPR's right to restriction of processing (Article 18) clashes with blockchain's distributed ledger?

☐ GDPR defines data processing as "any operation or set of operations which is performed on personal data or on a set of personal data, whether or not by automated means" (GDPR Article 4(1)). GDPR incurs greater data control power to data subjects by giving them the right to restriction of processing, that is, "The data subject shall have the right to obtain from the controller restriction of processing" (GDPR Article 18) if the data subject feels the data may be inaccurate or there is "unlawful" processing of the personal data. However, the data as a part of the ledger in a blockchain network is distributed amongst the nodes participating in the network. Besides the data controller, every participant in the network can process the data which averts data privacy desired by the regulation. In simple terms, every participant maintains a local copy of the ledger. Anyone can store and process the data, because of this local copy held in his or her computer, while maintaining their anonymity. This directly contradicts GDPR's privacy policies where a centralized data controller and processor has the power to store, collect and process the data. (GDPR Article 24)[9].

Q3.3: Can encrypted personal data be stored on a blockchain? Are encrypted personal data on a blockchain anonymous enough to fall outside the scope of GDPR?

☐ GDPR does not apply to anonymous data as stated in GDPR Recital 26[10]. The threshold for anonymization under the regulation is high and only results "from processing personal data in order to prevent identification" irreversibly [2]. A typical blockchain network aims to achieve anonymity using cryptography, precisely, public-key cryptography and hashing. However, the identity and data in a blockchain is in fact, 'pseudonymous'. According to Andreas M. Antonopoulos[11], Bitcoin is mistakenly characterized as 'anonymous' currency [3]. Identity is tied to a pseudonym, that is, the public key. Pseudonymous data, however, falls under the scope of the law. Data is pseudonymous if it can be tied to other available information to identify the data subject, else the data is considered anonymous (GDPR recital 26).

Q3.4: In a blockchain who is identified as data controller and data processor?

☐ According to GDPR Article 13, data subjects have the right to know "the identity and the contact details of the controller"[12]. GDPR Article 4 (7) and Article 4 (8) define that in order to process data, data controllers are required

---

[9] GDPR Article 24, https://gdpr-info.eu/art-24-gdpr/.
[10] GDPR Recital 26, https://gdpr-info.eu/recitals/no-26/.
[11] https://antonopoulos.com/.
[12] GDPR Article 13, https://gdpr-info.eu/art-13-gdpr/.

to determine "the purposes and means of the processing of personal data" and data processors are required to process "personal data on behalf of the controller". GDPR's accountability directs a controller to be responsible for legal and lawful processing of personal data (GDPR Article 5). A *public permissionless* blockchain is perfectly decentralized as there is no inherent power inequality between the nodes. Thus, *permissionless* blockchain networks require no obvious identifiable data controller to direct and co-ordinate the working of the blockchain network and it falls directly under the scope of GDPR. In a *permissioned* blockchain network, identity of the data controller is less of an issue. GDPR Article 26(1)[13] also defines joint controllers "where two or more controllers jointly determine the purposes and means of processing, they shall be joint controllers". In a permissioned blockchain, a plurality of controllers can govern the network with pre-defined rules of consensus, which is exactly how a *federated* blockchain network works.

Q3.5: How does GDPR's territorial scope clashes with blockchain?

☐ According to GDPR Article 3 territorial scope, the regulation applies to personal data processing of the citizens who are a part of EU. In GDPR Chap. 5, "Transfer of personal data to third countries or international organization", the law defines that personal data transfer to countries and controllers outside EU are allowed only if the controller conforms to GDPR or provides an identical level of data protection (GDPR Article 45(1))[14] and where "enforceable data subject rights and effective legal remedies for data subjects are available". The regulation applies to controllers who are not established in the EU but process personal data of the citizens in EU. *Public* blockchains do not provide adherence to these principles and data movement in them are cross-bordered. In a *public* blockchain, anyone can join the network as a node and create transactions. *Public* blockchain provides no geographical border to its network, which comprises a number of uncontrolled nodes, free to trade data and thus the allows cross-border data processing. Compliance with GDPR's territorial scope is more feasible in a *private permissioned* blockchain.

4   Towards GDPR Compliant Blockchain

This Section states the potential solutions to the conflicts addressed in Sect. 3 between GDRP and blockchain in data driven cooperation.

Q4.1: How to enable GDPR's right to erasure and rectification in a blockchain?

☐ We look at the potential solutions to enable data modification in blockchain.

---

[13] GDPR Article 26, https://gdpr-info.eu/art-26-gdpr/.

[14] GDPR Article 45, https://gdpr-info.eu/art-45-gdpr/.

Storing Data Off-Chain. A potential solution to allow data adjustability in blockchain is storing the personal data off-chain with restricted access control. The reference to this data is kept along with its hash and other metadata including the claims and permissions regarding this data on the blockchain [4]. The blockchain is a medium of enabling trust between parties and delivering proof for transactions. The proof will be done off-chain through conventional methods where the data controller decides if the party requesting the data has authorized access to it [5]. After GDPR came into play, off-chain data storage in the blockchain is now seen as a possible workaround.

A number of off-chain data storage solutions for blockchain have emerged recently. My Health My Data (MHMD), a *private permissioned* blockchain[15], is a project funded by the EU, stores personal data off-chain. Other such blockchain networks include the Bitcoin Lightning Network [6] that uses off-chain exchange of bitcoins between nodes through micropayment channels[16]. Æternity blockchain [7] uses state channel technology[17] for transactions and smart contracts to be executed off-chain. Liquidity exchange built on top of Liquidity network [8] allows off-chain exchanges, which although being a decentralized network is scalable to a centralized exchange.

State Tree Pruning and Smart Contract Self-destruct in Ethereum. State tree pruning[18], similar to automatic memory management in volatile resources, is a method of removing data in the Ethereum blockchain. However, the drawback is that it is intended for minimizing states in the block by removing unused records and removal does not depend on participant's demand. The only way to remove code from the blockchain is when a contract at that address performs the "selfdestruct" operation[19]. The storage and code is removed from the state. Even if a contract is removed by "selfdestruct", it is still part of the history of the blockchain and probably retained by most Ethereum nodes. So using "selfdestruct" is not the same as deleting data from a hard disk.

Chameleon Hashes. Using "chameleon" hash functions [9] to frame an editable blockchain (or redactable blockchain) has been explored [10]. The hash of the data stored in the blockchain retains the integrity of the data. Any changes to the data changes the hash of the data in the block which implies data tempering. This changes the block header hash and eventually breaks the chain (link) between the subsequent blocks. Also referred to as trapdoor hash functions, "chameleon" hash function has an additional secured private key, known as trapdoor key using which the original data can be updated and written back

---

[15] www.myhealthmydata.eu/.

[16] https://medium.com/@super3/introduction-to-micropayment-channels-5beb3bb2 24c1.

[17] https://blog.stephantual.com/what-are-state-channels-32a81f7accab.

[18] https://blog.ethereum.org/2015/06/26/state-tree-pruning/.

[19] https://solidity.readthedocs.io/en/v0.5.0/introduction-to-smart-contracts.html? highlight=self%20destruct.

into the blockchain. However, the updated data has the same hash value as the original data. This enables imposing GDPR's right to erasure and right to rectification by allowing users to rewrite or delete past blocks of information without breaking the blockchain.

μ**chain.** Recently, authors have introduced a new mutable blockchain, called μchain [11]. The main features of μchain include maintaining alternative versions of data records, using consensus to approve a valid history and its inherent capability to conceal alternative versions of history. In a given set of transactions, only a single transaction is marked as "active", while all the remaining ones represent alternative inactive transactions. A set of transactions can be extended to add new versions of transactions. Thus, transactions can be updated by the sender if it requires any rectification which is the "active" transaction. Decryption keys are available only for the "active" transactions, and the inactive transactions are all kept hidden by encryption. This allows data subjects with the option to exercise their right to rectification.

Q4.2: How to identify data controller and data processor in a blockchain?

☐ GDPR is established on the notion of an identifiable data controller to determine "the purposes and means of the processing" (GDPR Recital 79)[20]. Here, we address how can such a controller and processor be established in the decentralized world of blockchain.

Network Administrator and Miners in `Permissioned` Blockchain. In a *permissioned* blockchain, the entity responsible for handling of personal data can be the data controller and data processor depending on the implementation specifics. The entity who determines the participation rights (authentication) and the access rights (authorization) of every participants in the blockchain network can be considered as the controller of the network. This entity can be the governing body, that is, "the natural or legal person" which "determines the purposes and means of the processing of personal data" (GDPR Article 4(7)). In a *federated* blockchain, a plurality of controllers can govern the network with predefined and transparent rules of consensus, that is, in case of joint controllers. The miners make a paramount contribution to the operation of the blockchain as they bear the responsibility of confirming and adding transactions into the blockchain. The transactions initiated by the participants in a blockchain are stored in a temporary 'pool of unconfirmed transactions' which is a collection of transactions waiting for their confirmation [3], that is, waiting to be processed by the miners. Therefore, we can consider miners as the data processors. Hence, in accordance with GDPR data controller definition (GDPR Article 4(7)), they cannot be reckoned as data controllers.

---

[20] GDPR Recital 79, https://gdpr-info.eu/recitals/no-79/.

Smart Contract. A blockchain network employing smart contracts protocol can operate it as a data processor. CNIL[21] explained in their report[22] that smart contract developers could be considered either data controllers or data processors accordingly. For a specific purpose and means for processing of personal data for that purpose identified by a participant or set of participants in the blockchain, a developer designs a smart contract solution for that purpose.

Here, the smart contract developer is processing the personal data on behalf of that participant through that smart contract. Here, that participant can be considered as the data controller (or joint controllers in case of plurality of controllers) whereas the smart contract developer as well as the smart contract itself can be determined as the data processor.

Q4.3: How to make personal data anonymous in a blockchain?

☐ Recalling GDPR Recital 26, anonymous data are not in the scope of the regulation. If the data on the blockchain is anonymous, it falls directly outside the scope of GDPR. In this Section, potential solutions to achieve anonymity are discussed.

Zero-Knowledge Proof. A solution to achieve anonymity in blockchain is Zero-knowledge proof [12]. It allows a verifier to validate the truth of a statement of a party (prover) without having any knowledge about the statement except that the statement is true. Zero-knowledge protocols supplements privacy in transactions in a blockchain where the transaction is validated without revealing the internal details of the transactions, that is, the sender, recipient and the content of the transaction (personal data). The entire blockchain network can agree on the validity of a transaction without learning about the content of the transaction.

Zero-knowledge protocols in blockchain use zk-snarks (Zero knowledge Succinct Non-Interactive Arguments of Kn-owledge) [13] to overcome multiple challenge interactions between verifier and prover to validate a transaction. Zk-snarks only requires a common string of characters known by the prover and verifier to validate a statement. Using the digital signature of the prover in blockchain as the common string, a transaction can be proved easily with low computational effort. The personal data in the transactions are decentralized and no personal data is stored on the blockchain, Due to the absence of actual data in the blockchain, participants cannot process the data which in turn, provides data privacy and restricts any unintended and "unlawful" processing of the data as desired in GDPR's right to restriction of processing as explained in Sect. 3.

---

[21] https://www.cnil.fr/en/home.

[22] CNIL report,https://www.cnil.fr/fr/Blockchain-et-rgpd-quelles-solutions-pour-un-usage-responsable-en-presence-de-donnees-personnelles.

Zcash[23] is a high profile cryptocurrency using zk-snarks. Ethereum's metropolis[24] protocol upgrade allowed users to use zk-snarks in their smart contracts. PIVX is another cryptocurrency using zk-snarks[25].

Ring Signatures and Stealth Addresses. Another solution to anonymization in blockchain is the use of ring signatures [14] and stealth addresses. Ring signatures hides the identity of the creator/sender of a transaction. A ring signature is a type of digital signature in which a group of possible signers are fused together to obscure the actual signature of the sender of the transaction. All the signers are equal and valid and hence, to a third party all the signers seem to be the sender but is unable to determine the identity of the actual sender of the transaction. Stealth addresses, enhances privacy by shielding the identity of the recipient in a transaction. A transaction in blockchain is essentially transformation of old outputs belonging to one wallet to new outputs in another wallet. Stealth address is recorded in every transaction to indicate the recipient of asset involved. However, any other party cannot determine the identity of the recipient by looking at the stealth address because a stealth address is not associated with the recipient's public address. Stealth addresses and ring signatures are used in Bytecoin[26] and Monero[27]. Monero also uses the technique of ring confidential signatures [15], which is a combination of ring signatures, to hide transaction amounts.

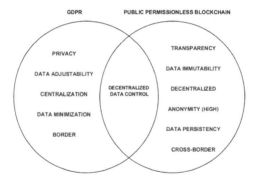

Fig. 2. GDPR vs *Public permissionless* blockchain

---

[23] Zcash, 2018, www.z.cash.

[24] https://blockgeeks.com/guides/ethereum-metropolis/.

[25] https://pivx.org/wp-content/uploads/2018/10/PIVX-White.pdf.

[26] Bytecoin, https://bytecoin.org/.

[27] Monero, https://ww.getmonero.org/.

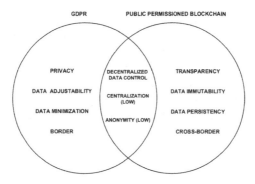

Fig. 3. GDPR vs *Public permissioned* blockchain

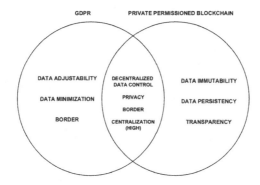

Fig. 4. GDPR vs *Private permissioned* blockchain

Fig. 5. GDPR compliance

5   Conclusion

This paper analyzed and discussed the significant privacy concerns and challenges to blockchain from the lens of collaborative data governance; precisely the rights of data subject, data controller and processor, pseudonymous personal data and the territorial scope of GDPR. The paper also highlights opportunities for the various types of blockchain to comply with GDPR or at least achieve partial compliance which itself is a step forward. As a result, we get a clear vision of the relationship between GDPR and *public* and *private* blockchain networks respectively. We illustrate their relationship through venn diagrams. Fig. 2 shows the relationship between GDPR and *public permissionless* blockchain. Fig. 3 and Fig. 4 illustrate the relationship between GDPR and *public permissioned* blockchain and *private permissioned* blockchain respectively. From the above comparison, we get a clear understanding of the potentials of GDPR compliance of the three different types of blockchain networks as shown in Fig. 5. We can observe from Fig. 5 that the increase in GDPR compliance is when the decentralization nature of the blockchain decreases. To demonstrate the compatibility of blockchain and GDPR, the possible solution discussed in this paper should be leveraged to the most significant extent possible in blockchain solution architectures.

References

1. Nakamoto, S.: Bitcoin: a peer-to-peer electronic cash system. Technical report (2008)
2. Finck, M.: Blockchains and data protection in the European union. Technical report 18-01 (2018)
3. Antonopoulos, A.M.: Mastering Bitcoin: Unlocking Digital Crypto-Currencies, 1st edn. O'Reilly Media Inc, Newton (2014)
4. Humbeeck, A.V.: The blockchain-GDPR paradox, Medium (2017)
5. Xu, X., et al.: A taxonomy of blockchain-based systems for architecture design, April 2017
6. Poon, J., Dryja, T.: The bitcoin lightning network: scalable off-chain instant payments (2016). https://lightning.network/lightning-network-paper.pdf
7. Hess, Z., Malahov, Y., Pettersson, J.: Æternity blockchain (2017)
8. Stiller, B., Bocek, T., Hecht, F., Machado, G., Racz, P., Waldburger, M.: Mobile Systems IV, University of Zurich, Department of Informatics, Technical report, January 2010
9. Krawczyk, H.M., Rabin, T.D.: Chameleon hashing and signatures, US Patent 6,108,783, August 22 2000
10. Ateniese, G., Magri, B., Venturi, D., Andrade, E.: Redactable blockchain-or-rewriting history in bitcoin and friends. In: 2017 IEEE European Symposium on Security and Privacy (EuroS&P), pp. 111–126. IEEE (2017)
11. Puddu, I., Dmitrienko, A., Capkun, S.: μchain: how to forget without hard forks (2017)
12. Goldwasser, S., Micali, S., Rackoff, C.: The knowledge complexity of interactive proof systems. SIAM J. Comput. **18**(1), 186–208 (1989)
13. Bitansky, N., Canetti, R., Chiesa, A., Tromer, E.: From extractable collision resistance to succinct non-interactive arguments of knowledge, and back again. In: Proceedings of the 3rd Innovations in Theoretical Computer Science Conference, ser. ITCS 2012. New York, NY, USA, pp. 326–349. ACM (2012). http://doi.acm.org/10.1145/2090236.2090263
14. Rivest, R.L., Shamir, A., Tauman, Y.: How to Leak a Secret. In: Boyd, C. (ed.) ASIACRYPT 2001. LNCS, vol. 2248, pp. 552–565. Springer, Heidelberg (2001). https://doi.org/10.1007/3-540-45682-1_32
15. Noether, S., Mackenzie, A., et al.: Ring confidential transactions. Ledger **1**, 1–18 (2016)

Cooperative Decision Making in Crowdfunding – Applying Theory of Behavior and Exemplary Empirical Validation

Valerie Busse[1,2(✉)], Christine Strauss[1] ⓘ, and Michal Gregus[2]

[1] University of Vienna, Oskar-Morgenstern-Platz 1, 1090 Vienna, Austria
valerie.busse@infinanz.de,
christine.strauss@univie.ac.at
[2] Comenius University, Odbojárov 10, Bratislava, Slovakia
michal.gregusml@fm.uniba.sk

Abstract. Cooperative issues gained attention with fast growing digitalization and social networks. Especially, research in advanced cooperative funding, i.e. crowdfunding, is rapidly increasing. Hence, this paper addresses behavioral issues in the highly complex decision-making processes from the viewpoint of various actors in crowdfunding. It provides a detailed overview of major behavioral models by focusing on *(i)* the theory or reasoned action, *(ii)* its application and *(iii)* its exemplary empirical validation. The empirical study examines the crowdfunding process by targeting 416 entrepreneurs and by analyzing their behavior towards Kickstarter.com and Indiegogo.com.

Keywords: Crowdfunding · Behavior · Theory of reasoned action · Cooperation

1 Introduction

Crowdfunding has gained importance as an alternative financing method in recent years. In several new crowdfunding online-platforms the platform providers as well as the entrepreneurs and the crowd have shown a tremendous engagement in the relatively new alternative funding method [1, 2].

Current research addresses questions on which factors contribute to the behavioural aspects of crowdfunding seen from three different viewpoints, namely the entrepreneurial perspective, the perspective of the crowd and the perspective of the intermediary, i.e. the crowdfunding platform. However, research attending the topic of behaviour in the interactions between these actors is still in a rather unexplored stage [1, 2]. These three main actors in the crowdfunding process, i.e. the entrepreneur, the intermediary, and the crowd, are interrelated in a triadic relationship. Throughout this relationship these three actors carry out several typical activities, perform characteristic tasks, and make various repetitive decisions. For the sake of target achievement within this triadic relationship, it is necessary, that actors cooperate with each other. The paper at hand addresses the cooperation in terms of attributes between one pair of actors, i.e.

© Springer Nature Switzerland AG 2020
Y. Luo (Ed.): CDVE 2020, LNCS 12341, pp. 93–103, 2020.
https://doi.org/10.1007/978-3-030-60816-3_11

the entrepreneur and the intermediary. Essential attributes between these two actors will be quantitatively tested on a well-known behaviour model through a survey with 416 participants.

The remainder of this paper is organized as follows: Sect. 2 provides a brief direction toward the subject matter by introducing classic approaches. Section 3 describes the adaption of theory of reasoned action on the crowdfunding process by testing six hypotheses based on a survey with 416 participants. Section 4 provides the empirical analysis, whereas Sect. 5 concludes with a summary of the findings and a discussion.

2   Theory of Reasoned Action

In order to evaluate determinants of consumer decisions, scientific research has developed a number of theories. Widespread theories are for instance behavioral perspective model of purchase and consumption (BPM) of Foxall (1992), three component attitude model of Rosenberg and Hovlands (1960), and Fishbein and Ajzen's (1975) theory of reasoned action (TRA) [6–8]. After analyzing these models, TRA has developed as the major theory to analyze customer behavior. The theory has been successfully proven by a great variety of empirical research [9]. Therefore, this research focuses on the TRA. This model explains the relationship between attitude and behaviors of human actions based on research in social psychology. TRA was implemented by Fishbein and Ajzen in 1967 and predicts the behavior of individuals based on their pre-existing intentions towards their behavior and attitudes [10], specifically, the attitude towards an object and the attitude towards a behavior with respect to that object. Fishbein and Ajzen (1980) state that "our ultimate goal is to predict and understand an individual's behavior" [10]. Therefore, TRA aims to understand a person's motivation and his/her individual behavior to perform an action [11, 12]. The theory is based on the assumption that individuals make rational and systematic use of information which is available to them [10]. Subsequently, the persons' intention to perform a behavior is the major predictor of whether or not the person actually performs that behavior [11]. Once this behavior is clarified, it is necessary to ask what determines this behavior [10]. Therefore, the target variable of the model is the behavior. It is assumed that the actual behavior of a person is determined by his or her intention to behave. The behavioral intention, according to the model, results from both, the personal attitude towards the behavior as well as the subjective norm which is a personal perception. Subjective norms are the sum of subjective social and normative beliefs and motivation that affect the intention to act. The attitude towards behavior results from the assumption about the beliefs of behavior and the evaluation of the result [10]. It is also important to distinguish clearly between the intention to behave and the behavior per se [10]. TRA has been thoroughly researched and successfully applied in various context; its causal relations have been empirically tested and are regarded as fundamentally confirmed (e.g. [13, 15]). The authors later developed TRA further into the theory of planned behavior (TPB) [15]. TPB consists of the same components as TRA but has been extended by perceived behavioral control as an additional component, considering both behavioral intentions and behavior. The constructs of the TRA depicted in Fig. 1 will be further explained in more detail.

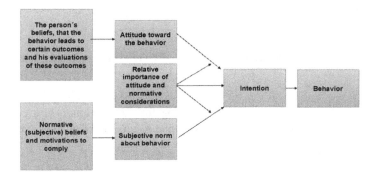

Fig. 1. Theory of Reasoned Action (TRA) (adapted from [10] p. 8)

According to Ajzen and Fishbein (2005), TRA assumes that people's *behavior* follows reasonably from their attitudes, beliefs and intentions. Behavior is the way in which one acts or conducts oneself especially towards others [15, 16]. Another pivotal element is *intention*, that shows to which extent an individual is likely to plan and invest effort in pursuing a given behavior [18]. Intention results from two belief-based concepts: attitude towards behavior and subjective norms about behavior. Fishbein and Ajzen (1980) define "behavioral intention as the agent's subjective probability that he or she will perform the behavior" [10, 20]. The third element is represented by *attitudes*, which may be positive, negative or neutral estimations of performing the behavior in future [17]. Schwartz (1992) defines attitudes as sets of beliefs about a certain object or an act which may lead to intention to carry out the act [21]. Therefore, attitudes are dependent on the strength of behavioral beliefs (if there is a probable outcome) as well as on the evaluation of potential outcome (if the outcome is positive) [9]. Subsequently, attitudes are key elements of the determination of behavioral intention by referring to how people feel towards any particular behavior [19].

As depicted in Fig. 1, Ajzen and Fishbein (1980) propose in their model that on the one hand, the person's beliefs, that their behavior leads to certain outcomes and his/her evaluation of these outcomes results in the attitude towards behavior [10]. On the other hand, the authors suggest that normative (subjective) beliefs and motivations to comply lead to a subjective norm about behavior. These attitudes and beliefs result in the intention of a person which leads to their direct behavior [10].

3   Applying TRA on Crowdfunding – an Empirical Study

In the presented approach we adapt the classic model of TRA for the purpose of analysing the cooperative relationships between the three main actors in crowdfunding; our study focuses on the cooperation between entrepreneur and intermediary (cf. Fig. 2).

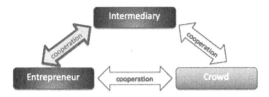

Fig. 2. Cooperation among the actors in the triadic relationship of crowdfunding (adapted from [22]).

Fishbein and Ajzen developed the following formal description of a customer's attitude towards a product. This formal description results in an equation, which reads as:

$$E_{ij} = \sum_{a=1}^{n} W_{ija} B_{ija}$$

E_{ij} ... entrepreneur i and his/her attitude towards the particular crowdfunding platform j

W_{ija} ... degree of beliefs of entrepreneur i that crowdfunding platform j has a certain attribute a (benefits, values, features) as a result of knowledge, experience or reputation

B_{ija} ... subjective evaluation of attribute a by entrepreneur i of particular crowdfunding platform j

n ... number of attributes a

3.1 Objective of Empirical Validation

The empirical validation aims to analyze if and to which extend TRA can be applied to the crowdfunding process of entrepreneur towards intermediary and therefore to determine the entrepreneurial attitude and their intention to use a crowdfunding platform. Kickstarter.com and Indigogo.com were used as the major platforms, as they provide the highest market share in the crowdfunding sector [1, 2].

3.2 Procedure of Data Collection

The online survey was conducted among 416 participants, who are familiar with the crowdfunding concept and have used or have intend to use a crowdfunding platform. From the 416 participants, data was used to test various hypotheses, from which we present six of them in this paper. Hence, even if participants stopped the survey at one point, data required for certain hypotheses was used. In order to ensure validity and reliability potential participants were invited from a list of contacts from the entrepreneurial center of the Vienna university of economics and business (WU

Gründungszentrum) as well as data from various social media groups, such as *Crowdfunding*, *Start-up Jobs*, or *Find your Co-Founder*. Participation in the study was voluntary and anonymous; links to the online questionnaire were promoted via a survey link in Facebook and LinkedIn-post as well as by direct e-mail within a time frame of two weeks. *Soscisurvey* was the applied tool enabling the online survey. In order to test the hypotheses different tests were used including: Spearman Correlation, Friedman Test and Wilcoxon Test. The data has been statistically analyzed using SPSS.

3.3 Development of the Survey

The first part of the online survey covers all socio-demographic factors such as gender, age, origin, principle knowledge of crowdfunding platforms. The second part aims to identify the W_{ija} and the B_{ija} based on Fishbein and Aizen's (1980) formal description. While W_{ija} denotes the degree of beliefs of the entrepreneur i that crowdfunding platform j has a certain attribute a (benefits, values, features) as result of knowledge or advertising, and B_{ija} denotes the subjective evaluation of attribute a by entrepreneur i of a particular crowdfunding platform j. The last part of the survey aims to generate knowledge of the subjective norm as well as his/her overall satisfaction with the platform.

The overall aim is to evaluate all entrepreneurs E_i with his/her attitude towards a particular crowdfunding platform j. Thus, we analyse three issues: (1) examine if TRA may be applied in the context of crowdfunding, (2) measure the overall attitude of participating entrepreneurs towards using crowdfunding platforms, and (3) support platforms by indicating crucial attributes to attract entrepreneurs interested in crowdfunding.

4   Analysis and Results

The following hypotheses are formulated in order to test the TRA in the crowdfunding process. Hypothesis 1 and 2 investigate the correlation between attitude and behavior according to the TRA based on Kickstarter.com and Indicgogo.com. Hypothesis 3 and 4 assume a correlation between the information from the community with respect to crowdfunding platform 1 (i.e. Kickstarter.com) or crowdfunding platform 2 (i.e. Indiegogo.com) and the intention to use said platform in the future. Hypothesis 5 assumes that the individual assessment of attributes is not equally distributed among all ten attributes. Hypothesis 6 is formulated in order to test, if platform 1 has a better reputation than platform 2. Each hypothesis consists of H1 and H0, where H1 is formulated as a positive statement.

Figure 3 depicts the application and integration of the set of hypotheses within the frame of the TRA model. It provides insights, which hypothesis relates to which component of TRA.

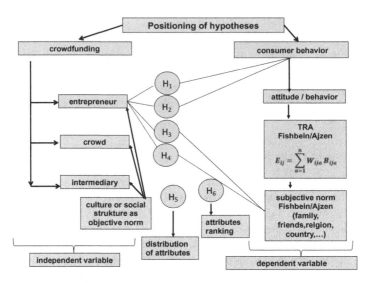

Fig. 3. Six hypotheses in the context of TRA

4.1   Hypotheses Testing

The previously formulated six hypotheses have been evaluated. The first hypothesis is proofed by the Spearman Correlation. The Spearman correlation measures the correlation between two variables. The value of a correlation coefficient may vary between $r = -1$ (negatively correlated), $r = 0$ (not correlated), $r = +1$ (positively correlated). Spearman correlation coefficient is also called rank coefficient because the correlation is not measured between two data points but between their ranks. The aim of applying the Spearman Correlation coefficient here is to test the first scientific hypothesis.

Hypothesis 1
H1: There is a positive correlation between the attitude towards a crowdfunding platform 1 (Kickstarter.com) and the intention to use said platform in the future. (The more positive an attitude towards a crowdfunding platform, the higher the intention of using a crowdfunding platform for his/her campaign in the future).
H0: There is no positive correlation between the attitude towards a crowdfunding platform 1 (Kickstarter.com) and the intention to use said platform in the future (Fig. 4).

This sample of all answered participants $N = 112$, which could be used to answer this hypothesis shows a significant positive correlation between variable 1, i.e. intention to use platform 1, and variable 2, i.e. attitude towards platform 1 ($r = 0,695$; $p < 0,001$, $N = 112$). The result of the Spearman Correlation coefficient r shows a relatively high value (0,695). This result leads to confirmation of H1 and rejection of H0. Subsequently, the sample data shows this positive correlation between the attitude towards platform 1 (Kickstarter.com) and the intention to use said platform. The result of Hypothesis 1 testing confirms the TRA of Fishbein and Ajzen and their scientific results that attitude towards behavior leads to intention to use a special service provider platform of crowdfunding.

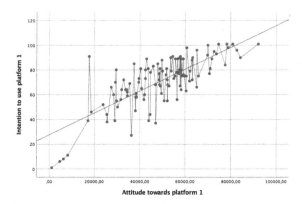

Fig. 4. Survey outcome using SPSS: Intention and attitude towards platform 1

Hypothesis 2

After testing the correlation coefficient r between attitudes towards platform 1 (Kickstarter.com) and intention to use this platform, in hypothesis 2 the correlation coefficient r concerning platform 2 (Indiegogo.com) will be tested.

H1: There is a positive correlation between the attitude towards a crowdfunding platform 2 (Indiegogo.com) and the intention to use said platform in the future. (The more positive an attitude towards a crowdfunding platform, the higher the intention of using a crowdfunding platform for his/her campaign in the future).

H0: There is no positive correlation between the attitude towards a crowdfunding platform 2 (Indiegogo.com) and the intention to use said platform in the future.

Spearman correlation coefficient shows for the sample of all answered participants $N = 102$ a significant positive correlation between variable 1, i.e. intention to use platform 2, and variable 2, i.e. attitude towards platform 2 ($r = 0,568$; $p < 0,001$, $N = 102$). The result of the Spearman correlation coefficient r has a relatively high value (0,568). This result implies the confirmation of H1 and the rejection of H0. Subsequently, the sample data shows this positive correlation between the attitude towards platform 2 (Indiegogo.com) and the intention to use said platform.

Hypothesis 3

Concerning TRA, Fishbein and Ajzen analyzed a strong influence from the so-called "subjective norm", that means that the entrepreneur believes, that specific individuals or groups think he/she should or he/she should not perform the behavior and his/her motivation to comply with specific reference. Subsequently, the questionnaire contained the question: Does additional information (advertisement, social media, friends and family etc.) drive you to use or no to use the platform. Figure 3 illustrates where the hypothesis is tested within the model.

H1: There is a positive correlation between the information from the community with respect to a crowdfunding platform 1 (Kickstarter.com) and the intention to use said platform in the future.

H0: There is no positive correlation between the information from the community with respect to a crowdfunding platform 1 (Kickstarter.com) and the intention to use said platform in the future.

This sample of all answered participants $N = 112$ shows a significant positive correlation between variable 1, intention to use platform 1 and variable 2 attitude towards platform 1 ($r = 0,512$; $p < 0,001$; $N = 112$). The result of the Spearman correlation coefficient r shows a relatively high value (0,512). This result leads to confirmation of H1 and rejection of H0.

Subsequently, the sample data shows a positive correlation between the additional information from the environment on platform 1 (Kickstarter.com) and the intention to use said platform. Therefore, it is to be noted that one of the major points of TRA (decisions are influenced by subjective norms) is hereby empirically proved.

Hypothesis 4

H1: There is a positive correlation between the information from the community with respect to a crowdfunding platform 2 (Indiegogo.com) and the intention to use said platform in the future.

H0: There is no positive correlation between the information from the community with respect to a crowdfunding platform 2 (Indiegogo.com) and the intention to use said platform in the future.

This sample of all answered participants $N = 102$ shows a significant positive correlation between variable 1, i.e. intention to use platform 2, and variable 2, i.e. attitude towards platform 2 ($r = 0,529$; $p < 0,001$, $N = 102$). The result of the spearman correlation coefficient r shows a relatively high value (0,529). This result leads to confirmation of H1 and rejection of H0.

Subsequently, the sample data shows a positive correlation between the additional information from the environment on platform 2 (Indiegogo.com) and the intention to use said platform. Therefore, it is again to be noted that one of the major points of TRA (decisions are influenced by subjective norms) is hereby empirically proved.

Hypothesis 5

Hypothesis 5 relates to ten attributes and its statistic distribution: (1) design, (2) usability, (3) market position, (4) trustworthiness, (5) reputation, (6) ease of navigation, (7) security, (8) coverage of industrial sectors, (9) cost of use, and (10) unrestricted access. In order to analyze the statistic distribution among the attributes, a Friedman Test is applied, which is a non-parametric test of mean score comparison. Simultaneously, the equal distribution will be tested.

H1: The assessment of attributes is not equally distributed among all ten attributes.

H0: The assessment of attributes is equally distributed among all ten attributes.

As this sample shows significant differences ($p < 0,001$; $N = 133$) H0 is rejected. The results of Friedman Test reveal that participants attach importance on security and trustworthiness of the webpage as the most important attributes followed by usability and reputation. The importance of unrestricted access as well as the importance of coverage of industrial sectors is ranked as the lowest compared to the other ten attributes (Fig. 5).

Hypothesis 6

The Wilcoxon Signed Rank Test is a non-parametric statically hypothesis test in order to compare two related samples: Comparison of attitudes of platform 1 and platform 2. E_{ij} = Entrepreneur i and his/her attitude towards particular crowdfunding platform j.

Due to expertise and market observation of the total crowdfunding market one can assume that the most popular crowdfunding platform worldwide, Kickstarter.com will have the highest reputation among all survey participants.

H1: Platform 1 has a higher reputation than platform 2.

H0: Platform 1 has not a higher reputation than platform 2.

The results of Wilcoxon Signed Rank Test shows that H1 is rejected. Other than intuitively assumed, the participants of the survey prefer Indiegogo.com over Kickstarter.com.

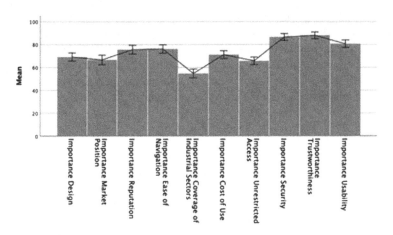

Fig. 5. Importance of attributes

5 Findings and Discussion

Our empirical study on the cooperatively performed crowdfunding activities of entrepreneurs and intermediaries to achieve the common goal of financing an idea or project validated the underlying model of the theory of behaviour. Especially, hypothesis 1 and hypothesis 2 showed a high positive correlation coefficient (between $r = 0,695$ and $r = 0,568$) between the attitude towards crowdfunding platform Kickstarter.com and Indiegogo.com and the intention to use these platforms in the future. Hypothesis 3 and hypothesis 4 showed both a positive correlation coefficient ($r = 0,512$ and $r = 0,529$) between the subjective norm and the intention to act. The validation of hypothesis 1 to hypothesis 4 illustrates the application of TRA towards a crowdfunding decision process. Up to now – to the authors' best knowledge – this fact has not been shown in other surveys. The proof of scientific hypothesis 5 shows as a result of the Friedmann Test the mean ranking of attributes by using crowdfunding platforms. The analysis of ten main attributes based on the cooperation between entrepreneur and intermediary, sourced by the quantitative data evaluation and their spreads of importance for the choice of a platform usage is a novel result. The proof of the scientific hypothesis 6 is the first application of TRA towards crowdfunding which is calculated as a total attitude (total benefit) of an entrepreneur by using a crowd-funding platform.

This paper provides evidence, that TRA can be applied in the context of crowd-funding (1) and shows a positive correlation between attitude and intention of all participators towards the two platforms (2).

The well-known theory specifies cooperative behaviour attributes between the entrepreneur and the intermediary, which provides platforms with crucial attributes to attract entrepreneurs interest in crowdfunding platforms (3). Results indicate, that platform provider should focus on trustworthiness and security mostly, but also consider factors such as ease of navigation, reputation and design as well as market position as highly important attributes in order to attract more entrepreneurs and optimize the cooperative behaviour between the entrepreneur and the intermediary. Further research could consider testing more attributes as well as include aspects of TPB or other conversant behaviour theories. Additional application-specific attributes focussing the other actors in the triadic relationship, i.e. the intermediary and the crowd, or the entrepreneur and the crowd could be analysed in further studies.

References

1. Busse, V.: Crowdfunding - an empirical study on the entrepreneurial viewpoint. In: Fatos, X., Barolli, L., and Gregus, M.: In: Advances in Intelligent Networking and Collaborative Systems, the 10th International Conference on intelligent Networking and Collaborative Systems, Bratislava, pp. 306–318 (2018)
2. Busse, V., Gregus, M.: Crowdfunding – an innovative corporate finance method and its decision-making steps. In: Barolli, L., Nishino, H., Miwa H. (eds.). Advances in Intelligent Systems and Computing, vol. 1035, pp. 544–555 (2019)
3. Peisl, T., Raeside, R., Busse, V.: Predictive Crowding: The role of trust in crowd selection. In: Proceedings 3E Conference Ireland. pp. 1–19 (2017)
4. Bauer, C., Mladenow, A., Strauss, C.: Fostering collaboration by location-based crowd-sourcing. In: Luo, Y. (ed.) CDVE 2014. LNCS, vol. 8683, pp. 88–95. Springer, Cham (2014). https://doi.org/10.1007/978-3-319-10831-5_13
5. Kryvinska, N., Strauss, C.: Conceptual model of business services availability vs. interoperability on collaborative IoT-enabled eBusiness Platforms. In: Bessis, N., et al. (eds.) Internet of Things and Inter-cooperative Computational Technologies for Collective Intelligence, Studies in Computational Intelligence, vol. 460, pp. 167–187, (2013)
6. Foxall, R.: The behavioral perspective model of purchase and consumption: From consumer theory to marketing practice. J. Acad. Mark. Sci. **20**(2), 189–198 (1992)
7. Rosenberg, M., Hovland, C.: Cognitive, affective, and behavioral components of attitudes. In: Rosenberg, M., Hovland, C. (eds.) Attitude Organization and Change: An Analysis of Consistency among Attitude Components, pp. 1–14. Yale University Publications, New Haven (1960)
8. Fishbein, M., Ajzen, I.: Belief, Attitude. An Introduction to Theory and Research (Addison-Wesley series in social psychology), Intention and Behavior (1975)
9. Busse, V., Angerer, T.: Analyse des Käuferverhaltens für dekorative Kosmetik - eine empirische Untersuchung für das Unternehmen L'Oréal, München, Wien, (2016)
10. Ajzen, I., Fishbein, M.: Understanding attitudes and predicting social behavior, New York, (1980)

11. Montano, D., Kasprzyk, D.: Theory of reasoned action, theory of planned behavior, and the integrated behavioral model. In: Glanz, K, Rimer, B., Viswanath, K. (eds.) Health Behavior: Theory, Research, and Practice 5th ed., pp. 95–124 (2015)
12. Doswell, W., Braxter, B., Cha, E., Kim, K.: Testing the theory of reasoned action in explaining sexual behavior among african american young teen girls. J. Pediatr. Nurs. **26**(6), 45–54 (2011)
13. Shimp, T., Kavas, A.: The theory of reasoned action applied to coupon usage. J. Consumer Res. **11**(3), 795–809 (1984)
14. Ajzen, I.: The theory of planned behavior. Organ. Behav. Hum. Decis. Process. **50**, 179–211 (1991)
15. Fishbein, M., Ajzen, I.: Theory-based behavior change interventions: comments on hobbis and sutton. J. Health Psychol. **10**(1), 27–31 (2005)
16. ULR: https://www.definitions.net/definition/Behavior, (seen on 24.07.2019, 10 pm)
17. Fishbein, M.: Attitude and the prediction of behavior. In: Fishbein, M. (ed.) Readings in attitude theory and measurement, pp. 477–493, New York (1967)
18. Hagger, M.: The reasoned action approach and the theories of reasoned action and planned behavior. In: Dunn, D. (ed.) Oxford Bibliographies in Psychology. Oxford University Press, New York (2019)
19. Madden, T., Ellen, P., Ajzen, I.: A comparison of the theory of planned behavior and the theory of reasoned action. Pers. Soc. Psychol. Bull. **18**(1), 3–9 (1992)
20. Konerding, U.: Formal models for predicting behavioral intentions in dichotomous choice situations. Methods Psychol. Res. Online **4**(2), 1–32 (1999)
21. Schwartz, S.H., Tessler, R.: A test of a model for reducing measured attitude-behavior discrepancies. J. Pers. Soc. Psychol. **24**(2), 225–236 (1972)
22. Busse, V., Strauss, C., Gregus, M.: Decision-making in crowdfunding – the value of behavioral issues in collaborative business environments. In: Luo, H. (ed.) CDVE 2019. LNCS, vol. 11792, pp. 219–228. Springer, Cham (2019). https://doi.org/10.1007/978-3-030-30949-7_25

FireBird: A Fire Alert and Live Fire Monitoring System Based on Social Media Contribution

Arijit Das[1], Rahul Dutta[2], Ayan Dey[2], Thomas Tamisier[3], and Sukriti Bhattacharya[3(✉)]

[1] Narula Institute of Technology, Kolkata, India
arijit1080@gmail.com
[2] University of Calcutta, Kolkata, India
rahul39dutta@gmail.com, adakc_rs@caluniv.ac.in
[3] Luxembourg Institute of Science and Technology, Esch-sur-Alzette, Luxembourg
{thomas.tamisier,sukriti.bhattacharya}@list.lu

Abstract. Social media renders real-time updates, which are, in many cases, much faster than the traditional media. Due to this reason, social media is rapidly becoming an essential aspect of emergency response and recovery. This paper proposes a collaborative approach for a more coordinated emergency response system during a fire incident from Twitter. The method is implemented in a visual tool, called `Firebird`. `Firebird` attempts to source first-hand situational information from Twitter feeds. Using a combination of NLP and deep learning techniques, `Firebird` offers real-time fire detection, fact-checking, and incident location sharing with the firefighters to speed up the response efforts at a scale close to real-time.

Keywords: Crowd sourcing · Twitter · Live fire detection · NLP · CNN · RNN.

1 Introduction

Since its inception in 2006, Twitter's popularity has escalated to over 300 million active users[1]. Besides being a communication channel for expressing social interests and emotions, Twitter's microblogging service supplements broadcasting and circulation of newsworthy events and trending topics [1,2]. The interactions in Twitter are short 140 characters micro-blogs called tweets. According to the 2018 Twitter Report[2], half a billion tweets are sent out each day. Twitter's data follows a data stream model on which data mining algorithms, streaming APIs[3] can be applied for analysis in the field of Natural Language Processing

---

[1] https://www.statista.com/statistics/282087/number-of-monthly-active-twitter-users/.

[2] https://mention.com/en/reports/twitter/.

[3] https://developer.twitter.com/en/docs/tweets/compliance/api-reference.

© Springer Nature Switzerland AG 2020
Y. Luo (Ed.): CDVE 2020, LNCS 12341, pp. 104–114, 2020.
https://doi.org/10.1007/978-3-030-60816-3_12

(NLP). Underpinned by near real-time nature of tweets acting as 'social-sensors', they are collected and filtered to detect natural disasters like earthquakes [3–5], crisis events like riots and fire incidents [6,7] and for detecting trending topics [8]. Extracting locations from tweets are essential to generate precise reports of such events. Research has been done on identifying locations from tweets using Named-Entity Recognition (NER) [9], toponym resolution [10] and geo-predication models [11].

This paper proposes a tool called Firebird that detects fire incidents from Twitter, fact-checks the event and reports for prevention. Using a combination of NLP and deep learning models, Firebird follows a pragmatic approach to handle fire incidents. Tweets having the keyword 'fire' are considered as tweets that potentially indicate such events. Firebird streams these tweets in real-time (Sect. 2.1), which are then preprocessed (Sect. 2.3) to make it analysis-ready. Later, analyzed and validated by Long Short Term Memory (LSTM) [12] and Convolution Neural Network [13] (CNN) models (Sect. 2.5). LSTMs effectively capture long-term memory dependencies without suffering from vanishing gradients, outperforms vanilla Recurrent Neural Network (RNN) in most NLP tasks [14]. That CNN model defined in [15] has been adapted because of its 93% accuracy that surpasses prior works like non-temporal fire detection [16] and at a lower complexity than earlier CNN based approach [17]. Moreover, the tool leverages (a) NASA Active Fire Data[4] which provides data that can be used to detect fires and (b) a voting algorithm as an alternative to the Active Fire Data (Sect. 2.5) to verify the fire incidents. Visualisation aspects can be elaborated from use of tweets images (Fig. 4) and location mapping (Fig. 3).

The paper is organized as follows: Sect. 2 explains the architecture of Firebird. Section 3 describes the flow chart of the tool along with case studies. Finally, the paper is concluded in Sect. 4.

2 Architecture

The architecture of Firebird is illustrated in Fig. 1. In this section, the authors describe in detail each component of the architecture - Twitter Streaming (Sect. 2.1), Data Collection (Sect. 2.2), Data Processing (Sect. 2.3), Supervised Learning (Sect. 2.5) Data Validation (Sect. 2.5) and Deployment (Sect. 2.6).

2.1 Twitter Streaming

Twitter streaming API allows us to consume tweets of interest without having to wait for it to download in real-time. The authors used Python Library Tweepy[5] to connect to the Twitter API to stream tweets that mention the keyword 'fire'.

---

[4] https://earthdata.nasa.gov/earth-observation-data/near-real-time/firms/active-fire-data.

[5] http://www.tweepy.org/.

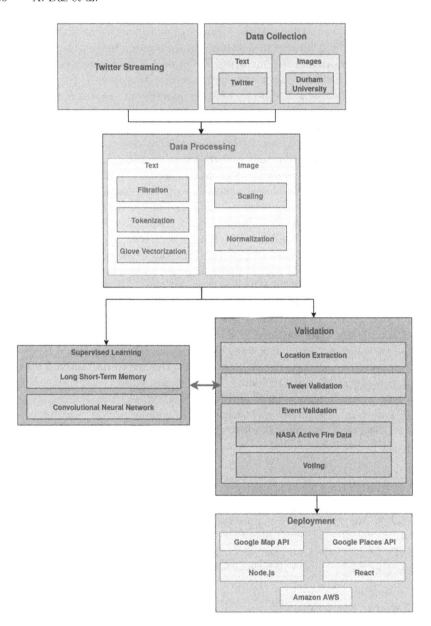

Fig. 1. Architecture of Firebird

2.2   Data Collection

The reliability and validity of the research depends on the process of collecting information from the relevant sources to find answers to the underlying research problem, to test the hypothesis, and to evaluate the final outcomes. This paper uses the textual data from public social interactions on Twitter as a potential complement to the fire incident. Tweepy API is used to collect 12998 tweets on January 19, 2020. The tweets have been labelled manually by the authors. These interactions often represent day-to-day events and can include location information, making them potentially fitting for use in the transportation-level deployment later in our process. The fire image dataset is collected from Durham University [18].

2.3 Data Processing

When building any intelligent systems based on tweet data, the tweets should be cleaned and preprocessed before being analyzed. The authors tried the following approaches for tweet preprocessing.

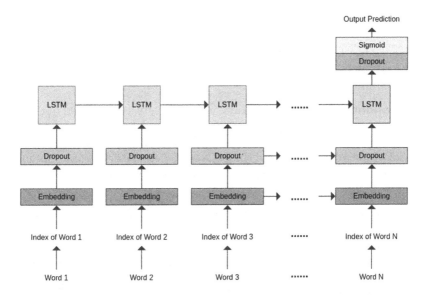

Fig. 2. LSTM Model

Filtration - The collected tweets undergo filtration to remove irrelevant data to reduces noises and include the tweets that describe the experience with the real fire incidents. Some basic filtration techniques on tweets are performed - URLs, Non-English words, emojis, punctuation are removed, and spellings are corrected (using Python `pyspellchecker`[6] library). Collected image data are scaled and normalized.

Tokenization -The filtered tweet undergoes tokenization to create a corpus that is vectorized and fed to the neural network model. Tokenization is almost implicit since the English language is already segmented. Each word is separated

---

[6] https://pypi.org/project/pyspellchecker/.

by space. Hence, the tokens are created by splitting the sentence on each space. Each individual word in the tweet is considered as an individual token. The tokens are further filtered to remove noise using Python `nltk.py`[7] library.

Vectorization - This project used, the pre-trained Global Vectors for Word Representation (GloVe[8]) model on the tokens for the word vectors. Henceforth, the data set is now ready for validation as explained in the following Section.

2.4 Supervised Learning

`Firebird`'s supervised learning models are underpinned by LSTM to model the features of tweets and CNN to model the features of the image data. The LSTM model used is illustrated in Fig. 2. This project adopted the exact CNN model defined in [19] due to highly accurate results.

2.5 Data Validation

Validation is two-fold, testing the tweet stream by the deep learning models and verifying the incidence mentioned in the positively tested tweet after extracting the location information.

Tweet Validation - The tweet stream (Sect. 2.1) acts as an unseen test dataset used to evaluate the model's performance on unseen data. A valid tweet is determined by both the LSTM and CNN models proposed in Sect. 2.3. Our LSTM model achieves 88% accuracy and the CNN model gives 93% accuracy on unseen tweets. Considering the gravity of the incident, tweet validation is crucial to forbade misleading consequences.

Location Extraction - Location information is decisive in understanding the impact of a fire incident at the granularity of point-of-interest [20,21]. The authors examined the practicability of applying Named Entity Recognizers to extract locations from the tweets of both geo-location and point-of-interest level.

Event Validation - The spread of misinformation is inherently human. Fire incidents can appear in the form of old, legitimate news articles being reshared months or years later, after another significant event. It's also worthwhile to check if the person or group that posted the incident claims is actually valid or not. The validation process strives to accomplish this fact-checking by `NASA Active Fire Data`. Using this service, `Firebird` checks if the Active Fire Data indicates a fire in the location previously extracted from the tweet. If it does, the occurrence of fire is confirmed; otherwise, a voting algorithm is applied to check if more than a 'threshold' number of tweets indicate the fire incident in that same location.

---

[7] https://www.nltk.org/.
[8] https://nlp.stanford.edu/projects/glove/.

Fig. 3. Deployment of `Firebird`

Fig. 4. Case 1: Only image indicates fire incident

2.6 Deployment

Upon detection of a fire incident, `Firebird` marks the location of the fire incident on a map as shown in Fig. 3 with respect to an example tweet shown in Fig. 4. Google Map API has been used to plot the map. In future, the authors will extend `Firebird` with fullstack application (using React and Node.js) hosted on Amazon AWS and, capable of notifying fire stations.

3   Case Study

In this Section, the architecture discussed above is expanded and the workflow of `Firebird` is described . Figure 5 illustrates the overall workflow of `Firebird` using a flowchart. Depending on the content of the tweet, distinct paths are followed in the workflow. For instance, the image in the tweet may indicate a fire incident but, the text may not or vice versa. Three such cases are illustrated in Figs. 4, 6, 7 and analyzed in Table 1. Due to page limitation, further cases are not analyzed.

Table 1. Case Study

Case	Tweet Data		Location Extraction		Tweet Validation		Event Validation		Fire incident	Path
	Text	Image	Location in Tweet	User Location	Image Validation	Text Validation	NASA Active Fire Data	Voting		
Figure 4	Available	Available	Available	Ignore	Valid	Ignore	N/A	Valid	Detected	$1 \to 2 \to 3$ $\to 4 \to 4.1.1$ $\to 4.1.2 \to 5$ $\to 5.1.1 \to$ $5.1.2 \to 6 \to$ $6.1 \to 7 \to$ $7.1 \to 8 \to 9$ $\to 10$
Figure 6	Available	Available	Available	Ignore	Invalid	Valid	N/A	Invalid	Not detected	$1 \to 2 \to 3$ $\to 4 \to 4.1.1$ $\to 4.1.2 \to 5$ $\to 5.1.1 \to$ $5.1.2 \to 5.2.1$ $\to 5.2.2 \to 6$ $\to 6.1 \to 7$ $\to 7.1 \to 10$
Figure 7	Available	Available	Unavailable	Available	Invalid	Invalid	Ignore	Ignore	Not detected	$1 \to 2 \to$ $3 \to 4 \to$ $4.2.1 \to 4.2.2$ $\to 5 \to$ $5.1.1 \to 5.1.2$ $\to 5.2.1 \to$ $5.2.2 \to 10$

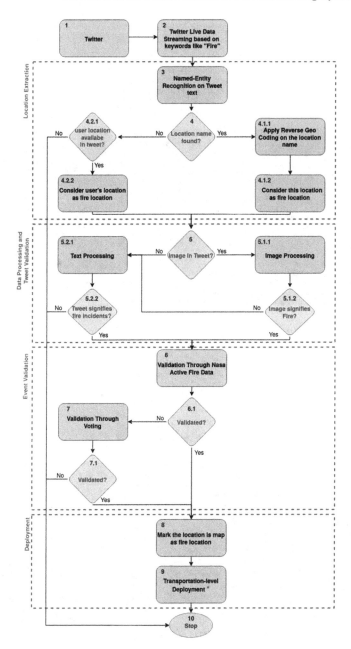

Fig. 5. Workflow of Firebird

Fig. 6. Case 2: Only text indicates fire incident

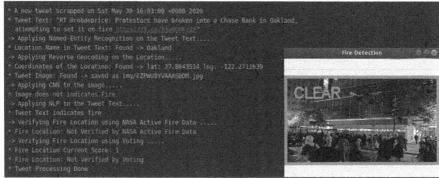

Fig. 7. Case 3: Both image and text does not indicate fire incident

4   Conclusion

Twitter streaming allows valuable insight into real-time events on such a global scale that brings significant research challenges. In this paper, the authors tackle such a challenge by developing and applying deep learning techniques to ensure that users have the best possible experience. This paper outlines the architecture and the steps followed by a proposed tool `Firebird` to detect fire incidents with unambiguity at the point-of-interest. Case studies have observed to justify the practicality of the proof-of-concept. In future work, the authors would like to integrate local fire stations with `Firebird`. One possible extension is using adaptive deep learning networks by dynamically adjusting the 'alert-words' and collecting the dataset accordingly to render better accuracy. It is expected that this research will lead to a better understanding of the potential for information from Twitter to add context to other real-time incident management systems. An Android application remains to be seen and warrant further exploration. It is expected that this research will lead to a better understanding of the potential for information from Twitter to add context to other real-time incident management systems.

References

1. Kim, S., Bak, J., Oh, A.H.: Do you feel what i feel? social aspects of emotions in twitter conversations. In: Sixth International AAAI Conference on Weblogs and Social Media (2012)
2. Java, A., Song, X., Finin, T., Tseng, B.: Why we twitter: understanding microblogging usage and communities. In: Proceedings of the 9th WebKDD and 1st SNA-KDD 2007 Workshop on Web Mining and Social Network Analysis, pp. 56–65 (2007)
3. Sakaki, T., Okazaki, M., Matsuo, Y.: Tweet analysis for real-time event detection and earthquake reporting system development. IEEE Transactions on Knowledge and Data Engineering **25**(4), 919–931 (2012)
4. Robinson, B., Power, R., Cameron, M.: A sensitive twitter earthquake detector. In: Proceedings of the 22nd International Conference on World Wide Web, pp. 999–1002 (2013)
5. Avvenuti, M., Cresci, S., Marchetti, A., Meletti, C., Tesconi, M.: Ears (earthquake alert and report system) a real time decision support system for earthquake crisis management. In: Proceedings of the 20th ACM SIGKDD International Conference on Knowledge Discovery and Data Mining, pp. 1749–1758 (2014)
6. Alsaedi, N., Burnap, P., Rana, O.: Can we predict a riot? disruptive event detection using twitter. ACM Trans. Internet Technol. **17**(2), March 2017. https://doi.org/10.1145/2996183
7. Terpstra, T., De Vries, A., Stronkman, R., Paradies, G.: Towards a realtime Twitter analysis during crises for operational crisis management. Simon Fraser University Burnaby (2012)
8. Benhardus, J., Kalita, J.: Streaming trend detection in twitter. International Journal of Web Based Communities **9**(1), 122–139 (2013)
9. J. Gelernter and S. Balaji, "An algorithm for local geoparsing of microtext," GeoInformatica, vol. 17, no. 4, pp. 635–667, 2013
10. Ghahremanlou, L., Sherchan, W., Thom, J.A.: Geotagging twitter messages in crisis management. The Computer Journal **58**(9), 1937–1954 (2015)
11. Han, B., Cook, P., Baldwin, T.: Text-based twitter user geolocation prediction. Journal of Artificial Intelligence Research **49**, 451–500 (2014)

12. Hochreiter, S., Schmidhuber, J.: Long short-term memory. Neural Comput. **9**(8) 1735–1780, November 1997. https://doi.org/10.1162/neco.1997.9.8.1735

13. Krizhevsky, A., Sutskever, I., Hinton, G.E.: Imagenet classification with deep convolutional neural networks. In: Advances in Neural Information Processing Systems 25, Pereira, F., Burges, C.J.C., Bottou, L., Weinberger, K.Q., Eds. Curran Associates Inc, pp. 1097–1105 (2012). http://papers.nips.cc/paper/4824-imagenet-classification-with-deep-convolutional-neural-networks.pdf

14. Sundermeyer, M., Schlüter, R., Ney, H.: LSTM neural networks for language modeling. In: Thirteenth Annual Conference of the International Speech Communication Association. 09 (2012)

15. Dunnings, A.J., Breckon, T.P.: Experimentally defined convolutional neural network architecture variants for non-temporal real-time fire detection. In: 2018 25th IEEE International Conference on Image Processing(ICIP). IEEE, pp. 1558–1562 (2018)

16. Chenebert, A., Breckon, T.P., Gaszczak, A.: A non-temporal texture driven approach to real-time fire detection. In: 2011 18th IEEE International Conference on Image Processing. IEEE, pp. 1741–1744 (2011)

17. Luo, Y., Zhao, L., Liu, P., Huang, D.: Fire smoke detection algorithm based on motion characteristic and convolutional neural networks. Multimedia Tools and Applications, **77**(12), 075– 092 (2018)

18. Dunnings, A.: Fire image data set for dunnings 2018 study - PNG still image set (2018)

19. Dunnings, A.J., Breckon, T.P.: Experimentally defined convolutional neural network architecture variants for non-temporal real-time fire detection. In: 2018 25th IEEE International Conference on Image Processing (ICIP). IEEE, pp. 1558–1562 (2018)

20. Lingad, J., Karimi, S., Yin, J.: Location extraction from disaster-related microblogs. In: Proceedings of the 22nd International Conference on World Wide Web, pp. 1017–1020 (2013)

21. Li, C., Sun, A.: Fine-grained location extraction from tweets with temporal awareness. In: Proceedings of the 37th international ACM SIGIR conference on Research & development in information retrieval, pp. 43–52 (2014)

Clustering of Time-Series Balance History Data Streams Using Apache Spark

Do Quang Dat and Phan Duy Hung[✉]

FPT University, Hanoi, Vietnam
dat18mse13010@fsb.edu.vn, hungpd2@fe.edu.vn

Abstract. Clustering customers, predicting account balances, scoring credits, detecting risk cash flows, etc. are the problems that have been focused on research in the banking sector. With the explosion of big data, these problems will take a new approach. This paper proposes a new solution based on historical information of balances to cluster customers. The work has implemented clustering algorithms for time series in a big data environment. In addition, stream data clustering was tested with positive results. The result of customer clustering helps to make marketing decisions, forecasting of customer deposits in the following month, etc.

Keywords: Modeling of group behavior · Big data exploration · Balance history · Customer clustering · Time-series · Stream data · Apache spark

1 Introduction

With the evolution of big data and data mining, the classical problem of marketing and risk management in banking are approached in new ways to be more effective. One of the most common problems is how to effectively cluster customers, because customer information is very diverse, with age, gender, job, salary, spending patterns, balance history, daily expenses, etc. This study focuses on clustering customers using their balance history as a time series.

There have been some studies regarding the matter. In 2017, the authors in [1] have taken up the challenge of missing data prediction in multivariable time series by employing improved matrix factorization techniques, the approaches are optimally designed to largely utilize both the internal patterns of each time series and the information. A tool for easily understanding large-scale time series was proposed by the authors in [2] who presented an introductory analysis of time series clustering with a focus on a novel shape-based measure of similarity, which is invariant, based on this measure we develop a Visual Assessment of cluster Tendency (VAT) algorithm to assess large time-series data sets and demonstrate its advantages in terms of complexity and propensity for implementation in a distributed computing environment under uniform time shift and uniform amplitude scaling of time series across multiple sources. For time series forecasting for scalable time-series, different methods proposed by the authors in [3, 4], and [5]. In [3], the authors presented different scalable methods for predicting big time series, namely time series with a high-frequency measurement. Different from authors in [3], the authors in [4] introduced a new approach for big data

© Springer Nature Switzerland AG 2020
Y. Luo (Ed.): CDVE 2020, LNCS 12341, pp. 115–124, 2020.
https://doi.org/10.1007/978-3-030-60816-3_13

forecasting based on the k-weighted nearest neighbor algorithm in the Apache Spark framework. The authors in [5] proposed a new distributed computing which used on time-series stock data in the distributed cluster.

The big data system designs for applications with time series are introduced in [6–8], and [9]. In [6], the authors presented an end-to-end architecture for a real-time testbed to analyze and cluster time series sensor data using an IoT architecture composed of Kaa (a middleware), Kafka (a realtime data messaging queue), Spark (an in-memory data analytics platform) and k-means (a clustering algorithm). The authors in [7] presented a latency-driven data controller, which aims to process as much data as possible, while processing these as fast as the application target latency and system capacity allow. The authors in [8] and [9] proposed methods for distributed indexing of time-series datasets. The authors in [8] proposed a demonstration of Spark-parSketch, a complete solution based on sketches/random projections to efficiently perform both the parallel indexing of large sets of time series and a similarity search on them. Unlike [8], the authors in [9] propose the TARDIS distributed indexing framework to overcome the scale problem of iSAX structure limitations.

The studies summarized above show the potential of applying time-series data research on big data platforms to customer clustering problem. This paper proposes a new approach based on historical information of balances as a time series to cluster customers. Clustering algorithms have discovered for time series on Apache Spark. Stream data clustering was tested with positive results. This result will be the input for marketing, risk management, etc. in banks. As an additional contribution, a dataset, which is stripped of customers' private information is available at Github [10]. It can also be used for other fields of research regarding time series and customers' behavior.

2 Data Description

The data set is taken from a bank's deposit account information. For each account, there is data about balance history in 48 months from January 2013 to January 2017. To assess customer clustering in real time, historical information of customer balances for 12 months is used as a sliding window. After each month, the window is up to one step and clustering is performed again. The total number of accounts collected is 976,289. However, 95% of the accounts are no longer active or the balance is very low, under 350 USD, and will not be used in this study because of their low significance. The number of remaining accounts with a high balance is 5,869. These accounts represent only 0.6% of the total but they contain 46.55% of the total balance of all deposit accounts.

For privacy reasons, all customer information and bank information have been discarded. Only the account balance details remain. Hence, the data for each customer is a sequence of 48 values, each being the balance at the beginning of the month.

3   Methodologies and Implementation

3.1   Methodologies

First, the original data is smoothed using the spline function to reduce sharp variations. Next, the data is normalized to the range of [0, 1]. This normalization aims to focus on finding customers with the same "behavior" every 12 months, and to reduce the effect of disparities in account balance values on cluster results. There will be some customers who have no transactions over a 12-month period will be standardized to value 1.

The clustering method is k-means based on Dynamic Time Warping Distance (DTW) [11]. DTW allows estimating distances between time series, in this case, time series of customer account balances for 12 months. The Silhouette index will be used to evaluate cluster information [12]. This is also the index to optimize the number of customer clusters after each clustering.

For monitoring cluster transition, there are several methods like MONIC [13] and MEC [14]. MONIC is an algorithm that was proposed for modeling and tracking clustering transitions. These transitions can be internal, related to each clustering process as a whole. MONIC provides information about changes in clusters such as whether clusters continue to exist or disappear, new clusters are created, or changes in clusters that occur during automatic clustering. Unlike MONIC, MEC which traces the evolution of clusters over time through the identification of the temporal relationship among them.

In this paper, we use MONIC for tracking cluster's transition between months. This paper selects a "survival threshold" that will vary from 0.4 to 0.7, a jump of 0.05. Other constants such as split threshold and size threshold unchanged from the original paper are 0.2 and 100, respectively. In addition to changing the survival threshold, the study also changed the tracking of cluster results after 1 month, 3 months, 6 months and 12 months to be able to analyze how the clustering frequency is effective and how the survival threshold value is appropriate in this problem.

3.2   System Installation

The deployment model includes main components (Fig. 1):

- Publisher: A simulator program to push monthly balance information of customers to the main program.
- Subscriber: A Spark Streaming service receives monthly balance information of customers and performs clustering on a monthly basis. Cluster results will be saved and analyzed when the process is finished.
- Messaging queue service: A component for communicating between Publisher and Subscriber, the balance information of the customer will be pushed into the queue by the Publisher and the Subscriber will receive the messages in the queue for processing.

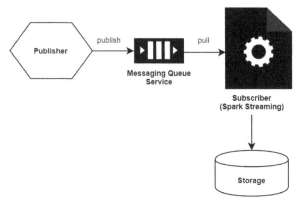

Fig. 1. Application installation model.

4   Result Analysis

After performing clustering, clustering results start from the 12th month with Silhouette values as shown in Fig. 2. After each clustering, the optimal number of clusters is 5 or 6, and the average silhouette value is approximately 0.85, which is a very high silhouette value when performing clustering.

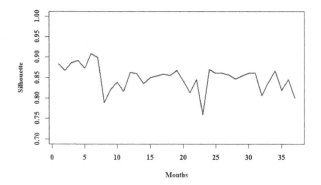

Fig. 2. Silhouette values over time.

For each 12-month window, the principal component analysis is calculated to provide insight into cluster results. Figure 3 shows some typical clustering results in several windows of the months such as 12, 18, 34, 30, 35 and 44. Although the results are presented in two dimensions, it also proves that clustering results are good.

The results of clustering continue to be analyzed based on the MONIC method. It can be seen that when the survival threshold increases, the number of clusters that survive in the next cluster (continue as a separate cluster or merge into another cluster) decreases. When the survival threshold is equal to 0.7, almost only one cluster is considered to survive. In contrast, when the survival threshold is equal to 0.4, many

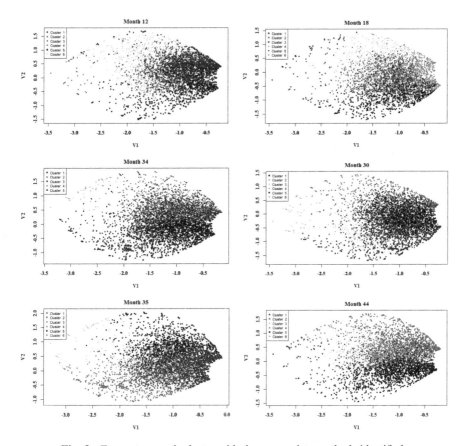

Fig. 3. Forecast on each cluster with the appropriate methods identified.

clusters are likely to survive in the next clustering (Fig. 4). When the survival threshold changes from 0.4 to 0.7, the number of clusters that continues to remain between successive clusterings decreases. While the number of clusters is split into other clusters, the number of lost or added clusters between consecutive clustering increases.

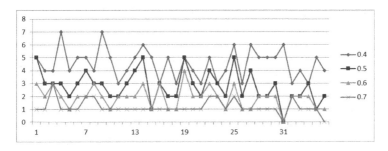

Fig. 4. Number of survival clusters over time and the survival threshold.

The number of survival clusters varies under the influence of the survival threshold and the time interval between two clusterings is shown in Fig. 5. For example, with a survival threshold of 0.4, if the interval between two clusters is a month, then more than half of the clusters continue to exist. Whereas if the time between clusters is 12 months, most of the clusters do not survive, that is, the cluster has completely changed in structure, or the customer has completely changed the behavior after about 12 months with other customers in the cluster they belong earlier. Similarly, when the time between clusters is 1 month, most customers still maintain their behavior compared to other members in the cluster.

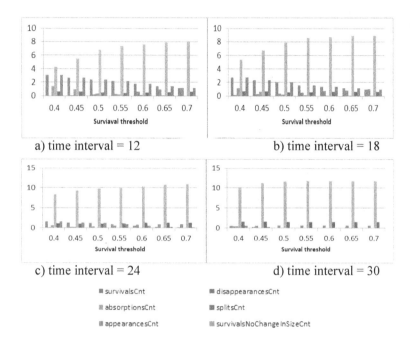

Fig. 5. Number of survival clusters over the survival threshold and the time interval between two clusterings.

From the above analysis, depending on the level of response (real-time), the application will determine the time interval between clusters as well as the value of survival threshold to optimize the monitoring of changes of clusters over time and devise strategies suitable for each customer cluster.

Figure 6 is an example of some of the cluster's survival or split changes over a 6-month period at time-points of 12, 18, 24 and 30 months.

The graph does not show all the changes of clusters between two clusters that only represent survival clusters, disappearance clusters, new emerging clusters, and split clusters. We can see that at two times clustering at time-point 12 and 18, cluster 3 at time-point 12 has disappeared in the result of clustering at time-point 18. At time-point 18, the two new clusters are clusters 2 and 5, while cluster 4 at time-point 12 splits the

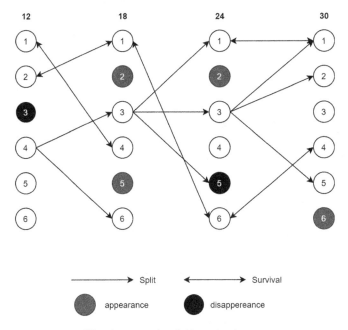

Fig. 6. Example of Cluster's change.

elements into clusters 3 and 6 at time-point 18. In addition, one cluster can survive through all time-points 12, 18, 24 and 30. The survival process is as follows 2(12) ⇔ 1 (18) ⇔ 6(24) ⇔ 4(30). This result is also shown in Figs. 7, 8 and 9. It is easy to see that the surviving cluster consists of customers who did not perform any behavior during the monitoring process.

With the above analysis, some meaningful conclusions can be drawn:

- Clustering customers based on behavior through the history of balances gives very positive results. Silhouette values for clustering are very high. The results of clustering when viewed on 2-dimensional space show the relative separation of clusters.
- When monitoring the change of clusters of consecutive clustering process by MONIC method, the frequency of clustering so that it is effective and consistent with the problem can be determined.
- Also from the process of tracking clustering using the MONIC method, a cluster of customers who did not perform or perform very few transactions was detected as an abnormal cluster.

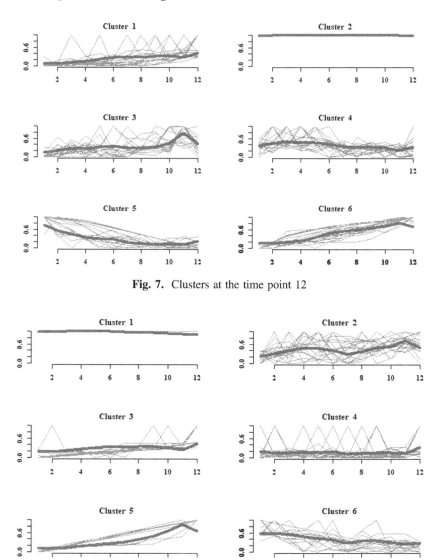

Fig. 7. Clusters at the time point 12

Fig. 8. Clusters at the time point 18

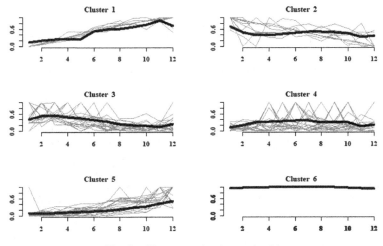

Fig. 9. Clusters at the time point 24

5 Conclusion and Perspectives

The paper proposes a new method for clustering customers based on the history of account balances and demonstrates the effectiveness of the method based on clustering data as well as statistics on real data. The work has implemented algorithms for time series in a big data environment. In addition, stream data clustering was tested with positive results. The tracking of clustering with MONIC method allows giving some meaningful results on the appropriate frequency for clustering as well as detecting abnormal clusters when tracking the variation between times of clustering.

The result of customer clustering can be used in marketing strategies, forecasting of affordability, or customer deposits in the following month, etc. The paper is also a valuable reference for problems in areas such as Knowledge Representation, Prediction, Time Series Analysis, etc.

References

1. Shi, W., et al.: Effective prediction of missing data on apache spark over multivariable time series. IEEE Trans. Big Data **4**(4), 473–486 (2018). https://doi.org/10.1109/tbdata.2017. 2719703
2. Iredale, T.B, Erfani, S.M., Leckie, C.: An efficient visual assessment of cluster tendency tool for large-scale time series data sets. In: Proceedings of the IEEE International Conference on Fuzzy Systems (FUZZ-IEEE), Naples, Italy, pp. 1–8 (2017)
3. Galicia, A., Torres, J.F., Martínez-Álvarez, F., Troncoso, A.: A novel Spark-based multi-step forecasting algorithm for big data time series. Inf. Sci. **467**, 800–818 (2018). https://doi.org/ 10.1016/j.ins.2018.06.010
4. Talavera-Llames, R., Pérez-Chacón, R., Troncoso, A., Martínez-Álvarez, F.: Big data time series forecasting based on nearest neighbours distributed computing with Spark. Knowl. Based Syst. **161**, 12–25 (2018)

5. Hussain, L., Banarjee, S., Kumar, S., Chaubey, A., Reza, M.: Forecasting time series stock data using deep learning technique in a distributed computing environment. In: Proceedings of the International Conference on Computing, Power and Communication Technologies (GUCON), Greater Noida, UP, India, pp. 489–493 (2018)
6. Talei, H., Essaaidi, M., Benhaddou, D.: An end to end real time architecture for analyzing and clustering time series data: case of an energy management system. In: Proceedings of the 6th International Renewable and Sustainable Energy Conference (IRSEC), Rabat, Morocco, pp. 1–7 (2018)
7. Bouslama, A., Laaziz, Y., Tali, A.: Scalable and real-time time series analytics: telemedicine as use case. In: Proceedings of the IEEE 5th International Congress on Information Science and Technology (CiSt), Marrakech, Morocco, pp. 70–73 (2018)
8. Oleksandra, L., Djamel-Edine, Y., Reza, A., Masseglia, F., Kolev, B., Shasha, D.: Spark-parSketch: a massively distributed indexing of time series datasets. In: Proceedings of the 27th ACM International Conference on Information and Knowledge Management (CIKM 2018). Association for Computing Machinery, New York, USA, 1951–1954 (2018). https://doi.org/10.1145/3269206.3269226
9. Zhang, L., Alghamdi, N., Eltabakh, M.Y., Rundensteiner, E.A.: TARDIS: distributed indexing framework for big time series data. In: Proceedings of the IEEE 35th International Conference on Data Engineering (ICDE), Macao, Macao, pp. 1202–1213 (2019)
10. https://github.com/ziczacziczac/customer-clustering/tree/master/data
11. Berndt, D.J., Clifford, J.: Using dynamic time warping to findpatterns in time series. In: Proceedings of the Workshop on Knowledge Discovery in Databases, Washington, pp. 359–370 (1994)
12. Rousseeuw, P.J.: Silhouettes: a graphical aid to the interpretation and validation of cluster analysis. J. Comput. Appl. Math. **20**, 53–65 (1987)
13. Spilioopoulou, M., Mtoutsi, I., Theodoridis, Y., Schult, R.: MONIC - Modeling and monitoring cluster transitions. In: Proceedings of the 12th ACM SIGKDD International conference on Knowledge discovery and data mining, Philadelphia PA, USA (2006)
14. Oliverira, M., Gama, J.: MEC: monitoring clusters' transitions. In: Proceedings of the 5th Starting AI Researchers' Symposium, Amsterdam, Netherlands (2010)

Integrated Evolution Model of Service Internet Based on an Improved Logistic Growth Model

Zhixuan Jia[1], Shuangxi Huang[2(✉)], and Yushun Fan[2]

[1] School of Software and Microelectronics, Peking University, Beijing, China
jiazhixuan@pku.edu.cn
[2] Department of Automation, Tsinghua University, Beijing, China
{huangsx,fanyus}@tsinghua.edu.cn

Abstract. Service Internet is a complex, networked, and comprehensive service system formed by a large number of service units in different networks through a highly cooperative relationship. It can effectively and accurately create value for service stakeholders, and provide basic theoretical support for service application in many different situations. Nevertheless, there is a lack of systematic research on the overall dynamic evolution of service Internet, which leads to the lack of relevant mathematical models and theoretical guidance on the control and optimization for the overall service Internet. Therefore, considering the system characteristics such as cooperation and competition in service internet, this paper puts forward an overall evolution model of service Internet based on the logistic growth model, and then makes a theoretical analysis of its life cycle and evolution path. Finally, we use real-world electronic technology industry cluster data to verify the proposed model. Experiment results show that our model can better reflect and predict the evolution trend of service Internet.

Keywords: Service Internet · Evolution · Cooperation and competition · Environmental factors · Logistic growth model

1 Introduction

With the rise of the concepts about network, intelligence and service, service Internet has emerged in many application fields, resulting in new business forms like technology service network, health care service network and so on [4]. Service Internet is a complex service system composed of cross-network, cross-domain and cross-border services, which is essentially a complex service ecosystem [5], as shown in Fig. 1. It supports network-based service cooperation and service competition, so as to realize the creation and value-added of related service value. Services in service Internet include not only web services, but also productive business services, life consumption services, etc. It has become a huge driving force for the upgrading of modern service industry.

© Springer Nature Switzerland AG 2020
Y. Luo (Ed.): CDVE 2020, LNCS 12341, pp. 125–130, 2020.
https://doi.org/10.1007/978-3-030-60816-3_14

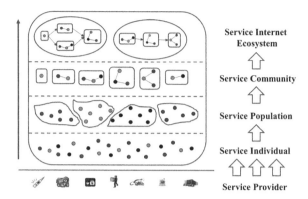

Fig. 1. Service Internet ecosystem

Although, in recent years, there are many research on the evolution of service system, most of them focus on web services [1]. Or, according to the characteristics of service system, they study its evolution mode and model from the micro perspective of service system [3]. However, at present, there are few studies on the evolution model of service Internet, which is based on the concept of big service, from the perspective of the whole system and considering the influence of external environment. As a result, there is still a lack of basic theoretical research on the cognition of the overall evolution rule and the integrated evolution model of service Internet. It makes the follow-up research on macro control of service Internet lack of relevant basic knowledge. Thus, it restricts the realization, application and development of service Internet.

Therefore, from the macro level of service Internet system, this paper constructs the integrated evolution model of service Internet based on the logistic growth model [2]. The life cycle and the paths of evolution are analyzed. We also use the real data to show that the proposed model has better explanatory and predictive performance for the evolution trend of service Internet.

2 Integrated Evolution Model of Service Internet

Model Description. As we all know, the resources of service Internet system are limited, and the value revenue it creates cannot be increased without limitation. Because it is also subject to various factors. It is restricted by external factors such as service infrastructure, service science and technology, service market capacity, service capital, service labor resources, etc. It will also be affected by the increase in the number of services within this system.

Service Internet system belongs to service ecosystem, which has the characteristics of general ecosystem. Therefore, its evolution trend is similar to the growth law for the number of organisms in the ecosystem. According to the logistic growth model, when a species enters a new environment, the number of this species shows an S-shaped growth trend. So we can use this model to describe the overall evolution process of service Internet system. The general form of the logistic growth model for service Internet is as follows:

$$\frac{dP}{dt} = rP(1 - \frac{P}{M})$$ (1)

where P is the service economic income created by the current service Internet. t represents the time unit. M represents the maximum economic benefit that service Internet can achieve in a certain time and under the state of environmental factors (capital, market, resources, etc.). r is the natural growth rate of the economic benefit for service Internet.

Considering the characteristics of cooperation and competition within service Internet system, and the characteristics of external environment factors outside the system, the original model is improved as follows:

$$\frac{dP}{dt} = rP(1 - \frac{\epsilon P^\sigma}{M}) + \eta$$ (2)

where ϵ indicates the different influence of external dynamic environment factors (capital, policy, market, and other socio-economic factors) on the overall economic benefits of service Internet. $\epsilon > 1$ indicates that the external social and economic factors have an inhibitory effect on the development of service Internet, and vice versa. σ represents the impact of competition and cooperation among services within service Internet on the overall evolution of the system, with a value greater than 0. When $\sigma < 1$, the model curve shows a lower convex growth, while $\sigma > 1$ model curve shows a upper convex growth. η is a constant compensation term.

In general, the improved model indicates the density restriction effect caused by service competition and service cooperation, and the influence of external social and economic factors.

Parameters Estimation Method. Nonlinear regression can guarantee the least square unbiasedness of the parameters to be estimated in the model curve, so we can get the best parameter estimation with the best accuracy. So in this paper, the nonlinear least square method is used to fit the model curve, and the parameters are initialized according to the following methods.

The first step is to set r as 0.2, ϵ as 1, σ as 1 and η as 0.1. Then, we choose to use the four point method to initialize the parameter M. According to the principle of equidistant time series, four groups of data $(t_1, y_1), (t_2, y_2), (t_3, y_3), (t_4, y_4)$ with equal time span $(t_1 + t_4 = t_2 + t_3)$ are selected, and the initial M value is calculated by Eq. (3).

$$M = \frac{y_2 y_3 (y_1 + y_4) - y_1 y_4 (y_2 + y_3)}{y_2 y_3 - y_1 y_4}$$ (3)

At last, the parameters r, ϵ, σ, η are estimated by iterative fitting of least square method. By this method, we can improve the iteration speed and accuracy.

3   Evolution Life Cycle and Path of Service Internet

Evolution Life Cycle Analysis. According to the S-curve of logistic growth model, there are four different stages in the evolution of service Internet.

Formation Period. At this time, it is the initial formation stage of service Internet system or the new development stage of service Internet system. The overall service value scale growth speed and value scale growth acceleration of service Internet system are increasing.

Growth Period. At this time, the economic growth rate of service Internet system continues to increase, while the acceleration of economic growth is getting smaller and smaller. Due to the continuous construction of service system, it attracts more and more services to move into this system. The competition and cooperation among services have been further enhanced, and the comprehensive development level of the system has been greatly improved.

Maturation Period. In this period, the internal structure of service Internet and the relationship and interaction between various components tend to be stable. The communication among service individuals tends to be frequent. The division of labor in the service chain is detailed. Service competition and cooperation are further strengthened.

Stabilization Period. The value of service Internet system has reached the largest scale in the current life cycle. Because of the prosperity and stability of the system, the service units, service populations and service communities enjoy the maximization of economic benefits.

Evolution Path Analysis. After the stabilization period of a life cycle, there are two types of evolution paths for service Internet system. The first one is the positive evolution. All kinds of services form a path dependence of continuous innovation through orderly and standardized competition & cooperation. It can expand service demands, and realize the continuous updating, transformation and structural upgrading of service Internet. The second is the retrogression. Service Internet falls into the path locking. The innovation momentum is insufficient. The integration ability of service resources is declining. And the overall system begins to stagnate or even decline. The evolution path of service Internet system depends on the service resource conditions in the environment, the service competition and cooperation in different periods, and the impact of environmental factors. Therefore, the evolution of service Internet system is likely to have bifurcations, as shown in Fig. 2.

4   Model Verification

Industrial cluster is a typical application case of service Internet [6]. Therefore, we use the real data of electronic technology industry cluster in a certain region

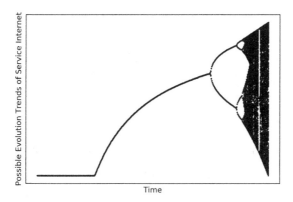

Fig. 2. Evolution path of service internet

of China from 1998 to 2017. The total output value of industrial cluster can be regarded as the total value scale of service Internet. We use the data of the first 15 years to estimate the parameters of these models. The parameters of our model are as follows. $r = 0.96$, $M = 146893.13$, $\sigma = 4.24$, $\epsilon = 1.94e-8$ and $\eta = -99.65$. Finally, we draw the prediction curves of these models and the real data curve on the same figure, as shown in Fig. 3. Via unused data, we carry out relevant tests to compare their prediction performance. The results are shown in Table 1.

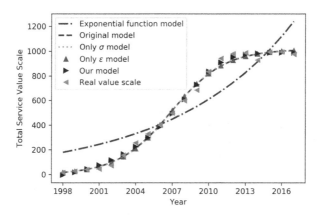

Fig. 3. Fitting performance comparison of different integrated evolution models

Therefore, it is not difficult to find that our model is superior to other models in fitting and prediction performance.

Table 1. Prediction performance comparison of evolution models for future evolution trend

Models	MAE	RMSE	Adjusted-R^2
Exponential function model	138.44	160.56	0.8055
Original model	24.44	31.10	0.9927
Only σ model	24.04	30.97	0.9923
Only ϵ model	24.42	31.11	0.9922
Our model	**20.67**	**25.60**	**0.9939**

5   Conclusion

According to the ecosystem characteristics of service Internet, considering the characteristics of its internal cooperation & competition and the influence of external environmental factors, this paper proposes an integrated evolution model of service Internet. This model can not only fit the real data curve well, but also has a good ability to predict the evolution trend of service Internet. This model is helpful for researchers to control and optimize service Internet in the future.

Acknowledgements. This research is supported by the National Key Research and Development Program of China (No. 2018YFB1402902).

References

1. Huang, K., Fan, Y., Tan, W.: An empirical study of programmable web: a network analysis on a service-mashup system. In: 2012 IEEE 19th International Conference on Web Services, pp. 552–559. IEEE (2012)
2. Jin, W., McCue, S.W., Simpson, M.J.: Extended logistic growth model for heterogeneous populations. J. Theor. Biol. **445**, 51–61 (2018)
3. Wang, X., Feng, Z., Chen, S., Huang, K.: DKEM: a distributed knowledge based evolution model for service ecosystem. In: 2018 IEEE International Conference on Web Services (ICWS), pp. 1–8. IEEE (2018)
4. Xu, H., Pan, Y., Li, J., Nie, L., Xu, X.: Activity recognition method for home-based elderly care service based on random forest and activity similarity. IEEE Access **7**, 16217–16225 (2019)
5. Xu, X., Sheng, Q.Z., Zhang, L.J., Fan, Y., Dustdar, S.: From big data to big service. Computer **7**, 80–83 (2015)
6. Zhang, K., Ma, B., Dong, P., Tang, B., Cai, H.: Research on producer service innovation in home-textile industrial cluster based on cloud computing platform. In: Proceedings of 2010 IEEE International Conference on Service Operations and Logistics, and Informatics, pp. 155–160. IEEE (2010)

A Data-Driven Platform for Predicting the Position of Future Wind Turbines

Olivier Parisot[✉]

Luxembourg Institute of Science and Technology (LIST),
5 Avenue des Hauts-Fourneaux, 4362 Esch-sur-Alzette, Luxembourg
olivier.parisot@list.lu

Abstract. Optimal location of wind turbines is a complex decision problem involving environmental, performance, societal and other parameter. This paper investigates the domain by describing Windturbines-Planner: by providing machine learning models trained on various data sources, the platform can help to anticipate the potential location of future onshore wind turbines in Luxembourg, France, Belgium and Germany.

Keywords: Wind turbines · Predictive analytics · Visualisation

1 Introduction

Nowadays, the production of renewable energy is more than ever an ecological and political priority. Therefore, each citizen can observe the installation of new wind turbines everywhere.

To understand this trend from a data-driven approach, we have developed WindturbinesPlanner – a platform to analyse and anticipate the location of potential future wind turbines in Luxembourg, France, Belgium and Germany.

By applying machine learning techniques on heterogeneous data sources, WindturbinesPlanner provides predictions that may be useful for politics and energy actors while considering social acceptance by the public [6]. Weather conditions like *wind speed* are obviously important to explain the location of onshore wind farms. Nevertheless, WindturbinesPlanner could help to understand to what extent other criteria may be important in the covered territories.

The rest of this article is organized as follows. Firstly, related works about wind turbines planning are briefly presented (Sect. 2). Secondly, the input data sources are detailed (Sect. 3). Thirdly, a data-driven prediction approach is described (Sect. 4). Finally, the implementation is presented (Sect. 5) and the results of preliminary experiments are discussed (Sect. 6).

2 Related Works

As the use of wind energy is a technology that is increasingly used worldwide, the scientific literature on this topic is very abundant.

© Springer Nature Switzerland AG 2020
Y. Luo (Ed.): CDVE 2020, LNCS 12341, pp. 131–136, 2020.
https://doi.org/10.1007/978-3-030-60816-3_15

For example, various computational methods for onshore wind farms placement have been proposed:

- Genetic algorithms have been developed to optimize the positioning of wind turbine in a single area [4,10].
- Geographic Information System (GIS) have been applied to determine the areas that could be interesting for wind energy development in Northeast Nebraska (USA) [9]; a recent solution consider spatial preferences for offshore/onshore and farms locations in Denmark [7].
- Other works rather focus on the design of algorithms to optimize the layout of wind turbines in dedicated farms [12].

Nevertheless, there is no advanced work about the deducing of wind turbines positions with a purely data-driven approach.

3   Data Sources

In order to build a meaningful and exploitable dataset for the prediction of the location of the next onshore wind turbines, different data sources have been aggregated for Luxembourg, Belgium, France, Germany:

- List of the current onshore wind turbines locations (for instance: 943 wind farms listed in France in April 2019)[1].
- Historical time series of daily minimal/maximal/average wind speed values: each time serie corresponds to a geolocated zone (with a width of 7.5 km), two years of data have been considered.
- STRM digital elevation model[2]: it may help to check if the topology is concretely considered before installing wind turbines.
- Cities positions and populations: it may help to check the distance between existing wind turbines and town centers, for instance.
- Points of Interests (POI) positions[3]: it may have a direct/indirect impact on wind turbines installation.

Combining these heterogeneous data sources, we have built an aggregated dataset with the following structure:

- Coordinates of the center of the geographical zone (latitude and longitude).
- Average elevation of the geographical zone.
- Average and Maximum wind speed on a recent time period.
- Distance between the geographical zone center and the nearest POI.
- Count of POI in the considered geographical zone.
- Distance between the geographical zone center and the nearest city.
- Population of the nearest city.
- Class to predict: does the geographical zone accommodate wind turbine(s)?

---

[1] https://data.open-power-system-data.org/renewable_power_plants/.
[2] https://fr.wikipedia.org/wiki/Shuttle_Radar_Topography_Mission.
[3] http://openpoimap.org/.

Additionally, different scales of precision were considered for the width of geographical zones: 7500/2500/1500/500 m (Fig. 1). To give an overview of the amount of data, considering a width of 500 m gives a dataset describing 2932088 geographical zones.

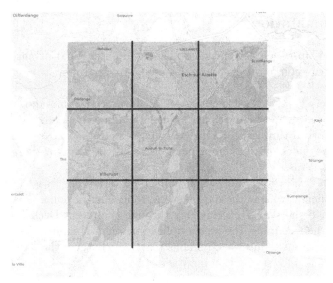

Fig. 1. Considering geographical zones near Audun-Le-Tiche (France): the large square has a width of 7500 m while the little squares have a width of 2500 m.

4 Approach

We considered the prediction of wind turbines location as a supervised classification problem with these characteristics:

- The input dataset is class-imbalanced [5] – there are much more zones without wind turbines (this kind of problem can be found in different domains like medical diagnosis or fraud detection).
- False positive should be *encouraged* in order to detect potentially interesting geographical zones to accommodate wind turbines.

Therefore, we have applied state-of-the-art machine learning techniques that are generally effective for class-imbalanced dataset [5]:

- Data Sampling coupled to well-known algorithms like Random Forest [1].
- Ensemble learning methods like Gradient Tree Boost [3].
- One-class Support Vector Machines [8] and One-class Neural Networks [2].

To check the efficiency of the predictive models obtained with these algorithms, we used the classical indicators: accuracy, precision, recall, F1. Additionally, we focused on the *False Discovery Rate* in order to control the proportion of potentially interesting geographical zones for wind turbines.

$$FalseDiscoveryRate = \frac{\text{False Positives Count}}{\text{False Positives Count} + \text{True Positives Count}} \quad (1)$$

5   Implementation

The proposed approach has been implemented into WindturbinesPlanner: a Backend for the computation and a Frontend for the interactive presentation of the results (Fig. 2).

More precisely, the Backend is a set of Javascript command-line tools to retrieve, preprocess and analyze the input data. Thus the predictive models are trained and served through a REST API. These scripts are based on LIMDU[4]: this library provides efficient implementations of the state-or-the-art machine learning algorithms.

The Frontend is a web application built upon the recent React framework[5]). In order to efficiently show the data (several thousands of points and polygons), we have applied the WebGL technology through the recent DeckGL framework [11]. Thus, when running the web application on a computer with a decent graphics card, the user interface remains reactive whatever the amount of data to display (thanks to the GPU computation).

In practice, a typical usage scenario of WindturbinesPlanner is the following: after selecting an geographical zone on the map, the end-user can investigate to check why an area is potentially favorable or unfavorable to accommodate wind turbines by showing (or hiding): the existing onshore wind turbines, the cities, the points of interests, the weather data and the potential future wind turbines for various scales precisions (from 7500 to 500 m) and different algorithms.

6   Experiments

Machine learning models have been trained and then integrated into WindturbinesPlanner for various configurations. To this end, the main dataset was splitted into a training dataset and a test dataset (*holdout* strategy).

According to the results (Table 1), we can observe that increasing the geographical precision of the prediction has the effect of greatly increasing the size of the resulting dataset. As a result, it affects the models training time (several minutes for a precision of 2500 m, much slower for 500 m).

Moreover, the experiments have shown that is easy to build accurate predictive models from the current datasets. To anticipate the installation of potential but not-yet-existing wind turbines, we think it's better to select highly accurate models that produce a *reasonable* rate of false negative by selecting a geographical zone width (for instance: 1500 m).

---

[4] https://github.com/erelsgl/limdu.
[5] https://reactjs.org.

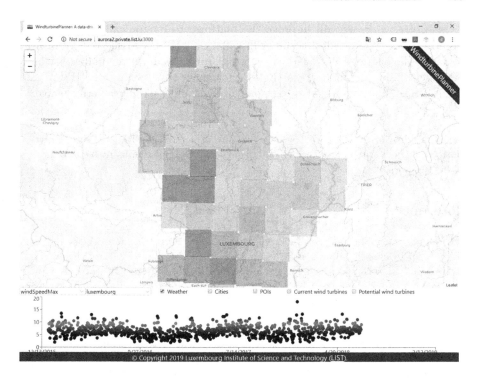

Fig. 2. WindturbinesPlanner provides an interactive map highlighting geographical zones that could contain wind turbines (green color) or not (red color). The predictions can be interpreted by inspecting the input data (wind speed, cities, points of interests). (Color figure online)

Table 1. Several machine learning models trained to predict if a geographical zone accommodates wind turbine(s). The indicators have been obtained with the test dataset.

Zone width	Dataset size	Algorithm	Accuracy	Precision	Recall	F1	False positive rate
7500	13036	XGBoost	0.94	0.68	0.93	0.79	0.31
2500	117278	SVN	0.99	0.98	0.99	0.99	0.01
1500	325786	SVN	0.99	0.84	0.99	0.91	0.15
500	2932088	SVN	0.99	0.27	0.70	0.40	0.72

7   Conclusion and Perspectives

In this paper, we presented the WindturbinesPlanner platform in order to anticipate the installation of next onshore wind turbines in a given geographical area. A meaningful dataset was built, machine learning models have been trained and an interactive user interface was developed.

In future work, we will improve the platform to dynamically highlight the evolution over time of wind turbines installation policies carried out by professionals in the energy sector. Moreover, we plan to speed-up the models learning phase by training the model on a High-Performance supercomputer (HPC). This should help refine predictions geographically without sacrificing performance.

Acknowledgments. This work was carried out as part of the FEDER Data Analytics Platform project (http://tiny.cc/feder-dap-project). Special thanks to Anne Hendrick for her support.

References

1. Bellinger, C., Sharma, S., Japkowicz, N., Zaïane, O.R.: Framework for extreme imbalance classification: SWIM—sampling with the majority class. Knowl. Inf. Syst. **62**(3), 841–866 (2019). https://doi.org/10.1007/s10115-019-01380-z
2. Chalapathy, R., Menon, A.K., Chawla, S.: Anomaly detection using one-class neural networks. arXiv preprint arXiv:1802.06360 (2018)
3. Friedman, J.H.: Greedy function approximation: a gradient boosting machine. Ann. Stat. **29**, 1189–1232 (2001)
4. Grady, S., Hussaini, M., Abdullah, M.M.: Placement of wind turbines using genetic algorithms. Renew. Energy **30**(2), 259–270 (2005)
5. Haixiang, G., Yijing, L., Shang, J., Mingyun, G., Yuanyue, H., Bing, G.: Learning from class-imbalanced data: review of methods and applications. Exp. Syst. Appl. **73**, 220–239 (2017)
6. Hevia-Koch, P., Ladenburg, J.: Where should wind energy be located? A review of preferences and visualisation approaches for wind turbine locations. Energy Res. Soc. Sci. **53**, 23–33 (2019)
7. Ladenburg, J., Hevia-Koch, P., Petrovic, S., Knapp, L.: The offshore-onshore conundrum: preferences for wind energy considering spatial data in Denmark. Renew. Sustain. Energy Rev. **121**, 109711 (2020)
8. Li, K.L., Huang, H.K., Tian, S.F., Xu, W.: Improving one-class SVM for anomaly detection. In: Proceedings of the 2003 International Conference on Machine Learning and Cybernetics (IEEE Cat. No. 03EX693), vol. 5, pp. 3077–3081. IEEE (2003)
9. Miller, A., Li, R.: A geospatial approach for prioritizing wind farm development in Northeast Nebraska. ISPRS Int. J. Geo-inf. **3**(3), 968–979 (2014)
10. Mosetti, G., Poloni, C., Diviacco, B.: Optimization of wind turbine positioning in large windfarms by means of a genetic algorithm. J. Wind Eng. Ind. Aerodyn. **51**(1), 105–116 (1994)
11. Wang, Y.: Deck.gl: Large-scale web-based visual analytics made easy. arXiv preprint arXiv:1910.08865 (2019)
12. Yang, K., Kwak, G., Cho, K., Huh, J.: Wind farm layout optimization for wake effect uniformity. Energy **183**, 983–995 (2019)

Cooperative Designing of Machine Layout Using Teaching Learning Based Optimisation and Its Modifications

Srisatja Vitayasak and Pupong Pongcharoen[✉]

Centre of Operations Research and Industrial Applications,
Department of Industrial Engineering, Faculty of Engineering,
Naresuan University, Phitsanulok 65000, Thailand
{srisatjav, pupongp}@nu.ac.th

Abstract. A variation of customer demand over time periods has resulted in production layout's efficiency especially in term of material handling cost. Machine re-location approach can help to maintain the flow distances but the costs related to the machine movement may be imposed. Cooperative redesigning of machine layouts between time periods was proposed to minimise both material handling and relocation costs. In this work, Teaching-Learning-Based Optimisation (TLBO) and its modifications were applied to solve non-identical machine layout redesign (MLRD) problem in multi-period multi-row configuration with demand uncertainty scenario. The computational experiments were carried out using eleven benchmarking datasets. The performance of the proposed methods was compared with the conventional Genetic Algorithm, Backtracking Search Algorithm. The effect of relocation cost on the layout design approach was also investigated.

Keywords: Layout redesign · Cooperative redesign · Teaching-Learning-Based optimisation · Demand uncertainty

1 Introduction

Uncertain material flow over multi-time periods in realistic production system has been resulted from product redesign, removal of the existing product, addition of the new product, renovation of production equipment, or the level of customer demand [1]. The production quantity and flow intensity between machines will unavoidably change along with the customer requirement, so the flow distances and costs may increase. Tompkins et al. [2] mentioned that "between 20 and 50% of the total operating expenses within manufacturing is attributed to material handling". Facility layout problem (FLP) deals with positioning of facilities (e.g. machines) on working area to minimise the movement between facilities, decrease material handling cost, and increase a system's efficiency and productivity. Nowadays, there are internal and external uncertainties [3] which can affect manufacturing performance. The contemporary layout is continuously improved in design approach.

FLPs are differences in term of characteristics e.g. layout design approaches, shop floor area, number and type of machines, number and type of products, and processing

© Springer Nature Switzerland AG 2020
Y. Luo (Ed.): CDVE 2020, LNCS 12341, pp. 137–147, 2020.
https://doi.org/10.1007/978-3-030-60816-3_16

sequences. Process layout designers usually work cooperatively with production engineers or decision makers for seeking the efficient layout under demand uncertainty. In design stage, designers and users work together on the necessary functions of the computer application. The flexible computer program can support various attributes of FLPs. In implement stage, users have a chance to identify the problem characteristics. Cooperative design in FLP can be adopted to address all users' requirements.

The FLP is non-deterministic polynomial hard problem. High computation time and memory are required to solve the problems, so metaheuristics approaches have been applied. Facility layout redesign (or re-layout) in uncertain environment have been investigated using metaheuristics for example, Ant Colony Optimisation [4], Genetic Algorithm [5], Particle Swarm Optimisation [6]. However, application of Teaching-Learning based Optimisation (TLBO) on machine layout redesign has not been found in Web of Science database.

Teaching-Learning based Optimisation (TLBO) was based on the philosophy of the teaching–learning process and contributed by Rao [7] in 2011 to solve mechanical design optimisation problems. TLBO has been examined on several fields, such as bearing design [8], flow shop scheduling [9], reactive power planning [10], line balancing [11]. Advantages of TLBO are a better performance with less computational effort and high consistency [7], free from algorithm parameters [12], ease of implementation [13], high-precision globally optimal solution [14], and fast convergence [15]. These motivates researchers to apply TLBO for problem solving.

The objective of this paper is to address the application of Teaching-Learning based Optimisation (TLBO) and modified TLBO for solving the non-identical machine layout redesign problem under demand variation in multi-period multi-row configuration. The remaining sections are organised as follows: Sect. 2 presents the machine layout redesign (MLRD) problem. Application of TLBO and its modifications on the MLRD problem is shown in Sect. 3 and Sect. 4, respectively. The experimental results and analysis are provided in Sect. 5 and followed by conclusions and future work.

2   Machine Layout Redesign Problem

Machine layout redesign (MLRD) involves with the reassignment of machines' locations corresponding to the demand uncertainty in each period to minimise total cost including material handling and relocating (or rearrangement) costs. A literature review based on FLP and ISI Web of Science database between period 2015 to 2018 showed that 35 of 141 papers studied demand variability in FLP. A number of papers on facility re-layout problem were 28. All of them presented the most efficient rearrangement of facilities in order to achieve objective(s). Representation of demand level can be function distribution [16–18] e.g. exponential, normal, and uniform.

Figure 1 shows three time-periods redesigning of non-identical machine layouts. Materials are transferred between machines in each row according to the processing sequences required for each products. Based on the demand level in period 2, sum of material handling cost on layout B and relocation cost for redesigning layout A to B are less than material handling cost on layout A, the layout A is therefore redesigned to be layout B. In period 3, layout C is same as layout B because total material handling cost by layout B corresponding to the demand level on period 3 is less than sum of material handling cost of a new layout and relocation cost for redesigning layout B. In contrast approach, the robust layout design aimed to minimise material handling cost in three periods, so there is only one layout for all periods.

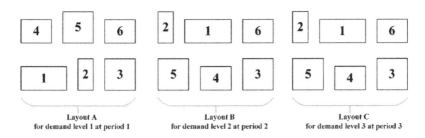

Fig. 1. Example multi-row layouts with 6 machines and 3 time periods

Machine movements between periods cause relocation costs associating with production stoppage and shifted machines [19]. Relocation cost incurred between periods can be calculated on total distance of machine movement [20] or the number of moved machines [21]. Trade-off between cost of excess material handling cost and re-layout cost under demand changes is carefully studied. The material handling cost (MHC) can be evaluated using Eq. (1). The relocation cost (RC) is defined by Eq. (2).

$$MHC \ for \ period \ k = C_{MH} \sum_{g=1}^{N} \sum_{i=1}^{M} \sum_{j=1}^{M} d_{ij} f_{ijgk} D_{gk} \tag{1}$$

$$RC \ for \ period \ k = C_R \sum_{i=1}^{M} DMM_{ik} \tag{2}$$

C_{MH} is the material handle cost per distance unit; P is the number of time periods; and k is a time period index ($k = 1, 2, 3, ..., P$); N is the number of product types; g is a product index ($g = 1, 2, 3, ..., N$); M is the number of machines; i and j are machine indices (i and $j = 1, 2, 3, ..., M$); d_{ij} is the distance from machines i to j ($i \neq j$); f_{ijgk} is the frequency of material flow of product g from machines i to j on period k; and D_{gk} is the customer demand of product g on period k. C_R is the relocation cost per distance unit of machine movement; and DMM is distance of machine movement for machine i in period k.

The following assumptions were made for the machine layout redesign (MLRD) problem: i) Non-identical rectangular-shaped machines were placed and arranged in multi-row configuration; ii) There was enough space on the shop floor area for machine placement; iii) Material flow distance between machines was determined using the rectilinear distance between the machines' centroids; iv) A gap between machines and rows was predefined and constant; and v) A machine was located in one orientation, where machine length was parallel to the x-axis, and machine width was parallel to the y-axis.

3 Teaching-Learning Based Optimisation on the MLRD Problem

Teaching-Learning based Optimisation (TLBO) [7] is categorised into a population-based metaheuristic. Search processes compose of Teacher phase and Leaner phase. In Teacher phase, the best solution in each generation (called Teacher) tries to share own knowledge with other solutions (Students or learners) to improve outputs. This mechanism relates to the quality of teacher and student, Teacher Factor (T_F), and random number. Each student c is modified by utilising the following equation.

$$X_{new,i} = X_{old,i} + r_i(X_{best} - T_F X_{old,i}) \tag{3}$$

$X_{new,i}$ was the new solution at i^{th} solution. $X_{old,i}$ was the existing solution at i^{th} solution. i was a solution index (i = 1, 2, 3, …, number of solutions or students). r_i was a random number in the range [0, 1] at i^{th} solution. T_F was a teaching factor. Rao et al. (2011) [7] suggested that the value of T_F can be either 1 or 2.

For Learner phase, each student (X_j) randomly interacts with each other (X_k). Learning process depends on the other learner's knowledge and can be formulated as Eq. (4) (if X_j is better than X_k) and Eq. (5) (if X_k is better than X_j) where j $\neq$ k.

$$X_{new,j} = X_{old,j} + r_j(X_j - X_k) \tag{4}$$

$$X_{new,j} = X_{old,j} + r_j(X_k - X_j) \tag{5}$$

j is a solution index (j = 1, 2, 3, …, number of solutions). k is a solution index (k = 1, 2, 3, …, number of solutions). $X_{old,j}$ is X_j and modified to be $X_{new,j}$. r_j is a random number in the range [0, 1] at j^{th} solution.

Problem data for MLRD are the number of machines (M), the dimensions of machines (width x length), the number of products (N), the machine sequences (M_S) and demand profile. Multi-row layout configuration relates to floor length (F_L), floor width (F_W), the gap between machines (G), and the number of periods (P). TLBO's common parameters include the population size (Pop) or number of solutions (Students), the number of generations (Gen). Before the computer aided program for MLRD was executed, the user can choose or fill layout design approaches (Robust or re-layout), floor width and length, gap between machines, material handling cost per unit, and TLBO types (TLBO or modified TLBOs). The TLBO flow chart for the MLRD problem is shown in Fig. 2 and described as follows: i) create the production quantity in each period associating with the demand profile; ii) initialise the candidate solutions according to Pop for period k. Each solution contains a number of arranged machines; iii) arrange machines row by row based on F_L F_W, and G; iv) calculate material handling cost (MHC) using Eq. (1) for all students; v) identify the best solution to be Teacher; vi) in Teacher phase, modify each student using Eq. (3); vii) evaluate the MHC of $X_{new,i}$ based on the product having maximum material flow cost; viii) accept $X_{new,i}$ if it was better than $X_{old,i}$ ix) adapt X_j using randomly selected X_k, and Eq. (4) or Eq. (5); x) decide whether $X_{new,j}$ is accepted or not by evaluating MHC; xi) select the best solution (The best layout); xii) for k $\geq$ 2, calculate relocation cost

(RC) using Eq. (2). If sum of MHC_k and RC_k is less than MHC_{k-1}, the redesigning is required; xiii) terminate the optimisation process according to *Gen* and *P*, respectively.

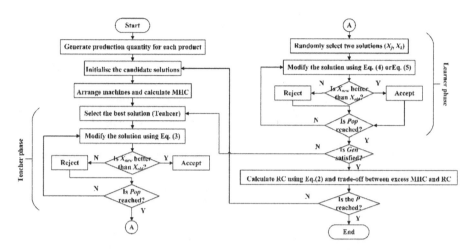

Fig. 2. Flow chart of TLBO for the MLRD problem

In Eq. (3), the T_F meant a number of swapping for X_{old}. If the T_F was equal to 1, one swapping is happened as illustrated in Fig. 3. Two positions of X_{old} were randomly chosen, and then swapped, so $T_F X_{old}$ was 8-9-1-2-3-5-6-7-4-10. Differences between X_{best} and $T_F X_{old}$ in Eq. (3), and X_j and X_k in Eq. (4) and Eq. (5) were based on a number of ordered pairs in swapping. For example, in Fig. 4, X_{best} and $T_F X_{old}$ are assumed as solution A and B, respectively. Position no. 1 in solution A was machine no. 5 whilst machine no. 5 in solution B was in position no. 6. So, machine no. 5 in position no. 6 of solution B was swapped with machine no. 8 in position no.1. The swapping processes were continued until solution B was similar to solution A. Hence, to get the solution A sequence from the solution B sequence, the number of swapping operations was six, including (8, 5) (9, 1) (9, 2) (6, 4) (7, 6) and (7, 10). If the random number was 0.81, the number of swaps was 6 * 0.81 = 4.86, which was rounded up to 5. The solution B was modified with five swaps: (8, 5) (9, 1) (9, 2) (6, 4) and (7, 6). The new solution B is 5-1-2-9-3-8-4-6-7-10.

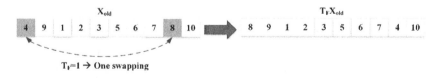

Fig. 3. Modifying the X_{old} with T_F ($T_F = 1$)

	Solution A										Solution B										
	5	1	2	9	3	8	4	6	10	7	**8**	9	1	2	3	**5**	6	7	4	10	1	I
	5	1	2	9	3	8	4	6	10	7	5	**9**	**1**	2	3	8	6	7	4	10	II
VI	5	1	2	9	3	8	4	6	**7**	**10**	5	1	**9**	**2**	3	8	6	7	4	10	III
V	5	1	2	9	3	8	4	**7**	**6**	10	5	1	2	9	3	8	**6**	7	**4**	10	IV

Fig. 4. Swap operation between solution A and solution B

4   Modifications of Teaching-Learning Based Optimisation

A kind of modified TLBO (MoTLBO) is proposed to enhance the solution quality. Teacher is the best student that is selected for improvement process in Teacher phase. Several factors affect students' comprehension such as instructional media, textbook, student skill, teacher skill, and number of students or teachers in each class. A number of teachers per class in Teacher phase is employed in TLBO modification. Two types of MoTLBO are: i) students were divided into several classes, each of which had a teacher (MoTLBO1); and ii) more than one teacher are arranged for a single class of students (MoTLBO2). The processes of MoTLBO1 and MoTLBO2 are shown in Fig. 5a and Fig. 5b, respectively.

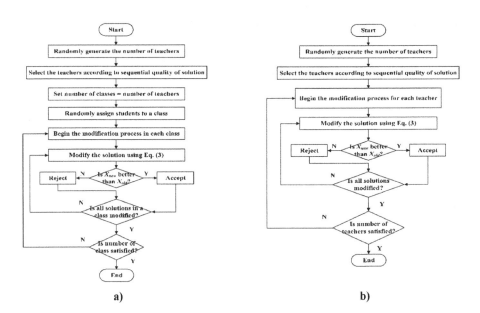

Fig. 5. Flow charts of Teacher phase for a) MoTLBO1 and b) MoTLBO2

In MoTLBO1, a number of classes are randomly generated according to number of teachers (*Num_T*), which was in range between 2 to maximum number of teachers

(*Max_T*). The *Max_T* was 10% of the population size. All students were randomly split to each class. A student was studied with one teacher. In contrast, there is only one class for MoTLBO2 that studied with a group of teachers according to *Num_T*. Each student had more learning opportunity through several teachers. The teachers in MoTLBO1 and MoTLBO2 were selected according to sequential quality of solutions.

5   The Experimental Results and Analysis

The proposed TLBO and MoTLBOs have been applied for eleven datasets [22] on MLRD problems. Each of them had different number of non-identical machines, product types, machine sequences, and demand profiles. Demand profiles were in form of empirical data or probability distributions (exponential, normal distribution, or uniform). The computational experiment was repeated thirty times under five time periods. The 10 M5N dataset means that ten machines are available for five types of product. The optimised TLBO parameters were investigated in the previous work [22] as shown in Table 1. Two experiments were conducted on a personal computer with an Intel Core i7 3.4 GHz CPU and 16 GB DDR3 RAM. The experimental results were analysed and described in the following subsections.

Table 1. Appropriate TLBO parameters for each dataset

Pop * Gen	Datasets
25 * 100	40M20N, 50M25N, 50M40N
50 * 50	10M10N, 20M10N, 20M20N, 20M40N, 30M30N, 40MM40N
100 * 25	10M5N, 30M15N

5.1   Performance Comparison on MLRD Problems

Changing the layout between periods involved relocation cost (RC). This cost was based on the distance of machine movement (DMM), which was set at 100 currency unit per metre. A total of computational runs was 11 datasets * 30 replications * 3 types of TLBOs (TLBO, MoTTLBO1, MoTLBO2) = 990. The results were analysed in term of mean and standard deviations (SD) of the sum of MHC and RC (unit: currency unit) and executing time (Time) (unit: second). Total costs for the re-layout are shown in Table 2, where the bold number means the lowest total cost in each dataset.

The average total cost obtained from MoTLBO2 was lower than both TLBO and MoTLBO1 except 10M10N and 20M40N datasets. The big-class learning with multiple teachers was more potential than small-class learning with a teacher. Each student has many times for knowledge enhancement respecting number of teachers. However, the mean computational times for MoTLBO2 was up to 60% higher than TLBO and MoTLBO1 in 50M40N dataset because of the increased number of learning iterations in Teacher phase. MoTLBO1 can generate solutions better than TLBO in seven datasets but there were no significantly statistical differences in mean of total cost with a 95% confidence interval or the P-value > 0.05 using the Student's t-test except

Table 2. Sum of material handling and relocation costs (unit: currency unit)

Dataset	Value	GA	BSA	MoBSA	TLBO	MoTLBO1	MoTLBO2
10M5N	Mean	318,834.4	324,228.7	319,128.7	321,186.7	319,199.6	**316,182.8**
	SD	12,896.8	11,793.3	10,573.8	12,571.9	9,540.4	9,542.5
	Time	66.0	26.0	29.0	68.0	67.0	171.0
10M10N	Mean	786,080.0	795,354.0	795,672.0	788,761.8	**784,530.0**	792,564.6
	SD	18,989.0	21,322.0	13,615.0	9,814.2	11,960.6	13,301.3
	Time	111.0	50.0	47.0	136.0	138.0	360.0
20M10N	Mean	1,655,451.5	1,706,707.9	1,672,990.6	1,613,516.3	1,613,064.6	**1,598,678.3**
	SD	27,792.8	21,633.4	25,570.7	29,971.0	22,500.0	20,764.9
	Time	236.0	88.0	105.0	240.0	247.0	485.0
20M20N	Mean	5,233,863.4	5,418,974.7	5,313,282.1	5,247,236.9	5,256,511.8	**5,218,014.4**
	SD	51,923.1	59,049.5	45,789.1	61,405.3	48,232.6	48,160.2
	Time	410.0	162.0	165.0	442.0	525.0	863.0
20M40N	Mean	**10,276,216.0**	10,602,08.1	10,395,917.1	10,348,080.9	10,385,053.9	10,357,122.6
	SD	74,198.0	82,150.9	64,450.4	102,961.5	100,121.9	106,008.8
	Time	845.1	209.0	214.0	711.5	839.7	1,262.3
30M15N	Mean	3,922,998.8	4,119,721.9	3,982,044.1	3,898,051.7	3,902,422.9	**3,818,302.9**
	SD	59,537.3	52,351.7	55,367.2	55,989.3	53,494.1	60,089.2
	Time	611.6	153.0	157.0	466.0	455.0	1,192.0
30M30N	Mean	8,361,651.0	8,712,238.0	8,396,821.0	8,307,893.6	8,275,552.6	**8,188,394.8**
	SD	89,134.0	133,221.0	88,876.0	82,911.8	111,406.3	83,310.7
	Time	637.2	272.0	273.0	664.2	738.7	1,285.9
40M20N	Mean	7,726,749.7	8,253,327.5	7,645,462.0	7,595,081.2	7,501,710.9	**7,388,217.4**
	SD	139,506.6	133,813.3	97,004.5	162,629.9	141,789.4	139,791.5
	Time	900.5	218.7	229.5	617.0	600.8	897.8
40M40N	Mean	14,381,572.3	15,353,287.1	14,199,333.9	14,325,337.5	14,182,384.4	**13,857,876.7**
	SD	257,817.2	246,171.8	227,414.4	299,964.8	206,264.4	243,270.3
	Time	1,474.2	395.6	3,998.0	1,132.7	974.7	1,691.6
50M25N	Mean	12,443,878.0	13,424,172.3	12,408,187.7	12,107,292.6	12,126,924.2	**11,881,854.4**
	SD	249,032.9	226,738.2	141,424.8	208,856.5	212,273.5	226,418.4
	Time	1,043.6	318.0	298.4	842.4	729.0	1,186.7
50M40N	Mean	18,729,876.0	19,936,087.0	18,618,543.0	18,406,258.3	18,367,713.4	**17,870,302.6**
	SD	238,603.0	294,974.0	242,379.0	232,246.0	222,736.7	293,692.9
	Time	1,005.8	365.9	417.6	1,016.6	1,139.0	1,631.5

40M40N dataset. Learning in small class did not benefit to students since the quality of a teacher in each class was different. The average computational times required by TLBO and MoTLBO1 were slightly different.

The results obtained from TLBO and two types of MoTLBO were compare with Genetic Algorithm (GA) [23], Backtracking Search Algorithm (BSA) [24], and modified BSA (MoBSA) [24]. TLBO can produce lower total cost than GA, BSA, and MoBSA in six of eleven datasets. The reason is that TLBO mechanism has twice evaluations of fitness function for all solutions due to the two phases (Teacher and

Learner), while a number of improved solutions in GA depend on crossover and mutation probabilities, and BSA uses the solutions obtained from the previous generation without consideration of solution quality. Besides, MoTLBO2 was more efficient than the others in almost datasets except 10M10N and 20M40N dataset. Modification based on a group of teachers in one class can promote TLBO performance. The raised executing time for MoTLBO2 may be inconsiderable because of technology development in computational resources. However, TLBO, MoTLBO1, and MoTLBO2 in 20M40N dataset gave higher total costs than GA. It may be resulted from the additional exploration in search process that was noticed from higher standard deviation than GA.

5.2 Different Layout Design Approaches in Demand Uncertainty

The layout under demand variation can be either robust or re-layout. Total costs obtained from each design approach could affect the user's implements. Comparison of total costs obtained from TLBO with two design approaches and varied relocation costs (RC) is shown in Table 3, where the minimum cost in each dataset are in bold. The RC based on DMM for 50-machine datasets was set at 0, 100, 200, and 400 currency unit. The MHC for robust layout referred to the previous work [22].

Table 3. Values of costs (currency unit) in each dataset

Dataset	Robust layout	Re-layout based on RC			
		0	100	200	400
10M5N	308,192.5	**306,115.4**	321,186.7	327,052.3	331,298.9
10M10N	771,372.8	**768,639.4**	788,761.8	796,643.9	804,442.0
20M10N	1,615,932.6	**1,593,454.8**	1,613,516.3	1,618,259.0	1,619,024.1
20M20N	5,293,133.1	**5,219,736.0**	5,247,236.9	5,259.189.2	5,268,853.3
20M40N	10,416,073.3	**10,312,072.0**	10,348,080.9	10,363,899.4	10,385,076.9
30M15N	3,883,961.1	**3,833,017.6**	3,898,051.7	3,911,644.5	3,914,268.5
30M30N	**8,219,945.7**	8,264,593.6	8,307,893.6	8,325,575.1	8,335,684.8
40M20N	**7,489,970.7**	7,534,378.9	7,595,081.2	7,603,403.9	7,604,551.3
40M40N	**13,876,258.6**	14,244,238.3	14,325,337.5	14,344,105.3	14,387,854.6
50M25N	12,175,637.4	**12,060,303.6**	12,107,292.6	12,112,715.3	12,114,318.4
50M40N	**18,280,861.2**	18,304,587.6	18,406,258.3	18,425,188.1	18,432,298.9

The results showed the total costs associated with the layout design according to the machine relocation. If there were no expenses for repositioning machines (RC = 0), the existing layout can be changed to achieve the minimum MHC. In contrast, Once the RC was increase, the total costs were higher. This situation leads to the robust design approach for 10M5N, 10M10N, 20M10N, and 30M15N datasets. For 20M20N, 20M40N, and 50M25N, redesigning the layout is the best alternative, although the RC increased to 400 currency unit per metre that there were almost no machine movements between periods. The layout design for 30M30N, 40M20N, 40M40N, and 50M40N datasets was always robust. This was caused by differences in number of machines and product types, machine sequences, and demand fluctuation. Investigation of the appropriate layout design approach did not only considered cost of machine movement, but also the problem characteristics were examined.

6 Conclusions

This paper presents the application of Teaching-Learning-Based Optimisation (TLBO) and its modifications for cooperative redesigning of multi-period machine layout under demand uncertainty. The design task was to minimise total costs including material handling and machine relocation costs. The statistical analysis on the computational results suggested that TLBO performed better than the conventional Genetic Algorithm, Backtracking Search Algorithm, and modified Backtracking Search Algorithm in six of eleven datasets. However, the TLBO required longer computational time since all solutions were improved in both Teacher phase and Learner phase. The efficient modified TLBO was based on the big-class with teachers in Teacher phase. This concept led to higher performance in nine of eleven datasets with longer computational time.

The effects of relocation cost on design procedure were reported. Relocation costs were varied with 0, 100, and 200 currency unit per distance of machine moved. Total costs were increase due to the relocation cost. This issue therefore suggested the reconsideration of the robust layout design approach. However, the layout cannot be redesigned in some datasets because of different attributes related to product types, demand profiles, and processing sequences. Future research may focus on other mechanisms for improvement of metaheuristics performance or investigate multi-objective machine layout design problem.

Acknowledgement. This work was part of the research project supported by the Thailand Research Fund under the grant number MRG6280168.

References

1. McKendall, A.R., Shang, J., Kuppusamy, S.: Simulated annealing heuristics for the dynamic facility layout problem. Comput. Oper. Res. **33**, 2431–2444 (2006)
2. Tompkins, J.A., White, J.A., Bozer, Y.A., Tanchoco, J.M.A.: Facilities Planning, 4th edn. John Wiley & Sons, Inc, Hoboken (2010)
3. Kulturel-Konak, S.: Approaches to uncertainties in facility layout problems: Perspectives at the beginning of the 21(st) Century. J. Intell. Manuf. **18**, 273–284 (2007)
4. Chen, G.Y.H., Lo, J.-C.: Dynamic facility layout with multi-objectives. Asia Pac. J. Oper. Res. **31**, 1450027 (2014)
5. Ghosh, T., Doloi, B., Dan, P.K.: An Immune Genetic algorithm for inter-cell layout problem in cellular manufacturing system. Prod. Eng. Res. Devel. **10**(2), 157–174 (2015). https://doi.org/10.1007/s11740-015-0645-4

6. Derakhshan Asl, A., Wong, K.Y.: Solving unequal-area static and dynamic facility layout problems using modified particle swarm optimization. J. Intell. Manuf. **28**(6), 1317–1336 (2015). https://doi.org/10.1007/s10845-015-1053-5

7. Rao, R.V., Savsani, V.J., Vakharia, D.P.: Teaching-learning-based optimization: a novel method for constrained mechanical design optimization problems. Comput.-Aid. Des. **43**, 303–315 (2011)

8. Panda, S., Panda, S.N., Nanda, P., Mishra, D.: Comparative study on optimum design of rolling element bearing. Tribol. Int. **92**, 595–604 (2015)

9. Shao, W.S., Pi, D.C., Shao, Z.S.: A hybrid discrete optimization algorithm based on teaching-probabilistic learning mechanism for no-wait flow shop scheduling. Knowl.-Based Syst. **107**, 219–234 (2016)

10. Bhattacharyya, B., Babu, R.: Teaching learning based optimization algorithm for reactive power planning. Int. J. Electr. Power Energ. Syst. **81**, 248–253 (2016)

11. Tang, Li., Wang, Y., Ding, X., Yin, H., Xiong, R., Huang, S.: Topological local-metric framework for mobile robots navigation: a long term perspective. Auton. Rob. **43**(1), 197–211 (2018). https://doi.org/10.1007/s10514-018-9724-7

12. Rao, R.V., Kalyankar, V.D.: Multi-objective multi-parameter optimization of the industrial LBW process using a new optimization algorithm. Proc. Inst. Mech. Eng. Part B-J. Eng. Manuf. **226**, 1018–1025 (2012)

13. Verma, P., Om, H.: A novel approach for text summarization using optimal combination of sentence scoring methods. Sādhanā **44**(5), 1–15 (2019). https://doi.org/10.1007/s12046-019-1082-4

14. Tuo, S.H., He, H.: Solving complex cardinality constrained mean variance portfolio optimization problems using hybrid HS and TLBO algorithm. Econ. Comput. Econ. Cybern. Stud. **52**, 231–248 (2018)

15. Singh, S., Ashok, A., Kumar, M., Rawat, T.K.: Adaptive infinite impulse response system identification using teacher learner based optimization algorithm. Appl. Intell. **49**(5), 1785–1802 (2018). https://doi.org/10.1007/s10489-018-1354-4

16. Pourvaziri, H., Naderi, B.: A hybrid multi-population genetic algorithm for the dynamic facility layout problem. Appl. Soft Comput. **24**, 457–469 (2014)

17. Samarghandi, H., Taabayan, P., Behroozi, M.: Metaheuristics for fuzzy dynamic facility layout problem with unequal area constraints and closeness ratings. Int. J. Adv. Manuf. Tech. **67**, 2701–2715 (2013)

18. Moslemipour, G., Lee, T.S., Loong, Y.T.: Performance Analysis of Intelligent Robust Facility Layout Design. Chin. J. Mech. Eng. **30**(2), 407–418 (2017). https://doi.org/10.1007/s10033-017-0073-9

19. Hosseini, S., Al Khaled, A., Vadlamani, S.: Hybrid imperialist competitive algorithm, variable neighborhood search, and simulated annealing for dynamic facility layout problem. Neural Comput. Appl. **25**, 1871–1885 (2014)

20. Montreuil, B., Laforge, A.: Dynamic layout design given a scenario tree of probable futures. Eur. J. Oper. Res. **63**, 271–286 (1992)

21. Corry, P., Kozan, E.: Ant colony optimisation for machine layout problems. Comput. Optim. Appl. **28**, 287–310 (2004)

22. Vitayasak, S., Pongcharoen, P.: Performance improvement of Teaching-Learning-Based Optimisation for robust machine layout design. Expert Syst. Appl. **98**, 129–152 (2018)

23. Vitayasak, S., Pongcharoen, P., Hicks, C.: Robust machine layout design under dynamic environment: Dynamic customer demand and machine maintenance. Expert Syst. Appl. X **3**, 100015 (2019)

24. Vitayasak, S., Pongcharoen, P., Hicks, C.: A tool for solving stochastic dynamic facility layout problems with stochastic demand using either a Genetic Algorithm or modified Backtracking Search Algorithm. Int. J. Prod. Econ. **190**, 146–157 (2017)

Making Sociological Theories Come Alive

Cooperative Work on Collective Memories Regarding Frontier Zones

Ursula Kirschner[(✉)]

Leuphana University Lüneburg, Universitätsallee 1, 21335 Lüneburg, Germany
kirschner@uni.leuphana.de

Abstract. The aim of this paper is to demonstrate how the medium film is able not only to challenge, but also to push toward further development of some of the basic assumptions in sociological spatial theories as used within cultural area research. In so doing, we wish to increase knowledge on a central epistemological question for the field of Spatial Turn, namely how field research, by using film and playing it back to the field, can be a vehicle for new methodology in making theories collectively come alive.

The paper reflects on thoughts about Frontier Zones developed from the interpretations of space and its history as presented by students of cultural studies. The students' interpretations are according to the theory of memory by Aleida Assman, to the understanding of the structure of power by Michel Foucault, and to the symbolic power and the habitus of the place by Pierre Bourdieu. In this sense, the concept of Frontier Zones contributes in two directions: in the practical experiments that seek to highlight and read the Frontier Zones that are expressed in the urban dynamics as well as to highlight the Frontier Zones between areas of knowledge seeking to understand and redefine them. The perception of the Frontier Zones allows us to recognize the levels of belonging, diversity and composition.

Keywords: Collective memory · Perception of urban space · Medium film for making theories come alive

1 Introduction

This research project was developed in cooperation with a Brazilian PhD candidate, who participated in two International Summer Schools on Frontier Zones in São Paulo in 2015 and 2017, coordinated by the Leuphana and the University of São Paulo. During these summer sessions 30 researchers, including architects, city planners, film makers, journalists, audio experts, social scientists and sociologists, met in São Paulo to collaborate and discuss how to explore the city. The method was strongly cooperative, working with students and teachers as well as with the people we filmed on the streets

---

All films are available under http://frontierzones.myqnapcloud.com/files?project=4. Please contact the author for receiving the login data.

© Springer Nature Switzerland AG 2020
Y. Luo (Ed.): CDVE 2020, LNCS 12341, pp. 148–157, 2020.
https://doi.org/10.1007/978-3-030-60816-3_17

of São Paulo. There is no neutral observer, only authors with different cultural and personal backgrounds.

In a single seminar at Leuphana University in Germany, we studied the produced Brazilian films with the intention of providing a methodology for analyzing urban space based on well-known theories.

The main objective of this project was to observe, reflect and discuss Frontier Zones through the production of audiovisual material. We chose the campus of Leuphana University for the case study, which served as military barracks beginning in the 1930s and was home to different armies before it was converted to a university in the 1990s. The zeitgeist of World War II is inscribed in these buildings. The starting point of our research was, that our behavior in all areas depends on and is closely linked to the acceptable social system of standards and values and to the derived behavioral expectations of the social environment [1].

This study examines the constructed space in regard to the interaction between erected structures and action. There is no distinction between the consideration of the territorial, material space on the one hand and the social interaction space of the participants on the other; instead there is correlated interaction between these two components of space. This is based on the assumption that the space is experienced subjectively and serves as a source of information perceived differently as a factor of the cultural socialization of a person. In this sense, we tried to capture the aura of our campus with different media. Benjamin a philosopher described an aura as "[a] strange web of space and time: the unique manifestation of a distance, however near it may be. To follow, while reclining on a summer's noon, the outline of a mountain range on the horizon or a branch, which casts its shadow on the observer until the moment or hour partakes of their presence - this is to breathe in the aura of those mountains, of this branch" [2].

Our intention was to sensitize the students to the social ambience, influenced by digital and analog media, and hence to identify with the place as well as with collective memory. These reflections were developed and debated throughout the process and after its presentation. Therefore, the students used the medium film to capture images and sound data and compiled them to create a specific statement according to a chosen theory. Nothing is close, nothing is frozen, and everything is fluid. Reflecting individually and collectively the film products, we experimented with the films in various spaces. For a cybernetic approach to analyzing the results in different environments, we produced making-ofs and making-ofs of making-ofs, with the intention of making the so-called "unmarked space" more visible. These layers are also necessary for the deeper understanding of the role that Frontier Zones play in this learning area.

The production of images is related to the production of collective memory and new imaginings in the digital age. In this way, it can be understood as a means of expression, reading, and representation of urban dynamics. Furthermore, the cooperative work on different theories, the attempt to visualize them with the medium film and turning theory into an experience is a new approach in teaching "Space and Sociology and Art" at the same time.

2 Research Approach

The theoretic research approach is based on Maran's analysis of "Architecture as societal space – the significance of social science theories for archeology." Maran explains that architecture on the one hand serves as the framework for social circumstances and on the other hand as a reflection thereof [3]. Applying socio-logical theories, he examines this "dual property" of architecture and reveals new perspectives for analyzing architecture and urban space applying a culture-scientific approach. Architecture is defined as the system of spatial relationships in which human interaction occurs. It is constructed of walls, free spaces, roofing, doors and atmospheric components such as protection from weather conditions, light, color, etc. Böhme defines atmosphere as "[…] the common reality of the perceiver and the perceived" [4]. Löw talks about the "duality of space" [5] and describes space not only as a backdrop but also as a space that is continuously evolving as a result of interaction. Thus the interpretation of the perception of a space is a factor of the socialization and culture of the interpreter. Bourdieu claims that each society creates the architectural spaces that it considers essential to its own social action – the habitus determines the habitat [6]. This would mean that space can be the image or the counter-image of a society. Foucault talks about heterotopias, which are strictly demarcated places like prisons, cemeteries, homes, brothels, theaters, military barracks, etc. Other social norms are manifest-ed here. Such heterotopias can occur temporarily in certain spaces, e.g. when a factory is repurposed to become a disco. Materials such as those used in construction are permanent. They store the traces of bygone times, subtly maintaining the old social norms, which can in turn be the "crystallization point for legitimizing new social drafts" [7].

When the former barracks were converted to a campus, economic and functional interests took precedence over maintaining a culture of remembrance. A decision was made to refrain from tearing down the old buildings, thus allowing traces of the past to serve as a reminder of a former culture. So when it comes to the university cam-pus, this could be considered "unintentional communication of the history" [8]. It occurs simply because people move around the "historically evolving architectural complexes" [9] and include structures from bygone eras is their own actions without really thinking about it [10].

The University campus provides reference points for these theories, which serve as the starting points for exploration of these theories.

3 The Methodology

Discovering "Frontier Zones" in urban areas and examining them from a variety of perspectives, we used the language of documentary film making as an exploratory way to analyze urban areas. This method is based on the thesis posed by the media scientists Horwitz, Joerges and Potthast. They propose that, through the use of images, film allows one to get "closer" to social realities than would be possible with text-based empirical social research [11]. We used this medium in the above-mentioned Summer School sessions as well [12]. This time we have added new milestones. Socio-theoretical theories were the starting point, which inspired the empiric work at the beginning and which were used for the written reflection in the end. Several experimental screenings on different surfaces in unusual spaces on the campus, for example on the façade of the new central building, designed by Libeskind, in a restroom, in catacombs, etc. were done. So we interacted with the campus like performance artists do. Making-ofs served as a starting point for discussions about what we have seen and how we feel. The outcome of our discussions flowed directly into the refinement of the film products and inspired us to create new ideas for the next screening.

The research student group, consisting of ten students from the Bachelor program, including two incoming students from Columbia and from Vietnam, belongs to the faculty of Cultural Studies. Most of them were familiar with the history of the campus, so they already had the knowledge necessary for the transfer process. We worked cooperatively in the sense that everyone captured images and sounds on the campus individually or in small groups but for the whole seminar group. At the same time making-of material was collected and all data was saved in a single archive that everyone could access and to which the students continuously added material. In the postproduction phase, small groups started open-mindedly selecting material from the archive according to a chosen topic and editing a first rough cut. Followed by discussions about how theory could be mediated with images and sounds, the theory began to come alive. Three screening sessions on campus in different environments were essential to the didactical impact as well as to facilitate better understanding of the theory. The first session was more about investigating the technical staff; the second one was experimental, where we tested the effects of the films (Fig. 1).

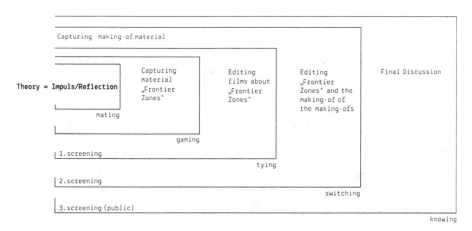

Fig. 1. Scheme of the methodology, based on Baecker (Compare Baecker, D.: Bauen, Ordnen, Abreißen im Formmodel des Sozialen. Die ›Architektur der Gesellschaft‹ aus system- und formtheoretischer Sicht. In: Fischer, J., Delitz, H. (eds.) Die Architektur der Gesellschaft (2009) Bielefeld, p.199)

The aim was to find a place that emphasizes or expresses in the best way the meaning of the content of the film. The third screening was public, so the students received feedback from different students and teachers about the cooperative work on bringing theory to life in their everyday environment (Fig. 1). The concept of this event showed that, when talking about Frontier Zones, we talk at the same time about "frontier crossings."

During the research study students had to change their perspectives several times: from a critical observer to a producer of films, to a scenographer and in the end to a scientist reflecting the process of making theory coming alive.

4   Narratives

The idea of situationism was applied to provide different input at a new level to visualization and to making theory come alive.[1] The situationists sought new methods to facilitate fundamental change of the current state of politics and society by thinking ahead. The value of conventional behaviors has to be diminished to be able to handle them creatively and experimentally and to be able to use them subversively [13]. The situationists aimed to produce situations and subsequently moods and new behaviors, and to "set against the reflection of the capitalistic lifestyle other, more desirable ways of life at every opportunity; [and] to use every hyper-political means to destroy the bourgeois concept of happiness" [14]. Thinking was to be revolutionized by constructing situations.

Spontaneously screening clips that critically examined the respective location on campus was a unique experience for all of the participants. We were all moving in a particular way between "permitted" and "prohibited" behavior in a Frontier Zone. Classmates passing by and viewing the clips were offered a new view of the everyday

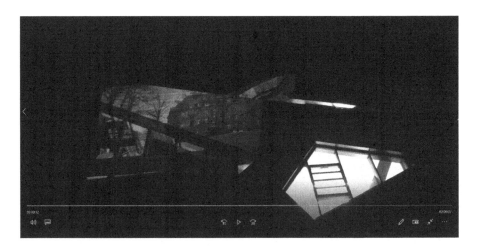

Fig. 2. Screenshot from the Making-of December 2018 (Source: Project Group)

---

[1] The Situationist International was an international organization of social revolutionaries made up of avant-garde artists and prominent in Europe from its formation in 1957 to its dissolution in 1972.

spaces within their social environment through these interactions. And it was quickly apparent which films clearly communicated their messages and which did not.

The screenings provided new interpretations of the space by revealing new situations. Figure 2 shows a projection of a brick barrack onto the modern zinc façade of the central building on campus. The film is cut up by the different levels of the diagonal façade as well as by the windows. The viewer's eyes wander from one surface to another and perception of the film becomes selective. If we would like to speak of the "habitus" of this building, it would be as a very elegant, clean but slanted structure, with edges and corners but also with many clear, restrictive rules. This is nearly the opposite comparing with the everyday life inside the barracks.

One of the films, screened as rear projection on the curtain of the dining room, was "Between the Spaces." The film was viewed from the main road outside as well as from inside and seized upon the idea of a Frontier Zone as a semipermeable membrane. Figure 3 shows the façade with screening from outside and shows a similar situation from the inside.

Fig. 3. Left: Glass-façade from Outside with Screening January 2019; Right: from Inside December 2018 (Source: Spindler, S.: Marching Present; Mährlein, J. and Project Group)

Another film deals with exclusion. It focuses on how the cleaning staff is seemingly systematically ignored in daily life at the university. "Just as physical space is defined by the reciprocal outwardness of the parts, social space is de-fined by the mutual exclusion (or differentiation) of the positions that form it, meaning the juxtaposition of social positions" [14]. In Bourdieu's version, spaces serve as means to achieving social differentiation. The voice narrating the visual impressions in the documentary is not just any voice, it is that of a cleaner who works at Leuphana University Lüneburg. Because they work at night, the cleaning staff is invisible during the day at German universities. The cleaner talks about her work and about the issues and objects she encounters every day, but she remains faceless until the end.

The documentary discussed here was presented for the first time in the women's restroom at the cafeteria, after a trial in the handicapped restroom in the central building.

Another screening took place in the catacombs (cellar). These rooms are not locked, but they are rarely visited. The rooms look the same as when they were built in the 1930s. Walls, doors, light fixtures and signs act as mementos, and the particular acoustics dominate the atmosphere. Films with "military" marching steps as the sound track were particularly stirring here (Fig. 4).

Fig. 4. Screenshots of the Making-of December 2018 (Source: Alster, F., Biermann-Firek, L. and Project Group)

5 Reflection on the Making-of Process

In cybernetics of the second order, an observation of the second order is the observation of an observation. In an observation of the second order, the "blind spot" becomes more visible, revealing what cannot be perceived in the selected position. "No observer can see his own blindness, but he can see the blindness of others, thus encountering a phenomenon that affects himself as well. The observation of the second order allows him to see his own blindness and, to a certain degree, to see that he cannot see. But only up to a certain point: The new observation perspective inevitably contributes its own specific blind spot that can only be seen from an additional and other perspective, and so on" [15].

By observing through a camera, by capturing situations, by editing and with effects such as crossfading, an attempt is made to achieve an overall picture or statement. However, perfection can never be achieved. But the "blind spot," "unmarked space" or lack of knowledge is reduced by the making-ofs and the making-ofs of the making-ofs, happening at the third level of observation.

Foucault describes military barracks as heterotopies. The extent to which daily life at a contemporary university can be characterized this way, or whether a new heterotopy emerges nowadays, served as a basis for discussion during one of the screenings (Fig. 5).

The video deals with Bourdieu's thesis of "habitus and habitat" as well as Assmann's approach "Buildings as warehouses of remembrances." The clock, a re-curring image in the film, sometimes run forwards and sometimes backwards, reflecting the present from the perspective of the past and the utopian future. Jefferson's declaration "I like the dreams of the future better than the history of the past" is prominently displayed in the foyer, in large letters over the stairs, directly above the screen – and the author has added a question mark to it. During the 8-min screening, interested students stopped their study and watched the film screening. But at the same time several employees firmly admonished us (see to Fig. 5) and asked us to leave. The collective experience was once again addressed when the group made the decision to proceed beyond the above film productions and to collaborate in creating making-ofs on "atmosphere," "irritants" and "perspectives". The atmosphere was determined by the external situations (space and people), the irritants were the result of inner feelings, and

Fig. 5. Making-of video of the 2. Screening in the Lobby of the Library November 2018 (Source: Project Group)

the perspectives were considered to be the spatial aspects - meaning from the outside - as well as the intellectual based on the various perspectives.

6   Conclusion

Film has always been an ideal way to obtain an overview of the transformational forces of urban development. If one thinks of space as motion in time, "[i]n space we read the time", this correlation becomes tangible. After all, film is also founded on motion in time [16].

Playing with the audio and visual elements moreover manages to show the invisible in its invisibility in a clarity of which no other medium is capable. So the medium documentary or experimental film reveals the invisible and ultimately serves as the starting point for the examination of current theoretical lines of thought [17].

While situationists wanted to produce situations and thus moods and new behaviors, we were searching for a way to bring to life sociological space theories in spaces, with the goal of minimizing the "blind spot." Our activities on campus were met with a wide range of reactions. They were not the primary focus of our research project, but we were also able to use them as additional evidence. This creative research process, in which the second step was inspired by the first, was strange for the students and some criticized it.

"One of the students concluded her paper by writing, "[t]he university was not constructed with the primary intention of creating a place of remembrance in former military barracks. But the campus still has the potential to create a culture of remembrance that feeds into people's thought patterns" [18]. Cooperative learning contributed to the collective culture of remembrance based on the architecture as well as new forms of critical analysis of the students' day-to-day life on the university campus. Therefor media plays an important role in the construction of collective urban memory, and while working with and on the campus we were touched by the history like a twig, which throws its shadow on the observer.

The concluding discussion was moderated by a student who asked the audience to close their eyes for a little while and ask themselves "Is there a place without a Frontier Zone?" There are Frontier Zones everywhere. The challenge is to describe them.

Acknowledgments. I would like to thank Maria Julia Stella Martins, the co-teacher in one part of the seminar. As a scientist and as a performance artist, she inspired the students to think and to experiment in new ways. Furthermore, I am very grateful for the enthusiastic participation of the students in the seminar "Urban Frontier Zones in Urban Spaces" 2018/19, Leuphana University Lüneburg. I acknowledge Luciana Santos da Roche for giving a lecture on urban sound.

References

1. Maran, J.: Architektur als gesellschaftlicher Raum. Zur Bedeutung sozialwissen-schaftlicher Theorien für die Archäologie. (2004). https://www.uni-heidelberg.de/md/zaw/akh/akh_texte/02maran121104.pdf. Accessed 21 April 2020
2. Benjamin, W.: A Short History of Photography. (1931/1972), p. 16. https://monoskop.org/images/7/79/Benjamin_Walter_1931_1972_A_Short_History_of_Photography.pdf. Accessed 06 Oct 2020
3. Schäfer, B.. In: Maran, J.: Architektur als gesellschaftlicher Raum. Zur Bedeutung sozialwissenschaftlicher Theorien für die Archäologie (2004). https://www.uni-heidelberg.de/md/zaw/akh/akh_texte/02maran121104.pdf, p. 2. Accessed 21 April 2020
4. Böhme, G.: Atmosphäre. Essays zur neuen Ästhetik. p. 34, Frankfurt am Main. (1995)
5. Löw, M. In: Maran, J.: Architektur als gesellschaftlicher Raum. Zur Be-deutung sozialwissenschaftlicher Theorien für die Archäologie (2004). https://www.uni-heidelberg.de/md/zaw/akh/akh_texte/02maran121104.pdf, p. 4. Accessed 21 April 2020
6. Bourdieu, P.: In: Maran, J.: Architektur als gesellschaftlicher Raum. Zur Bedeutung sozialwissenschaftlicher Theorien für die Archäologie (2004). https://www.uni-heidelberg.de/md/zaw/akh/akh_texte/02maran121104.pdf, p. 7. Accessed 21 April 2020
7. Assmann A. In: Maran, J.: Architektur als gesellschaftlicher Raum. Zur Bedeutung sozialwissenschaftlicher Theorien für die Archäologie (2004). https://www.uni-heidelberg.de/md/zaw/akh/akh_texte/02maran121104.pdf, p. 7. Accessed 21 April 2020
8. Welzer, H.: Das soziale Gedächtnis. In: H. Welzer (ed.) Das soziale Gedächtnis. Geschichte, Erinnerung, Tradierung. Hamburg., p. 18, (2001)
9. Maran, J.: Architektur als gesellschaftlicher Raum. Zur Bedeutung sozialwissen-schaftlicher Theorien für die Archäologie, p. 7, (2004). https://www.uni-heidelberg.de/md/zaw/akh/akh_texte/02maran121104.pdf. Accessed 21 April 2020
10. ibid, p. 7
11. Horwitz, M.; Joerges, B.; Potthast, J. (eds.): Stadt und Film. Versuch zu einer „Visuellen Soziologie". Discussion Paper FS-II 96-503. Berlin: Wissenschaftszentrum, Berlin 1996. URL: http://bibliothek.wz-berlin.de/pdf/1996/ii96-503.pdf (translated by the author). Accessed 29 April 2020
12. Kirschner, U.: Urban transdisciplinary co-study in a cooperative multicultural working project. In: Luo, Y. (ed.) CDVE 2018. LNCS, vol. 11151, pp. 145–152. Springer, Cham (2018). https://doi.org/10.1007/978-3-030-00560-3_20

13. Debord, G.: Rapport über die Konstruktion von Situationen und die Organisations- und Aktionsbedingungen der internationalen situationistischen Tendenz. In: Pierre Gallissaires, Hanna Mittelstädt und Roberto Ohrt (eds.): Der Beginn einer Epoche, p. 37, Hamburg (1995)
14. ibid, p. 43
15. Bourdieu, P.: Ortseffekte. In: Bourdieu, Pierre u.a. (Hg.): Das Elend der Welt. Zeugnisse und Diagnosen alltäglichen Leidens an der Gesellschaft. (translated by the author) Konstanz, p. 160 (1997)
16. Esposito, E.: Die Beobachtung der Kybernetik. Über Heinz von Foerster, Ob-serving Systems. (translated by the author) In: Dirk Baecker (eds.): Schlüsselwerke der Systemtheorie, p. 105 (2016)
17. Kirschner, U.: A Hermeneutic Interpretation of Concepts in a Cooperative Multicul-tural Working Project, SIGraDi 2017: XXI Congreso de la Sociedad Ibero-americana de Gráfica Digital. Ibaceta, M. R. (Hrsg.). Blucher, S. 610–615 6 S. (Blucher Design Proceedings; Band 3, Nr. 12) (2017). https://doi.org/10.5151/sigradi2017-094
18. Petersen, A.: "Visibility of Unseen (Voices)" Analyse und theoretische Einordnung, witten homework (unpublished) (2019)
19. Biermann-Firek, L.: (2019) Von Kaserne zum Campus – Der Habitus schafft das Habitat? witten homework (unpublished)

Designing a Culturally Inspired Mobile Application for Cooperative Learning

Philemon Yalamu[✉], Wendy Doube, and Caslon Chua[✉]

Swinburne University of Technology, Melbourne, Australia
{pyalamu,wdoube,cchua}@swin.edu.au

Abstract. Cooperative learning is shown to build positive relationships among students and improve one's achievement. In most cases, studies focus on improving the type of learning technologies and other associated challenges pertaining to infrastructural needs. Little attention is given to understand specific knowledge that could enable advancement in learning, particularly in places that are culturally diverse with traditional knowledge. If cultural underpinnings are not carefully considered, it may hinder students to collaborate. This work adopted a user-centered approach to gain user needs and requirements to design and test a mobile application that fosters cooperative learning. The study also discovered the importance of having cultural elements and the need for having a system that recognizes and supports cooperative learning.

Keywords: Interface design · Cooperative learning · Cultural elements

1 Introduction

Often tertiary institutions in developing nations are faced with numerous challenges hindering academic progress. There is this concern of the growing technology gap between developed and developing nations, and technology leapfrogging has become a common paradigm emerging in some developing nations in their race to stay abreast of the changes [1, 2]. Studies have also shown ways in which education technologies could help leapfrog progress in education [3]. For a developing nation, a significant barrier to education is its cultural diversity. Taking Papua New Guinea (PNG) as an example, students are raised in different ethnicities, each having their own cultural differences [4]. Eighty percent of the population lives in rural areas with varying cultural influences that are usually brought into formal education [4–6]. As such, students' participation in formal learning activities is likely to be impacted, lowering their performances below the expected standards. Consequently, these may contribute to the lack of quality outcomes resulting in low employment rates for university graduates [7].

Research has shown that technology can eliminate barriers in education when used properly [3]. In tertiary education settings, cooperative learning is essential however may not work if cultural underpinnings that hinder students to collaborate are not carefully considered.

To address this issue, a requirement gathering and user studies were conducted, aimed at identifying cultural obstructions to cooperative learning. These studies

© Springer Nature Switzerland AG 2020
Y. Luo (Ed.): CDVE 2020, LNCS 12341, pp. 158–166, 2020.
https://doi.org/10.1007/978-3-030-60816-3_18

investigated ways to utilize technology through the understanding of traditional requirements of university students from PNG. Upon completion of the requirements gathering, a mobile application prototype of a Learning Management System (LMS) was designed and implemented having learning activities that can support cooperative learning.

This paper presents the findings of the requirements gathering and user studies of a mobile application prototype that incorporates cultural elements and foster cooperative learning. User-centered approach [8] was adopted in these studies to ensure that the needs of the target users are identified.

2   Methods

This work was divided into three parts, namely (1) understanding the user, (2) investigating context, tasks, and design, and (3) user study.

2.1   Understanding the Users

Understanding the user involved getting requirements from the users to ensure the design conforms to their specific needs [8, 9]. This is done using a requirement gathering study involving three cohorts of one university in PNG. Three sets of separate questionnaires were used on these cohorts to get a broader understanding of the user requirements. Two follow up focus group discussions were conducted, one for students and the other for lecturers to enable us to obtain more inputs from the participants. It was important to segregate participants into their appropriate categories to gain a more profound understanding of their experiences and expectations. The responses were collected to make an informed design decision.

2.2   Investigating Context, Task and Design

To gain an understanding of the context and tasks, literature on academic achievements, LMS interfaces, cultural diversity, and cultural sensitive technologies were reviewed [10–13]. All information gained from the review was used to develop the understanding of cultural elements to be incorporated into the mobile application prototype. A technology review of LMS interfaces used in higher education in developing nations was also conducted [14–16]. This review provides insights into creating tasks and requirements appropriate to design the prototype. Moreover, the technology review of ten LMS platforms; five of which were identified through requirement gathering study while five were identified through investigation of online popularity ranking, resulted in the identification of the type of LMS interface to be developed and investigated appropriate interface design for the mobile application. It also identified existing interface elements that are present in an LMS.

2.3   User Study

The user study conducted involved getting user feedback about the design decisions through user interactions with the various interface elements incorporated into the mobile application. The prototype was coded using existing web application technologies, to enable interactive user interactions. Three learning activities were set up to allow participants to interact with the interface [17]. The interface prototype was tested on university students from PNG, the Pacific Islands, and other international English As Second Language (EASL) students. In addition, comments and user observations from the interactions were noted.

3   Results

We start by analyzing the results of the user requirements. Combining these results with the review of literature, we came up with a mobile application prototype of an LMS that incorporate identified interface elements and tasks. Finally, the results of the user study were analyzed and discussed.

3.1   The Users

In understanding the users, we presented the results from the three sets of survey questionnaires to get a broader understanding of the user requirements. We also presented the two focus group discussions. These results consistently showed the need of cultural elements in an LMS. We further noted that these cultural elements relate to the interest of cooperative learning. In addition, the results showed a preference in the use of mobile devices when accessing an LMS.

Survey Questionnaire Results

Three survey questionnaires were designed for three different participant cohorts namely, students, lecturers, and administrators. The student and lecturer questionnaires were divided into two sections whereas the administrator questionnaire had only one section. The first section of student and lecturer questionnaires captures demographic information while the second section investigates various teaching and learning experiences from the perspective of both the content users and content creators. However, the administrator questionnaire provided questions for a semi-structured interview and was completed by the interviewer during the interview.

The responses generally outlined cultural influences that are relevant to cooperative learning such as the choice of gender preference in group discussions, the size of group they preferred, and aspects of reverence which showed the students' respect for their elders to be a prominent cornerstone in PNG's traditional cultures. Examples include females prefer to work with other females, students prefer to work in small groups than large groups and teachers could hardly be questioned as they are considered elders and are respected. In a similar study, Kelegai and Middleton [4] pointed out that students do not ask lecturers questions nor participate unless they were asked to.

Other responses also outlined the importance of images which had been used in traditional learning and has the potential to engage students in cooperative learning.

Traditional learning is defined as how the participants experience learning prior to their formal schooling. Berk [18] pointed out that these learners rely highly on their experiences as they participate in practical work.

Focus Group Results

Two focus group sessions, one for students and one for lecturers, were designed to provide an avenue for additional data to be collected. The questions investigated various ways in which traditional knowledge and technology could assist teaching and learning. Each focus group used the same questions in their discussions. Participants in each group spent a few minutes to individually write down answers to the three questions before sharing them with others. This was to reduce the risk of groupthink and ensure the opinions of each participant is heard instead of being influenced by the opinions of others in the group [19].

In the student focus group, male students shared their experiences about cultural beliefs relating to restrictions prohibiting men to associate themselves with women in traditional society and how this influences male students who come into the university. This affects the way male and female students interact with each other in group discussions. For example, a male student stated, "…males are seen to be of higher status than female in the village". This is likely associated with the patrilineal background that comprises most of the cultures in PNG where males retain hereditary statuses [20, 21].

The lecturer focus group touched on the importance of traditional knowledge suggesting, it gives foundation to basic knowledge which students can formalize through learning in the classroom. An example given was in reference to lime making. A science male lecturer explained, "In traditional lime-making process along coastal PNG, raw elements such as coral reef or seashells are burnt and crushed to form lime. This (traditional) process usually focused mainly on learning the end-product (lime). However, in the contemporary classes, the scientific knowledge behind the process is usually covered which gives an in-depth understanding of how lime is made". This demonstrates a cooperative learning approach integrating traditional and contemporary learning methods. The ideology of culture being an important factor in learning enhancements was debated by a female lecturer who argued that technology is the solution, therefore cultural barriers should not be of concern. However, this was refuted by another male lecturer stating, "…I think it is relevant because we really need to study traditional knowledge and how people are engaged in traditional knowledge in order to help us identify a relevant technology that suits the kind of style of learning and from that, we can embrace that particular technology to use in the delivery of teaching and learning".

This information provided us with insights on how different users perceive the importance of culture in relation to technology.

3.2 The Context, Task and Design

The results from the survey questionnaires and focus group discussion enabled us to gather a broader understanding of the user requirements. We were able to develop a prototype that incorporates cultural elements in a mobile application prototype of an LMS, and tasks that support cooperative learning.

Context and Task

We defined three tasks namely tutorials, a quiz, and games. This was designed to capture feedback from the users using surveys, focus groups and interviews, and the technology review.

Having a tutorial, more specifically video tutorial, is the feedback that was obtained. Participants suggested video tutorials be produced for courses and lectures to assist learning. This will help address problems such as timetable clashes and limited lecture rooms. It will also allow students to form small groups when viewing the tutorial for collaborative learning.

The quiz was one of the highly preferred online activities uncovered during the requirements gathering. Quiz provides an opportunity for trivia-like activities where students form groups and try to answer questions. The intent of the quiz was designed to be a learning activity rather than an assessment activity. Learning is further supported with provision to gain badges for success in answering quiz questions.

Finally, the game experience is included as practice-based learning like traditional learning, where knowledge is passed on through interactions and observances of celebrations. The game is designed to provide such interactions and can be extended to allow students to interact with each other.

The incorporation of these tasks into the design enables users to be able to use the system in cooperative learning.

Prototype Design

Three levels of interactions were implemented as shown in Fig. 1. Level one holds the main page, level two contains links to activities, and level three consists of respective interactive activities and have their own sub-sections.

As part of the interface design, a quick access menu is provided that gives access to all the pages in the prototype. It also acts as the primary navigational menu for the prototype. Figure 2(a) shows the quick access menu on the main page.

Level one contains links to the three activities. As shown in Fig. 2(a), the interface presents buttons to access the tutorials in videos and notes, the quiz questions, and games. Each of these sections have their own sub-sections to allow contents to be accessed separately. Both sections and sub-sections will be presented in a non-linear format except for the quiz which is organized in a linear format.

Level two comprises of links to the specific learning activities for tutorial, quiz and games. Each of these levels have their own sections and sub-sections and access to this level is linear. Figure 2(b), 2(c) and 2(d) are the interfaces for tutorials, quiz and games.

Finally, level three contains the learning activities for tutorials, quiz and games. Tutorials are provided in both English and Pidgin, where Pidgin is the cultural element. The quiz utilized cultural symbols as badges, while games adopted a cultural theme.

3.3   User Study

A mobile application prototype was designed and implemented with the three learning activities. The results captured feedback on the importance of cultural elements and support for cooperative learning. The user study was done with 22 university students from PNG, the Pacific Islands, and other international English As Second Language

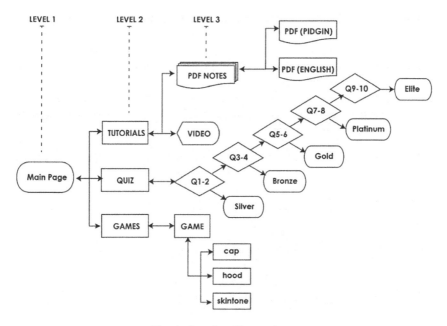

Fig. 1. Levels of Interactions.

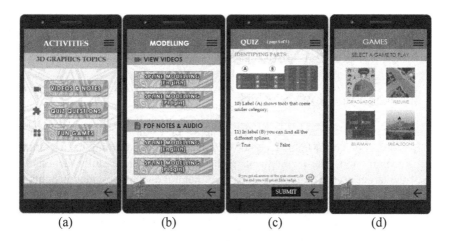

Fig. 2. Interface examples of the app prototype.

(EASL) students. The students were given tasks to complete and a post-questionnaire to get their feedback from the experience. Their interactions were also observed during the process.

For the discussion, we have provided the game experience activity as an example. The game provides an example of practical engagement in learning which involved the user to interact with various features on the interface as part of their learning. In some traditional societies, learning is a practical process [22]. This understanding was captured in the Likert scale rating of the game experience. Ninety percent of participants rated their gaming experience as supportive of practice-based learning, identical to the ones used traditionally. The other ten percent rated that their culture did not support learning by practice as in the game experience.

Participants also gave their overall comments on the game experience. As shown in Fig. 3, the interpretation of comments as word cloud indicates that learning in a cultural setting is as equivalent to the game experience.

Fig. 3. Participants' comments on the game experience

4   Conclusion and Future Work

This paper presented a user-centered design approach in developing a mobile application prototype of an LMS that could enrich cooperative learning in a culturally diverse student cohort. The requirements gathering process successfully identified the needs of the target user. The focus groups were helpful as they provided insights into understanding the users' cultural perspectives and contexts. This also provided an avenue for intuitive responses from the participants. Getting views from the two cohorts; lecturers and students, gave a two-dimensional view of the cultural influences affecting the students. These findings highlight the importance of cultural elements and the need of cooperative learning support.

By providing tutorial in both English and Pidgin, the participants in the user study acknowledged that having a local language not only helped them learn content but also helped them learn English. Using a common first language to work together, students can understand and discuss what they have gone through [23]. In addition, a study by Singhanayok and Hooper [24] indicates that high and low achieving students performed better in cooperative learning tutorials. Information from the requirements gathering indicated that quizzes are vital to enhance learning and that quizzes are the best option because it enables the brain to think and work fast. By incorporating cultural elements in the quiz in the form of badges, the participants from the user study indicated that these provide a sense of belonging. Moreover, the sense of belonging provides an environment for the students to engage in cooperative learning. A study by Jensen, Moore [25] showed that students' performance on the cooperative potion of quiz was significantly better than the individual component. Results from the game experience shown relevance to traditional learning methods in indigenous cultures which allows for practical engagement in learning. Particularly, gamification as a persuasive technology, could be used to match the user's personality to specific techniques that can engage students in a collaborative learning [26]. Overall, the cultural features such as images and symbols have been found to have lasting impressions and could promote cooperative learning.

For our future work, we aim to look at developing a framework of incorporating cultural elements in LMSs that would aid cooperative learning. In addition, the option of cultural preference for collaboration would also be explored. We will also investigate how gamified activities with cultural elements can empower cooperative learning in a collaborative environment.

References

1. Fong, M.W.L.: Digital divide: the case of developing countries. Issues in Informing Science Information Technology, vol. 6, p. 471+ (2009)
2. Davison, R., et al.: Technology leapfrogging in developing countries–an inevitable luxury? Electr. J. Inf. Syst. Dev. Countries **1**(1), 1–10 (2000)
3. Vegas, E., Ziegler, L., Zerbino, N.: How Ed-Tech Can Help Leapfrog Progress in Education. Center for Universal Education at The Brookings Institution (2019)
4. Kelegai, L., Middleton, M.: Information technology education in papua new guinea: cultural, economic and political influences. J. Inf. Technol. Educ.: Australia **1**, 11–23 (2002)
5. Hinafa, S., Halim, A.: Niugini Agrisaiens, p. 16 (2014)
6. BBC News. Papua New Guinea country profile (2019). https://www.bbc.com/news/world-asia-pacific-15436981
7. EMTV online. Graduates unemployment an emerging problem in PNG (2017). http://www.emtv.com.pg/graduates-unemployment-an-emerging-problem-in-png/
8. ISO 9241-210, Ergonomics of human-system interaction - Part 210: Human-centred design for interactive systems, ISO 9241-210:2010(E), Editor, International Organization for Standardization: ISO Online (2010)
9. Abras, C., Maloney-Krichmar, D., Preece, J.: User-Centered Design. Bainbridge, W. Encyclopedia of Human-Computer Interaction. Thousand Oaks: Sage Publications, **37**(4), 445–456 (2004)
10. Panthee, R.K.: Inviting Citizen Designers to Design Learning Management System (LMS) Interfaces for Student Agency in a Cross-Cultural Digital Contact Zone (2014)
11. Callahan, E.: Interface design and culture. Ann. Rev. Inf. Sci. Technol. **39**(1), 255–310 (2005)
12. Khaslavsky, J.: Integrating culture into interface design. In: CHI' 1998 Conference Summary on Human Factors in Computing Systems, Los Angeles, California, USA, pp. 365–366. ACM (1998)

13. Gillies, R.M., Boyle, M.: Teachers' Reflections on Cooperative Learning: Issues of Implementation. Teach. Teach. Educ. **26**(4), 933–940 (2010)

14. Pappas, C.: The Top Open Source Learning Management Systems [2019 Update] (2015). https://elearningindustry.com/top-open-source-learning-management-systems

15. Dravis, P.: Open source software: perspectives for development, The World Bank (2003)

16. Wolfer, J.: Choreographing computer literacy-crafting demonstrations to engage the general education student. In: International Conference on Engineering and Computer Education, pp. 34–38 (2007)

17. Yalamu, P., Chua, C., Doube, W.: Does indigenous culture affect one's view of an LMS interface: a png and pacific islands students' perspective. In: Proceedings of the 31st Australian Conference on Human-Computer-Interaction, Association for Computing Machinery: Fremantle, WA, Australia, pp. 302–306 (2019)

18. Berk, R.A.: Teaching strategies for the Net Generation. Transform. Dialogues: Teach. Learn. J. **3**(2), 24 (2009)

19. Humphreys, S.J.: Ethics committee membership selection: a moral preference tool. Res. Ethics **6**(2), 37–42 (2010)

20. Encyclopaedia Britannica. Papua New Guinea. Daily life and social customs (2019). https://www.britannica.com/place/Papua-New-Guinea/Daily-life-and-social-customs

21. Fingleton, J.: Rethinking the need for land reform in Papua New Guinea (2019)

22. Facing History And Ourselves. Traditional Education. Stolen Lives: The Indigenous Peoples of Canada and the Indian Residential Schools (2020). https://www.facinghistory.org/stolen-lives-indigenous-peoples-canada-and-indian-residential-schools/historical-background/traditional-education

23. Bismark Tefeh, J.: Examining the Role of First Language in Learning a Second Language: An Overview of Code Switching in the English Language Classroom. Nairobi J. Humanit. Soc. Sci. **3**(4), 145–156 (2019)

24. Singhanayok, C., Hooper, S.: The effects of cooperative learning and learner control on students' achievement, option selections, and attitudes. Educ. Tech. Res. Dev. **46**(2), 17–36 (1998)

25. Jensen, M., Moore, R., Hatch, J.: Cooperative learning: Part I: cooperative quizzes. Am. Biol. Teach. **64**(1), 29–34 (2002)

26. Challco, G.C., Mizoguchi, R., Bittencourt, I.I., Isotani, S.: Gamification of collaborative learning scenarios: structuring persuasive strategies using game elements and ontologies. In: Koch, F., Koster, A., Primo, T. (eds.) SOCIALEDU 2015. CCIS, vol. 606, pp. 12–28. Springer, Cham (2016). https://doi.org/10.1007/978-3-319-39672-9_2

CLASS-O, A Cooperative Language Assessment System with Ontology

Chakkrit Snae Namahoot[1]([✉]) [iD], Michael Brückner[2] [iD],
and Chayan Nuntawong[3] [iD]

[1] Faculty of Science, Naresuan University, Phitsanulok, Thailand
chakkrits@nu.ac.th
[2] Naresuan University International College, Naresuan University,
Phitsanulok, Thailand
michaelb@nu.ac.th
[3] Faculty of Science and Technology, Nakhon Sawan Rajabhat University,
Nakhon Sawan, Thailand
chayan@nsru.ac.th

Abstract. This paper describes the design, development and test of a novel Computerized Adaptive Testing (CAT) system for English language based on a testing process using features of Item Response Theory and an Ontology of English Language (ELO). The testing process employs a variable branching procedure to deliver the best next test item to the examinee based on the ability level shown so far. The formative assessment part is based on ELO, which acts as knowledge base for giving efficient and detailed feedback to the examinee. The summative part of the feedback consists of the percentage of correct answers regarding the three sections covered in the test: vocabulary, reading comprehension, and structure. It includes the proficiency level and places examinees into one of three groups: high, medium and low proficiency. After the test has terminated, each examinee contributes to a new version of the item bank by feeding back the individual response parameters, which refines item data for subsequent tests.

Keywords: Computerized adaptive test system · Item response theory · English language ontology · Variable branching model

1 Background and Previous Work

Feedback has been found of major importance for successful teaching and learning [1, 2] both in traditional classroom settings and in more autonomous online learning environments. The immediacy, frequency and the quality of the feedback are important factors for successful learning [3, 4, 5]. Regarding the first factor we can state that computer systems have the capability of delivering feedback immediately after completion of tasks and sub-tasks [6]. In a computer-assisted classroom, the frequency of feedback depends on the frequency of testing or assignments. The quality of feedback is related to the teacher's ability to assess and construct valuable feedback, whereas computer-assisted feedback is seen as inferior. Computerized Adaptive Test

© Springer Nature Switzerland AG 2020
Y. Luo (Ed.): CDVE 2020, LNCS 12341, pp. 167–177, 2020.
https://doi.org/10.1007/978-3-030-60816-3_19

(CAT) systems have gained attention in the testing community because of the enhanced capabilities of computers in terms of hardware and software [7]. Moreover, the rise of appropriate methods supporting CAT has considerably contributed to the application of CAT; examples are the Item Response Theory (IRT) framework and variable branching models [8, 9]. Whereas these methods improve the test management and the validity of test results in terms of summative assessments (points gained by the examinees and disjunct ability levels), one important part of feedback is missing: formative assessment, which guides the examinee after having taken a test administered by CAT to weaknesses in such fields as vocabulary, structure, or reading comprehension. In this research, we applied a linguistic ontology of English Language to analyze the fields of weakness in examinees' responses and provide appropriate and detailed formative feedback besides the traditional summative feedback with points and proficiency classification.

The following scenario illustrates the use of an application like CLASS-O, the Computerized Language Assessment System with Ontology. We consider a cohort of examinees at a test center for admitting students to higher education institutions. This cohort typically includes individuals, like examinee A, of low to medium proficiency levels, so for this purpose the item bank should reflect this observation. Examinee A takes the test and gets the test results in form of a summative evaluation (percentage of correct or incorrect answers) and a formative assessment (feedback on the weak points in the responses, e.g. use of pronouns). With this information, examinee A can now work on improving the specific weaknesses before taking the test again.

Traditional CAT systems return the test results in form of points or proficiency levels. Information about weaknesses, or knowledge gaps, the examinee has shown during the test is missing in those tools. The proposed system addresses this lack of formative assessment by using an ontology covering English language features in a comprehensive way to support substantial and immediate formative feedback to the examinees after completing their tasks and sub-tasks in an English language proficiency test administered via CAT.

The rest of this paper is organized as follows: Sect. 2 outlines the design methods and approach used in this research. Section 3 details the system architecture and its components. Results of the system test are presented and discussed in Sect. 4. Finally, conclusions are drawn in Sect. 5, and an outlook on further work regarding CLASS-O is given.

2   Design Methods and Approach of CLASS-O

CLASS-O is a CAT system that employs Item Response Theory and lets the examinee pass the ability assessment to estimate the individual knowledge level of English language (Fig. 1). We apply Item Response Theory (IRT) because we want to provide feedback on the basis of test items and not only on test scores. IRT is a probabilistic test theory which supports the analysis of which latent variables (e.g. personality traits) can be inferred from manifest categorial data (e.g. responses to test items). The questions come from an item bank with more than 300 items covering vocabulary, structure, and reading comprehension. Five experts checked the original items and classified the level of difficulty for each item as an initial parameter into high, medium and low. The latent variable derived from the examinee's responses is the individual proficiency level of English language. A variable branching algorithm is applied to sequence the set of test items for the examinee. CLASS-O can handle both kinds of tests: fixed number of items and variable number of items to be presented to the examinees. The 3-Parameter IRT model (detailed in Sect. 3) calibrates the test items independent of the examinees and enables the placement of examinees on an absolute scale. The three parameters are item discrimination, item difficulty, and probability for correct guessing, which are explained in the next section.

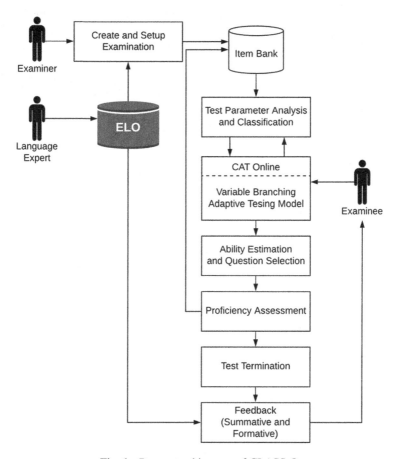

Fig. 1. Process architecture of CLASS-O

The variable branching component determines, which is the best item to show next based on the examinee's current ability level. We apply variable branching to ensure suitability of the item selection given the ability of the examinee. Then, the examinee provides the response, which CLASS-O uses to compute a new ability based on all responses so far. Here, the system uses maximum likelihood method. The examinee's test stops after the stopping condition is reached: either the number of questions or a defined standard error (see Sect. 3 for details).

After CLASS-O has determined the stopping condition, the proficiency level is evaluated and fed back to the examinee together with a detailed analysis of weaknesses using shown during the test using the English Language Ontology (ELO). The ELO consists of English language structural components, which are to provide guidance for the formative assessment and feedback after test completion. The item parameters gained by the examinee's responses are used to update item parameters in the item bank. In a sense, the examinees act as the developers of the subsequent versions of the item bank.

The English ontology (ELO) has been designed and developed during the last three years. The area of linguistic ontologies has gained attention in the last decade [10]. ELO was evaluated by five professionals and experts of teaching English as a Second Language (ESL).

The English ontology is structured into four main classes: Punctuation, Word Use, Sentence Elements and Parts of Speech, which are further divided into detailed concepts of linguistics, as shown in the schematic diagram of Fig. 2.

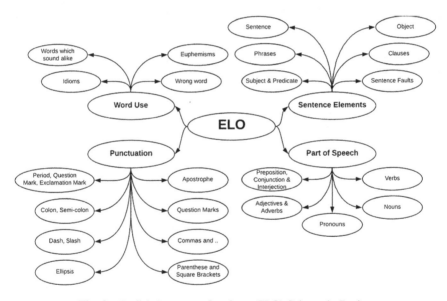

Fig. 2. English Language Ontology (ELO) Schematic Design

3   System Components

This section details the system architecture and its components (Fig. 1).**The Test Parameter Analysis and Classification of CLASS-O uses** IRT and an item bank of more than 300 questions, which is designed and evaluated to be optimal for examinees with low to medium proficiency levels. The parameter values are analyzed using the item response from all the examinees and classified into three values: discrimination, difficulty and guess values. The analysis of all three parameters proceeds until appropriate parameters can be summarized and the analysis is finished. The parameters can be analyzed applying Eq. (1)–(4) given by [11] as follows.

a is the probability of the item discrimination value; for the analysis of the initial item the value will be set close to 0,

b is the probability of the item difficulty; for the exam analysis the initial value will be set close to 0,

c is the probability value of guessing the item correctly, for the exam analysis the initial value will be set close to 0.

In practice, we will set parameters a, b, and c to 0.0001 when starting the first value analysis.

The discrimination parameter is evaluated according to Eq. (1).

$$a(i) = a + \frac{\sum_1^n (obs(i) - pr)/(pr * qr))D(th(i) - b)qr(pr - c)/(1 - c)}{\sum_1^n \frac{D(th(i)-b)qr(pr-c)/(1-c)^2}{pr*qr}} \tag{1}$$

The difficulty value analysis is shown in Eq. (2).

$$b(i) = b + \frac{\sum_1^n (obs(i) - pr)/(pr * qr)) * (-D * a * qr * (pr - c)/(1 - c))}{\sum_1^n \frac{(-D*a*qr*(pr-c)/(1-c))^2}{pr*qr}} \tag{2}$$

Equation (3) defines the parameter for guessing items correctly.

$$c(i) = c + \frac{\sum_1^n (obs(i) - pr)/(pr * qr))qr/(1 - c)}{\sum_1^n \frac{(qr/(1-c))^2}{(qr/(1-c))^2/pr*qr}}, , \tag{3}$$

where $a(i)$ is the discrimination value of item number i, $b(i)$ is the difficulty of the item i, $c(i)$ is the test guess of item i correctly, n is the number of test respondents according to item i, $obs(i)$ is the answer value for item i, correct answer is 1, wrong answer is 0, pr is the probability of the correct answer, qr is the complementary value of pr, which is 1-pr, D is the constant value, which is equal to 1.7, th is the examinee ability, for exam analysis, the value will be set to close to 0 (in practice, we will set it to 0.0001 when starting the first value analysis). In this step, the exam analyzes the parameters a, b and c, which will take the results of all the test of the item to be analyzed by converting the correct answer to 1 and the wrong answer to 0 and storing it in the obs [] array. Then the initial parameters (a_{in}, b_{in}, c_{in}) are set to 0.0001 and the ability value is stored in the th [array]. In the analysis, the maximum number of turns is limited to 200 cycles, and the function of exam analysis is used to calculate the final parameters (a_{out}, b_{out}, c_{out}). Then the initial parameters will be compared with the final parameters to find the difference of these parameters with following conditions:

If the difference between a_{in} and a_{out}, b_{in} and b_{out}, c_{in} and c_{out} is less than 0.0001

Then the test parameters of this item are considered equal to a_{out}, b_{out}, and c_{out}

Else (greater than 0.0001)

Update the a_{in} value to be equal to a_{out}, $b_{in} = b_{out}$, $c_{in} = c_{out}$
and begin the analysis process of parameters a, b and c again

However, in practice, endless loops may occur when the difference cannot be determined. Therefore, we set the maximum of 200 cycles in accordance with the theory. When the analysis cycle is completed, the test parameters of this item are set equal to a_{out}, b_{out}, and c_{out}.

The Ability value analysis of examinees uses IRT with three parameters above and takes all the correct and wrong answers in sequence of tests for the ability analysis. The ability results have values ranking from -3 to $+3$. If the value is closer to the side -3, it will indicate that examinees have low ability in that field. If the ability value is close to 0, it means the examinees have a medium level of ability and if the ability is approaching $+3$, the examinees have a high ability.

To assess the ability of the examinee, there must be at least one correct answer and at least one wrong answer in the test. This is according to the joint probability analysis technique [8]. The analysis can be calculated from Eq. (4)

$$(\theta) = \theta + \frac{\sum_1^n (obs - pr)D\left(\frac{a}{1-c}\right)(p-c)/p}{\sum_1^n D^2 a^2 \left(\frac{1-p}{p}\right)\left(\frac{p-c}{1-c}\right)^2}, \tag{4}$$

where θ is the ability of the examinees in the first round of analysis, the value is set to 0.0001 n is the number of items (exams) that the examinees have answered, and p is the probability of answering the exam correctly.

Variable Branching Adaptive Testing Model is a multi-stage strategy [12] which is a multi-step test, a test that has a number of measurement steps, and assessing the examinees of more than two or more. The variable branching adaptive tests do not have the test organization structure because the test parameters, information on test responses and standard error values as are used as the conditions for selecting the test including the end of the test.

For multi-step tests of variable branching test will not be able to determine the certain path or structure of the test. The exam (test) that is used in this type of test must pass the analysis of the three parameters consisting of the difficulty level, discrimination and the correct guessing values of the test. From the three parameters above, the position value will be analyzed to give the most information value of answering to that item. This position value will be used to choose the question (question selection). Every test answer has an answer check, analyze the ability level of the examinees, analyze information value of test answering, and analyze the standard error values. If the tolerance values are small to an acceptable level, for example, for tolerances smaller than 0.0001, the test will be stopped, and the ability of the examinees will be estimated. However, if the test still has unacceptable deviations, the test will not be terminated and will continue until the error is reduced to the specified size. However, in practice, there is a limit to the maximum number of exams used in the exam cycle. This type of testing is necessary to use Computerized Adaptive Test (CAT) to support operations.

Computerized Adaptive Test (CAT) means computer technology that helps to improve the examination efficiency, analyzing exam questions, grading and reporting results, including the use in building the exam bank. CAT is the use of computers in adaptive tests that are suitable for the ability of the examinees. This process can estimate examinee ability by selecting suitable questions for examinees from correct or wrong answering in each question. For example, if examinees answer question correctly then the more difficulty and ability score they can get. If the system can estimate the true ability of the examinees reliably (with a low discrepancy), the examination system will end, exam results are recorded and reported on the computer screen. CAT has 3important components for system operations: test starting point, item (exam) selection and ability estimation, and test termination criteria.

- Test starting point is the selection of the first item (initial item), which is preferable to choose the item that is at a medium level [13]. The selection of the first item is not important for the adaptive test to estimate ability of the examinees. From the beginning of the experiment with tests with different levels of difficulty, found that it almost does not affect the accuracy of the estimation of the true ability (θ) after the use of 20 questions or more.
- Item selection and ability estimation

The ability estimation method (θ) using the Maximum Likelihood Estimation (MLE) method is commonly used to select the exam which can be described as follows [14, 15].

1. Select items (exams) that have difficulty equal to the estimated competency level (θ) (Match b_i to (θ)) by checking all items. To select an item that has a b_i value similar to the estimated value (θ) at that time and use that item as the next item. This method has the advantage of being easy to calculate.
2. Choose the item that has the highest information position value (m_i) that is close to the competency level (θ) (Match m_i to (θ)). This method takes the guess value into consideration to select the test. The m_i calculation formula for the 3 parameters is calculated as the Eq. (5)

$$m_i = b_i + \frac{1}{Da_i} ln \left[\frac{1 + \sqrt{1 + 8c_i}}{2} \right],$$ (5)

where m_i is information position value, ln is a natural logarithm and other variables are previously defined in above equations.

- Test termination criteria can be used for both specifying the exact number of exams or the standard error setting of the ability estimation of the examinees. In practice, CAT testing should continue until the estimation (θ) has a specified standard error; the standard error (SE (θ)) decreases to an acceptable level, and thus the test should stop. Before analyzing the standard error, the highest information value must be analyzed at the position of the proficiency value of examinees $I_i(\theta)$ and then use the information value to find the standard error again. Analysis of the maximum information value at the position of the ability of the examinees can be calculated using Eq. 6 and the standard error analysis of test answers can be calculated from Eq. 7.

$$I_i(\theta) = D^2 a_i^2 \frac{\left[1 - 20c_i - 8c_i^2 + (1 + 8c_i)^{3/2}\right]}{8\left(1 - c_i^2\right)}, \tag{6}$$

where $I_i(\theta)$ is the highest information value of item i at the position of the ability of the examinees; the other variables are previously defined in above equations.

$$SE(\theta) = \frac{1}{\sqrt{I(\theta)}}, \tag{7}$$

where SE (θ) is the standard error of the estimation (θ) and I (θ) is the information of the exam used for ability of examinees (θ).

From our analysis, the use of standard error gives better results than the use of the test information values for the test termination criteria.

4 Results and Discussion

In this section, we discuss two examples of an examinee who has taken CAT twice and got both low and high score in the first and second test, respectively. There are two main interfaces: language proficiency assessment of the examinee's test history (Fig. 3) and the feedback (summative and formative) following the weakness analysis (Fig. 4).

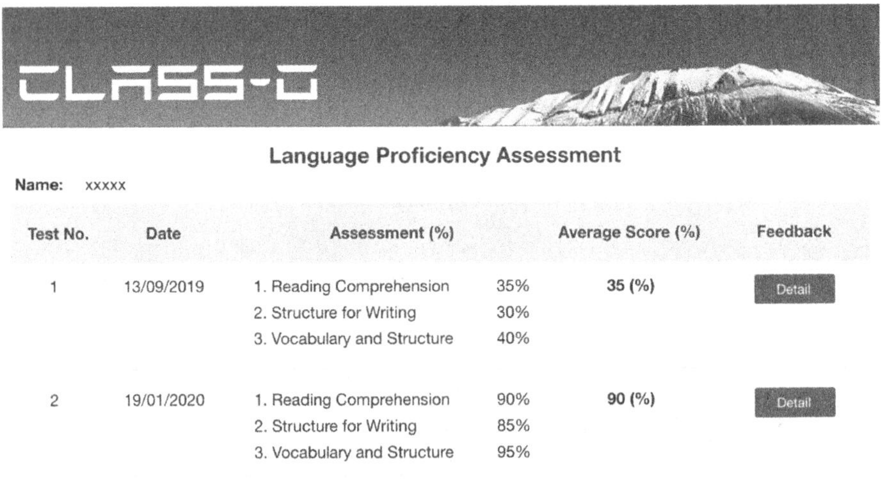

Fig. 3. Language proficiency assessment of the examinee's test history

Figure 3 shows the language proficiency assessment, which consists of the test no., test date, proficiency assessment, the average score per test and the feedback with details. After the test has terminated, the examinee can log in and check the test results and assessments. For example, in Fig. 3 the system shows that this examinee has been

Feedback (Summative and Formative)

| Name: | xxxxx | | Test Date: | 13/09/2019 | | Test No. | 1 |

Weakness Topic	Wrong Answer (%)	**Detail of Weakness**
		Topic: Pronouns
Pronouns	30	**A pronoun** (I, me, he, she, herself, you, it, that, they, each, few, many,
Nouns	24	who, whoever, whose, someone, everybody, etc.) is a **word that takes**
Verbs	15	**the place of noun**
Part of Speech	11	**Example 1:** Joe saw Jill, and he waved at her, the pronouns he and
Word Use	10	her take the place of Joe and Jill, respectively.
		Example 2: Jill hesitated whether **she** should go to school.
		More Details and Examples

Fig. 4. Feedback (summative and formative) after the weakness analysis

test twice (the first test was on 13 October 2019 and the second was on 19 January 2020) with the percentage of scores assessment in three different parts of the test (Reading Comprehension, Structure for Writing and Vocabulary and Structure) and an average score to compare with each test improvement. The assessment and the average score of the first test was low (an average score was only 35%). However, from the second test the examinee improved proficiency by getting high scores with 95%, 95% and 90% in Reading, Structure, and Vocabulary, respectively (90% of average score). The system also shows the feedback (summative and formative) of the weakness analysis (Fig. 4) by clicking at the button "detail" (Test no. 1) of the feedback column.

Figure 4 shows the feedback of each test (test no. 1 in this case) for improvement which consists of weakness topics, percentage of wrong answers and detail of weakness in each topic. As can be seen, there were five topics that the examinee needs to improve from the first test ranking from the highest to lowest of wrong answering percentage: Pronouns, Nouns, Verbs, Parts of speech, and Word use with 30%, 24%, 15%, 11%, and 10% of wrong answering respective. The examinee can see the details of weaknesses by clicking on each of the weakness topics (left side). after which the details will show up on the right side of the interface together with explanations and examples. To get to this screen, the examinee clicked on the "Pronouns" topic, and then the system detailed this topic. If the examinee wanted to see more information and details about the topic, a click on "More Details and Examples" would show more on this.

In addition, the weakness topic was randomly collected 100 test labs in total for 300 examinees and was analyzed by counting the frequency of the topics that examinees answered incorrectly. The result shows that the top five topics leading to wrong answers were Parts of speech, Reading Comprehension, Verbs, Pronouns, and Word use with frequencies of 7016, 4956, 3023, 1816 and 1321, respectively.

5 Conclusion and Future Work

This paper reported the results of a design-and-create research for a computerized adaptive test employing item response theory to administer tests of English language proficiency. The tests were performed for grouping Thai graduates intending admission to further studies.

There are some limitations in this research. Both the reliability (i.e. the extent to which a test measures consistently) and the validity (i.e. the extent to which a test measures what it is supposed to measure) of the test presented here have not been thoroughly examined yet due to limited data.

It should be noted that our approach does not target a major problem of such broad high-stakes (i.e., important for individual participants' educational and working lives) language tests in Thailand: using these tests "as a benchmark in a context where learners share a common L1 (which is not English) is clearly problematic, since, without a substantial body of evidence to support this usage, neither test is likely to be demonstrably valid (i.e. for use in that particular context or domain)" [16].

Future work includes (1) improving test characteristics regarding the writing part of the test; examinees will have to key in correct words and not only select correct answers, (2) the use of an ontology matching tool to inform examinees on parts of corresponding course specifications, which they should review for effective improvement.

References

1. Sadler, D.R.: Beyond feedback: Developing student capability in complex appraisal. Assessment Eval. High. Educ. **35**, 535–550 (2010)
2. Hepplestone, S., Holden, G., Irwin, B., Parkin, H.J., Thorpe, L.: Using technology to encourage student engagement with feedback: a literature review. Res. Learn. Technol. **19** (2), 117–127 (2011)
3. Evans, G.E., Allen, G., Bender, T., Cluett, W.: We never talk: peer to peer observation and formative feedback as steps to evolving academic culture. In: Proceedings 2017 Canadian Engineering Education Association (CEEA 2017), Paper 174 (2017)
4. Vawter, L., Martens, A.: Categorizing software feedback in current language software. In: 2019 IEEE 19th International Conference on Advanced Learning Technologies (ICALT), pp. 258–260 (2019)
5. Fox, J.: Using Portfolios for Assessment/Alternative Assessment. In: Shohamy, E., Or, I.G., May, S. (eds.) Language Testing and Assessment. ELE, pp. 135–147. Springer, Cham (2017). https://doi.org/10.1007/978-3-319-02261-1_9
6. Rietsche, R., Duss, K., Persch, J.M., Söllner, M.: Design and Evaluation of an IT-based Formative Feedback Tool to Foster Student Performance. In: 39th International Conference on Information Systems, San Francisco, pp. 1–17 (2018)
7. Van Groen, M.M., Eggen, T.J.H.M.: Educational test approaches: the suitability of computer-based test types for assessment and evaluation in formative and summative contexts. J. Appl. Test. Technol. **21**(1), 12–24 (2020)
8. Hambleton, R.K., Swaminathan, H., Rogers, H.J.: Fundamentals of Item Response Theory. SAGE Publications, Newbury Park, C.A. (1991)

9. de Ayala, R.J.: The Theory and Practice of Item Response Theory, 2nd edn. Guilford Publications, New York (2008)
10. Schalley, A.C.: Ontologies and ontological methods in linguistics. Lang. Linguist. Compass **13**(11), 1–19 (2019)
11. Rudner, L.M.: An On-line, Interactive, Computer Adaptive Testing,Tutorial. Computer Adaptive Testing Tutorial. http://echo.edres.org:8080/scripts/cat/catdemo.html. Accessed 15 Mar 2020
12. Weiss, D.J.: Strategics of adaptive ability measurement. University of Minnoseta, Mineapolis (1974)
13. Lord, F.M.: A theoretical study of the measurement effectiveness of flexilevel test. Educ. Psychol. Meas. **31**, 805–813 (1971)
14. Urry, V.W.: Tailored testing: A successful application of latent trait theory. J. Educ. Meas. **14**, 181–196 (1977)
15. Reckase, M.D.: An interactive computer program for tailored testing based on the one-parameter logistic model. Behav. Res. Methods Instrum. **6**, 208–212 (1974)
16. O'Sullivan, B.: Language Testing: Theories and Practices. Palgrave Macmillan, UK (2011)

Comparing Machine Learning Algorithms to Predict Topic Keywords of Student Comments

Feng Liu[1], Xiaodi Huang[1], and Weidong Huang[2(✉)]

[1] Charles Sturt University, Albury, NSW 2640, Australia
liufeng121@gmail.com, xhuang@csu.edu.au
[2] University of Technology Sydney, Ultimo, Australia
weidong.huang@uts.edu.au

Abstract. Student comments as a kind of online teaching feedback in higher education organizations are becoming important which provides the evidence to improve the quality of teaching and learning. Effectively extracting useful information from the comments is critical. On the other hand, machine learning algorithms have achieved great performance in automatically extracting information and making predictions. This research compared the performance of three statistical machine learning algorithms and two deep learning methods on topic keyword extraction.

Keywords: Student comments · Machine learning · Topic keywords extraction · Naïve bayes · LogR · SVM · CNN · Att-LSTM

1 Introduction

As a type of important feedback, student comments posted on a forum provide valuable information for teaching and learning. The object of this research is to make use of student subject comments for enhancing teaching quality. Student comments are regarded as a way of online communication to discuss about the subject learning issues. The participants include the lecturer, the tutor, and the students.

The importance of students' feedback has been acknowledged at universities for quality plans and policy [1]. It provides some evidence for teaching plan review and makes student learning more efficient. Nowadays, higher education as a service industry was recognized over the years and valued to meet the expectations of their stakeholders to re-evaluate the approaches in education systems [1, 2]. Based on the reasons above, this research has achieved the topic keywords extracted from the student comments to improve teaching.

Topic keywords are the core words by the content, and they indicate the main ideas of documents [3]. As an important part of the task in NLP, topic keyword extraction has been researched by researchers for several decades. It is a research topic for the last decades in Natural Language Processing (NLP). Buitelaar et al. [4] analyzed the trend of NLP tasks from the top conferences of LREC and ACL. They considered that "Statistical Machine Translation" is the most successful research topic in NLP, and also

© Springer Nature Switzerland AG 2020
Y. Luo (Ed.): CDVE 2020, LNCS 12341, pp. 178–183, 2020.
https://doi.org/10.1007/978-3-030-60816-3_20

provided some insight for keyword extraction and other NLP research directions. Traditionally, identifying topic keywords from a text or a document manually by domain experts is a complex and tedious task. With the big-data, data mining and machine learning approaches constructed many effective models, and some researchers have used different ways to extract keywords from the corpus automatically.

Keyword extraction is one of the text classification problems. Its methods usually have two steps: (1) generating the candidate topic keywords by some heuristics; and (2) identifying the correct topic keywords from candidate words using supervised, unsupervised methods or other leaning scenarios [5]. The methods can be divided into statistical strategies, linguistic approaches, and machine learning approaches.

In this paper, we compare several machine learning methods, such as Naïve Bayes, Logistic Regression, Support Vector Machine, Convolutional Neural Networks, and Long Short-Term Memory, to predict the topic keywords from student subject comments.

2 Related Work

Topic keywords are extracted from a text or document, which is a high generalization of a paragraph or a document, and an accurate description of the document content [6]. However, there are often many language fragments or documents without topic keywords, which makes further analysis and processing of the documents difficult. There are many methods for keyword extraction, and with the application of various new algorithms, the accuracy is continuously improved. Overall, different methods have been used individually in an ensemble way. Despite their differences, the methods have the same purpose and attempt to use a heuristic to locate a set of words to present their topic and describe information from the text [7]. By summarizing all the methods in the supervised learning type, keyword extraction contains the following two main steps:

Selecting the candidates from the text and selecting them through Heuristics Rules are often used to identify and keep the number of candidates as a small data set. With the improvement of Heuristics Rules, many practices have proved that it performs very well in the extraction of topic keywords or phrases [8].

The candidates are subject to several different algorithms to find the valid topic keywords or phrases. The topic keywords and phrases in the document are generated when the candidates are graded according to the word frequency statistics, and the candidates with high scores are selected as the topic keywords. The algorithm models that have been trained are also used to identify the topic keywords again, such as various machine learning algorithms.

3 Method

This research compares several methods to extract the keywords from student subject comments to predict their topic. The approaches include Naïve Bayes, Logistic Regression, Support Vector Machine, Convolutional Neural Networks, and Long Short-Term Memory with Attention mechanism.

Naïve Bayes is a simple effective and well-known algorithm, which makes use of Bayes probability theory and statistics, with good performance on high dimensionality of input [9]. As a classical statistical algorithm, Logistic Regression (LogR) especially performs well in binary classification. Support Vector Machine (SVM) is one of the classifying algorithms of machine learning, a linear model for classification and regression problems. Convolutional Neural Networks (CNN) is a simple neural network algorithm, a forward feed deep neural network. "Convolution" is a mathematical operation, a specialized linear operation [10]. Long Short-Term Memory (LSTM) is a particular type of RNN, specialized in remembering information for an extended period. The Attention mechanism was proposed initially in the field of computer vision in the 1990s, but people started to research on it after a paper published by Google Mind team in 2014 [11]. Recently some researchers attempted to combine the LSTM with the Attention mechanism for NLP tasks, and the ensemble method had a great performance. We compared the several approaches for the student subject comments dataset to discuss performance of each algorithm.

4   Experiments and Results

In this experiment, we developed the program by Python with TensorFlow and Natural Language Toolkit to compare the five algorithms on the two datasets. The models were trained by using Facebook Recruiting III - Keyword Extraction (FR-III-KB) and ITC-114 student comments and prediction part of the ITC-114 topic keywords.

4.1   Datasets

ITC-114 is a subject about Database Systems for Information Technology students at Charles Sturt University. For the online communication, every subject has a website for students and teachers. Stakeholders can comment about this course on the page, which is similar to subject forums. The student comment dataset was collected by the ITC 114 subject team of Charles Sturt University. According to ethical principles, the dataset removed all personal information and retained a few items of every comment, such as Forum, Thread, Topic, and Comment post. The content of this dataset is related to the subject studying and teaching questions and discussions, which include greetings, subject textbook, assessments, SQL, DBMS tools, database design, and final exam, etc. It covered two years from session 3 of 2015 to session 3 of 2017, and 450 recordings were labeled manually in this dataset. Table 1 shows more details about ITC-114 dataset.

FR-III-KB dataset was provided by Kaggle and was released by the Stack Exchange group. All data is licensed under the "CC-BY-SA" license. The content of this dataset is knowledge about information technology, which includes programming, math, website design, database design, SQL, database maintenance, etc. The dataset contains four columns, ID, Title, Body, and Tags. ID is the unique identifier for each question, Title is the question's title, Body is the question description, Tags are the keywords of the question. In this dataset, there are 19.07% recordings about database knowledge. More details are shown in Table 2.

Table 1. Details of ITC-114

Description	Amount
Number of participants	169
Topics	344
Words of shortest recording	2
Sentences of shortest recording	1
Sentences of longest recording	6
Words of longest recording	92
Total number of recording	793

Table 2. Details of FR-III-KB

Description	Amount
Minimum labelled keywords	2
Maximum labelled keywords	18
Words of shortest recording	7
Sentences of shortest recording	1
Sentences of longest recording	4
Words of longest recording	89
Total of database recording	1,189,290

The project dataset was constructed by combining the 1189290 records of the Database knowledge text from FR-III-KB with the 793 records of the ITC-114 dataset, which are shuffled for the final dataset to this project, and the dataset was separated into three parts: the training set, validation set, and testing set as shown in Table 3.

Table 3. THE ENTIRE DATASET

Category	Training	Validation	Test
FR-III-KB	830503	118929	237858
ITC-114	405	45	345
This project	830908	118974	238203

4.2   Data Pre-Processing

Data pre-processing is an integral step for machine learning models construction, which keeps the high-quality data for the model training and validation. The text process task includes removing format tags and stopping words, converting letters, restoring abbreviations and removing punctuation, etc. In this stage, we select some word features to generate candidate keywords, such as word position, word frequency, posterior probability, candidate keyword length, part of speech, the occurrence, line position, parabolic position, standard deviation etc. For deep learning algorithms, the model received the text as vectors by word embedding technique.

4.3   Comparisons Results and Performance

In the experiments, we have compared the five machine learning algorithms on predicting the topic keywords on the dataset of student comments. Neural Network algorithms performed better than the traditional machine learning algorithms. They took more time on their processing, however. As shown in Table 4, Att-LSTM has obtained the highest performance with respect to the metrics of precision, recall, F1 score, and accuracy. CNN performed a little bit lower than Att-LSTM, but higher than Naïve Bayes, Logistic Regression, and Support Vector Machine on the keyword topic extraction task. Naïve Bayes, Logistic Regression, and SVM need to select the features manually for their model training. Such features selection affected their performance, but they had less training and prediction time.

Table 4. Comparisons of the five algorithms

Approaches	Precision	Recall	F1-Score	Accuracy (%)
Naïve Bayes	0.1076	0.04	0.056	73.8647
LogR	0.269	0.8143	0.0521	75.4780
SVM	0.297	0.819	0.0573	77.6895
CNN	0.632	0.5	0.6343	81.22
Att-LSTM	0.8523	0.83	0.8395	84.01

5   Concluding Remarks

In this paper, we have compared the five different types of machine learning algorithms for extracting topic keywords from the student comment dataset. These methods are selected from classical statistical approaches of linear models and two popular deep learning algorithms. All the methods are compared on the dataset and evaluated by four metrics, and the benefits of each method are discussed. The statistical algorithms can be trained fast, while their performance depends on the features selected. Deep learning algorithms have great accuracy, but they need more training time. For the two compared approaches of deep learning, Att-LSTM has the best performance with respect to every metric. Each single approach has limitations for the topic keyword extraction task. But the combination mechanism method is better than any single approach. Moreover, the quality of the dataset also affects the results.

The contribution of this work lies in using machine learning approaches to extract the topic keywords from the student comments for predicting the topics. As such, we can summarize the online subject communication information for learning and teaching in higher education organizations. Machine learning approaches have achieved good performance in many areas in the past years [5, 9, 12, 13]. For the educational aspect, it is still limited, however. In universities, many text tasks are important parts of daily works and usually time-consuming. As demonstrated in our work, this is where machine learning algorithms can help.

References

1. Nair, C.S.: Evaluation of subject, teaching and research. In: Higher Education Research and Development Society of Australia Conference, pp. 481–489 (2002)
2. Ilias, A., Hasan, H.F.A., Rahman, R.A. Yasoa, M.R.B.: Student satisfaction and service quality: any differences in demographic factors? Int. Bus. Res. vol. 1, 4 (1997)
3. Beliga, S., Meštrović, A., Martinčić-Ipšić, S.: An overview of graph-based keyword extraction methods and approaches. J. Inf. Organ. Sci. **39**(1), 1–20 (2015)
4. Buitelaar, P., Bordea, G., Coughlan, B.: Hot topics and schisms in NLP: Community and trend analysis with saffron on ACL and LREC proceedings. In 9th Edition of Language Resources and Evaluation Conference (LREC 2014) (2014)
5. Hasan, K.S., Ng, V.: Automatic keyphrase extraction: A survey of the state of the art. In: Proceedings of the 52nd Annual Meeting of the Association for Computational Linguistics, vol. 1, pp. 1262–1273 (2014)
6. Witten, I.H., Medelyan, O.: Thesaurus based automatic keyphrase indexing. In: Proceedings of the 6th ACM/IEEE-CS Joint Conference on Digital Libraries (JCDL' 2006), pp. 296–297. IEEE (2006)
7. Kadhim, A.I.: Survey on supervised machine learning techniques for automatic text classification. Artif. Intell. Rev. **52**(1), 273–292 (2019). https://doi.org/10.1007/s10462-018-09677-1
8. Hasan, K.S., Ng, V.: Automatic keyphrase extraction: A survey of the state of the art. In: Proceedings of the 52nd Annual Meeting of the Association for Computational Linguistics, vol. 1, pp. 1262–1273, June 2014
9. Kim, S.B., Han, K.S., Rim, H.C., Myaeng, S.H.: Some effective techniques for Naïve bayes text classification. IEEE Trans. Knowl. Data Eng. **18**(11), 1457–1466 (2006)
10. Goodfellow, I., Bengio, Y., Courville, A.: Deep Learning, pp. 326–380. MIT press, New York (2016)
11. Mnih, V., Heess, N., Graves, A.: Recurrent models of visual attention. In: Advances in Neural Information Processing Systems, pp. 2204–2212 (2014)
12. Liao, X., Huang, X., Huang, W.: ML-LUM: A system for land use mapping by machine learning algorithms. J. Comput. Lang. vol. 54 (2019)
13. Liao, X., Huang, X., Huang, W.: Visualization of farm land use by classifying satellite images. In: Luo, Y. (ed.) CDVE 2018. LNCS, vol. 11151, pp. 287–290. Springer, Cham (2018). https://doi.org/10.1007/978-3-030-00560-3_40

Logging and Monitoring System for Streaming Data

Nguyen Ngoc Chung and Phan Duy Hung$^{(\boxtimes)}$

FPT University, Hanoi, Vietnam
chung18mse13005@fsb.edu.vn, hungpd2@fe.edu.vn

Abstract. Logging and monitoring data is very important during the development process as well as the operation of information systems. As the data grows to TB every day, this problem becomes more complicated. Companies can generally buy big data analytics platforms or build it by themselves. Whether buying or building, it is important to have a realistic expectation of time and budget needed to successfully implement, roll out and provide ongoing support. There was a lot of confusion and frustration as the data platform market grew. Suppliers sell their capabilities instead of the actual needs of their customers. Contrary to that trend, some companies would like to build the platform using open source systems such as Apache Flume, Apache Spark Streaming and some other auxiliary technologies at a reasonable cost. This study analyzes requirements, introduces system architecture, and builds a logging and monitoring system for streaming data. The work is also a real project in the field of advertising.

Keywords: Log analysis · Monitoring · Apache flume · Apache spark streaming · Advertisement

1 Introduction

Collecting and monitoring the data generated during the development and operation of the systems can help the process of analysis, making strategic decisions for many companies. For example, during the operation of the system, statistics and descriptions of the failures allow early warning of infrastructure-related problems. Based on the warning content, the operator may have appropriate repair solutions so that the system can operate stably. For web systems, server metrics need to be monitored to allow automation scenarios for system scaling ability. The system will scale-out when high traffic and scale-in when low traffic. Another typical system that requires the continuous collection and monitoring of system parameters is the e-commerce system, managers need to see a user's log of actions taken on the website. Information that can be used to personalize user interfaces, predict and analyze user's behavior, etc. Moreover, when the data required to log increases up to TB every day, the analysis and visualization of data also arise a lot of complex problems.

This paper presents applied research for the Deha solution company's Adlink advertising system [1]. Adlink system includes modules such as advertising management, campaign management, user management and authorization, output tracking, and

© Springer Nature Switzerland AG 2020
Y. Luo (Ed.): CDVE 2020, LNCS 12341, pp. 184–191, 2020.
https://doi.org/10.1007/978-3-030-60816-3_21

payment (Fig. 1). Tracking the effectiveness gained from each ad to optimize costs is very important. Managers need visual charts and recommendations, on which basis they can make timely decisions about whether to pause, resume ads, or even stop a campaign.

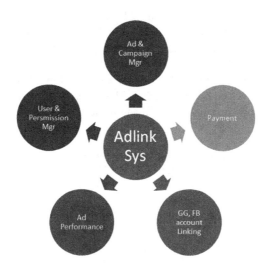

Fig. 1. Adlink system.

The system requires scalability as the number of customers changes can upload up to 10,000 ads to Google and Facebook. At the same time, the system needs to be able to monitor the effectiveness of these ads by querying periodically to Google, Facebook to get results. Do a simple calculation as follows: 10 k (ads) * 2 (request API per minute) * 4kbytes (size of API result) * 60 (min per h) ∼ 4Gbytes data per hour.

Such a large amount of data requires a big data infrastructure that supports streaming data and does the two main tasks of collecting and providing monitoring tools for data analysis.

While researching solutions to build the solution for the Deha solution company, several related studies were found.

Some research related to service integration platforms by utilizing Apache Flume, Apache Spark Streaming. Apache Flume can be used to perform transfer logs, and Apache Spark Streaming can be used for capturing log and analyzing log. As in the study of real-time processing using Apache Flume [2], the authors study Flume's architecture and to be able to read and analyze Twitter data. The work shows that Apache Flume is well suited for real-time data processing. In another study, the authors also used Flume as a tool to collect and transfer huge data from Twitter to Hadoop's HDFS storage system, which is used to evaluate the number of tweets about candidates in 2017 Ecuadorian presidential election [3]. On the side of Apache Spark Streaming, in the research paper "Evaluation of distributed stream processing frameworks for IoT applications in Smart Cities" [4], the authors point out that Spark Streaming has good scaling out and can handle high throughput and suitable for loading, extracting and converting data. In addition to the above studies, the study of "Dynamic Hashtag Interactions and Recommendations: An Implementation Using Apache Spark Streaming and GraphX" [5] also shows that Spark Streaming can also be used in a machine learning problem, which could potentially be applied to our actual systems in the future.

The above studies confirm that the Hadoop ecosystem with Flume, Spark Streaming provides powerful tools to help build in-house infrastructure systems that can collect data from multiple sources, storing, monitoring and analyzing to extract the necessary information for managers and it is good for Adlink management problem.

The remainder of the paper will be organized as follows: Sect. 2 describes the system requirements, system design and implementation presented in Sect. 3, and finally, conclusions and perspectives are made in Sect. 4.

2   System Architecture and Requirements

2.1   Architecture Overview

With the visions of building a large data collection and monitoring system, capable of scaling out well, operating independently of the current business system, the system architecture is proposed as Fig. 2 follows:

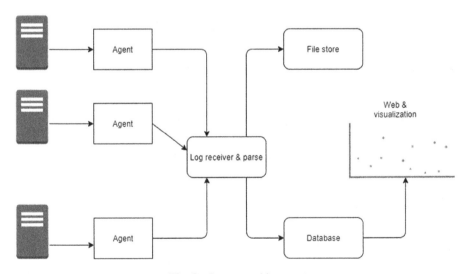

Fig. 2. System architecture

The system consists of main components as below:

- **Log Agents** are installed on application servers to collect and transfer log data to the Streaming Process component. These agents will use the configuration file generated by the Web Manager component.

- **Log receiver & parser component** performs real-time data analysis and saves aggregated data into the database.
- **Storage component** saves log data to file system for reuse when needed.
- **Database component** stores data after analysis which will be used for the Visualization component.
- **Web Manager & visualization component** presents data in the form of graphs, trigger warning base on predefined conditions.

2.2 System Requirements

The system has two main types of users that are system normal users, administrators. The functional requirements of each user are described in Table 1.

Table 1. Functional requirements.

Type	Content
Administrator	Manage User & privilege
	Generate and store configuration file for agents following predefined templates
	Login, Logout
Normal user	View dashboard
	View visual chart report
	Installation & Starter: Download and install the necessary libraries, predefined profiles and start the log agent

After using the system to create configuration files for the Flume agent, users will use it to proceed with their server configuration. Then, when the Flume agent is started, the log data in the specified directories will be transferred to the streaming processing component (receiver & parser). In this module, the log streams will be analyzed and converted into data types that the visualization will use to display the graphs.

3 System Design and Implementation

3.1 Servers

Based on the system architecture as well as the technologies selected, server configurations for system deployment (production) are listed in Table 2. Note that the system is flexible and scalable because it is deployed on Cloud AWS, so the table gives the minimum list for the system to work.

3.2 Apache Spark Streaming

Apache Spark Streaming is an extension of the core Apache Spark API that provides scalable, high-throughput and fault-tolerant stream processing of live data streams [6].

Table 2. List of servers used in the system.

No	Configuration			Type	Number	Function	Environment
	CPU (Cores)	RAM (Gb)	HDD (Gb)				
1	4	16	256	Virtual	1	Hadoop NameNode	Production
2	4	8	10240	Virtual	3	Hadoop DataNode	Production
3	4	16	1024	Virtual	1	Database	Production
4	4	8	100	Virtual	1	Web	Production

Data ingestion can be done from many sources like Kafka, Apache Flume, Amazon Kinesis or TCP sockets and processing can be done using complex algorithms that are expressed with high-level functions like map, reduce, join and window. Finally, processed data can be pushed out to file systems, databases and live dashboards. Its key abstraction is Apache Spark Discretized Stream or, in short, a Spark DStream, which represents a stream of data divided into small batches. DStreams are built on Spark RDDs, Spark's core data abstraction. This allows Streaming in Spark to seamlessly integrate with any other Apache Spark components like Spark MLlib and Spark SQL.

3.3   Apache Flume

Flume is a distributed, reliable, and available service for efficiently collecting, aggregating, and moving large amounts of log data [7]. It has a simple and flexible architecture based on streaming data flows. It is robust and faults tolerant with tunable reliability mechanisms and many failovers and recovery mechanisms. It uses a simple extensible data model that allows for online analytic application.

In this work, Apache Flume is used for transfer logs to HDFS as well as Apache Spark Streaming (Fig. 3). Just a simple configuration with a few steps is okay. This helps to build the system mainly in the analysis of log data.

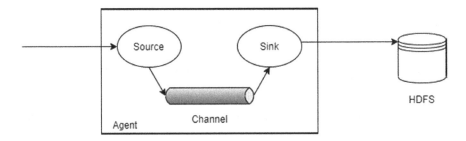

Fig. 3. Flume's operation.

The system uses a push approach, which means that the flume agent actively pushes the log onto Spark Streaming for processing log data (Fig. 4).

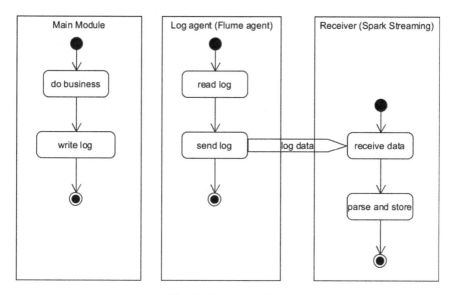

Fig. 4. Data processing.

According to this model, Flume Agent will actively read the log files in the specified folder and then transmit these log streams with Spark Streaming. The receiver then will analyze the log stream and continue to store data to the database or to HDFS.

3.4   Website Design

Regarding the representation of data in the form of graphs and charts, there are many tools like Apache Superset [8], Kibana [9], Grafana [10], etc.

All tools support various forms of data representation, but the data needs to be modified to suit the input format of each tool. This work has built Website management using PHP Laravel [11] and graphs using the Javascript library (ChartJS) [12].

Figures from 5 to 7 show the results after analyzing the log of different applications, including number of ad impressions, number of ad clicks, number of error transactions, number of successful transactions.

These results can help managers to make decisions. For example, Fig. 5 shows that the number of impressions for the ad with the orange line is significantly lower than the red line. If the cost for the orange line is higher than the cost for the red line, the corresponding ad to the orange line should stop. While from Fig. 6, on the 11th day, the output is low, Modifications to the image of the ad were subsequently made to increase the attractiveness. As a result, the number of clicks and the number of transactions increases.

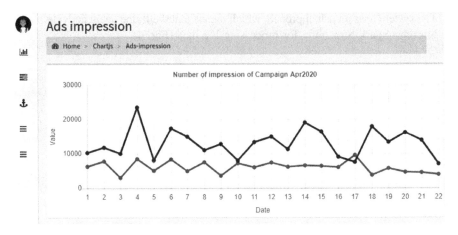

Fig. 5. Ads Impression.

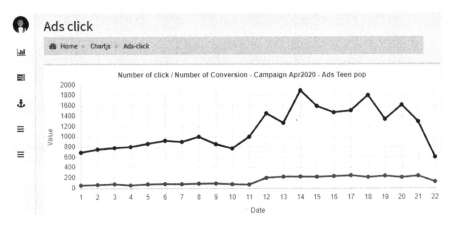

Fig. 6. Ads Click.

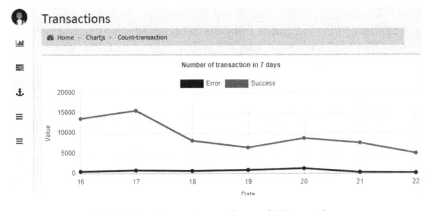

Fig. 7. Error Transaction vs Successful Transaction.

4 Conclusion and Perspectives

The paper presents the design and implementation of a system for logging and monitoring the streaming data. The system operates independently in parallel with the actual advertising system. The solution builds on open-source software Apache Flume, Apache Spark Streaming and some other open frameworks and libraries such as PHP Laravel, ChartJS, etc.

The system design allows for flexible scaling out. During the monitoring process, managers can rely on charts and analyzes to make strategic decisions. The system ensures the initiative of the business with a team of professional programmers available.

This solution is also fully applicable for similar company models and is also a good reference for research directions of Software engineering, Information System, etc.

References

1. Deha solution. https://deha.co.jp/
2. Srinivasa, K.G., Siddesh, G.M., Srinidhi, H.: Apache Flume, Network Data Analytics, pp 95–107 (2018). https://doi.org/10.1007/978-3-319-77800-6
3. Tenesaca-Luna, G.A., Imba D., Mora-Arciniegas, M.B., Segarra-Faggioni, V., Ramírez-Coronel, R.L.: Use of apache flume in the big data environment for processing and evaluation of the data quality of the twitter social network. In: Botto-Tobar, M., Barba-Maggi, L., González-Huerta, J., Villacrés-Cevallos, P., Gómez, O.S., Uvidia-Fassler, M. (eds) Information and Communication Technologies of Ecuador (TIC.EC). TICEC 2018. Advances in Intelligent Systems and Computing, vol. 884. Springer, Cham (2019). https://doi.org/10.1007/978-3-030-02828-2_23
4. Nasiri, H., Nasehi, S., Goudarzi, M.: Evaluation of distributed stream processing frameworks for IoT applications in Smart Cities. J. Big Data 6(1), 1–24 (2019). https://doi.org/10.1186/s40537-019-0215-2
5. Sharma, S.: Dynamic hashtag interactions and recommendations: an implementation using apache spark streaming and GraphX. In: Sharma, N., Chakrabarti, A., Balas, V.E. (eds.) Data Management, Analytics and Innovation. AISC, vol. 1042, pp. 723–738. Springer, Singapore (2020). https://doi.org/10.1007/978-981-32-9949-8_51
6. Spark Streaming Programming Guide (2020). https://spark.apache.org/docs/latest/streaming-programming-guide.html
7. (2020). https://flume.apache.org/
8. (2020). https://superset.incubator.apache.org/
9. (2020). https://www.elastic.co/kibana
10. (2020). https://grafana.com/grafana/
11. (2020). https://laravel.com/docs/7.x
12. (2020). https://www.chartjs.org/docs/latest/

Active Learning with Crowdsourcing for the Cold Start of Imbalanced Classifiers

Etienne Brangbour[1,2]([⊠]), Pierrick Bruneau[1], Thomas Tamisier[1], and Stéphane Marchand-Maillet[2]

[1] Luxembourg Institute of Science and Technology, Esch-sur-Alzette, Luxembourg
{etienne.brangbour,pierrick.bruneau,thomas.tamisier}@list.lu
[2] University of Geneva, Geneva, Switzerland
{etienne.brangbour,stephane.marchand-maillet}@unige.ch

Abstract. We present a novel cooperative strategy based on active learning and crowdsourcing, dedicated to provide a solution to the cold start stage, i.e. initializing the classification of a large set of data with no attached labels. The strategy is moreover designed to handle an imbalanced context in which random selection is highly inefficient. In this purpose, our method is guided by an unsupervised clustering, and the computation of cluster quality and impurity indexes, updated at each active learning step. The strategy is explained on a case study of annotating Twitter content w.r.t. a real flood event. We also show that our technique can cope with multiple heterogeneous data representations.

Keywords: Active learning · Imbalanced classification · Cold start

1 Introduction

Learning a classification model usually proceeds by fitting a model (e.g. feedforward neural networks [16], deep convolutional networks [20], SVM [26]) using independent labelled training and validation data sets. Trained models are then used in a production environment, where labels are unknown and to be predicted. However, in real applications, the labels are often implicit, i.e. experts and users are able to tell to which class a given data item belongs to, but this operation is time consuming and costly. Large data sets are hence initially completely unlabelled, or only a small portion is labelled.

Methods from the active learning domain come as support in such situations [27]. In brief, starting from an initial classification model estimated using a small subset of labeled data (comparatively to the amount of unlabelled data that has been collected), the core of active learning is to design strategies for sampling data items from the large unlabelled collection in a way that will be most likely to improve the classifier. Such data are submitted for annotation by oracle, per batches or one by one. Returned labelled elements are integrated to the model

© Springer Nature Switzerland AG 2020
Y. Luo (Ed.): CDVE 2020, LNCS 12341, pp. 192–201, 2020.
https://doi.org/10.1007/978-3-030-60816-3_22

training set and the classification model is retrained. The procedure is iterated until some convergence criterion is matched, or a predefined maximum amount of annotation is reached.

The oracle in charge of attributing labels to the selected elements can take different natures such as a server with limited access, but most likely one or several human beings, expert or not, in an interactive and collaborative system. In a case that requires a massive amount of annotation such as social media analysis, it is possible to introduce crowdsourcing as an oracle [2]. However, crowdsourcing introduces problems such as fuzzy labeling [23], that can be safely assumed as controlled in the context of this paper.

Within this general scheme, methods from the active learning domain are distinguished mostly according to their sampling strategy [27]. For instance, uncertainty sampling strategies query elements in region where a tentative classifier, trained with the small labeled data set, is the least confident. Query-by-committee uses ensembles of models to reduce disagreement among models.

Imbalanced training sets are problematic for learning classification models. For simplicity, elements from the minority class(es) are called *positive*, and elements from the majority class(es) *negative*. Some ways to circumvent this imbalance issue have been proposed in the literature [9]. However, in the context of active learning, this yields a *chicken and egg problem*: sampling an initial training set at random is highly likely to yield only negative elements. The initial resulting classifier will hence be poor, harming any active learning strategy. This leads to poor convergence, that contradicts the spirit of active learning that aims at *efficient labelling*.

We consider such a cold start context, that can be reasonably assumed to be highly imbalanced. More specifically, the relevant content (or positive class) is expected to be the minority class, whereas there will be a wealth of irrelevant content. This is a typical *needle in the haystack* problem. Our intuition is to guide the selection strategy of an active learning process by a clustering structure. Using a clustering structure as a canvas for active learning has already been considered in the literature [19], but to our knowledge, never as a solution to a cold start issue in an imbalanced classification context.

2   Proposed Active Learning Strategy

Let us consider a partially labelled data set $X = \{x_n\}_{n \in [\![1,N]\!]}$. Individual x_n can be assumed as numerical vectors, so X is the corresponding matrix. We also consider C possible ground truth classes for elements, indexed with integers from 1 to C. In the context of this paper, we limit our interest to $C = 2$ (i.e. imbalanced problem with rare positive elements), but the technical description in this section can be generalized straightforwardly. We build the set $t = \{t_n\}_{n \in [\![1,N]\!]}$ of partial labels, with 0 as the placeholder for missing labels, and $t_n \in [\![1,C]\!]$ otherwise. The set of labelled elements is then $\{n|t_n > 0\}$.

Let us also assume a clustering algorithm has been applied to X, yielding K clusters, and a set of N cluster labels $y = \{y_n\}_{n \in [\![1,N]\!]}$ with $y_n \in [\![1,K]\!]$. A stage of an active learning process consists in selecting elements to be annotated by an oracle (e.g. user in an interactive setting), and update the selection strategy according to the response. Let us suppose we are able to compute two indexes at any stage of the process, for any cluster $k \in [\![1, K]\!]$:

- Cluster quality $q_k \in [0, 1]$. Intuitively, q_k being close to 1 indicates a highly compact and well separated cluster. Common cluster quality metrics are the Silhouette index [25], the Calinski-Harabasz index [8], the Davies-Bouldin index [10], and the cluster conductance [1].
- Impurity estimate $p_k \in [0, 1]$. Intuitively, p_k being close to 1 indicates a cluster with uniformly random known ground truth labels, whereas p_k close to 0 indicates clusters with only 1 known ground truth label. Common metric that relate clusters to a ground truth are the Adjusted Rand Index [17], the Adjusted Mutual Information [29], Homogeneity [24] and the Fowlkes-Mallows index [14].

The rationale of the proposed method is to collect annotation labels that would be possibly propagated reliably within clusters, using e.g. k-nearest neighbors classifiers, or label propagation techniques such as [31]. Also, we want to sample preferably in high quality clusters, as propagation in them is likely to be more effective. Regarding impurity, we will preferably sample in clusters with high estimated impurity, as more labels will be hereby needed for reliable propagation. Though the most interesting from the application point of view, if a cluster has low p_k w.r.t. the positive class, and high q_k, we may propagate the positive label reliably, so further queries from elements in this cluster are unnecessary. Impurity is initially assumed to be maximal in all clusters, and can hence only be potentially reduced as the active learning process progresses.

At each active learning step, data items to be annotated by the oracle are sampled in clusters which hold the highest $p_k + q_k$. p_k is updated according to the oracle feedback. The underlying assumption is that clusters with high q_k will be quickly associated to low p_k, hence a small number of labels can be reliably propagated. Reciprocally, clusters with lower q_k will be associated to higher p_k, hence concentrating the annotation effort.

The proposed active learning loop and query strategy is summarized in Fig. 1. The fact that we want to rate clusters individually limits the possible candidates taken from the literature in supervised (i.e. that relate cluster labels to a ground truth class) and unsupervised (i.e. use only the cluster distribution in the data representation space) cluster quality criteria. We must have a criterion that scales in $[0, 1]$ for each cluster, which occurs when the considered criterion aggregates cluster-wise values, e.g. using average, minimum or maximum functions. In the next two subsection, we show that Adjusted Mutual Information and cluster conductance enforce this property, and use them in the context of our active learning strategy afterwards.

2.1 Impurity Criterion

For now, we assume we have no missing labels in the ground truth t. In the supervised case, we consider $P_y(k)$ the probability of cluster label k, and $P_t(c)$ the probability of true label c, formally:

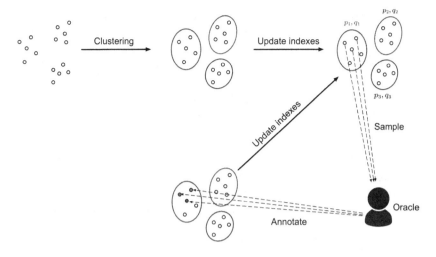

Fig. 1. Proposed active learning loop and query strategy.

$$P_y(k) = \frac{\sum_n^N \mathbb{1}_{y_n=k}}{N}, \qquad P_t(c) = \frac{\sum_n^N \mathbb{1}_{t_n=c}}{N}$$

H_y and H_t are the respective entropies. Likewise, we define:

$$P(k,c) = \frac{\sum_n^N \mathbb{1}_{y_n=k\&t_n=c}}{N}$$

The Mutual Information (MI) and Adjusted Mutual Information (AMI) [29] between the clustering and the ground truth class are then defined as:

$$\mathrm{MI}(y,t) = \sum_{k=1}^K \sum_{c=1}^C P(k,c) \log \frac{P(k,c)}{P_y(k)P_t(c)} \tag{1}$$

$$\mathrm{AMI}(y,t) = \frac{\mathrm{MI}(y,t) - \mathbb{E}[\mathrm{MI}(y,t)]}{\mathrm{mean}(H_y, H_t) - \mathbb{E}[\mathrm{MI}(y,t)]} \tag{2}$$

where $\mathbb{E}[\mathrm{MI}(y,t)]$ is obtained using k-combinations under the assumption of random cluster assignments. High MI means the clustering is close to recovering the ground truth. As Eq. (1) is summed over possible cluster labels, MI and AMI can be decomposed per cluster as:

$$\mathrm{MI}_k(t) = \sum_c P(k,c) \log \frac{P(k,c)}{P_y(k)P_t(c)} \tag{3}$$

$$\mathrm{AMI}_k(t) = \frac{\mathrm{MI}_k(t) - \mathbb{E}[\mathrm{MI}_k(t)]}{H_t - \mathbb{E}[\mathrm{MI}_k(t)]} \tag{4}$$

where $\mathbb{E}[\mathrm{MI}_k(t)]$ restricts the k-combinations calculations to a single cluster. We note that $\sum_k \mathrm{MI}_k(t) = MI(y,t)$, but $\sum_k \mathrm{AMI}_k(t) \neq \mathrm{AMI}(y,t)$ in general, as the point of AMI is to rescale the criterion in $[0, 1]$. As AMI_k will be maximal when only one true label is observed in the cluster, a possible impurity criterion is $p_k = 1 - \mathrm{AMI}_k$.

This naturally extends to the case where t includes missing labels. As $\lim_{x \to 0} x \log x = 0$, when no label falls in cluster k we have $\mathrm{MI}_k(t) = 0$, which ensures the criterion is smooth, and yields maximal associated impurity p_k with absence of ground truth information as required previously.

2.2 Cluster Quality Criterion

Few unsupervised quality criteria can be decomposed per-cluster in a straight-forward manner. The conductance [1] offers this possibility, while having been recognized as showing good agreement to supervised criteria in the context of graph clustering [13], and no explicit requirement of spherical clusters. Using it requires converting pairwise distances d_{ij} to edge weights (or similarities) w_{ij} scaled in $[0, 1]$, which can be easily performed e.g. using $w_{ij} = e^{-d_{ij}^2}$.

Let k be a cluster index. Let also I_k the set of members of cluster k, i.e. the subset of $[\![1, N]\!]$ so that $i \in I_k$ iif $y_i = k$. The conductance of cluster k is defined as:

$$\Phi_k = 1 - \frac{\sum_{i \in I_k, j \notin I_k} w_{ij}}{\min(a_k, a_{\bar{k}})} \tag{5}$$

with $a_k = \sum_{i \in I_k, j \in [\![1,N]\!]} w_{ij}$ and $a_{\bar{k}} = \sum_{i \notin I_k, j \in [\![1,N]\!]} w_{ij}$. Maximal conductance means a dense and well separated cluster. Per-cluster conductance already ranges in $[0, 1]$, e.g. the overall conductance of a clustering is obtained by averaging per-cluster conductance. This means conductance can be used as a cluster quality criterion q_k. Also, conductance accounts for cluster size, i.e. intrinsically to its definition, small outlying but compact clusters will have low conductance. We verified this is indeed the case with validation experiments using UCI data sets [12].

3 Application Use Case

3.1 Spatio-Temporal and Social Media Context

In the context of the Publimape project (*Public information mapped to Environmental Events*, see Sect. 5), that addresses the exploitation of geo-localized information from social media, we focus on the detection of Twitter posts created by users witnessing floods during and after the Harvey tropical storm that occurred in 2017 in Texas, USA [21]. In this context, the positive (and scarce *a priori*) class is the set of posts matching our focus, and the negative class is everything else (including general discussions and news, jokes, memes, advertisement).

As Twitter analysis is more relevant in urban areas, we focused on Houston urban surroundings. Using the Twitter APIs, we collected a corpus of 7.5M tweets. In order to increase the potential recall of the relevant posts, we did not use textual query filters, and collected all content matching the spatio-temporal bounds displayed in Fig. 2a, that encompass the storm and ensuing floods. The spatial area of interest has been determined according to prior analyses of Hurricane Harvey impacts [21]. Details about the corpus collection, pre-processing, and descriptive analysis are described to further extent in [5]. However, increasing recall comes with a higher risk of collecting irrelevant content, thus increasing the imbalance problem that motivated the approach described in this paper. Indeed, among 6571 manually annotated tweets sampled randomly in our corpus, we found only 7.6% tweets from the positive class.

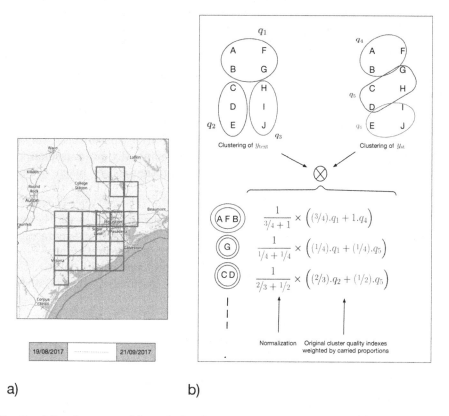

Fig. 2. *a)* Spatio-temporal bounds for the Twitter corpus collection. *b)* Illustration of the Cartesian product between clustering vectors y_{text} and y_{st} translated into cluster quality index combination.

3.2 Data Representation

In our experiments, we use a subset of 25k tweets extracted at random from our corpus. We analyze Twitter posts from two perspectives: their textual content, and their spatio-temporal coordinates. Applying classification or clustering algorithms to textual content typically requires a preprocessing step, where the piece of text is *embedded* in a high-dimensional numerical space, hence facilitating further calculations. Common such embeddings are TF-IDF [18], which is based on word frequencies, and Word2Vec [22], which exploits word co-occurence. Prior work on the corpus described above used the TF-IDF representation space [4]. In the latter, the objective has been to estimate flooding probabilities across space and time, discretized in spatio-temporal cells. However, this representation space is sparse, and Twitter posts are short and not curated, with many word variants due to, amongst other origins, misspelling errors, abbreviations or parts of speech. This issue was previously tackled using a spatio-temporal cell structure to perform the stacking of tweets [4]. But in this paper we address the labelling of individual tweets, which calls for another approach.

For the experiments, we use a character-based language model, trained for a hashtag prediction task [11]. Specifically, we use the 500-dimensional output vectors trained as specified in [11] as textual embedding. Transferring such latent representations trained for another task is a common practice in the machine learning literature, e.g. the last layers of convolutional models trained on general-purpose benchmarks are reused in a flood-related task in [7]. As the ultimate objective is to estimate flooding probability in spatio-temporal cells, spatio-temporal coordinates are also a relevant representation space. Intuitively, we would like to propagate tweets labels in a spatio-temporally aware fashion.

We extracted clusters using the two representation spaces taken independently. Hence, according to definitions used in Sect. 2, we obtain two cluster label vectors, y_{text} and y_{st} (where st stands for *spatio-temporal*). y_{st} is extracted using Gaussian mixtures estimated using the EM algorithm [3], with the number of cluster chosen heuristically as the number of days that separates the first tweet from the last in the dataset. y_{text} is obtained using Affinity Propagation [15] combined to local scaling [30] in order to cope with local variations of data density in the language model space. y_{text} features 47 clusters, and y_{st} 24 clusters.

3.3 Combining Cluster Quality Indexes

Combining heterogeneous representation spaces as described in the previous section can be related to subspace clustering [28]. However, in our case the aim is to use spatio-temporally homogeneous clusters, so we rather consider the Cartesian product of two clustering structures. Formally, we build $y_{\text{text}\times\text{st}}$ out of independent cluster label vectors. 1128 clusters result from this product, with many singletons or very small clusters.

p_k indexes only depend on the distribution of ground truth classes in clusters, so they can be computed in clusters of the Cartesian product in a straightforward way. However, q_k indexes depend on a data representation space, which is composite in our application context. We propose to reuse q_k computed w.r.t. textual and spatio-temporal representation spaces separately, and average and weigh them according to the portion of the original cluster they carry in the Cartesian product (see illustration in Fig. 2b).

For high-dimensional data, distance-based criteria suffer from the curse of dimensionality. Indeed, the distribution of pairwise distances follows a χ^2 distribution with the dimensionality d as parameter [6]. As $\mathbb{E}(x) = d$ for $x \sim \chi_d^2$, the expected distance grows linearly as the underlying dimensionality increases, which lead to ill-behaved criteria (e.g. BIC in [6]). A possibility exposed here is to remap distances according to $F_{\chi_c^2}^{-1}(F_{\chi_d^2})$, with $c < d$. We use this technique to ensure that indexes computed using different representations (e.g. space-time or textual embeddings) can be compared, and be combined meaningfully. In our context, we use $d = 500$ and $c = 3$, so that textual and spatio-temporal representation spaces are reconciled.

4   Conclusion

A first important point in this paper has been to expose the peculiarities when trying to combine active learning methods to imbalanced classification problems. We motivated the use of clustering in this context, and described an approach based on the combination of impurity and cluster quality indexes, re-evaluated at each active learning iterations. In addition, we disclosed a way to combine the information carried by multiple subspaces, illustrated by our use case about extracting spatio-temporally aware information from a Twitter corpus.

Once a sufficient number of labels is acquired (i.e. in the range of thousands), language models can be fine-tuned to the task at hand. The approach exposed in this paper can be used to efficiently bootstrap this fine-tuning step. It can then be re-applied after updating the textual representation space and reusing previously collected labels.

A limitation in the previous approach is that the clustering structure may be poorly aligned with the positive label density. Ideally, we would like the granularity of the clustering structure guiding the active learning strategy to adapt to the label feedback. An idea would be to exploit the dendrogram resulting from a hierarchical clustering method, such as Hierarchical Agglomerative Clustering (HAC). However, combining dendrograms is not trivial, and cannot be performed according to a Cartesian product as exposed in this paper.

Acknowledgements. This work was performed in the context of the Publimape project, funded by the CORE programme of the Luxembourgish National Research Fund (FNR).

References

1. Almeida, H., Guedes, D., Meira, W., Zaki, M.J.: Is there a best quality metric for graph clusters? In: Gunopulos, D., Hofmann, T., Malerba, D., Vazirgiannis, M. (eds.) ECML PKDD 2011. LNCS (LNAI), vol. 6911, pp. 44–59. Springer, Heidelberg (2011). https://doi.org/10.1007/978-3-642-23780-5_13

2. Anthony, B., Derek, G., Pádraig, C.: Using crowdsourcing and active learning to track sentiment in online media, pp. 145–150. https://doi.org/10.3233/978-1-60750-606-5-14. http://www.medra.org/servlet/aliasResolver?alias=iospressISSNISBN&issn=0922-6389&volume=215&spage=145

3. Bishop, C.: Pattern Recognition and Machine Learning. Information Science and Statistics, 1st edn. pp. xx, 738. Springer, New York (2006)

4. Brangbour, E., et al.: Computing flood probabilities using Twitter: application to the Houston urban area during Harvey. In: 9th International Workshop on Climate Informatics (2019)

5. Brangbour, E., et al.: Extracting localized information from a Twitter corpus for flood prevention. arXiv:1903.04748 (2019)

6. Bruneau, P., Otjacques, B.: A probabilistic model selection criterion for spectral clustering. Intell. Data Anal. **22**(5), 1059–1077 (2018)

7. Bruneau, P., Tamisier, T.: Transfer learning and mixed input deep neural networks for estimating flood severity in news content. In: MediaEval Multimedia Evaluation Workshop (2019)

8. Caliński, T., Harabasz, J.: A dendrite method for cluster analysis. Commun. Stat. **3**(1), 1–27 (1974)

9. Chawla, N., Bowyer, K., Hall, L., Kegelmeyer, W.: SMOTE: synthetic minority over-sampling technique. J. Artif. Intell. Res. **16**, 321–357 (2002)

10. Davies, D., Bouldin, D.: A cluster separation measure. IEEE Trans. Pattern Anal. Mach. Intell. PAMI, 1(2), 224–227 (1979)

11. Dhingra, B., Zhou, Z., Fitzpatrick, D., Muehl, M., Cohen, W.: Tweet2Vec: Character-Based Distributed Representations for Social Media. arXiv:1605.03481 (2016)

12. Dua, D., Graff, C.: UCI machine learning repository (2017). http://archive.ics.uci.edu/ml

13. Emmons, S., Kobourov, S., Gallant, M., Börner, K.: Analysis of network clustering algorithms and cluster quality metrics at scale. PLOS One **11**(7), e0159161 (2016)

14. Fowlkes, E.B., Mallows, C.L.: A method for comparing two hierarchical clusterings. J. Am. Stat. Assoc. **78**(383), 553–569 (1983)

15. Frey, B., Dueck, D.: Clustering by passing messages between data points. Science **315**(5814), 972–976 (2007)

16. Glorot, X., Bengio, Y.: Understanding the difficulty of training deep feedforward neural networks. In: AISTATS, pp. 249–256 (2010)

17. Hubert, L., Arabie, P.: Comparing partitions. J. Classif. **2**(1), 193–218 (1985)

18. Joachims, T.: Text categorization with Support Vector Machines: Learning with many relevant features. In: Nédellec, C., Rouveirol, C. (eds.) ECML 1998. LNCS, vol. 1398, pp. 137–142. Springer, Heidelberg (1998). https://doi.org/10.1007/BFb0026683

19. Kang, J., Ryu, K.R., Kwon, H.-C.: Using Cluster-Based Sampling to Select Initial Training Set for Active Learning in Text Classification. In: Dai, H., Srikant, R., Zhang, C. (eds.) PAKDD 2004. LNCS (LNAI), vol. 3056, pp. 384–388. Springer, Heidelberg (2004). https://doi.org/10.1007/978-3-540-24775-3_46

20. Krizhevsky, A., Sutskever, I., Hinton, G.: ImageNet classification with deep convolutional neural networks. Adv. Neural Inform. Process. Sys. **25**, 1097–1105 (2012)

21. Matgen, P., et al.: Integrating Data Streams from in-situ Measurements, Social Networks and Satellite Earth Observation to Augment Operational Flood Monitoring and Forecasting: the 2017 Hurricane Season in the Americas as a Large-scale Test Case. AGU Fall Meeting Abstracts 31 (2017)

22. Mikolov, T., Chen, K., Corrado, G., Dean, J.: Efficient Estimation of Word Representations in Vector Space. arXiv:1301.3781 (2013)
23. Nowak, S., Rüger, S.: How reliable are annotations via crowdsourcing: a study about inter-annotator agreement for multi-label image annotation. In: Proceedings of the International Conference on Multimedia Information Retrieval - MIR'10, p. 557. ACM Press. https://doi.org/10.1145/1743384.1743478. http://portal.acm.org/citation.cfm?doid=1743384.1743478
24. Rosenberg, A., Hirschberg, J.: V-Measure: a conditional entropy-based external cluster evaluation measure. In: Proceedings of the 2007 Joint Conference on Empirical Methods in Natural Language Processing and Computational Natural Language Learning (EMNLP-CoNLL), pp. 410–420 (2007)
25. Rousseeuw, P.: Silhouettes: a graphical aid to the interpretation and validation of cluster analysis. J. Comput. Appl. Math. **20**, 53–65 (1987)
26. Scholkopf, B., Smola, A.: Learning with Kernels: Support Vector Machines, Regularization, Optimization, and Beyond. MIT Press, Cambridge, MA, USA (2001)
27. Settles, B.: Active learning literature survey. Technical report. University of Wisconsin-Madison Department of Computer Sciences (2009). https://minds.wisconsin.edu/handle/1793/60660
28. Vidal, R.: Subspace clustering. IEEE Sig. Proc. Mag. **28**(2), 52–68 (2011)
29. Vinh, N., Epps, J., Bailey, J.: Information theoretic measures for clusterings comparison: variants, properties, normalization and correction for chance. J. Mach. Learn. Res. **11**(95), 2837–2854 (2010)
30. Zelnik-Manor, L., Perona, P.: Self-tuning spectral clustering. In: Advances in Neural Information Processing Systems 17, pp. 1601–1608. MIT Press (2005)
31. Zhu, X., Gharamani, Z.: Learning from labeled and unlabeled data with label propagation. Technical report. CMU-CALD-02-107, Carnegie Mellon University (2002)

A Dynamic Visualization Platform for Operational Maritime Cybersecurity

Hanning Zhao$^{(\boxtimes)}$ and Bilhanan Silverajan

Tampere University, Tampere, Finland
{hanning.zhao,bilhanan.silverajan}@tuni.fi

Abstract. Increasing cyberattacks in the maritime industry have high-lighted the need for innovative approaches for effective cybersecurity responses. Considering the multiple stakeholders involved in maritime, collaboration and information sharing are essential for responding to cyber incidents and mitigation. However operational cybersecurity awareness is currently very low. This short paper presents the ongoing development of a dynamic security visualization platform for operational maritime cybersecurity. The platform can flexibly support collaboration among multiple stakeholders in the port ecosystem, while introducing multiple security roles to increase situational awareness. It also provides interfaces for communication among these roles as well as offering composable visualization widgets that can be customized to user needs.

Keywords: Maritime cybersecurity · Operational Visualization · Cooperative Platform

1 Introduction

The maritime industry is essential to the global economy, and is rapidly entering a new era of digital transformation to increase operational intelligence. Harbours are aggressively engaged in activities to enhance their infrastructure with the integration of Industrial Internet of Things (IoT) and autonomously operating equipment. Two examples are Singapore's Tuas Mega Port project, which includes unmanned vehicles, drones and cranes, as well as the port of Rotterdam, which is developing a digital "twin" replica of operations using IoT sensors, Augmented Reality (AR) and Artificial Intelligence (AI) [5,8].

Maritime cybersecurity awareness however, is comparatively low against other industries such as aviation, rail and logistics. Many ports, and shore-based fleet operation systems still depend on legacy or outdated technology, and insecure practices abound such as using default or easy-to-guess credentials for operation centers and bridge control systems. Phishing attacks as well as ransomware and malware infections are increasingly being reported around the world targeting harbours [3]. Because of its inherent nature of being a multi-stakeholder industry, an attack on one actor can have very severe repercussions

© Springer Nature Switzerland AG 2020
Y. Luo (Ed.): CDVE 2020, LNCS 12341, pp. 202–208, 2020.
https://doi.org/10.1007/978-3-030-60816-3_23

on many related companies in the manufacturing, logistics and cargo handling industries [1].

The maritime industry has also been accused of being slow to respond to these threats. Even when endpoint protection is present, at times cybersecurity incidents go undetected for long periods of time, and communicating these incidents among different stakeholders occurs verbally or informally as SMS, phone or even fax messages. Therefore better ways of observing operational security threats, and increased collaboration among various parties to co-ordinate and combat them, are needed.

This short paper describes ongoing work in a national project to increase maritime cybersecurity awareness and visualize operational cybersecurity for small and medium sized Finnish ports, primarily serving cargo traffic. A user-friendly cybersecurity visualization platform is being developed to identify perceived threats and risks to port assets, as well as the rapid detection and collaborative responses to emerging cybersecurity attacks. "Port assets" in this paper refer not only to hardware and software systems and associated infrastructure at the terminal itself, but also include the sensors, gateways, smart devices (such as cameras and radar equipment) situated close-by in the navigational channels near the port (called the fairway). The design utilizes a variety of visualization widgets to assist multiple security roles, beyond the network monitoring and analysis, towards delivering an overall picture of cybersecurity management.

The paper's structure is as follows: Sect. 2 presents related work. Section 3 outlines the aims and main requirements of the platform. Section 4 describes the ongoing design. Section 5 concludes the paper.

2   Related Work

Research in cybersecurity visualization for the maritime domain is limited, although visualization research in other cybersecurity domains have resulted in a diverse range of visualization tools. For network security, McKenna et al. [6] proposed an interactive dashboard called BubbleNet for aiding network analysts and managers to identify patterns of anomalous network behaviour. The design provides inspiration of using visualization to facilitate the communications between multiple stakeholders. BubbleNet only visualizes the alerts in a worldwide map without allowing any further actions by users. Arendt et al. [2] developed Ocelot, the security dashboard for supporting cyber analysts in dynamic network management and defence. It primarily assists analysts with threats and quarantines compromised cyber assets from other healthy network. However, as the dashboard has been implemented solely for network analysis, it lacks the ability for visualizing other cyber assets and for collaborations. Another immersive solution for cybersecurity was proposed by Kabil et al. [4]. The platform is developed in a virtual environment with 3D visualizations and mostly used for training and data analysis. This work indicates the visualizations for collaboration among multiple user roles, though the 3D interfaces are quite limited and only can host simple scenarios. The Azure security center of Microsoft is a unified infrastructure of cybersecurity for organizations to manage policy and compliance, security estates and protect against threats [7]. It provides open source tools for monitoring security posture and organizations can customize the solutions based on their business goals.

3   Aims and Platform Requirements

The aim of the platform is two-fold: Firstly to visualize the operational cybersecurity for real-time situational awareness in a port based on the role of the human user. Secondly, to provide customisable and dynamic interfaces and tools to effectively coordinate and communicate incident responses with multiple stakeholders. The following requirements are being targeted:

1. *Multiple port assets and stakeholders.* Considering the diversity of maritime infrastructure and services, the platform should prepare for the analysis of heterogeneous security incidents to evaluate the status of harbour-side, fairway and fleet operational cybersecurity. It also needs to deliver dynamic visualizations for facilitating the collaboration and information sharing among port stakeholders while assisting their respective operations.
2. *Real-time visualization.* The platform should enable real-time monitoring of the cybersecurity posture specific to the port environment and its assets. By visualizing such real-time data across the harbour and fairway environment it gives human operators situational awareness and understanding of ongoing cyber incidents and empowers them to respond faster. That also leads to a timely analysis of threats and attacks and devising efficient countermeasures.
3. *Consider supply chain trust.* The majority of port equipment, systems and services are obtained and integrated from multiple companies and manufacturers in the port ecosystem. Thus the security in the system supply chain is another challenging aspect in the maritime context. This should be included and visualized for communication and investigation amongst the multiple stakeholders responsible for cyber risks in the life-cycle of assets.
4. *Flexibility and Scalability.* The design of visualizations should provide customize services based on the needs and roles of different stakeholders. The cybersecurity team can work with other stakeholders, including vessel owners and operators, to maintain robust operational security. Well-defined interfaces for visualizing security data from third parties should be provided by the platform, in addition to integrating and interoperating with services of existing port systems.

4   Platform Design

In this section, the platform design is described in terms of role based visualization. Then a scenario in which multiple stakeholders collaborate to respond to a potential malware infection is presented.

Role-Based Visualizations. The platform serves as a comprehensive dashboard for real-time monitoring and evaluating the security posture of the port.

Three roles for stakeholders are currently defined for which a range of dynamic visualizations tailored to the specific needs of each role are provided:

- *Security analysts*, who are cybersecurity specialists responsible for investigating the threats and attacks. Each stakeholder in the port can have their own team of security analysts. They flag threats, attacks and corrective responses undertaken on port assets to operators and report incidents to their responsible managers.
- *Terminal operators*, focus on the holistic view of security posture and handle reports from security analysts. Each terminal only has 1 team of operators who may or may not have a cybersecurity background. They will be informed of the major risks, threats and the overall performance of port assets.
- *Managers*, responsible for maintaining the overall cybersecurity of each stakeholder and communicating with other stakeholder security teams as well as terminal operators.

For each role, the platform provides dynamic and customizable visualizations to support collaboration. For example, the designed visualizations allow analysts to investigate the threats and incidents. However, the interfaces for terminal operators includes the summary of security posture and major alerts. Figure 1 depicts the partial platform populated with several visualization widgets: Fig. 1(a) is mainly for terminal operators while Fig. 1(b) shows the interfaces for analysts to inspect port assets and report incidents. The interfaces in Fig. 1(a) provide terminal operators an awareness of the overall port cybersecurity posture by displaying a comparative analysis of threats and incidents along with their tendency. It also provides monitoring widgets of port assets associated with risks and alert widgets which consist of the latest incidents informed by analysts and managers. Alerts are highlighted with different colours presenting the severity level to deliver more effective operations. For analysts, Fig. 1(b) illustrates visualization widgets for attack types and vulnerability analysis. The

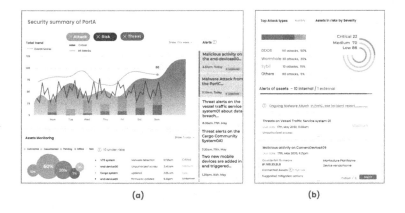

(a)   (b)

Fig. 1. Several views of the platform for terminal operators and analysts.

interfaces also support analysts communicating to other stakeholders after investigating potential malicious behaviour. One example depicts a shared incident of an unauthorized access to the vessel traffic service system. Another incident reveals the security risks of the supply chain, where a sensor of a fairway camera has been discovered with counterfeit firmware. The analysts can classify such risks and take actions towards mitigation. Then they can flag this device to notify operators and report the incident to managers who communicate with other stakeholders such as manufacturers and vendors. Manufacturers can immediately respond to such faults by replacing the firmware and investigating other potential risks in production lines.

Collaborative Cybersecurity Defence of Ports. The platform's design takes into account the necessary interfaces for supporting sharing cybersecurity incident reports and well as the coordination of incident responses and defences among the multiple stakeholders in the maritime domain. As an example, consider a cybersecurity incident report received by one or more managers at the port which details an active malware infection either at another port, or within the systems and devices of one of the stakeholders. The communication workflow among the multiple roles is described in Fig. 2(a). Managers will coordinate responses at the port by initially sharing the incident report to their team of analysts. Figure 1(b), described earlier in this section, illustrates the notifications and correlated alerts received by analysts from their manager. Analysts subsequently perform a vulnerability assessment of port assets under their control which could potentially be targeted by a similar attack and keep both managers as well as operators informed about undertaken responses. Figure 2(b) depicts how potentially risky and insecure port assets are flagged to provide terminal operators an up-to-date view of the current state of operational cybersecurity. This allows terminal operators to comprehend easily which port systems should be monitored more carefully in the short to medium term, while analysts remedy the situation. The platform would also allow managers to simultaneously observe and coordinate with other managers and associated teams of analysts in the port, if a larger-scale action is deemed necessary.

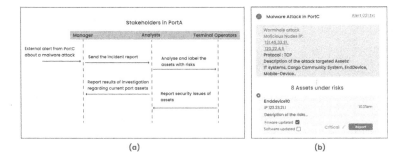

(a)   (b)

Fig. 2. Communication workflow and interfaces for analysts to flag risky assets.

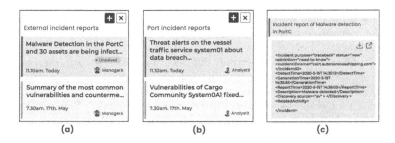

Fig. 3. The widgets of incident reports and details of one report.

The dashboard space provided by platform is designed to be editable by all the users belonging to the different roles, and be flexibly customised with different visualization widgets depending on their needs. Figures 3(a) and (b) provide widgets for managers depicting incoming incident reports and responses from both external stakeholders as well as from security analysts. Figure 3(c) shows a snippet of an incident report.

5 Conclusion and Further Research

In this paper we presented the initial results of a platform for improving multi-stakeholder collaboration and communication for maritime cybersecurity. Future work includes conducting user tests and design of interfaces, widgets and other functionality, such as automated response sharing and handling.

Acknowledgement. DIMECC Sea4Value FFN program funded this work.

References

1. Greenberg, A.: The Untold Story of NotPetya, the most devastating cyberattack. http://web.archive.org/web/20190412165908/https://www.wired.com/story/notpetya-cyberattack-ukraine-russia-code-crashed-the-world/
2. Arendt, D.L., et al.: Ocelot: user-centered design of a decision support visualization for network quarantine. In: 2015 IEEE Symposium on Visualization for Cyber Security (VizSec), pp. 1–8. IEEE (2015)
3. Johnson, J.: Ports of Barcelona and San Diego hit by cyber attacks. http://web.archive.org/web/20190411124543/https://www.imarest.org/themarineprofessional/item/4473-ports-of-barcelona-and-san-diego-hit-by-cyber-attacks
4. Kabil, A., Duval, T., Cuppens, N., Le Comte, G., Halgand, Y., Ponchel, C.: 3D CyberCOP: A Collaborative Platform for Cybersecurity Data Analysis and Training. In: Luo, Y. (ed.) CDVE 2018. LNCS, vol. 11151, pp. 176–183. Springer, Cham (2018). https://doi.org/10.1007/978-3-030-00560-3_24
5. Maritime Singapore Connect: 5 Things You Should Know About The New Tuas Mega Port. https://www.maritimesgconnect.com/features/spotlight/5-things-you-should-know-about-new-tuas-mega-port

6. McKenna, S., Staheli, D., Fulcher, C., Meyer, M.: Bubblenet: a cyber security dashboard for visualizing patterns. Comput. Graph. Forum **35**, 281–290 (2016). Wiley Online Library
7. Microsoft: Overview of the Microsoft 365 security center. https://docs.microsoft.com/en-us/microsoft-365/security/mtp/overview-security-center?view=o365-worldwide
8. Campfens, V., Dekker, C.: Turning Rotterdam into the World's Smartest Port with IBM Cloud & IoT. http://web.archive.org/web/20190301165941/https://www.ibm.com/blogs/think/2018/01/smart-port-rotterdam/

Collaborative Visual Analytics Using Blockchain

Darius Coelho[1]([⊠]), Rubin Trailor[2], Daniel Sill[3], Sophie Engle[2], Alark Joshi[2],
Serge Mankovskii[3], Maria Velez-Rojas[3], Steven Greenspan[3],
and Klaus Mueller[1]

[1] Stony Brook University, Stony Brook, NY 11790, USA
`dcoelho@cs.stonybrook.edu`
[2] University of San Fransisco, San Francisco, CA 94117, USA
[3] New York, USA

Abstract. Blockchain, a decentralized, distributed and encrypted ledger, was created to eliminate the need for a central trusted entity. Blockchains provide users with a secure, trusted, auditable, and immutable record of transactions and are applicable to systems that require a trustworthy record of information. Our work explores the use of blockchain in collaborative visual analytics systems where users share and store a record of the visual analysis of some data. We built *Share.va*, a framework that allows users to store and share the states of visual analytics dashboards through a blockchain. We apply *Share.va* to an existing visual analytics dashboard and conduct a pilot study to understand the effectiveness and limitations of blockchain in collaborative visual analytics.

Keywords: Collaborative visualization · Provenance · Blockchain

1 Introduction

In the collaborative analysis of data, analysts need to share data analysis tools, visualizations, and maintain a shareable history of their explorations. Such an auditable record is essential to shared decision making [5]. At the same time, to ensure trust among collaborators, their content must remain private and secure when being shared [8]. For example, in the collaborative analysis of medical records, multiple doctors and medical technicians may need to analyze a patient's sensitive data in order to diagnose the patient. Here, the patient needs to ensure that only trusted doctors and technicians analyze and share the data. The inherent properties of blockchain make it a viable candidate to support such scenarios. It's encryption based distributed consensus mechanism ensures that the blockchain only logs trusted updates and the log is authentic and unchangeable.

D. Sill, S. Mankovskii, M. Velez-Rojas and S. Greenspan—Independent Researcher, This research was conducted while the authors were at CA Technologies, USA.

© Springer Nature Switzerland AG 2020
Y. Luo (Ed.): CDVE 2020, LNCS 12341, pp. 209–219, 2020.
https://doi.org/10.1007/978-3-030-60816-3_24

In our work, we aimed to explore the viability of a blockchain back-end for collaborative visual analytics (C-VA) systems. Most literature on C-VA systems do not address the need for security and trust among collaborators. Using blockchain can address such issues, however, CV-A systems are highly interactive and require low latency communication and can be affected by the established performance issues with blockchain [10]. Our work explores the limits of blockchain in such systems.

We built *Share.va*; a framework that uses blockchain to log changes and insights derived through visual analytics dashboards. We also designed a visual metaphor to represent each collaboratively created state stored on the blockchain thus aiding the navigation of the blockchain. We demonstrate and evaluate the capabilities of our framework through a case study. Here, we retrofit an existing visual analytics dashboard used by social scientists with *Share.va*. We then observed the scientists collaboratively analyze their data both synchronously and asynchronously as well as record the analysis on the blockchain. By observing the scientists collaborate with the dashboard, we learned about the limitations of blockchain during real-time collaboration and how users worked around them.

2   Background

Blockchain was originally introduced to support the bitcoin cryptocurrency [7], but its ability to establish trust in a decentralized environment has led to many applications in the finance, health, and education sectors [3]. As explained by Swan [9], it is fundamentally a distributed ledger database that shares and synchronizes all records of digital transactions across multiple entities. Transactions are recorded into a block and added in a sequential manner so every block contains a hash to the previous block. This means every ledger entry is re-traceable across the full history of the blockchain. Before a transaction is added to the blockchain, all relevant parties need to agree that the block is valid. Once there is agreement on the validity of a block and it is recorded, it cannot be changed. These properties make blockchain a suitable technology that can be applied to any system that requires a trustworthy record of information [11].

Prior to implementing our framework, we first ensured that blockchain is suitable for our application by addressing the five key questions to determine the appropriateness of blockchain use [3]. First, users are required to have a shared database of datasets and insights in collaborative visual analytics. Next, they must be able to write to this database to add transformed data or insights. Additionally, in scenarios such as the medical analysis example, the patients need to trust that their information was only reviewed by approved doctors and other related individuals. In such cases, blockchain's disintermediation protocol ensures trust among collaborators. It does so by removing the need to trust a central entity as in traditional databases managed on a central server. Finally, the blockchain's ability to store an ordered, immutable and auditable record of the analysis inherently provides provenance of the analysis.

3   The Share.va Framework

Share.va is designed for web-based collaborative visual analytics dashboards and addresses the general requirements of or most C-VA systems[4]. It enables users to share interactions, data filters, annotations, and notes. It also allows users to make use of heterogeneous dashboards, i.e. dashboards that have different visual configurations but analyze the same data. Every user interaction leads to a change in the dashboard state which our framework logs to a back-end blockchain thus storing the provenance of an analysis. The blockchain can later be polled for prior dashboard states.

3.1   Representing Dashboard States

To represent a dashboard's shared state, we designed a specific data structure that supports the use of heterogeneous dashboards as well as sensemaking tools. The structure is concise due to the size limitation of blockchain and consists of three main subparts - data, view, and metadata. As we target web-based dashboards, the state is stored as a JSON with each subpart being stored as a field in this JSON. Each subpart is explained below:

Data: The data subpart of the state stores the data (or a pointer to it), and any functions that are used to manipulate the data along with the function parameters. These functions are often triggered by user interactions. They can be as simple as a list of filters over each data attribute or they could be more complex such as a clustering or layout algorithm. Changing a function's parameters can trigger a change in the visualizations, for example it may cause points to be highlighted or repositioned. Additionally, user-generated notes are stored in this subpart. Notes are the insights collaborators have gained at a particular

```
metadata :{                data:{                          view:{
    id:1001,                   datasetName:"Chicken-Quad1",     rankChart:
    creator:"user1",           dataAttributes:                  {
    collabStatus:{             [                                   algorithm: "elo",
        user1:"present",          "Time", "Count", "Action",       scale: "Count"
        user2:"absent",           "Initiator", "Receiver"          loc:{x:0.3,y:0.5,w:0.20,h:0.4}
        :                      ],                                  }
    }                          dataFilters:                      :
    changeInfo:{               [                                  :
        changeType:"View",        {                              annotations:
        changePane:"rankChart",     attr:"Count",                [
    }                               min:18 ,                        {
}                                   max:202                            creator: "user1",
                                  },                                   chart: "rankChart",
                               ],                                     x: 0.42,
                               notes:                                 y: 0.26,
                               [                                      text: "This is unusual"
                                  {                                 }
                                     creator:"user1",             ]
                                     stateID:1001,                }
                                     text:"Chicken one doesn't..."
                                  }
                               ],
                            },
```

(a) Meta-data   (b) Data   (c) View

Fig. 1. An example of the three dashboard state components from our case study.

dashboard state during their analysis. Although collaborators can have different dashboard views (with heterogeneous dashboards) the data insights would be the same as the functions applied to the data are always shared. Notes are essential to asynchronous collaboration as they communicate a user's thought process to his or her collaborators.

View: The view subpart stores information about the visual properties of the dashboard. The view is stored as a list of visual components, their locations in the dashboard, and annotations associated with them. The annotations, like the notes, are used for sensemaking but are more specific to the chart and often point to particular data points. Additionally, transforms that are chart specific are not essential for data sharing can also be maintained as part of the view, for example zoom levels or axis scales. When using heterogeneous or personalized views, the user can choose to ignore this view subpart of a shared state and use a personalized view. For example, a visual component that shows an overview of the data may either use a scatter plot or a parallel coordinate plot. By ignoring the view component one user could use a parallel coordinate plot and the other a scatter plot to visualize the same data, they could even use the scatter plot at different zoom levels.

Meta-data: While the data and view subparts reflect changes made to the content, an essential requirement for collaborative sense-making is knowing who made that change and when it was made. The meta-data section of the state is used to store this information. Additional information about the state is also maintained here such as which collaborators were present during the creation of the state and the type of change that led to the creation of the state (a data or view change). This meta-data is primarily used by history glyphs we designed to help users navigate states on the blockchain. The glyph is shown in Fig. 2. It is based on a dining table metaphor. A wireframe of the dashboard in the centre is the "dining table" and the arc segments along the circumference are the "seats" around this table. The arcs represent collaborators that were present during a state's creation and the circle behind the wireframe is colored and connected to the creator's arc. Panels in the wire-frame are highlighted to indicate in which panel a change occurred

An example of the state of a dashboard used in our case study is shown in Fig. 1. Here, the meta-data section (Fig. 1a) of the state stores the state's identifier in the *id* field, its creator in the *creator* field, the status of collaborators (present or absent) during the state's creation in the *collabStatus* field, and the type of change the state caused and the visualization it affected in *changeInfo* field. The data section (Fig. 1b) of the state stores a pointer to the dataset being analyzed in the *datasetName* field. The list of attributes in the dataset, the filters applied to them, and user notes are also stored in the *dataAttributes*, *dataFilters*, and *notes* fields of the data section. Adding or modifying a filter will cause a data change that is reflected across all visualizations. The view section (Fig. 1c) of the state has a list of fields that store the location and visual properties of the dashboard's visual elements. For example, the *rankingChart* field stores the normalized location and size of a line chart used to represent ranks of animals in

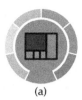

(a)   (b)

Fig. 2. The history glyph which help users navigate states on the blockchain. In (a) all seven collaborators were present when a change was made to the top left panel (dark gray highlight) while in (b) one collaborators was absent (green segment) when a change was made in the panel on the right (dark gray highlight) (Color figure online).

the *loc* sub-field. It also has an *algorithm* sub-field which allows users to select a ranking algorithm and a *scale* sub-field to select the kind of scale, in this dashboard the user could choose between item count and clock time. Since the view section can be ignored by collaborators, they could use different ranking algorithms and scales for this chart while collaborating with each other. The view section also stores annotations made to the dashboard in the *annotations* field.

Blockchain Implementation. Due to the complexity of our framework's data structure as well as other constraints and criteria, it was necessary to seek out the appropriate blockchain implementation from the many emerging options. We reviewed the available blockchain implementations (MultiChain, OpenChain and ScaleChain) to find one that best aligned with our needs. It should be noted that at the time of evaluation, promising candidates such as Hyperledger were rejected based on their maturity level but these may now be equally suitable for use in the framework. We had two primary design goals: (1) store data in a JSON object and (2) process client requests asynchronously.

We selected MultiChain, an open source system that stood out since it fulfilled our requirements as well as allowed us to store the largest size of data in the blocks. It provides a stream feature that allows raw text data to be written to the blockchain. This gave us the ability to encode our application data in JSON format, while still leveraging the auditable features of the blockchain. Additionally, MultiChain provides a permission management system that allows admins to grant read or write permissions to the blockchain. In our use case, the creator of a collaborative session is the admin who can then add collaborators to that session. Based on the permission a collaborator has, he or she can either contribute (write) to an analysis or only review (read) an analysis. The assignment of permissions is tracked by the blockchain ledger, much like a coin would be. This means that the assignment of read and write permissions would benefit from being traceable and auditable as well. A downside is that MultiChain uses JSON-RPC which requires synchronous communication with a client thereby making the client unresponsive until MultiChain replies to it. To overcome this issue, we implemented a Java program that acts as an interface between Multi-

Chain and the client. Here we use the REST architecture to communicate with the client asynchronously while communicating MultiChain synchronously.

Writing to the Blockchain. Having selected an appropriate blockchain implementation, we explored the possible methods of using it to store and share states among collaborators. In *Share.va*, a dashboard state is stored as a blockchain transaction and we employed two methods of storing this state - appending states and updating states - which are explained as follows:

Appending States: Appending a state is straightforward. For every user action, the current state of the user's dashboard is generated; this is essentially the entire JSON state described previously. This state is then sent to the blockchain and stored as a single transaction. As users generate annotations and notes, the number of items stored in the annotation and notes fields of the state increases. This increases the packet size of items being stored to the blockchain which can degrade the overall performance.

Updating States: Updating a state is a more involved process; for every user action, only the fields that have changed in the JSON are dispatched. The blockchain, however, is append-only and so does not allow stored states to be modified. Therefore, the latest state is duplicated and the changes are merged. This modified state is then appended to the blockchain.

Both methods are supported in the current implementation of *Share.va*. However, we recommend using the update method when one collaborator's interface is lagging. This causes less disruption for collaborators whose interfaces are not lagging. For example, if a user's interface is lagging, he would essentially be working on an older state of the dashboard. Now if he is five updates behind his collaborators, then using the append state method would cause collaborators to receive a state that has the five changes undone and a new change added which is effectively six changes. On the other hand, when using the update state method, the collaborators would receive just a single change that may not make sense to the collaborators since it was based on an older version of the state. While both methods cause disruptions, using updates is not as jarring as appending states with a lagging user. This is because with the update method the collaborators would always receive a single incorrect change while the append method can cause the collaborators to receive multiple incorrect changes.

4   Blockchain Performance

Before conducting our case study, we tested the response time of the blockchain while varying the number of users. The results are shown in Table 1. These response times are much slower than traditional databases and can cause problems when the frequency of user interactions is very high. Specifically, states can appear to be rejected when the blockchain receives too many requests before it finishes creating a new block. Consider the case of one or more users performing two or more interactions in under one second. As shown in the update

Table 1. The time taken to read and write (with the append and update methods) a block to the blockchain as the number of collaborators increase.

No. of users	1	2	3	4	5	6	7	8	9
Read time (s)	0.85	0.86	1.21	1.41	1.58	1.75	2.43	13.43	28.23
Append time (s)	0.58	0.58	0.59	0.59	0.63	0.63	1.78	7.72	20.49
Update time (s)	1.35	1.35	1.35	1.35	1.45	1.47	3.06	17.89	54.12

method, it takes the blockchain 1.35 s at the very least to create a block. Thus only the first interaction in the one second period is logged to the blockchain with the others timing out. Such high response times are unacceptable in highly interactive environments such as multiplayer games, but as we show in our case study visual analytics tasks have a significantly higher threshold. Additionally, asynchronous collaboration does not suffer from these issues as requests to the blockchain would be infrequent.

5   Case Study

To demonstrate and evaluate Share.va, we tested it on a real-world application. We took an existing dashboard used by social scientists [2] and augmented it with Share.va. The Share.va enabled dashboard, shown in Fig. 3, allowed scientists to load one of many datasets that contain an interaction record of an animal group and analyze it collaboratively.

5.1   Procedure

In this study, two social science professors (P1 and P2) and their research assistant (A1) who are familiar with the original dashboard used the Share.va enabled version of the dashboard. They collaboratively explored a new unstudied dataset acquired by them. The study consisted of three sessions. In the first session participants P1 and P2 performed a joint exploration of the datasets. The second session was an individual analysis of the data by A1 that was unrestricted. This was a deeper analysis than in the first session. In the final session, P1 and P2 jointly reviewed the dashboard states and insights generated by A1 during session 2. The sessions were conducted over a period of one week with the participants being allowed to use the interface independently during the course of the week. The first session lasted for 28 min and the third for 42 min and an author moderated the sessions and provided minimal help to the users. The second session was an independent analysis in which the participant could take as much time as she wanted. This second session was not moderated but A1 was able to contact the author for technical support when needed and her interactions could be reviewed through the blockchain. Prior to the first session, participants were given a demo of the Share.va enabled dashboard. The demo showed the participants how to use the various features that support collaboration. After the demo

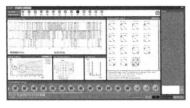
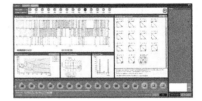

(a) P1's dashboard   (b) P2's dashboard

Fig. 3. A snapshot of our participants' dashboards during the case study. Here the collaborators are synchronizing the data but not the view, this can be observed in the right panel where (a) shows P1 using the compressed state space and (b) using the full state space. The single item selected in (a) (gray circular highlight) maps to 9 items selected in (b).

the participants were asked to perform three practice tasks: change a visual representation, add an annotation and add a note. During the two sessions with P1 and P2 we recorded their screens and verbal communications. Additionally, we had a post session interview with the participants and asked them about their experience. All participants used desktop computers running with 27 in. screens at a resolution of 1920 by 1080 and ran our tool on a browser of their choice. Verbal communication was supported by a commercial VoIP service which is not part of our current system.

5.2   Observations

During the first and third sessions which were synchronous collaborations between P1 and P2, we observed that right before or during an interaction with the dashboard they always verbally indicated which dashboard item they were looking at or interacting with. They did this because their mouse pointer's position was not shared due to the high-latency of the blockchain. We also observed that during the analysis, P1 and P2 would take turns performing a set of interactions and they would often have small discussions between interactions. The turn taking behavior was primarily due to each participant hypothesizing an insight and trying to verify it through a set of interactions while the other participant observed and discussed the changes in the visualization. The small discussions between interactions actually complimented the blockchain's high latency as they gave the blockchain enough time to record an interaction before processing the next request. Finally, we observed that P1 and P2 did not make use of notes they made handwritten notes instead. Additionally, they only used annotations when they could not verbally indicate an item's position.

In the second session, A1 performed an asynchronous analysis which was later reviewed by P1 and P2 in the third session. As A1 interacted with the dashboard alone, she did not face any latency issues. All her interactions were recorded and she did not have to undo or redo any part of her analysis. During her analysis, she applied multiple filters to the data and annotated visualizations with her observations at every stage of her analysis. She also made notes for P1 and P2. During session three, P1 and P2 spent the first half of the session reviewing A1's analysis. They first located the start of her analysis recording on the blockchain using the history glyphs. They then reviewed each of her actions by sequentially loading each state she created. Again, here one participant loaded the states while the other just viewed the dashboard and discussed A1 findings. Thus the blockchain never received two or more concurrent read requests. Also, since they spent time discussing each state, the blockchain had enough time to process each read request and was never overloaded.

6   Discussion

6.1   Latency

The main issue with blockchain is that it is slow due to its computational requirements. Our performance test showed that the blockchain could only allow a maximum of six users without rendering the system unfit for synchronous collaboration. The fastest time to read or write from the blockchain was just above half a second but on average it was longer. Most groupware applications would suffer from such a high response time. However, it might be acceptable for C-VA. Studies in information visualization have shown that most human cognitive tasks take one second or less [1]. On the other hand, Liu et al. [6] show that a 500ms delay in an interactive visualization has a significant effect on mouse movements and brushing but not in other tasks such as zooming and panning. Delays also cause users to change their interaction strategies. Our study participants adapted to delays by resorting to a turn taking behavior as well as filling time between interactions with discussions. The delays in a blockchain with a greater number of users are much larger but such delays have not been tested in C-VA. We hypothesize that users would also change strategies here and we plan to test this in future work. However, when using *Share.va* asynchronously, the study participants did not run into any performance related issues. This leads us to believe that blockchain might be more suitable for collaborative data analyses that are asynchronous or turn-based such as the case where a doctor and lab technician take turns analyzing a patient's data.

6.2   Space Limitations

The blockchain's storage constraint is another issue we had to deal with when designing *Share.va*. Most implementations support the storage of a few bytes of data which is insufficient for most C-VA systems. Today data being analyzed can exceed hundreds of gigabytes thus making it is impossible to store on a blockchain. In our case study, every user had a local copy of the dataset and only data transformation functions were shared and stored on the blockchain. Thus the security and authenticity of the dataset itself is not guaranteed by the blockchain; instead users need to rely on a third-party to secure the dataset.

6.3 Linearity

Another challenge with applying blockchain to C-VA is that it stores blocks in a linear manner and it does not support branching. On the other hand, in C-VA at a certain point analysts may choose to branch off into different paths of analysis. Due to the linear nature of blockchain only one branch can actively be shared and appended to the blockchain in real time. To support branching on a single chain, additional branches would need to be temporarily cached and appended to the blockchain sequentially at a later stage. This effectively makes the other branches asynchronous analyses. Thus blockchain is more suitable for collaborative analyses without branching or asynchronous turn-based collaboration.

7 Conclusion

In this paper we presented Share.va: a proof-of-concept framework that supports secure C-VA using a blockchain back-end. To the best of our knowledge, this is the first system to apply blockchain in this fashion. We tested our framework in a real world scenario by having a group of social scientists use our system to analyze their data collaboratively. While this study yielded insight in how our method and system is used in practice, it also revealed some of the system's limitations, and of blockchain technology applied for the purpose of C-VA overall. We found that while our use of blockchain in this way was viable for smaller numbers of users or for asynchronous collaboration.

Acknowledgments. This work was supported in part by NSF I/UCRC 1650499: Center for Visual and Decision Informatics (CVDI) Site at SUNY Stony Brook, CA Technologies, a Broadcom Company, USA, NSF grant IIS 1527200, and MSIT (Ministry of Science and ICT), Korea, under the SUNY Korea's ICT Consilience Creative program (IITP-2020-2011-1-00783) supervised by the IITP.

References

1. Card, S.K., Mackinlay, J.D., Shneiderman, B. (eds.): Readings in Information Visualization: Using Vision to Think. Morgan Kaufmann Publishers Inc., San Francisco (1999)
2. Coelho, D., Chase, I., Mueller, K.: Peckvis: a visual analytics tool to analyze dominance hierarchies in small groups. IEEE Trans. Vis. Comput. Graph. **26**(4), 1650–1660 (2020)
3. Gatteschi, V., Lamberti, F., Demartini, C., Pranteda, C., Santamaria, V.: To blockchain or not to blockchain: that is the question. IT Prof. **20**(2), 62–74 (2018)
4. Isenberg, P., Elmqvist, N., Scholtz, J., Cernea, D., Ma, K.L., Hagen, H.: Collaborative visualization: definition, challenges, and research agenda. Inf. Vis. **10**(4), 310–326 (2011)
5. Kane, B.T., Toussaint, P.J., Luz, S.: Shared decision making needs a communication record. In: Proceedings of the 2013 Conference on Computer Supported Cooperative Work, CSCW 2013, pp. 79–90. ACM, New York (2013)

6. Liu, Z., Heer, J.: The effects of interactive latency on exploratory visual analysis. IEEE Trans. Vis. Comput. Graph. **20**(12), 2122–2131 (2014)
7. Nakamoto, S.: Bitcoin: a peer-to-peer electronic cash system (2008)
8. Shen, H., Dewan, P.: Access control for collaborative environments. In: Proceedings of the 1992 ACM Conference on Computer-supported Cooperative Work, CSCW 1992, pp. 51–58. ACM, New York (1992)
9. Swan, M.: Blockchain: Blueprint for a New Economy. O'Reilly Media, Inc., Sebastopol (2015)
10. Xu, X., et al.: A taxonomy of blockchain-based systems for architecture design. In: IEEE International Conference on Software Architecture, pp. 243–252, April 2017
11. Zyskind, G., Nathan, O., Pentland, A.: Decentralizing privacy: using blockchain to protect personal data. In: 2015 IEEE Security and Privacy Workshops, pp. 180–184, May 2015

The Development of an Asynchronous Web Application for Family Social Media Communication

Thanathep Thaithae$^{(\boxtimes)}$, Apichaya Towsakul$^{(\boxtimes)}$,
and Pornsuree Jamsri$^{(\boxtimes)}$

Faculty of Information Technology, King Mongkut's Institute of Technology
Ladkrabang, Bangkok, Thailand
{59070066,59070186,pornsuree}@it.kmitl.ac.th

Abstract. In Asia countries, a family usually encourages their children to acquire a better education in a prestige university even though it is far from their hometown. The distance can affect to family relationship for this opportunity in life. A social media becomes one of the communication channels which usually insufficient to maintain proper communication and relationships due to the downside of synchronous communication. KUMAMI, a multi-platform web application, is developed by using an asynchronous communication. A solution to provides a better experience while communicating among family members with familiar features, members status, family notes. This method reduces expectation of an immediate response in the family as ordinary social media platforms.

Keywords: Family communication · Asynchronous communication · Social media · Web application · Cooperative family

1 Introduction

Social media has become one of the popular choices [1] in communication because of its easy accessibility and a wide range of usage [2]. However, when a family is relying on social media to interact and stay in touch with family members. It can cause difficulty in terms of privacy and tension between family members when information is posted by individuals on a social media timeline. Parents can feel they are not knowledgeable enough to catch up with their children's lives and children feel parents are invading their privacy [3].

The unique characteristic of synchronous communication that various social media platform are built on [2] that focus on giving immediate response to users, also provides a user, especially children, a sense of being monitored [4] and feel likes it takes more effort to keep parents updated everything in their lives [3].

Previous studies [2–4] indicated that synchronous communication in family can cause family members having a misperception of their children's behaviors, and children can feel uncomfortable to disclose their daily life. As a consequence, asynchronous communication can be a choice to use for family communication. It can

Y. Luo (Ed.): CDVE 2020, LNCS 12341, pp. 220–229, 2020.
https://doi.org/10.1007/978-3-030-60816-3_25

strengthen family relationships by not displaying information immediately. This research proposes the KUMAMI, an asynchronous web application, can work better as a family social media platform and strengthen cooperative family members relationship. Its aim is for usage by children (18–23 years old) and parents (35–55 years old) who live at a distance from each other. Previous studies and information from a focus group gave the research team insight on iteration design to develop a web application prototype multiple times regarding user requirements and benefits to enable better communication among family members.

2   Related Work

2.1   The Family Communication Platforms

The root cause of technology usage as a family communication medium is that parents and children grow up in different generation. There is a gap of parents who start using technology later than their children. Parents can find difficulty in using these applications [3]. They can, thus, feel left behind in family group interaction [5].

Most social media platforms rely on synchronous communication. Users, unfortunately, can feel frustration with a conversation partner because they expect an immediate response [3]. Users who interact through synchronous communication, as a study has shown, find it harder to coordinate with people who do not interact in an expected time that will cause communication chaos [6]. Asynchronous communication, however, showed a promising result as an effective communication method by giving more flexibility and control over the task [7] compared to synchronous communication.

To make communication and cooperative between family members more efficient, the study examined how people could feel a sense of comfort by knowing the presence of family members through interpersonal awareness information consisting of activity, location, and well-being [8]. In addition, a connectivity of how information could transfer to a conversation partner, reciprocity of user's behavior to various surroundings, and perceivable volume of information for an individual [9] should be taken into account when designing a better approach for communication within a family.

2.2   Teenager Perception Towards Technology and Privacy Issue

By observing teenage children's behavior when talking about their potential risk experiences in online society with their parents shows that they usually feel embarrassment, discomfort, and distressed due to the nature of parents exaggerations over their accounts [10]. Also when parents try to be involved with their children's online experience by using surveillance application it causes negative reactions. The monitoring of access, content and browsing, have shown children feel their privacy is invaded causing their aggravation in communicating with their parents [4].

In addition, another study illustrated that the comfort and boundaries of communication on the Internet is defined by teenagers' opinions of it as a communication place where teenagers usually separate their contacts to maintain relationships easily with different groups [11].

2.3   Popular Social Network Platforms

An initial study has examined the motivation and behavior of college students using various platforms and discovered that they mostly use the platforms as entertainment and attractive appearance rather than for social interaction [2].

Social media functionalities [1] in regard to selected popular social media platforms are listed in Table 1.

- Instagram is an image-based social media platform focusing on media content such as photos and videos.
- Between is a communication platform for a couple. It emphasizes on maintaining the presence of each other and keeping track on essential aspects of the relationship.
- Facebook is a social media platform that focuses on sharing stories in daily lives with a curated circle of friends. Most popular for all ages.
- Twitter is a social media platform with the goals on sharing a short personal story and trending news worldwide.
- Snapchat is a communication platform that targets sharing short video clips to a small circle of friends. Most popular for teenage users.

Table 1. A comparison of cross-functionality in social media.

Functionality	Instagram	Between	Facebook	Twitter	Snapchat
Display status messages	✓	✗	✓	✗	✓
Push notification	✗	✗	✗	✗	✗
Using hashtag	✓	✗	✓	✓	✓
Display earlier media	✓	✓	✓	✗	✓

Most popular social media platforms are built for a large audience rather than focusing on communication between people in a small group as family members.

3   Research Design

3.1   A Focus Group

Our research begins with information from divided users into 2 focus groups 1) parents and 2) children. To gather initial requirements and bring it into design criteria, the research was conducted in about 40–70 min with 5 persons per group. The participants discussed together the provided semi-structured interview questions. The focus group is designed for collecting information from each group in 4 aspects 1) communication technology choice 2) user perspective towards communication process 3) communication needs 4) following each group's social media by another party.

3.2   Design Guideline

The design thinking process [12] utilized as a guide is shown in Fig. 1, a platform designed and developed followed this process. The start is from empathize, to define, to ideate, to test, and to prototype steps, respectively, in designing a prototype. The process helps to understand the actual problem, define the actual gap before initiating KUMAMI platform with multiple testing and a number of prototypes. It is not only this process, but also gathering and evaluating data from multiple sources while testing and validating concept ideas to conceive a more concrete solution for KUMAMI.

Fig. 1. Design thinking process

Other further steps in the research design for a prototype included these usage factors: no restriction; security and privacy; sharing selected information; having different communication groups for personal lives; and make communication effortless, less tiring, and more enjoyable.

3.3   System Overview and System Architecture

The system consists of members who are part of a particular family group. Each family group interacts in their own private space, which cannot be accessed by other families. There is a created group by one family member with a password for access into the right group. A platform of each group will be receiving and displaying content that is stored in the database. See Fig. 2 for details.

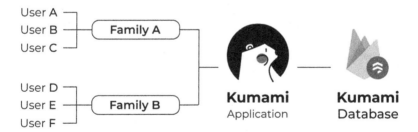

Fig. 2. System overview of KUMAMI

Tools that we use to design and develop the platform consists of Figma, which is a design tool for user interface design. We were also using Node.js and React Framework for developing a web application that could serve on multi-platforms.

KUMAMI's system architecture as shown in Fig. 3 contains two main components 1) a multi-platform web application that operates on firebase hosting, and 2) an API server which serves every request that originates from a web application.

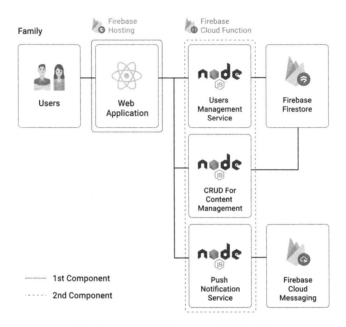

Fig. 3. System architecture of KUMAMI

4 Prototype

The prototype "KUMAMI" is a responsive web application that is designed on both operating systems, Mac and Windows, and for browsers on mobile devices. It is compatible with iOS and Android. This prototype is developed with a total of 10 features. However, this section demonstrates 5 selected outcomes as examples of features.

4.1 Log in

The prototype starts with "Login" to KUMAMI and could be done on the first page shown in Fig. 4 to begin the web application. The user enters an email that has been registered on KUMAMI and presses login to access the application.

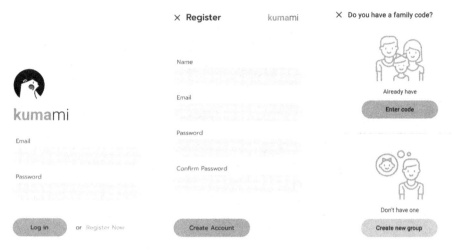

Fig. 4. Login feature   Fig. 5. Register feature   Fig. 6. Setup feature

4.2   Register and Set up

The new user needs to register for the first time to use KUMAMI. To register an account on KUMAMI requires basic information such as an email, name, and password as shown in Fig. 5.

After register, the user will be asked to set up an account to a new family group or join an existing group as shown in Fig. 6. For the user to join a group, they need a family code. This code is retrieved from the menu bar by other users in the group, simply by entering the family's name.

4.3   Main Screen

This "Main Screen" works as a homepage of any website or a dashboard of an application. The main screen consists of three sections: 1) the status bar shows the family member's latest status; 2) status feed shows the latest status of each member in chronologically order; and 3) family's note to access another section of the application as shown in Fig. 7.

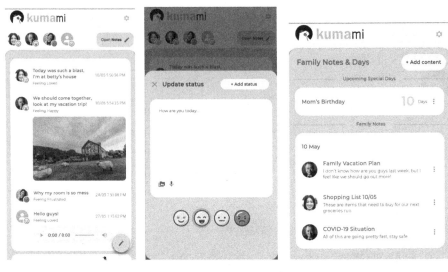

Fig. 7. Main screen   **Fig. 8.** Posting new status   **Fig. 9.** Family special day

4.4 Posting New Status

Besides a status message, posting a new status of each user by adding text, an audio clip or a photo with the smartphone is possible. Furthermore, users have an option to indicate an emoticon of their current status to let other members know how they feel at that time as shown in Fig. 8.

4.5 Family Special Day and Family Notes

The family note consists of two parts. First is the special day's countdown for reminding of an anniversary or other special days recorded into the platform. Second is a family note section that can be used for news or planning together for an entire family as shown in Fig. 9.

For a "Family Notes", an entire family has permission to edit, delete, update any content on this page. This is a way to stimulate the sense of sharing a space for a whole family to collaborate together.

5 Results and Evaluations

5.1 Design Iterations

Throughout the research period, we have designed and improved our application design for a total of 3 iterations that reflect the features in each prototype.

The first iteration as in Fig. 10 (a), is from studying previous research and a rough result of a focus group sharing various types of media such as short video clips and pictures that happened during the day. In the second iteration as in Fig. 10 (b), we adjusted some features intensely based on data from focus group interviews and insights on sharing status information and giving users a sense of comfort and ease from knowing other users' status and activity. The third iteration as in Fig. 10 (c), is to adjust the design to make it suitable for actual development.

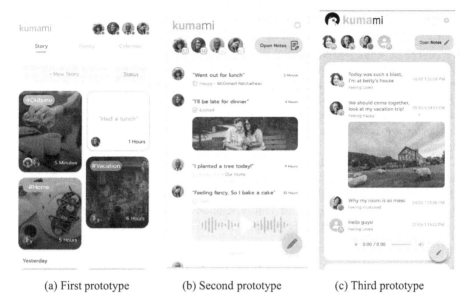

    (a) First prototype   (b) Second prototype   (c) Third prototype

Fig. 10. KUMAMI Main Screens of 3 Iterations (a) first prototype, (b) second prototype, and (c) third prototype

5.2 Target Groups Evaluations

In using KUMAMI with three selected families over a one-week period, we have gathered data by discussion with them on how they feel and their perceptions of asynchronous communication. The participants in the parents' group pointed out "KUMAMI is an intuitive platform that makes communication much more effective and effortless." They felt more comfortable by observing their child through the status system rather than making frequent phone calls to check-up on their children's situation. For children, the participants addressed that "KUMAMI gives them a privacy level that makes them feel comfortable sharing their daily lives with their parents rather than using personal social media such as Facebook." These were examples from our testing of the second prototype.

5.3 Area of Improvement

The performance of this web application has a significant impact on user experience and satisfaction. Some users suggested adding a feature that could open up more intuitive application of family communication, such as video clips and location tagging. These substantive recommendations are meaningful for future development.

6 Conclusion and Future Research

The multi-platform web application KUMAMI allows family members that were living apart to stay connected and cooperative with each other through asynchronous web application by using multiple media such as text, video clips, and audio as a message system corresponding to the previous research to prioritizes in maintaining a sense of awareness and comfort by using a specific set of information [3]. Using asynchronous communication reduced the expectation of parents' immediate response to help their children. The children, thus, gained a better attitude towards their parents. The platform gave parents a better understanding of their children and better experience of communication with them.

In the future, KUMAMI can be extended by adding more features including short video clips and geographical data as suggested by users. There is another possibility to add a YouTube link as well. Therefore, KUMAMI can be seen to offer a bright future towards strengthening cooperative family relationships through communication and this can also be useful other user groups.

References

1. Hellemans, J., Willems, K., Brengman, M.: Daily active users of social network sites: facebook, twitter, and instagram-use compared to general social network site use. In: Martínez-López, F.J., D'Alessandro, S. (eds.) Advances in Digital Marketing and eCommerce. SPBE, pp. 194–202. Springer, Cham (2020). https://doi.org/10.1007/978-3-030-47595-6_24
2. Ghosh, A.K., Badillo-Urquiola, K., Guha, S., Laviola Jr, J.J., Wisniewski, P.J.: Safety vs. surveillance: what children have to say about mobile apps for parental control. In: Proceedings of the 2018 CHI Conference on Human Factors in Computing Systems - CHI'2018 (2018). https://doi.org/10.1145/3173574.3173698
3. Alhabash, S., Ma, M.: A Tale of Four Platforms: Motivations and Uses of Facebook, Twitter, Instagram, and Snapchat Among College Students? Social Media + Society 3:205630511769154 (2017). https://doi.org/10.1177/2056305117691544
4. Davis, K., Dinhopl, A., Hiniker, A.: "Everything's the Phone": understanding the phone's supercharged role in parent-teen relationships. In: Proceedings of the 2019 CHI Conference on Human Factors in Computing Systems - CHI'2019, pp. 1–14 (2019). https://doi.org/10.1145/3290605.3300457
5. Muñoz, D., Cornejo, R., Gutierrez, F.J., et al.: A social cloud-based tool to deal with time and media mismatch of intergenerational family communication. Future Gener. Comput. Syst. **53**, 140–151 (2015). https://doi.org/10.1016/j.future.2014.07.003
6. Schuler, R.P., Grandhi, S.A., Mayer, J.M., Ricken, S.T., Jones, Q.: The doing of doing stuff: understanding the coordination of social group-activities. In: Proceedings of the 32nd Annual ACM Conference on Human Factors in Computing Systems - CHI'2014, pp. 119–128 (2014). https://doi.org/10.1145/2556288.2557388

7. Bhattacharya, A., et al.: Engaging teenagers in asynchronous online groups to design for stress management. In: Proceedings of the Interaction Design and Children on ZZZ - IDC'2019, pp. 26–37 (2019). https://doi.org/10.1145/3311927.3323140

8. Neustaedter, C., Elliot, K., Greenberg, S.: Interpersonal awareness in the domestic realm. In: Proceedings of the 20th Conference of the Computer-Human Interaction Special Interest Group (Chisig) of Australia on Computer-Human Interaction: Design: Activities, Artefacts and Environments - OZCHI'2006, pp. 15–22 (2006). https://doi.org/10.1145/1228175.1228182

9. Chatting, D., Kirk, D.S., Yurman, P., Bichard, J.-A.: Designing for family phatic communication: a design critique approach. In: Proceedings of the 2015 British HCI Conference on - British HCI'2015, pp. 175–183 (2015). https://doi.org/10.1145/2783446.2783566

10. Wisniewski, P., Xu, H., Rosson, M.B., Carroll, J.M.: Parents just don't understand: why teens don't talk to parents about their online risk experiences. In: Proceedings of the 2017 ACM Conference on Computer Supported Cooperative Work and Social Computing, pp. 523–540 (2017). https://doi.org/10.1145/2998181.2998236

11. Nouwens, M., Griggio, C.F., Mackay, W.E.: WhatsApp is for family; messenger is for friends. In: Proceedings of the 2017 CHI Conference on Human Factors in Computing Systems, pp. 727–735 (2017). https://doi.org/10.1145/3025453.3025484

12. Kolko, J.: The divisiveness of design thinking. Interactions **25**, 28–34 (2018). https://doi.org/10.1145/3194313

Analysis of Scholarship Consideration Using J48 Decision Tree Algorithm for Data Mining

Sanya Khruahong[✉] and Pirayu Tadkerd

Department of Computer Science and Information Technology,
Faculty of Science, Naresuan University, Phitsanulok, Thailand
sanyak@nu.ac.th, pirayut59@email.nu.ac.th

Abstract. Consideration of scholarships is a common occurrence in educational institutions such as in a university. The scholarship selection committees play an essential role in judgment, which must pay attention to considering issues efficiently. However, they may make mistakes because an applicant's information is complicated. This research proposes a scholarship analytic for the award of a student scholarship at university by using Data Mining techniques. The study was designed with seven variables on 468 samples, which were only selected with complete attributes from 2,549 student documents by a decision tree, J48 and J48graft algorithm with percentage split method at 20%, 30%, and 60%, k-fold cross validation both 5-folds and 10-folds. The development model's results found that the model created by a decision tree with the J48 algorithm and percentage split method at 66% is most effective, with the precision value at 77.35%. Therefore, we choose to model with the J48 algorithm by percentage split method at 66% to develop the web application, which is useful for students to assess themselves before applying and will decrease the committee's workload for the assessment of student's scholarship applications.

Keywords: Prediction model · Data mining · Decision tree

1 Introduction

The scholarship provides financial support for students who want to study at a college, university, or other academic institution. Many students still need scholarships while they are at the educational institute. Various criteria are used for scholarship awards, such as academic reports, athletic skills, financial need, or some combination of approaches. So, there are different criteria to be considered in each type of scholarship. For example, for the academic awards, generally, the committee will use a minimum Grade Point Average (GPA.) of the student. Athletic scholarships are usually based on the athletic performance of a student. Therefore, the grants will be decided for suitable students if they can pass scholarship conditions. The criteria for the award of a scholarship should reflect the purposes of the founder of the award. Besides, problems in screening student qualifications to match scholarship conditions are severe. For the award of each scholarship, it is still the duty of the university staff to check that students meet the criteria for the award of the scholarship. Also, to make the

© Springer Nature Switzerland AG 2020
Y. Luo (Ed.): CDVE 2020, LNCS 12341, pp. 230–238, 2020.
https://doi.org/10.1007/978-3-030-60816-3_26

scholarship consideration more effective there is a need to find some techniques to improve work efficiency.

Data mining is the process of finding patterns in massive datasets; it leads to the discovery of interesting, unexpected, or valuable structures in large databases [1, 2]. Data mining techniques are deployed to analyze vast amounts of information to find novel and beneficial patterns that might otherwise remain undiscovered [3, 4]. Data mining has been applied in several businesses, to which many pieces of research have been addressed. Using data mining and machine learning in diabetes mellitus (DM) research has adopted large volumes of accessible diabetes-related data for obtaining knowledge [5]. The advent of biotechnology, with the vast amount of data produced, along with the increasing amount of Electronic Medical Records (EMR) is expected to give rise to further in-depth exploration toward diagnosis. This article is informative, but researches only focused on biotechnology. Moreover, Data mining was applied to predictive analytics with information on public health data through the National Health and Morbidity Survey for predicting obesity [6]. This paper used J48 algorithm to measure the accuracy rate, which focuses on the food information that is bought from the store. If the daily activity data can be combined in the analysis, it may make the quality of forecasting more accurate.

Predictive Analytics is a mathematical process that aims to predict future situations by analyzing patterns for forecasting future results [7, 8]. As data is added in the system, it will be validated or revised with the statistical analysis. Predicting data has been used for a long time. Forecasting requires useful data because of the accuracy of the predictions depend on correct data, such as the forecast for rain that will fall from the weather data of the Thai Meteorological Department. In 2014, Naota Hanasaki and the researchers' team presented a quasi-real-time hydrological simulation system to predict the flooding of the Chao Phraya River in Thailand [9]. The simulation described a dam's limited performance, which applied recent meteorological data and was made up to two days before the present. However, all data should be checked for quality before being put into the process, such as precipitation data in the river, which may lead to getting a more precise prediction.

In this paper, we describe how to deploy the J48 decision tree algorithm for Data mining to analyze factors affecting scholarship consideration and how to support the investigation to find the relationship of data. The scholarship data analysis methods are an excellent way to find measures for determining student scholarships. This research uses the information from the Student Affairs Division in the university, which is the information that consists of information for students applying for scholarships in several academic years. The result uses web development, which we hope can screen students who meet the conditions specified in the scholarship because the web application is developed for students to evaluate the scholarship condition by themselves. It can reduce the committee's workload for evaluation.

This paper is organized as follows: Sect. 2 briefly summarizes the related works which reveal technology and are detailed in this section. Section 3 describes the research methodology and how it analyzes the scholarship data. Finally, we summarize, discuss the results, and suggest future work.

2 Related Works

This section details relevant literature related to this research. We describe related work covering Data Mining. Secondly, the Decision Tree with the J48 algorithm and the Weka application are described.

2.1 Data Mining

Data mining techniques are used in many research areas, including mathematics, cybernetics, genetics, and marketing [10, 11]. Data Mining is an essential introduction to the statistical methods needed to analyze complex data sets. Data Mining or Knowledge Discovery in Databases (KDD) is a technique to automatically search vast amounts of data, analyzing knowledge from big data by using algorithms from statistics on machine learning and pattern recognition for definition [12]. Moreover, it can search for images with guidelines and the relationships that are hidden in that data set by using recognition statistics, Machine learning, and mathematical principles. It is widely used for precise predictions. There is an algorithm of Data Mining for classification [13, 14] such as Decision tree and neural networks, which is used for forecasting.

Data mining is one technique that was applied to many prediction systems for finding the best selection. Educational data mining was developed for guides for course redesign, which is beneficial for the practice of the scholarship of teaching in the university [15]. However, this article may be the concept of getting the recommendation information for communication between lecturers and students. It needs more data in other dimensions, such as course management or history of instructors' teaching. Furthermore, the Data mining technique was applied to analyze with structured business data to extract financial risk events from news articles [16]. Nevertheless, it may be difficult to get news articles covering the content area of finance for analysis.

2.2 Decision Tree Algorithm

Classification of data purpose is used in grouping similar data objects together for a data mining and knowledge management method [17, 18]. Although there are many classification algorithms, the decision tree is the most commonly used because it is easier to understand compared to other classification algorithms. The decision tree is one of the most powerful and widely applied techniques for classification and prediction. The tree modeling of data supports the making of predictions about new data. For example, C4.5 algorithm, one of the decision tree methods, was developed for prediction to select the scholarship grantee, which is determined from external factors and internal students [19]. Moreover, C4.5 decision tree is built for the evaluation model of a higher educational scholarship, which can be achieved by using an efficient and fair scholarship [20]. This method may be difficult for getting data collection.

Additionally, J48 decision tree (J48DT) methodology is used extensively in medical predictions. For instance, it was applied with medicinal records of patients for predicting the dengue [21], and J48 approach contributed to diabetes risk factors to classify patients with diabetes mellitus [22]. Both articles may lead to diverse individual techniques. J48 Decision Tree and J48graft are the classification tree-based techniques known as the most common machine learning method [23, 24]. The purpose of J48 and J48graft are to build a tree for binary classification variables. The root node consists of all input data, the internal nodes branches are connected with decision function, and the leaf nodes give the output of a given input data. J48DT is the optimal choice for classification accuracy compared to other standard decision tree methods. Therefore, J48 and J48graft become a concept that is presented in this paper.

2.3   Weka Application

Weka is the application of Data Science or data mining tasks with GUI and easy to use [25, 26]. The algorithms can be implemented directly into a dataset. Weka includes tools for data pre-processing, classification, regression, clustering, association rules, and visualization. This paper employed this software for training of the student data set.

After the literature review, we found that scholarship consideration in the university can be deployed with the J48 decision tree algorithm for analyzing student scholarship consideration.

3   Research Methodology

This section describes how to implement for analyzing scholarship consideration by using the J48 decision tree algorithm followed by data collection, data preparation, modeling for forecasting, and web development, as shown in Fig. 1.

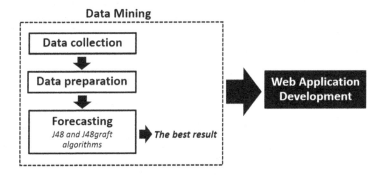

Fig. 1. Shows the process of research methodology

3.1   Data Collection

Data Mining needs to collect information; this paper obtained information from the Student Affairs Division Naresuan University Student. This information was data of students who received scholarships in the academic year 2016 – 2018, with 468 samples, which are only selected with complete attributes from 2,549 student documents. In this process, selecting the factors of determining scholarship consists of the year, faculty, Grade Point Average (GPA), family income, number of members in the family that request scholarships, and the result was that they received funding. The data format was collected in Microsoft Excel, in which all data was checked that can be used for analysis. Some detail may be non-value or unsuitable for analyzing. Therefore, the initial data has to be scrutinized, some columns selected that have complete information. In this data set, the column has complete information, including year, faculty name, GPA, family income, amount of Student loans for education, number of family members, and status of receiving the scholarship.

Table 1. Attributes name for using to analyze in Weka

Attributes Name	Description
YEAR	Current student's year
FACULTY	Student's faculty
GPA	Current student's GPA
SALARY	Total of family income
STUDENTLOAN	Amount of student loans for education
FAMILY	Number of members in the family
SCHOLARSHIP	Scholarship Name
STATUS	Scholarship result of student

Some students' information may not be used for analysis, such as the student ID column and the student's name, which cannot convert data into numbers or disadvantages. So, this data is prevented from being analyzed in Weka application. All attributes are discrete data, cleaning data, and eliminating unnecessary attributes, as shown in Table 1.

3.2 Data Preparation

After importing all the sample data into Microsoft Excel, we prepared the data by selecting the factors related to the analysis and which has a relationship with the first and the dependent variables. The researcher converted data into numbers to select the inputs using Pearson's Correlation Coefficient, after data conversion, and then put the data into SPSS (Statistical Package for the Social Sciences) program to analyze Pearson's Correlation Coefficient as shown in Fig. 1. The inputs used for the analysis of scholarships, consisting of 7 attributes, are *YEAR, FACULTY GPA, SALARY, STUDENTLOAN, FAMILY,* and *SCHOLARSHIP,* which will be used in Weka next.

Correlations

		STATUS	YEAR	GPA	SCHOLARSHIP	FAMILY	FACULTY	SALARY	STUDENTLOAN
STATUS	Pearson Correlation	1	-.114*	.092*	-.011	.055	-.005	-.079	.046
	Sig. (2-tailed)		.013	.046	.819	.233	.911	.090	.324
	N	468	468	468	468	468	468	468	468
YEAR	Pearson Correlation	-.114*	1	-.421**	.015	-.032	.033	.033	-.111*
	Sig. (2-tailed)	.013		.000	.752	.493	.480	.480	.016
	N	468	468	468	468	468	468	468	468
GPA	Pearson Correlation	.092*	-.421**	1	.063	.082	.129**	-.030	-.006
	Sig. (2-tailed)	.046	.000		.171	.077	.005	.511	.891
	N	468	468	468	468	468	468	468	468
SCHOLARSHIP	Pearson Correlation	-.011	.015	.063	1	.035	.052	-.197**	.053
	Sig. (2-tailed)	.819	.752	.171		.456	.262	.000	.249
	N	468	468	468	468	468	468	468	468
FAMILY	Pearson Correlation	.055	-.032	.082	.035	1	-.026	-.014	.036
	Sig. (2-tailed)	.233	.493	.077	.456		.579	.760	.440
	N	468	468	468	468	468	468	468	468
FACULTY	Pearson Correlation	-.005	.033	.129**	.052	-.026	1	-.005	-.020
	Sig. (2-tailed)	.911	.480	.005	.262	.579		.921	.668
	N	468	468	468	468	468	468	468	468
SALARY	Pearson Correlation	-.079	.033	-.030	-.197**	-.014	-.005	1	.014
	Sig. (2-tailed)	.090	.480	.511	.000	.760	.921		.755
	N	468	468	468	468	468	468	468	468
STUDENTLOAN	Pearson Correlation	.046	-.111*	-.006	.053	.036	-.020	.014	1
	Sig. (2-tailed)	.324	.016	.891	.249	.440	.668	.755	
	N	468	468	468	468	468	468	468	468

Fig. 2. Show the Pearson Correlation Analysis results

3.3 Modeling for Forecasting

This research created a model for the analysis of scholarships using the Decision Tree technique using J48 and J48graft algorithms. The method of modeling is as follows:

1. Import the information which is exported from SPSS in the CSV file or Attribute-Relation File Format (ARFF) to Weka application.
2. Create a model by data classification uses Decision Tree J48 and J48graft. This paper contributed two methods for constructing and testing the model.
- Method of segmentation checking with K-Fold Cross Validation Method, using 5-Fold and 10-Fold Cross-Validation.
- Process of dividing data randomly with Percentage Split Method using Decision Tree, J48, and J48graft algorithms divide data by 20%, 30%, and 66%, respectively, and Artificial Neural Network Technique divides data by 20%, 30%, and 66% respectively.

As can be seen in Table 2, the results of the decision tree model's test use J48 algorithm with random division with 20%, 30%, and 66% data sharing, with accuracy values of 51.07%, 50.30%, and 77.35% respectively. The 5-Folds and 10-Folds segmentation checks have an accuracy of 58.27% and 59.56% respectively, and the J48graft algorithm using random division with 20% data segmentation, 30%, and 66% accuracy of 51.06%, 50.31%, and 76.72%, respectively. With the 5-Folds and 10-Folds segmentation checking methods, the accuracy is 54.49% and 5.78%, respectively.

Table 3 shows the results from testing the artificial neural network model using a random division method with data division of 20%, 30%, and 66% with accuracy values of 50.27%, 47.87%, and 50.31%, respectively. In addition, with the 5-Folds and 10-Folds segmentation inspection methods, the accuracy is 54.49% and 55.78%, respectively Fig. 2.

Table 2. Accuracy performance value from the decision tree model

Classifier	Test options	Accuracy
J48	Percentage split 20%	51.07
	Percentage split 30%	50.30
	Percentage split 66%	77.35
	Cross validation 5-folds	58.27
	Cross validation 10-folds	59.56
J48graft	Percentage split 20%	51.06
	Percentage split 30%	50.31
	Percentage split 66%	76.72
	Cross validation 5-folds	54.49
	Cross validation 10-folds	55.78

Table 3. Accuracy performance value from the test of the neural network model

Classifier	Test options	Accuracy
Multilayer Perceptron	Percentage split 20%	50.27
	Percentage split 30%	47.87
	Percentage split 66%	50.31
	Cross validation 5-folds	50.00
	Cross validation 10-folds	46.79

3.4   Web Development

The model created by the decision tree technique can measure efficiency by using Percentage Split 66%, which is the most efficient method with an accuracy value of 77.35%, which is the most suitable model for web development. Web application analysis of scholarships uses data mining techniques to find the best value in the model. This application can be displayed with a responsive web on all devices such as laptops, tablets, or smartphones. Users can easily use this; students can validate their eligibility by inputting their information on web forms by themselves. So, they can show they are suitable to apply for the scholarships correctly, which may lead to a much better opportunity to be considered for university scholarships.

4   Conclusion and Future Work

This research proposes the scholarship analytic for the student's scholarship application at university. We found that Models constructed using J48 Decision Tree techniques by measuring the efficiency using the Percentage Split 66% method is the most effective method. The accuracy is 77.35%, which has more precision than other models. Therefore, this result is used to develop the web application, in which students can evaluate their potential by themselves before applying. Web application for students is easily accessed from any device via a web browser on a computer, tablets, or mobile phones to fill out and view scholarship results. Although the initial decision to fund belongs to the selection committees, this method is beneficial for the committees to decrease their workloads because they are required to waste time considering the students who are less well qualified to receive grants.

Nevertheless, the results of this assessment may not cover all kinds of scholarships, because we have some constraint information. In the future, much more data should be acquired, which can improve the precision of the analytic.

References

1. Han, J., Pei, J., Kamber, M.: Data Mining: Concepts and Techniques. Elsevier, Netherlands (2011)
2. Hand, D.J.J.D.s.: Principles of data mining. **30**(7), 621–622 (2007)
3. Tan, P.-N., Steinbach, M., Kumar, V.: Introduction to Data Mining. Pearson Education India, London (2016)
4. Ge, Z., Song, Z., Ding, S.X., Huang, B.: Data mining and analytics in the process industry: the role of machine learning. IEEE Access **5**, 20590–20616 (2017)
5. Kavakiotis, I., Tsave, O., Salifoglou, A., Maglaveras, N., Vlahavas, I., Chouvarda, I.: Machine learning and data mining methods in diabetes research. Comput. Struct. Biotechnol. J. **15**, 104–116 (2017)
6. Noor, N.L.M., et al.: Predictive analytics: the application of J48 algorithm on grocery data to predict obesity. In: 2018 IEEE Conference on Big Data and Analytics (ICBDA). IEEE (2018)
7. Harth, N., Anagnostopoulos, C.: Quality-aware aggregation & predictive analytics at the edge. In: 2017 IEEE International Conference on Big Data (Big Data), pp. 17–26. IEEE (2017)
8. Gunasekaran, A., et al.: Big data and predictive analytics for supply chain and organizational performance. J. Bus. Res. **70**, 308–317 (2017)
9. Hanasaki, N., et al.: A quasi-real-time hydrological simulation of the Chao Phraya River using meteorological data from the Thai Meteorological Department Automatic Weather Stations. Hydrol. Res. Lett. **8**(1), 9–14 (2014)
10. Roiger, R.J.: Data Mining: A Tutorial-based Primer. CRC Press, United States (2017)
11. Ivezić, Ž., Connolly, A.J., VanderPlas, J.T., Gray, A.: Statistics, Data Mining, and Machine Learning in Astronomy: A Practical Python Guide for the Analysis of Survey Data. Princeton University Press, New Jersey (2019)
12. Fayyad, U.: Knowledge discovery in databases: an overview. In: Lavrač, N., Džeroski, S. (eds.) ILP 1997. LNCS, vol. 1297, pp. 1–16. Springer, Heidelberg (1997). https://doi.org/10.1007/3540635149_30
13. Thomas, J., Princy, R.T.: Human heart disease prediction system using data mining techniques. In: 2016 International Conference on Circuit, Power and Computing Technologies (ICCPCT). IEEE (2016)
14. Agaoglu, M.: Predicting instructor performance using data mining techniques in higher education. IEEE Access **4**, 2379–2387 (2016)
15. Baepler, P., Murdoch, C.J.: Academic analytics and data mining in higher education. Int. J. Sch. Teach. Learn. **4**(2), 1–9 (2010)

16. Bhadani, S., Verma, I., Dey, L.: Mining financial risk events from news and assessing their impact on stocks. In: Bitetta, V., Bordino, I., Ferretti, A., Gullo, F., Pascolutti, S., Ponti, G. (eds.) MIDAS 2019. LNCS (LNAI), vol. 11985, pp. 85–100. Springer, Cham (2020). https://doi.org/10.1007/978-3-030-37720-5_7

17. Priyam, A., Guptaa, R., Ratheeb, A., Srivastavab, S.: Comparative analysis of decision tree classification algorithms. Int. J. Curr. Eng. Technol. ISSN 3(2), 334–337 (2013)

18. Saritas, M.M., Yasar, A.: Performance analysis of ANN and Naive Bayes classification algorithm for data classification. Int. J. Intell. Syst. Appl. Eng. 7(2), 88–91 (2019)

19. Sugiyarti, E., Jasmi, K.A., Basiron, B., Huda, M., Shankar, K., Maseleno, A.: Decision support system of scholarship grantee selection using data mining. Int. J. Pure Appl. Math. 119(15), 2239–2249 (2018)

20. Wang, X., Zhou, C., Xu, X.: Application of C4. 5 decision tree for scholarship evaluations. Procedia Comput. Sci. 151, 179–184 (2019)

21. Saravanan, N., Gayathri, V.: Classification of dengue dataset using J48 algorithm and ant colony based AJ48 algorithm. In: 2017 International Conference on Inventive Computing and Informatics (ICICI). IEEE (2017)

22. Perveen, S., Shahbaz, M., Guergachi, A., Keshavjee, K.: Performance analysis of data mining classification techniques to predict diabetes. Procedia Comput. Sci. 82, 115–121 (2016)

23. Pham, B.T., Bui, D.T., Prakash, I.: Landslide susceptibility assessment using bagging ensemble based alternating decision trees, logistic regression and J48 decision trees methods: a comparative study. Geotech. Geol. Eng. 35(6), 2597–2611 (2017)

24. Meena, G., Choudhary, R.R.: A review paper on IDS classification using KDD 99 and NSL KDD dataset in WEKA. In: 2017 International Conference on Computer, Communications and Electronics (Comptelix). IEEE (2017)

25. Russell, I., Markov, Z.: An introduction to the Weka data mining system. In: Proceedings of the 2017 ACM SIGCSE Technical Symposium on Computer Science Education (2017)

26. Sultana, M., Haider, A., Uddin, M.S.: Analysis of data mining techniques for heart disease prediction. In: 2016 3rd International Conference on Electrical Engineering and Information Communication Technology (ICEEICT). IEEE (2016)

Centralized Access Point for Information System Integration Problems in Large Enterprises

Mai Minh Hai and Phan Duy Hung[✉]

FPT University, Hanoi, Vietnam
hai18MSE13022@fsb.edu.vn, hungpd2@fe.edu.vn

Abstract. The role of information systems is extremely important for a business, especially those operating in the field of technology. The information system works with people, information technology and processes to accomplish business objectives. In the development process of large companies, the member units create many applications to serve their purposes. Increasing the number of applications or portals consumes employees' time, and they may eventually be unable to keep track of all the necessary or useful information. That is why it is necessary to build a centralized and intelligent information access point for large organizations. The paper presents such a solution for the largest software company in Vietnam, the FPT software company. The paper describes the architectures and technologies applied to build an access point that brings whole new experiences to all employees. By integrating smart features based on artificial intelligence, the work contributed to enhancing performance and quality of work for 28,000 internal users. The approaches and results of the paper are completely applicable to similar large company models.

Keywords: Information system integration · Centralized & intelligent access point · Microservice · Artificial intelligence (AI)

1 Introduction

The process of developing management information systems usually forms and develops step by step along with the development of enterprises. The pressures for implementing an enterprise information system could be globalization, overcapacity, and reengineering, dealing with changing environments, etc. Enterprise information systems are implemented for the purposes of the integration of business processes, cycle time reduction, faster information transactions, Improvements in financial management, making tacit process knowledge explicit.

For large companies, as the number of applications increases, users spend more time to remember and perform the login. In addition, information on system usage is not well managed if the applications are independent.

This study examines the applications built on the information systems of Vietnam's largest software company, the FPT Software [1]. The company has about 40 on premise applications being used by more than 28,000 programmers, employees worldwide. These applications cover many key business areas, helping support the day-to-day

© Springer Nature Switzerland AG 2020
Y. Luo (Ed.): CDVE 2020, LNCS 12341, pp. 239–248, 2020.
https://doi.org/10.1007/978-3-030-60816-3_27

management and administration of the company such as Human Resources, Sales & Marketing, Accounting & Finance, Delivery, Administrators, etc. Applications are developed using different platforms and technologies, integrated through the Application Programming Interface (API).

While researching solutions to build a centralized and intelligent access point for FPT software company, several related studies were found. Some research related to service integration platforms by utilizing Service Oriented Architecture (SOA) [2, 3], Enterprise Service Bus (ESB) [4, 5], meta-analysis [6]. Rini Priantari and al. in [6] see that the use of different and non-standard information technology in an organization will produce silo data that affects things like, non-uniform data formats, data duplication, and information. To overcome this problem, the different information technologies integration is carried out. The study gives a information technology (IT) integration metanalysis were carried out in an organization to gain an understanding of the architecture or layers, technology and integration platform features. In a study conducted by Singh [5], the best model has been proposed in designing the integration platform by conducting studies on existing integration platform research. Furthermore, research related to data integration platforms has been carried out using ESB, web services, and XML [7, 8]. Based on this research, solutions for designing data integration platforms are available by integrating RDMS and application platforms or service integration by utilizing SOA and ESB.

This paper introduces UniGate, which serves as a single access point, integrates all information channels, services and applications as a solution. UniGate uses microservice architecture, supports web and mobile platforms. With UniGate, the notification and approval of many systems are concentrated, and users can access to a user manual, frequently asked questions (FAQs), and are supported 24/7 through AI Bot. On the business side, the process of system integration will help information be fully managed, ready for exploitation on big data and management decisions.

The remainder of the paper is organized as follows. Section 2 describes system requirements. The system design and implementation are presented in Sect. 3. Then, conclusions and perspectives are made in Sect. 4.

2 System Architecture and Requirements

2.1 Architecture Overview

UniGate is the result of applying and integrating different technologies and architectures for the FPT Software management information system. The architecture of UniGate is described in Fig. 1.

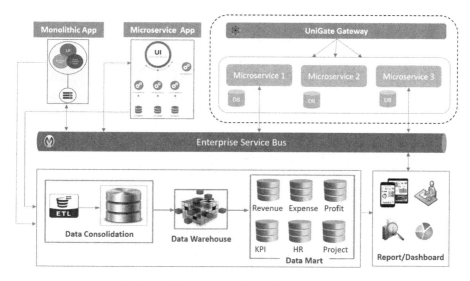

Fig. 1. Architecture overview of UniGate system.

The UniGate system consists of main components as below:

- Operation Systems: Including monolithic applications & microservice applications, which are used for Human Resource, Delivery, Finances, Marketing, etc.
- Integration System: Including an infrastructure of enterprise service bus. ESB is used for integrating services in the application landscape, allows different applications to communicate with each other by acting as a transit system for carrying data between applications.
- Data Consolidation: Combining data information from operation systems in many different formats, unifying and storing it in a raw database. The area sits between the data source(s) and the data target(s), which are often data warehouses, data marts, or other data repositories.
- Data warehouse/Data Mart: Storing data from operation systems, used for reporting and analyzing.
- Report/Dashboard: Providing analysis and summary reports to support decision-making.
- UniGate application: unique interface between the user and Unigate, which is integrated with artificial intelligence. Through this interface, users can work with services within the enterprise easily without the need for separate portals or applications for each service.

2.2   System Requirements

The system has three main types of user that are system normal users, managers and administrators. The functional requirements of each user are described in Table 1.

Table 1. Functional requirements.

Type	Content
Administrator	Create/Manage schedule
	Manage applications: Add new, Edit, Delete
	Manage app status: Disable, Enable
	Manage User Profile: Create, Edit, Remove, Upload Image
	Monitor API: Search API, View API status
	View log: View, Export
Manager	All functions of normal users
	Approval: View all ticket need to Approval
Normal User	Manage application: View, Add/remove favorites, Search
	Notification: View notifications from all systems
	Chatbot: Conversation between users and an AI bot
	Ticket: Log ticket support
	Landing Page: View report/dashboard

3   System Design and Implementation

3.1   Servers

The system consists of many servers configured in Table 2.

Table 2. List of servers used in the system.

No	Configuration			Type	Number	Function	Environment
	CPU (Cores)	RAM (Gb)	HDD (Gb)				
1	16	16	500	Virtual	1	Application	TEST
2	16	16	500	Virtual	1	Database	TEST
3	16	32	500	Virtual	1	Application/Database	UAT
4	16	32	500	Virtual	1	Application/Database	PRE/PRODUCTION
5	16	32	1024	Virtual	3	Database	PRODUCTION
6	16	32	500	Virtual	1	API Gateway	PRODUCTION
7	16	32	1024	Virtual	3	Microservice	PRODUCTION
8	16	32	1024	Virtual	1	Chatbot	PRODUCTION

3.2   Monolithic and Microservice Applications

Some applications in the system have all the business components packaged together, distributed and deployed as a whole, this development and deploy pattern is called monolithic [9, 10]. To realize the highly available and flexibly, the monolithic application deployed as a whole, and the load balancing carrying out at the front end using a load balancer. When it comes to the monolithic architecture system, we cannot make replicated the relevant component or module for extending, and deploying the entire application across multiple nodes will a cause waste of resources.

Some existing applications will be migrated as well as new applications that will use the microservice architecture [9, 10]. The microservice architecture is a lightweight, miniaturized development and operation mode. Each microservice deployed independently and follow the single responsibility principle, different microservice can use different technology stack, and update independently. In the UniGate system, microservice applications are developed based on JHipster, a development platform to generate, develop and deploy Microservice applications [11].

A typical JHipster application will include three components. First, JHipster Registry is an essential component in the microservices architecture because it connects all the other components and provides the communication between these components. Second, the microservice application which will provide the backend capabilities through exposing the API. Third, the microservices gateway is the frontend of the whole system which will include all the APIs of every microservice application in the system. UniGate's microservice architecture is described in Fig. 2:

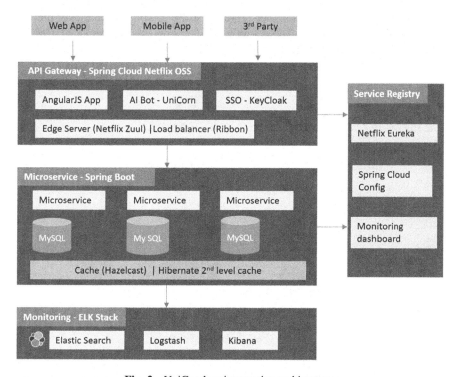

Fig. 2. UniGate's microservice architecture.

UniGate has an API Gateway that handles web traffic and also acts as a front-end application. It uses several common microservices of available information system (permission, organization, Single Sign On (SSO)) and has three new microservices:

Application Management, Notification, UniCorn. All microservices are registered in Service Registry. UniGate uses ELK Stack (Elasticsearch, Logstash, Kibana) [12] for managing and tracking log. Some of the main features of UniGate are:

- Centralize all notifications
- Integrate SSO using Keycloak, an open-source software product to allow single sign-on with Identity Management and Access Management [13]
- Integrate UniCorn - an AI bot that will be described below
- Plug/Un-plug application, allow users to manage applications, easy to add or remove applications that appear on the list
- Full-text search using Elastic Search for searching user guide, FAQ and other documents

3.3   AI Bot

AI Bot that integrates with UniGate is a chatbot which provides support service for all internal user of the FPT Software information system. The chatbot is called UniCorn. It allows users to chat and request many supporting services, offers both live chat and chatbot. The supporter can stop a bot response so he or she can take over the conversation. UniCorn is based on RASA - an open-source AI Bot platform [14]. UniCorn architecture is described in Fig. 3:

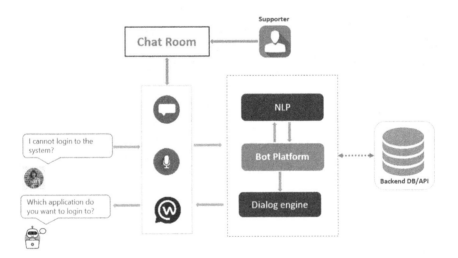

Fig. 3. UniCorn Bot architecture.

UniCorn has many intelligent features. It is a self-learning bot and be integrated with enterprise apps and legacy systems. UniCorn supports conversation channels across text, voice and custom channels and in multi-lingual. This AI Bot can be fully deployed on both on-premise and cloud environments.

3.4   Enterprise Service Bus

ESB is a standardized integration platform that combines messaging & web service. This platform provides a dependable and scalable infrastructure that connects disparate applications and IT resources, mediates their incompatibilities, orchestrates their interactions, and makes them broadly available as services for additional uses. Mule ESB [15] (community version) is used as the integration platform in the FPT Software information system (Fig. 4):

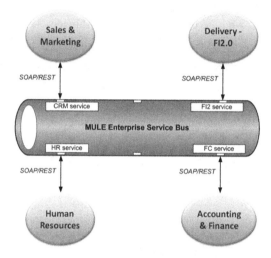

Fig. 4. Integration platform (ESB).

3.5   Data Consolidation and Data Warehouse

Data consolidation is the process that combines all data wherever it may live, removes any redundancies, and cleans up any errors before it gets stored in a data warehouse. Oracle Data Integrator [16] is used to extract all data from FPT Software operation systems, transform and load it into a centralized raw database.

Data warehouse is a subject-oriented, integrated, nonvolatile, time-variant data set for decision making support in enterprise management. Data warehouse can across time and space boundaries of the enterprise, integrating the data of different companies and different processing systems to provide a unified view, which can access more comprehensive information about company operation and customer behavior. Microsoft SQL Server [17] is used to implement the Data Warehouse solution for the FPT Software.

In this solution, the online analytical processing (OLAP) tool is an integral part. It based on the data warehouse and can perform the on-line data access and analysis for specific questions. The company used SQL Server Business Intelligence Development Studio (BIDS) [18] for this task. The goal is to meet the decision-making support or the particular query and reporting demand under the multi-dimensional environment.

A data mart is a subset of a data warehouse oriented to a specific business line. Data marts contain repositories of summarized data collected for analysis on a specific section or unit within the organization, some data mart have been built are Revenue, Expense, Profit, KPI, Project, etc. by Month, Quarter, Year.

3.6   Website Design

The main screen of the Web application is in Fig. 5. Figures from 6 to 7 show some statistics of the amount of traffic and user interaction with the system: the number of users accessing the system, the total number of users accessing over time, and the location of employees who are using the system worldwide.

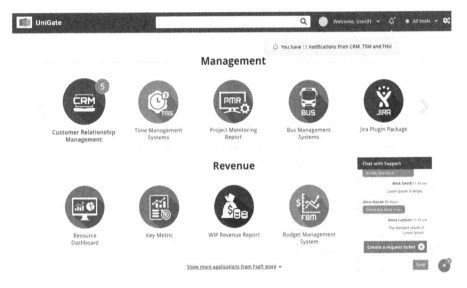

Fig. 5. UniGate main screen.

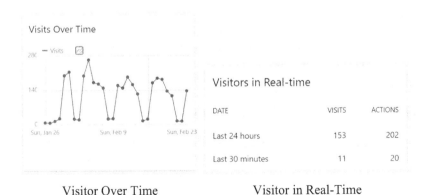

Visitor Over Time   Visitor in Real-Time

Fig. 6. Statistics of the amount of traffic and user interaction with the system.

Fig. 7. Visitor map.

4   Conclusion and Perspectives

The implementation of a centralized and intelligent access point for large organizations is essential. The paper presents the information system integration solution for the FPT software company in Vietnam. The paper describes the architectures and technologies applied to build an intelligent access point that brings whole new experiences to all employees.

Micro-service applications are based on the JHipster framework. Future integration of the framework with automated source generation is expected to accelerate application development by 30%. In addition, JHipster also can be integrated with the ability to test performance so that applications can be verified their own load capacity before releasing products.

This solution is also fully applicable for similar company models and is also a good reference for research directions of Software engineering, Information System, etc.

References

1. FPT Software. https://www.fpt-software.com/about-fpt-software/. Accessed 01 Feb 2020
2. Hahn, M., Saez, S.G., Andrikopoulos, V., Karastoyanova, D., Leymann, F.: Development and evaluation of a multi-tenant service middleware PaaS solution. In: Proceedings of the IEEE/ACM 7th International Conference on Utility and Cloud Computing, London, pp. 278–287 (2014). https://doi.org/10.1109/ucc.2014.37
3. Llambías, G., Ruggia, R.: A middleware-based platform for the integration of bioinformatic services. In: Proceedings of the XL Latin American Computing Conference (CLEI), Montevideo, pp. 1–12 (2014). https://doi.org/10.1109/clei.2014.6965178

4. Delgado, A., González, L., Ruggia, R.: A process-aware inter-organizational service integration platform to support collaborative organizations. In: Proceedings of the IEEE International Conference on Services Computing (SCC), San Francisco, CA, pp. 844–847 (2016). https://doi.org/10.1109/scc.2016.120
5. Singh, P.M., Van, S.M., Wieringa, R.: Reference architecture for integration platforms. In: Proceedings of the IEEE 21st International Enterprise Distributed Object Computing Conference (EDOC), Quebec City, QC, pp. 113–122 (2017). https://doi.org/10.1109/edoc.2017.24
6. Priantari, R., Kurniawan, N.B.: Integrated IT service platform: systematic literature review and meta-analysis. In: Proceedings of the International Conference on Information Technology Systems and Innovation (ICITSI), Bandung - Padang, Indonesia, pp. 562–567 (2018). https://doi.org/10.1109/icitsi.2018.8696013
7. Fan, J., Xu, C., Xiong, L.: Data transformation of ESB based on the data model for integration. In: Proceedings of the 9th International Conference on Fuzzy Systems and Knowledge Discovery, Sichuan, pp. 2645–2651 (2012). https://doi.org/10.1109/fskd.2012.6233914
8. Qiu, D., Liu, J., Zhao, G.: Design and application of data integration platform based on web services and XML. In: Proceedings of the 6th International Conference on Electronics Information and Emergency Communication (ICEIEC), Beijing, pp. 253–256 (2016). https://doi.org/10.1109/iceiec.2016.7589732
9. Furda, A., Fidge, C., Zimmermann, O., Kelly, W., Barros, A.: Migrating enterprise legacy source code to microservices: on multitenancy, statefulness, and data consistency. IEEE Softw. 35(03), 63–72 (2018). https://doi.org/10.1109/MS.2017.440134612(2018)
10. Velepucha, V., Flores, P., Torres, J.: Migration of monolithic applications towards microservices under the vision of the information hiding principle: a systematic mapping study. In: Botto-Tobar, M., León-Acurio, J., Díaz Cadena, A., Montiel Díaz, P. (eds.) ICAETT 2019. AISC, vol. 1066, pp. 90–100. Springer, Cham (2020). https://doi.org/10.1007/978-3-030-32022-5_9
11. https://www.jhipster.tech/. Accessed 01 Feb 2020
12. https://www.elastic.co/what-is/elk-stack. Accessed 01 Feb 2020
13. https://www.keycloak.org/. Accessed 01 Feb 2020
14. https://rasa.com/. Accessed 01 Feb 2020
15. https://www.mulesoft.com/platform/soa/mule-esb-open-source-esb. Accessed 01 Feb 2020
16. https://www.oracle.com/middleware/technologies/data-integrator.html. Accessed 01 Feb 2020
17. https://www.microsoft.com/en-us/sql-server/sql-server-downloads. Accessed 01 Feb 2020
18. https://www.microsoft.com/en-us/sql-server/sql-business-intelligence. Accessed 01 Feb 2020

Cooperation Between Performance and Innovation Engine: An Exploratory Study of Digital Innovation Labs in Family Business

Melina Schleef[1] , Jasper Steinlechner[1], Christine Strauss[2] ,
and Christian Stummer[1(✉)]

[1] Bielefeld University, Universitätsstr. 25, 33615 Bielefeld, Germany
{melina.schleef, jasper.steinlechner,
christian.stummer}@uni-bielefeld.de
[2] University of Vienna, Oskar-Morgenstern-Platz 1, 1090 Vienna, Austria
christine.strauss@univie.ac.at

Abstract. Digital innovation laboratories (DILs) constitute a promising approach to supporting a firm's digital transformation. Whereas the firm's existent departments, which form the so-called performance engine, can keep focusing on daily operations, the DIL representing the innovation engine executes digital innovation tasks. Cooperation between the performance engine and the innovation engine—including, but not limited to, the continuous exchange of information—is critical for the success of such an organizational setting. As research in this specific field of cooperative organization is still scarce, we employed an explorative case-study approach based on interviews with managers from DILs in family firms. Family business was chosen because it plays a prominent role in the German economy and it shall identify its own best practice in facing the digital future. We investigated on drivers, challenges, and organizational issues for establishing and operating such DILs. The findings provide valuable insights for practitioners in family business and may serve as a starting point for further research to examine differences between DILs in family and non-family business.

Keywords: Digital innovation labs · Cooperation between performance and innovation engine · Cooperative organization · Explorative case study

1 Introduction

The upcoming era of smart products and services poses severe managerial challenges, as these innovations not only provide novel functionalities for customers but will transform both markets and companies [6, 19, 20]. Smart products and services are likely to affect business processes, sales channels, supply chains, or even the core business models of incumbent firms. Digital innovation laboratories (DILs) provide a promising organizational measure to handle a firm's digital transformation, as they enable the maintenance of existing processes in the departments of the "performance engine", which have been shaped over decades in order to continuously increase productivity and efficiency, while establishing an "innovation engine" in close cooperation.

© Springer Nature Switzerland AG 2020
Y. Luo (Ed.): CDVE 2020, LNCS 12341, pp. 249–259, 2020.
https://doi.org/10.1007/978-3-030-60816-3_28

DILs are business units inside or outside a firm that aim at enhancing creativity and facilitating collaboration in order to foster the development of new products, services, or business models that particularly focus on digitalization. Their specific role as a potential managerial means for preparing a company for the upcoming digital age has gained practical relevance only lately. Our work aims at contributing to this relatively young stream of research.

In doing so, we focus on family business because it plays a particularly prominent role in Germany, with a share of approximately 90% in all German firms [23]. In addition, there is evidence that German family firms may cut their own path to face the digital future [5]. Accordingly, our work focuses on research questions concerning *(i)* the drivers for establishing DILs in family business, *(ii)* challenges in operating them as part of a cooperative organization, and *(iii)* organizational issues of such DILs.

Our findings support (top) managers who intend to strengthen their company's digital innovation capabilities and foster its sustainability by establishing a DIL as a cooperative-based organizational unit. At a more operational level, innovation managers who are already responsible for running such a DIL might benefit from examples of how others have tackled this challenge. Finally, researchers could utilize our exploratory results as a starting point for further research.

2 Background

2.1 Digital Innovation Laboratories

More often than not, incumbents fail to suitably deal with disruptive innovations and new technologies [3]. In order to execute the necessary innovation tasks, Govindarajan and Trimble [11] suggested a collaborative approach by the establishment of a dedicated team of internally and externally recruited employees (i.e., to establish an innovation engine). Tension between the performance and innovation engine might arise because of contrary objectives: whereas the performance engine focuses on achieving daily operative goals, the innovation engine develops new processes and products.

Among the alternatives of organizing this innovation team and embedding it in the overall organization, innovation laboratories (ILs) representing the innovation engine are suggested when the innovation initiative has a long-term perspective [8]. Although there is no undisputed definition for ILs yet, it is widely agreed that they have *(i)* their own physical (creativity-enhancing) environment; *(ii)* human, creativity, financial, and technical resources; and *(iii)* facilitation services to guide the innovation process. Prior works studied various characteristics of ILs (e.g., with respect to the influence of the physical space's design on creativity) and corresponding pros and cons (e.g., the reinforcement of corporate commitment to innovation or the encouragement of dissenting working methods leading to instability within the firm), or they compared different properties of ILs in different countries [e.g., 1, 9, 14, 15]. Most recently, Fecher et al. [7] explored team formation in and performance of ILs and Memon et al. [17] investigated the structural and functional diversity of ILs. The research methodology applied in most instances was explorative—that is, findings were derived from case studies based on interviews.

As far as DILs are concerned, research on their specific role as a means for coping with challenges stemming from digital transformation in numerous markets is relatively scarce but is gaining increasing interest among both researchers and practitioners. For example, Holotiuk and Beimborn [12] compared the DILs of nine firms in Germany with respect to intra-organizational exchange and integration. They characterized DILs as a dedicated organizational unit that combines the firm's exploration efforts into focusing on digital innovation. In doing so, a DIL is typically separated from the entire organization in terms of communication, mindset, and location, but still connected through transfer of knowledge and employees.

2.2 Innovation and Digitalization in Family Business

Although family business is presumed to be as innovative as non-family business, it may differ in several aspects. For example, long-term commitment, intergenerational involvement, and familiness are considered typical competitive advantages that positively affect innovation output; in contrast, risk aversion, a reservation of using investment capital, and insistence on retaining control might hamper innovation capacity [for an overview, see 2, 24]. Moreover, Werner et al. [24] showed that innovative power often declines from one generation to the next, which might contribute as an additional restraint for old-established family business.

In general, managers tend to avoid disruptive innovations in order to not risk possible damage to their career or reputation [3]. This is true even more so for family business, which is predisposed for relying on evolutionary innovations because of its general risk aversion. Consequently, managers in family firms must be particularly sensitive with respect to the opportunities and consequences arising during the digital transformation. DILs might be a measure to ensure that critical developments are not missed out on.

Nevertheless, research on digitalization in family business is rather limited. However, there is anecdotal evidence from an interview with Nils Kreimeier—an editor of the business magazine Capital, which has co-produced a ranking of DILs in German firms [22] —that DILs in family business differ from DILs in non-family business.

3 Research Design

3.1 Research Approach and Data Collection

Our study was based on a qualitative approach—namely, a case study using interviews, which is considered a suitable method for examining family business [13]. As no prior studies were concerned with DILs in family business, our study design was explorative.

All participating family firms are from the German region of East Westphalia-Lippe, which is well-known for its family-owned "hidden champions." Although these firms—namely, Claas KGaA mbH, Goldbeck GmbH, Schüco International KG, and Phoenix Contact GmbH & Co. KG—operate in diverse industrial sectors (i.e., agricultural engineering equipment, construction industry, building supplier, and electrical engineering, respectively), they have in common their engineering or technical focus (see Table 1 for an overview).

Table 1. Description of interviewees and associated companies

No.	Family firm	Industry	Firm's characteristics	Interviewee's position
1	Claas KGaA mbH [4]	Agricultural engineering equipment	Founded: 1913 Annual revenue: € 3.9 bn Employees: 11,500	Head of Digital Transformation
2	Goldbeck GmbH [10]	Construction industry	Founded: 1969 Annual revenue: € 2.9 bn Employees: 7,000	Director of Goldbeck US Inc./ Head of VDC & BIM Department
3	Schüco International KG [21]	Building supplier	Founded: 1951 Annual revenue: € 1.7 bn Employees: 5,400	Head of Schüco Startup Space/Member of Schüco Digital Board
4	Phoenix Contact GmbH & Co. KG [18]	Electrical engineering	Founded: 1923 Annual revenue: € 2.5 bn Employees: 17,600	Vice President Corporate Development & New Business

We conducted semi-structured interviews with DIL managers either face-to-face or by phone. For the development of the interview guide, previous works by Bustamante et al. [1] and Fuzi et al. [8] were taken into account. The interview guide referred to five areas regarding their respective DIL: establishment, organization, employees' working styles, drivers and challenges, and expected future development. The interviews were conducted between August 2019 and November 2019 and took 30 to 45 min.

3.2   Data Analysis

The interviews were transcribed and coded using the software MAXQDA. As a general rule, we followed the guidelines provided by Mayring [16]. The three research foci—drivers, challenges, and the organization related to DILs in family business—were used as a first guide to code. Following Mayring's inductive category development approach, we finally identified nine categories: industrial sector characteristics, family influence, digital transformation, innovation team, organization, strategic embedment, cooperation with start-ups, drivers and challenges, success and future expectations. In order to ensure data reliability, two authors individually have coded the interviews.

4   Findings

The main findings regarding the drivers and challenges for establishing DILs in family business as well as the organization of these DILs and their integration in family business are summarized in Table 2.

Table 2. Findings

Drivers for DILs in family business	• Initiation by top management or family owners • Facilitation of cooperation with other firms • Development of employees' expertise in digital transformation • Empowerment of employees • Speed-up internal development of new technologies • Improvement of efficiency of a firm's digital processes • Acceleration of a firm's growth • Improvement of a firm's competitiveness • Attraction of young talents
Challenges for DILs in family business	• Management of information exchange between performance engine and DIL • Establishment of interdisciplinary cooperation • Identifying appropriate (external or internal) managers • Strengthening authority of DIL management • Performance measurement and proof of DIL's success • Overcoming intra-organizational resistance
Organization of DILs in family business	• Establishment as independent department • Location in proximity to headquarter • Recruiting most DIL employees from other internal departments • Hiring a few DIL employees with specific expertise externally

In the following, findings are explained in more detail and illustrated through quotations. Note that all quotations are translated from German. The respective interview numbers refer to Table 1 (e.g., "Interview 2" relates to the director of Goldbeck).

4.1 Drivers for DILs in Family Business

DILs were typically initiated by the top management or family owners. Hence, the idea of establishing a DIL follows a top-down approach. The final decision is always made in accordance with the family or the CEO, respectively.

> "… I developed a concept of how the firm can address digitalization and how it can establish a special unit in the future and presented the concept to the management board. Subsequently, [the DIL] was established." (Interview 3)

A first reason for establishing a DIL is found in the demand to further the employees' expertise in digital transformation. To this end, DILs provide a protected space for the employees to experience digitalization and enable trial and error in organization-related digitalization tasks and empower them to implement related projects.

> "… the topic of empowerment, how to qualify the employees. We can talk much about digitalization, but if the employees do not have a comprehension of how to deal with digital topics

and how to approach digital business models as well as if they are not given the possibility of trying something out, [facing digitalization] it will not succeed." (Interview 1)

"… to establish space for experiments but aiming at generating additional value for the firm." (Interview 4)

Further, DILs are expected to make a firm's digital processes more efficient, simpler, and faster; moreover, they supposedly facilitate company growth—for example, by developing new business models and extending the firm's portfolio.

"… to make internal processes more efficient, simpler, and faster, there are possibilities of developing new business models…" (Interview 3)

A DIL may also foster the digital transformation in family business so that it can remain internationally competitive and extend its lead for economically more difficult times. Hence, DILs contribute to sustainable competitiveness.

"… to remain competitive in the future." (Interview 3)

"… in good times that are characterized by sufficient money and resources, it is important to think about the future." (Interview 2)

Moreover, DILs facilitate cooperation with other firms. They provide space for establishing networks and support in order to obtain new insights from the industry. Accordingly, family firms set a special focus on cooperation with start-ups.

"… to find partners who have a similar mindset […] and to start a common project." (Interview 2)

"… access to markets, new technologies, new business models in cooperation with start-ups …" (Interview 4)

Finally, DILs help to increase brand awareness and the perception of family business as an attractive employer. A large number of family firms are located in a rather rural area that is not appealing for young professionals and, thus, DILs may also help attracting young talent who otherwise would not have selected a family firm and provide them with a modern work environment.

"… to be attractive to new young employees and to keep them in the firm in our region, this is more challenging than in Berlin." (Interview 1)

4.2   Challenges for DILs in Family Business

The management of the cooperation and information exchange between the performance engine and the DIL poses a prime challenge. As a means to enable ambidexterity, family firms attempt to balance the exploration of digital innovations (enabled by the DIL) and exploitation of generating long-term value (enabled by the performance engine). However, although the innovation engine and the performance engine are separated, they still require to be engaged in a constant exchange and working cooperation.

"... not that the one hand does not know what the other one is doing. Instead, it should be something that is complementary ..." (Interview 4)

A related challenge is interdisciplinary collaboration within the DIL team where different cultures might collide and result in conflicts. In addition, different ways of working may lead to problems of acceptance of the DIL within the family firm.

"So, many cultures within [the firm] and numerous divisions get together and not everything works out in a rose-colored way." (Interview 1)

"... but there are also people who furiously refer to the coffee drinkers of the [DIL], who hang around on their beanbags." (Interview 1)

Another major managerial challenge in establishing DILs lies in identifying an appropriate DIL manager: If an internal manager is selected, the manager is familiar with the family firm as well as the industry and shares mutual trust with the family firm. Otherwise—that is, if an external DIL manager is selected—the manager brings in new ideas and a different perspective to the firm.

"... there has to be trust [and the DIL manager] must not be a digitalization weirdo who comes from somewhere and preaches the new world ..." (Interview 1)

"... previously, I have been working at [another company] for eleven years and I was looking for a new challenge [...] and we arranged that I will switch to Goldbeck and establish an innovation lab in the Silicon Valley." (Interview 2)

Although DILs usually have a designated DIL manager who is supposed to make decisions, often family owners—mostly representing the top management—interfere, thereby undermining the authority of the DIL management.

"But if the management board is not committed to it, it becomes more difficult to deal with these topics." (Interview 3)

Further, measuring the DIL's success is difficult because its contribution to the overall success of a firm cannot be easily quantified by conventional performance figures. Instead, other indicators must be applied—such as, for example, the DIL's acceptance in the family firm, the improvement of everyday tasks, or a gaining of knowledge regarding future sectoral trends.

"But we do not have a directly measurable value ..." (Interview 3)

"... whether we have improved [the employees'] daily routines." (Interview 2)

Finally, overcoming resistance from within the firm (but outside the DIL) is necessary, since employees may refuse innovations that are associated with digital transformation.

"Most of the organization is resistant to change and needs a clear statement from the top management." (Interview 1)

4.3   Organization of DILs in Family Business

Almost every DIL we visited in the course of this study is implemented as a fairly independent department but is still embedded in the parent company (as opposed to being established as formal subsidiary companies). The reason for this is that it is more straightforward to transfer new knowledge from the DIL into the core business.

> "We want to bring the digital transformation into the core business and, hence, we believe that an independent limited liability company does not pursue the appropriate goal and secludes itself and does its own thing." (Interview 1)

Most of the DILs are located near their respective headquarters. However, there is also a case in which a different strategy is implemented.

> "… and we like it that we did not position [our DIL] in Berlin." (Interview 1)

> "… to establish a [DIL] in the Silicon Valley." (Interview 2)

The DIL team is composed of both internal and external employees. Most employees come from internal departments which facilitates the cooperation with the performance engine's employees since these internal DIL employees have extensive knowledge regarding the industry and the family firm. Usually, they seek an opportunity to further develop their competency and gain valuable experience. A few employees with specific expertise are hired externally.

> "… in fact, they are all long-term employees." (Interview 2)

> "Of course, we have some externally hired employees here, too." (Interview 1)

5   Managerial Implications

Our case study provides insights from successful DILs in family business. Findings serve as a first guide regarding the establishment of DILs and how to tackle corresponding challenges.

For top management, the description of drivers and challenges of DILs might contribute to making an informed decision for or against the establishment of such a DIL. For the more operational management level, the case studies provide several hints on how to successfully establish a DIL and meet associated challenges: First, DILs require a suitable manager with industry-specific knowledge. An internal manager would benefit from additional firm-specific knowledge, whereas an external manager would add an external perspective and might bring in new ideas. Second, the cooperation and information exchange between the performance engine and the DIL must be secured. This can be supported by staffing with internal employees who are familiar with each other and by locating the DIL close to the headquarter; other measures (e.g., regular meetings, company intranet, or employee newsletters) might apply as well. Third, DILs and their employees often experience rejection and criticism from other business units (i.e., the performance engine). Continuous exchange between the performance engine and the DIL, a transparent culture, and open-mindedness regarding new working methods on the part of top management may serve as effective countermeasures.

6 Conclusion

This paper presented an explorative study on the drivers, challenges, and the organization of DILs in family business. We performed semi-structured interviews with four top managers of engineering- and technical-oriented Germany-located companies. A major finding from our interviews is that the main function of DILs in family firms lies in supporting the digital transformation of the incumbent company (e.g., with respect to new business processes and models). Consequently, close cooperation between the performance engine and the DIL is vital in order to *(i)* support in-house acceptance of an organizational unit, which follows entirely different principles and evaluation criteria than other units, and *(ii)* transfer crucial knowledge (as well as specific results and findings) from the DIL into the core business. In contrast, DILs in non-family firms are presumably more oriented toward (short-term) profit, potential spin-offs, etc.

Further, we identified several starting points for future research. First, it could be worthwhile to examine alternative strategies in locating the DIL. In this regard, we found two different approaches—that is, locating the DIL close to headquarters versus locating it at some remote hub of new technology such as in Silicon Valley. The effects of both approaches on the cooperation between the performance engine and the DIL shall be investigated. Second, there is an antagonism between the often rather risk-averse attitude in family firms and the need to prepare these fairly traditional firms for a digital future. Identifying the means to overcome this conflict is certainly an interesting topic for future work. Third, research on cooperative issues seems to be particularly important and fruitful. Corresponding research can refer to various issues of cooperation: *(i)* clearly-defined measures to maintain cooperation between the performance engine and the DIL (e.g., design of a collaborative working environment, hybrid evaluation and performance measurement, incentives), *(ii)* the role of DILs in initiating and coordinating cooperation with innovative start-ups, and *(iii)* cooperation and participation of DILs in research networks.

References

1. Bustamante, F.O., Reyes, J.I.P., Camargo, M., Dupont, L.: Spaces to foster and sustain innovation: towards a conceptual framework. In: Proceedings of the IEEE International Conference on Engineering, Technology and Innovation/ International Technology Management Conference (ICE/ITMC), Belfast, United Kingdom, pp. 1–7. IEEE (2015)
2. Calabrò, A., Vecchiarini, M., Gast, J., Campopiano, G., De Massis, A., Kraus, S.: Innovation in family firms: a systematic literature review and guidance for future research. Int. J. Manage. Rev. **21**(3), 317–355 (2019)

3. Christensen, C.M.: The Innovator's Dilemma. Harvard Business School Press, Boston (1997)
4. Claas Homepage: About Claas. https://www.claas-group.com/the-group/about-claas/overview Accessed 27 Mar 2020
5. Cravotta, S., Grottke, M.: Digitalization in German family firms: some preliminary insights. J. Evol. Stud. Bus. **4**(1), 1–25 (2019)
6. Dawid, H., et al.: Management science in the era of smart consumer products: challenges and research perspectives. Cent. Eur. J. Oper. Res. **25**(1), 203–230 (2017). https://doi.org/10.1007/s10100-016-0436-9
7. Fecher, F., Winding, J., Hutter, K., Füller, J.: Innovation labs from a participants' perspective. J. Bus. Res. **110**, 567–576 (2020)
8. Fuzi, A., Gryszkiewicz, L., Sikora, D.: A spectrum of urban innovation intermediaries: from co-working to collaboration. In: Proceedings of the ISPIM Innovation Conference, Stockholm, Sweden, pp. 1–6 (2018)
9. Gey, R., Meyer, L.P., Thieme, M.: A conceptual framework for describing the phenomenon innovation laboratory: a structurational viewpoint. In: Proceedings of the XXIII International RESER Conference, Aix en Provence, France, pp. 1–17 (2013)
10. Goldbeck Homepage: The company. https://www.goldbeck.co.uk/fileadmin/Redaktion/Downloads/Unternehmen/Dokumente/The_company_2019.pdf Accessed 27 Mar 2020
11. Govindarajan, V., Trimble, C.: The Other Side of Innovation: Solving The Execution Challenge. Harvard Business Review Press, Boston (2010)
12. Holotiuk, F., Beimborn, D.: Temporal ambidexterity: how digital innovation labs connect exploration and exploitation for digital innovation. In: Proceedings of the International Conference on Information Systems (ICIS), paper 3232, Munich, Germany, pp. 1–17 (2019)
13. Leppäaho, T., Plakoyiannaki, E., Dimitratos, P.: The case study in family business: an analysis of current research practices and recommendations. Fam. Bus. Rev. **29**(1), 159–173 (2016)
14. Lewis, M., Moultrie, J.: The organizational innovation laboratory. Creativity Innov. Manage. **14**(1), 73–83 (2005)
15. Magadley, W., Birdi, K.: Innovation labs: an examination into the use of physical spaces to enhance organizational creativity. Creativity and Innov. Manage. **18**(4), 315–325 (2009)
16. Mayring, P.: Qualitative Inhaltsanalyse, 12th edn. Beltz, Weinheim (2015) [in German]
17. Memon, A.B., Meyer, K., Thieme, M., Meyer, L.P.: Inter-InnoLab collaboration: an investigation of the diversity and interconnection among innovation laboratories. J. Eng. Technol. Manage. **47**(1), 1–21 (2018)
18. Phoenix Contact Homepage: Facts and figures. https://www.phoenixcontact.com/online/portal/pc?1dmy&urile=wcm%3apath%3a/pcen/web/corporate/company/subcategory_pages/Data_and_facts/32019ead-971d-45de-b0d3-638b8968671f Accessed 27 Mar 2020
19. Porter, M.E., Heppelmann, J.E.: How smart, connected products are transforming competition. Harvard Bus. Rev. **92**(11), 64–88 (2014)
20. Porter, M.E., Heppelmann, J.E.: How smart, connected products are transforming companies. Harvard Bus. Rev. **93**(10), 96–114 (2015)
21. Schüco Homepage: Company. https://www.schueco.com/de-en/company Accessed 27 Mar 2020
22. Sindemann, T.: Konzerne auf den Spuren von Startups 2019: Der steinige Weg zu substantieller digitaler Innovation. https://www.infront-consulting.com/publikationen Accessed 27 Mar 2020 [in German]

23. Statista: Anteile der Familienunternehmen in Deutschland an allen Unternehmen, an der Gesamtbeschäftigung und am gesamten Umsatz. https://de.statista.com/statistik/daten/studie/234891/umfrage/familienunternehmen-in-deutschland-anteil-an-unternehmen-beschaeftigten-und-umsatz/Accessed 27 Mar 2020 [in German]
24. Werner, A., Schröder, C., Chlosta, S.: Driving factors of innovation in family and non-family SMEs. Small Bus. Econ. **50**(1), 201–218 (2018). https://doi.org/10.1007/s11187-017-9884-4

Dynamic Network Visualization of Space Use Patterns to Support Agent-based Modelling for Spatial Design

Dario Esposito$^{(\boxtimes)}$ and Ilenia Abbattista

Polytechnic University of Bari, 70125 Bari, Italy
dario.esposito@poliba.it, abbattistailenia@gmail.com

Abstract. Urban planning practice and architectural design increasingly adopt agent-based models and simulations to support decision-making for spatial design. Nonetheless, although essential, a reliable representation of human spatial behaviour in a socially rich context is still challenging. The study presents a framework built on a Dynamic Network Visualization of space use patterns based on a Post Occupancy Evaluation in the case study of a hospital ward, which is intended to develop an agent-based spatial analysis. A functional and organizational redesign of the ward plan is proposed following the analysis of social and spatial behaviour of agents. The outlined methodology aims to prepare the development of a multi-agent software simulation to validate the proposed redesign from a human-centred perspective. Findings indicate the relevance of the proposed approach starting from organizational contexts with complex workflows where cooperation between agents is widely exist, such as in healthcare environments. The framework is structured as a methodology to support the practice of architectural design and urban planning for the realization of more efficient and sustainable cities.

Keywords: Dynamic Network Visualization · Agent-based modelling · Spatial design

1 Introduction

In strategic spatial planning, an increasing interest in the knowledge of human behaviour in spatial intelligence has emerged. This is essential for the development and management of human life spaces [1]. However, understanding the role of the environment in human behaviour performance in early design stages poses a major difficulty for practitioners, particularly due to the unpredictable impact that a physical setting produces on human decisions. It could lead to delays in job task accomplishment,

---

Author Contributions: Conceptualization, methodology, formalization, review and editing D.E.; investigation and visualization D.E. and I.A.; writing – introduction, background, and conclusions D.E.; writing - case study and results D.E. and I.A. All authors have read and agreed to the published version of the manuscript.

Y. Luo (Ed.): CDVE 2020, LNCS 12341, pp. 260–269, 2020.
https://doi.org/10.1007/978-3-030-60816-3_29

dissatisfaction, stress and user safety hazards, e.g. health risks such as falls, injuries or diseases [2].

In the present study the case study of a healthcare environment is investigated. Indeed, the relative complexity of hospitals on one hand, and their straightforward, standardized use pattern on the other, make them advantageous for our aim, since they can provide a comprehensive observed data set on which to set the proposed methodological framework. Moreover, it is intriguing since hospitals deal with the constant pressure of ensuring cost efficiency and so target areas include the optimization of processes and flow and the reduction of admission waiting times. However, it is difficult to find an optimal plan to manage resources and to assess the impact of built space on procedures and in this regard, an agent-based approach could be valuable. Furthermore, the choice of this case study should have a limited impact on the validity of the study because the methodology can be easily transferable to other domains.

In this background, the aim of the present study is to propose the use of a Dynamic Network Visualization (DNV) of human social and spatial behaviour to build an agent-based spatial analysis in order to inform the development of a multi-agent simulation. The DNV method is based on a Post Occupancy Evaluation (POE) conducted in an Italian hospital. A functional space analysis and an observation of users' behaviour were developed to explicitly represent space use patterns through the DNV spatially shown on the ward plan map. The produced output supported an agent-based spatial analysis which was used to propose a functional redesign of the unit, which in turn is intended to be the layout to be tested with the multi-agent simulation. The case study revealed potential and possible applications for the proposed framework which is developed to be of support to the architectural design and urban planning practices. Future studies will focus on model formalization for software implementation to simulate space use scenarios.

2 Background

Agent-based approaches model systems as a collection of entities called agents. These are appropriate to describe what is happening in dynamic real-world situations. Several definitions of the term "agent" exist, ranging from a basic "something that perceives and acts" ([3] pg. 59), to more software-oriented descriptions, which see agents as computational systems that inhabit a complex, dynamic environment and sense and act autonomously to realize a set of goals or tasks for which they are programmed [4].

Agent-based modelling (ABM) offers comparative advantages with respect to other modelling techniques, which makes it well-suited to applications at a micro-geographic setting, as in the field of urban and architectural studies. A core advantage of simulations based on ABM is their capacity to represent agents' spatial locations and movements in an explicit context, which is crucial to human spatial behaviour in a built environment [5].

Several applications of ABMs in hospital environments address system performances, examining patient flows and admission waiting time, staff workload, economic indicators, patient flow and other operational issues [6–10]. They proved that ABM is suitable to model a healthcare environment. This is largely a consequence of being able to address almost all the system's components relative to spatial description and the agents' ability for social and physical interaction [11]. However, regardless of the suitability of using ABM to describe some aspects of humans in space, ABM is still limited to representing more complex activity patterns of interaction (e.g. agents-agents-space) because of the high requirement for an accurate formalization of a real-time emulation of the coordinating process of human cognition and decision-making [12].

Correspondingly, Network Science has emerged as a cross disciplinary field of study to model many physical and real-world systems. In social contexts, this formalization depicts people and their relationships with graph structures, where actors are represented by nodes and interactions by edges [13]. Such networks are tools for conceptualizing social and spatial relations at various timescales and levels of aggregation. When it is important to understand their evolution in time, dynamic networks are drawn which undergo structural changes over time [14]. Methodologically, these aggregate continuous-time relational data and visualize how they are related and when changes arise in individual relations through a series of networks. Their visualization helps to visually comprehend the dynamics taking place in a network, e.g. to promptly assess the quality and quantity of the dynamics represented, in order to facilitate the process of knowledge elicitation [15].

Extending a DNV representation of micro-dynamics of small size social networks into a map-based spatial layout is the proposed way to render continuous networks of spatial relations into discrete patterns of events. This is aimed to bridge the gap with ABM, offering a formal representation which acts as a baseline on which to develop multi-agent simulations. The case study investigates this arrangement in order to meaningfully integrate both the approaches.

3 Case Study

Hospitals are human-centred buildings designed to treat patients, where a wide array of expertise is used and procedures are devised to maximize the number of patients to be treated in the most efficient ways. They exploit a wide variety of users and functions that are carried out in the same location, although all sub-systems, namely environment, personnel and technology share the common objective to guarantee that patients regain their health and are not harmed further during their stay in the hospital. There may be conflicts between the sub-systems themselves, for instance if they are competing for the same space to conduct different activities at the same time [16]. Therefore, even if they can be considered as highly specialized "machines", a balance to meet the different behaviours of users (patients, visitors and staff members) within hospitals is constantly being researched.

The focus on a single hospital ward setting allows us to reduce the overall complexity of human spatial behaviour to a fully expressive case, which is more manageable for an ABM. Spatially speaking, hospital wards can be divided into specific areas by type and by location, such as patient care spaces, departmental areas (nursing units, diagnostic and treatment units) and public areas (corridors, lobbies, waiting rooms) [17]. This is a feature of particular interest for building use understanding by means of the proposed DNV of space use patterns. To visualize the representation of how a building fits the needs and activities of its intended users, an observation and analysis of human behaviour in built environments was adopted, based on the POE paradigm [18]. This was used to investigate our case study and to explore the potential and limits of its interpretation for the proposed framework.

The survey was carried out in the video-laparoscopic and emergency surgery ward of the Policlinico hospital of Bari (Italy), where we collaborated with the internal healthcare staff and management. The department covers an area of about 1,300 square meters. Patients stay in two-bed rooms with an en-suite bathroom. There are two entrances for users: one for doctors' surgeries, located at the bottom of the building and an entrance for all other areas, located on the main side of the building. The layout in which agents operate represents the real-world layout of the hospital ward floor plan (see Fig. 1).

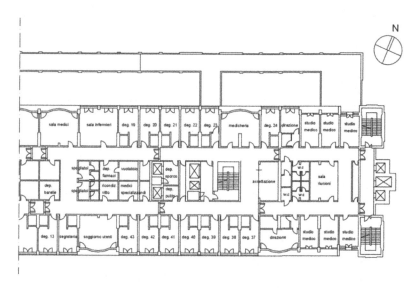

Fig. 1. Video-laparoscopic and emergency surgery ward plan.

For the purposes of capturing observable situations produced and driven by behavioural relationships between people and space, a variety of research techniques were adopted. Data was collected on user activities with direct-experience observations, i.e. monitoring what happens, tracking people and interviewing medical and administrative staff, patients and visitors. A quantitative method was used to gather data on the numbers and flow of patients, recording healthcare workers' (HCW) arrival and exit times, doctors' activities and several treatment events. The observation of HCWs spatial behaviour focused on main hospital practices, the interaction between patients and staff and the movement and flow of personnel and visitors. The

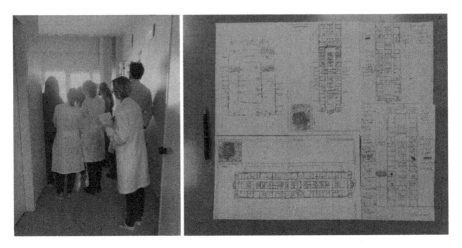

Fig. 2. Shadowing of hospital procedures and data collection sheets.

observation period lasted 75 h over 7 days during a period of 3 weeks in which 18 staff were followed by 6 students (see Fig. 2).

Qualitative methods such as interviews and questionnaires were involved in the data gathering process for the purposes of understanding the decision-making processes behind observed situations. Interviews were carried out with HCWs (doctors, nurses, medical staff), visitors and hospital directors to gain knowledge about current workflows and daily life in the department. A series of meetings were held with the unit director, who explained to the observer the list of procedures performed during treatments, the ratio and functions of daily life situations occurring in ward space. The information obtained was enriched with the study of spatial distribution of ward functions. This thorough analysis of ward space, care procedures and spatial behaviour allows us to establish schematic occupancy schedules (i.e. highly detailed lists of activities) from which users can be assessed by type and other essential understanding of the actual use of space can be derived.

This analysis was transposed in a network-based series of events with a DNV of the time to space mapping which visualizes agents' interactions in time-steps. This was developed as a series of successive snapshots for every 5 min of static networks which highlight structural changes of the social graph. This method was purposely enriched with its implementation on the ward plan to represent the space use patterns, i.e. to visualize how space is used and shared by agents. We made a short video clip to graphically represent the animation of everyday activities on a typical morning within the ward. This is available at the following weblink https://www.youtube.com/watch?v=8atUopyh4LQ. The video-based animation uses graphical attributes of shape and colour to portray each type of agent, allowing for the visualization of their movements in the places around them and their interactions between them by using interconnecting lines (see Fig. 3).

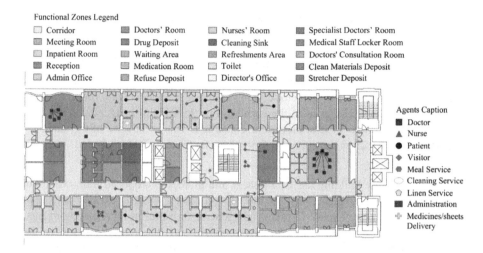

Fig. 3. Screenshot of the animation of the DNV of daily functioning.

Mapping and visualizing social structures allowed us to exploit key actors and their functional relationships, properties of interactions and distances, dynamic evolution of agents relations, cluster and hierarchy formation and action distribution. Moreover, linking DNV with the spatial layout makes a clear sense of the functional relationship between agents and space, allowing for an immediate understanding of the quantity and indirect quality of spatial occurrences and movements. Thus, the dynamic visual representation indicates what is going to happen, where, and by whom. All this fits well with the operational description of agents' spatial behaviour on which a multi-agent simulation can be conveniently developed.

4 Results

The proposed framework has shown to be able to account for many cases of the building use scenario. It can represent different kinds of agents interacting with space and forming groups to cooperate with each other, allowing for a fair description of rationales behind building uses. The functional description of space and the agents' typological features allowed us to understand the decision flow leading to actions and its variation due to contextual circumstances. Indeed, several occurrences observed can be fully represented with the proposed methodology, such as the following:

– People moving around the ward to reach a destination and to meet others, following available paths.
– Situations where a healthcare worker leaves her staff station before moving to the central medicine room to prepare medicines. Afterwards, she moves through the patients' rooms to distribute these. If the patient is absent, the agent adapts her behaviour, moving towards the next patient's room.
– Processes of action execution in relation to proximity between agents. For instance, in a situation where visitors enter the ward to meet their relatives undergoing

treatment, they walk through the hallway to reach the patient's room, where a social interaction will take place for a certain amount of time. When a visitor encounters an HCW, the unplanned meeting drives the visitor to interrupt HCW scheduled duties in order to start a social interaction in that same place.

- Execution of actions in relation to their spatial compatibility. For instance, when there is the occurrence of a doctor coming to check the patients in a room, it forces the visitor to leave and wait in the corridor until he has finished.
- Execution of actions in relation to time constraint. This is the case of the tendency to start a conversation during the activity flow, for instance, during rounds to check patients.

Examining these building use occurrences and more, the proposed framework can provide good visual explanations for the use processes, workflows and functional organization of spaces. Such a formalization scheme is useful in representing agents' spatial behaviour scenarios with temporal ordering and duration of events for the effective generation of an ABM for human spatial simulation [19]. This can help to incorporate a formal representation of activity development to address the effects of organizational intervention into design project practice. Indeed, this analysis supported the proposal of a functional redesign of ward spaces.

Taking into account design, functional, organizational and behavioural aspects, this was developed in order to separate areas with different level of infection risk, so as to improve the prevention and control of infection spread [20]. Indeed, the framework allows us to clearly envision issues concerning interferences between flows of HCWs, patients and visitors which might affect pathogen propagation. To this end, the following reorganization was proposed (see Fig. 4).

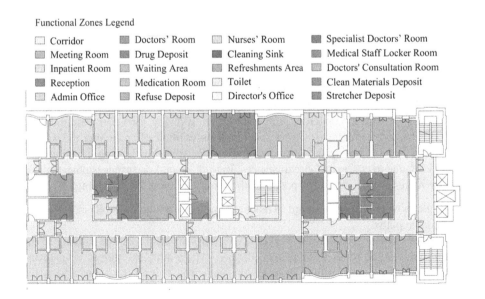

Functional Zones Legend

☐ Corridor	▨ Doctors' Room	▨ Nurses' Room	▨ Specialist Doctors' Room
▨ Meeting Room	▨ Drug Deposit	▨ Cleaning Sink	▨ Medical Staff Locker Room
☐ Inpatient Room	▨ Waiting Area	▨ Refreshments Area	▨ Doctors' Consultation Room
▨ Reception	▨ Medication Room	☐ Toilet	▨ Clean Materials Deposit
▨ Admin Office	▨ Refuse Deposit	☐ Director's Office	▨ Stretcher Deposit

Fig. 4. Redesigned plan with redistribution of ward spaces.

The framework developed for the case under study shows how the design choices and organization of spaces can impact on spatial behaviour, and thus how, conversely, it is possible to operate on the built environment to minimize the negatives and maximize the positives, e.g. appropriate practices and procedures [21]. A further purpose is to develop a formalized multi-agent simulation of workflows and space use scenarios, which will be interesting and useful in evaluating the potential of the proposed framework through the detailed testing and validation of the proposed spatial redesign [22].

5 Conclusions

ABMs and simulations are frequently used as decision support systems in healthcare management and design, being a simplified replica of a real-world system in order to predict its functioning by asking "what-if" questions [23]. This process offers the potential to identify improvements and new understanding of how a healthcare environment operates. It may also help to reduce the costs of planned interventions and the risk of errors in implementing changes [24]. The suitability of developing an agent-based version of hospitals is supported by the limitation that a hospital environment makes it unfeasible to manipulate the real world of people due to logistics, expense and the ethical implications of full-scale trials. Conversely, the proposed framework is an inexpensive method that does not place patients at risk and, at the same time, allows us to draw a number of conclusions, while remaining aware of all the premises and assumptions made in its design.

The present study develops an observation from a POE of the hospital ward workflow which was visualized through a DNV method applied on the ward plan, in order to allow for the ABM to consider the complexity of the spatial use of the built environment and to replicate it without losing important and detailed data. The presented framework represents the evolution of relational data in a visually accessible, scalable and effective way, which leads to an intuitive grasp and gives sufficiently accurate information to support functional redesign proposals and to inform a multi-agent simulation which can explicitly convey the continuous motion of agents. This will be developed in the near future so as to validate the redesign.

The broader picture is that providing an understanding of how urban spaces (as well as buildings) are used in a design phase has the potential of envisioning the various consequences of implementing specific solutions. It can also help to forecast the environment's capacity to support activities and to satisfy users' functional needs. It can aid both designers in making decisions that could impact on the lives of the users of future buildings as well as decision makers in evaluating alternative redevelopment project proposals before moving onto the construction phase. On a wider scale, human spatial behaviours could be integrated into the design process in order to understand and assess the impact of a built-up environment on its inhabitants, so as to understand their needs and address the constraints and issues of the context. At the same time, the ability to improve an understanding of the potential impact of physical and social settings of a built environment on its inhabitants could lead experts to develop and live in a more sustainable life environment.

Acknowledgments. We wish to thank Professor Angela Pezzolla, Professor Dino Borri and Professor Domenico Camarda for their valuable methodological assistance. We are grateful to the nurses, doctors and hospital managers of the Policlinico hospital of Bari (Italy) for their availability.

References

1. Esposito, D., Abbattista, I., Camarda, D.: A conceptual framework for agent-based modeling of human behavior in spatial design. In: Jezic, G., Chen-Burger, J., Kusek, M., Sperka, R., Howlett, Robert J., Jain, Lakhmi C. (eds.) Agents and Multi-Agent Systems: Technologies and Applications 2020. SIST, vol. 186, pp. 187–198. Springer, Singapore (2020). https://doi.org/10.1007/978-981-15-5764-4_17
2. Schaumann, D., Pilosof, N.P., Date, K., Kalay, Y.E.: A study of human behavior simulation in architectural design for healthcare facilities. Ann. Ist. Super. di Sanità. **52**, 24–32 (2016). https://doi.org/10.4415/ANN_16_01_07
3. Norvig, P., Russel, S.: Artificial Intelligence: A Modern Approach. Prentice Hall (2010)
4. Weiss, G., ed.: Multiagent Systems: A Modern Approach to Distributed Artificial Intelligence. The MIT Press (2000)
5. Crooks, A.T., Patel, A., Wise, S.: Multi-agent systems for urban planning. Technol. Urban Spat. Plan. Virtual Cities Territ, pp. 29–56 (2014) https://doi.org/10.4018/978-1-4666-4349-9.ch003
6. Kanagarajah, A.K., Lindsay, P., Miller, A., Parker, D.: An exploration into the uses of agent-based modeling to improve quality of health care. Unifying Themes Complex Syst., pp. 471–478 (2008) https://doi.org/10.1007/978-3-540-85081-6
7. Cabrera, E., Taboada, M., Iglesias, M.L., Epelde, F., Luque, E.: Optimization of healthcare emergency departments by agent-based simulation. Procedia Comput. Sci. **4**, 1880–1889 (2011). https://doi.org/10.1016/j.procs.2011.04.204
8. Spry, C.W., Lawley, M.A.: Evaluating hospital pharmacy staffing and work scheduling using simulation. Proc. - Winter Simul. Conf. **2005**, 2256–2263 (2005). https://doi.org/10.1109/WSC.2005.1574514
9. Hutzschenreuter, A.K., Bosman, P.A.N., Blonk-Altena, I., van Aarle, J., La Poutré, H.: Agent-based patient admission scheduling in hospitals, (2008)
10. Mielczarek, B., Uziałko-Mydlikowska, J.: Application of computer simulation modeling in the health care sector: a survey. Simul. **88**, 197–216 (2012). https://doi.org/10.1177/0037549710387802
11. Laskowski, M., Demianyk, B.C.P., Witt, J., Mukhi, S.N., Friesen, M.R., McLeod, R.D.: Agent-based modeling of the spread of influenza-like illness in an emergency department: A simulation study. IEEE Trans. Inf Technol. Biomed. **15**, 877–889 (2011). https://doi.org/10.1109/TITB.2011.2163414
12. Kennedy, W.G.: Modelling human behaviour in agent-based models. In: Agent-Based Models of Geographical Systems, pp. 167–179 (2011)
13. Moody, J., McFarland, D., Bender-DeMoll, S.: Dynamic Network Visualization. Am. J. Sociol. **110**, 1206–1241 (2005). https://doi.org/10.1086/421509
14. Zaidi, F., Muelder, C., Sallaberry, A.: Analysis and visualization of dynamic networks. Encycl. Soc. Netw. Anal. Min., pp. 58–69 (2018) https://doi.org/10.1007/978-1-4939-7131-2_382

15. de Vries, H., Biesmeijer, J.C.: Self-organization in collective honeybee foraging: emergence of symmetry breaking, cross inhibition and equal harvest-rate distribution. Behav. Ecol. Sociobiol. **51**(6), 557–569 (2002). https://doi.org/10.1007/s00265-002-0454-6

16. Jiménez, J.M., Lewis, B., Eubank, S.: Hospitals as complex social systems: agent-based simulations of hospital-acquired infections. In: Glass, K., Colbaugh, R., Ormerod, P., Tsao, J. (eds.) Complex 2012. LNICSSITE, vol. 126, pp. 165–178. Springer, Cham (2013). https://doi.org/10.1007/978-3-319-03473-7_15

17. Brodeschi, M., Pilosof, N.P., Kalay, Y.E.: The definition of semantic of spaces in virtual built environments oriented to BIM implementation. Caad Futures **2015**, 331–346 (2015)

18. Zimring, C.: Post-occupancy evaluation: issues and implementation. In: Handbook of environmental psychology, pp. 306–319 (2002)

19. Simeone, D., Kalay, Y., Schaumann, D., Hong, S.: Modelling and simulating use processes in buildings. Proc. eCAADe **31**, 59–68 (2013)

20. Esposito, D., Schaumann, D., Camarda, D., Kalay, Y.E.: Multi-agent modelling and simulation of hospital acquired infection propagation dynamics by contact transmission in hospital wards. In: Demazeau, Y., Holvoet, T., Corchado, J.M., Costantini, S. (eds.) PAAMS 2020. LNCS (LNAI), vol. 12092, pp. 118–133. Springer, Cham (2020). https://doi.org/10.1007/978-3-030-49778-1_10

21. Esposito, D., Schaumann, D., Camarda, D., Kalay, Y.E.: A multi-agent spatial-cognition model to represent infection spread in hospitals. Cogn. Process. **19**, 38–39 (2018). https://doi.org/10.1007/s10339-018-0884-3

22. Esposito, D., Schaumann, D., Camarda, D., Kalay, Y.E.: A multi-agent simulator for infection spread in a healthcare environment. In: Demazeau, Y., Holvoet, T., Corchado, J.M., Costantini, S. (eds.) PAAMS 2020. LNCS (LNAI), vol. 12092, pp. 408–411. Springer, Cham (2020). https://doi.org/10.1007/978-3-030-49778-1_36

23. Esposito, D., Schaumann, D., Camarda, D., Kalay, Y.E.: Decision support systems based on multi-agent simulation for spatial design and management of a built environment: the case study of hospitals. In: Gervasi, B., et al. (ed.): In: 20th International Conference on Computational Science and Its Applications ICCSa 2020. Lecture Notes in Computer Science. Springer (in press) (2020)

24. Friesen, M.R., McLeod, R.D.: A survey of agent-based modeling of hospital environments. IEEE Access. **2**, 227–233 (2014). https://doi.org/10.1109/ACCESS.2014.2313957

Challenges Related to 4D BIM Simulation in the Construction Industry

Jeanne Campagna-Wilson and Conrad Boton$^{(\boxtimes)}$ [ID]

École de Technologie Supérieure, 1100, rue Notre-Dame Ouest,
Montréal, Canada
jeanne.campagna-wilson.1@ens.etsmtl.ca,
conrad.boton@etsmtl.ca

Abstract. This research explores the points of view of practitioners regarding the challenges associated with 4D BIM in Quebec. Quantitative and qualitative data were collected, through an online survey and interviews with various professionals, to understand the current challenges associated with the use of 4D simulation in the construction industry. The importance of certain challenges, from the perspectives of different professionals, are determined, particularly in terms of organization and contracts, IT infrastructures and software, and staff training. The results proposed a new perspective based on the opinions of professionals in the construction industry in Quebec regarding the issues surrounding 4D simulation.

Keywords: 4D simulation · Building information modeling · Challenges · BIM

1 Introduction

The architecture, engineering and construction (AEC) industry is experiencing a major digital shift in recent years, with the growing adoption of IT-based solutions to improve the quality and the productivity of construction projects. Among these solutions, building information modeling (BIM) seems to play an important role [1, 2] with important impact on the way construction projects are managed [3]. 4D simulation, now considered one of the main BIM uses [4], consists of linking a three-dimensional (3D) model to the scheduling of activities to visualize the construction process over time. Its added value has been assessed through multiple studies, demonstrating its benefits for different needs such as construction planning and constructability analysis [5], education, communication and collaboration support [6, 7], or site installation and logistics management [8, 9].

However, while the potential benefit of the 4D simulation is perceived as high by practitioners, the adoption rates remain low [4, 10] and, in Quebec, few general contractors use 4D simulation to simulate the evolution of construction work, a phenomenon also observed in several other regions of the world. Several factors can be found in the literature to explain this reality, in particular the low demand from clients [11], some organizational challenges [12], the levels of experience and knowledge of users [13], the return on investment perceived as being uncertain, and the unsuitable

© Springer Nature Switzerland AG 2020
Y. Luo (Ed.): CDVE 2020, LNCS 12341, pp. 270–278, 2020.
https://doi.org/10.1007/978-3-030-60816-3_30

delivery methods used by the industry for construction projects [12]. Some technical challenges associated with the software currently available on the market can also slow down the adoption of 4D simulation, by reducing the effectiveness or efficiency of its use. These include, by name, the limited functionality of activity sequencing [14, 15], the limited visualization capacities offered [13, 16], the lack of interoperability between the existing software and the difficult automation of the link between objects in 3D models and activities in the schedule [17], in particular caused by certain modeling techniques and the absence of shared standards. However, there is no study that deals with the importance of the challenges associated with 4D simulation within the construction industry in Quebec, so as to allow effective actions to be taken for a better dissemination.

As part of this study, to better understand the factors hampering the adoption of 4D simulation in Quebec, practitioners in the industry were invited to express their views on various issues associated with the use of BIM and 4D simulation, through an online survey and semi-structured interviews.

2 Related Works

There was an increase of only 3% in the rate of BIM adoption in Canada between 2013 and 2015, which is well below the expected rate of 20% [18]. The use of 4D simulation remains far below its potential, and its adoption was not done systematically or rigorously in the construction industry, similarly to the reality of other countries [14, 16]. Indeed, although the 4D simulation has many benefits to offer to the construction industry, the adoption of this technology is difficult [19], mainly because of organizational and project-specific barriers [20].

Several studies show a correlation between customers' demand for BIM and the adoption of this technology by companies. According to a study carried out in the United Kingdom to identify the barriers to the adoption of 4D simulation, a majority of the professional respondents say they have experienced BIM technology in the course of their duties following a client request [12]. The same study shows that the contractors are particularly influenced by requests made by clients. Besides, according to a survey report by McGraw-Hill Construction, most of the companies that do not use BIM identify the lack of demand as the main reason for not using BIM [21], also identified as a barrier to BIM adoption in several other studies [18].

The implementation of BIM and the associated methods and practices imply many changes in the organizational culture of a company [18]. In other words, the business process, the technologies used, the employee routines, the workflows, etc. may be affected [18]. These changes also have a significant impact on work procedures, especially planning tools, which can cause some doubt among planners who are experienced in using conventional planning methods as to the reliability of the technical aspects of 4D simulation [22]. The resistance to change and the well-established corporate cultures would, therefore, be barriers to the implementation of information technologies such as BIM or 4D simulation [12, 23]. Among the main obstacles to implementing 4D simulation, there are also the challenges associated with the lack of skills and abilities among the users [13, 18]. According to the National BIM Report

2017, 73% of companies surveyed consider the lack of internal expertise to be a significant barrier [24]. Indeed, without the expertise of experienced managers and users, the benefits of 4D simulation cannot reach their full potential. This is why the experience of the staff is an important factor in the decision that a company can make regarding the adoption of 4D simulation [12].

Implementing BIM or 4D simulation in a business, like any other similar technological approaches, requires financial investments as well as investments in time. The financial investments include those required for the acquisition of a sufficiently efficient IT infrastructure, the purchase of specific software licenses and the training of the personnel [12]. As for the investments in time, these relate rather to the time required for employees to adapt to the revised work procedures as well as to the new tools and supports involved. According to several studies, the costs to invest and the time required to develop staff skills are indeed significant barriers to the implementation of BIM [12, 21, 24].

Different players intervene at different times and collaborate differently with each other depending on the delivery method with which the project is managed. To benefit as much as possible from the advantages of the BIM approach, the integration of manufacturers in the design phase must be possible. Thus, it is not all the delivery methods, nor all the types of contracts that foster its use [12]. In the case of 4D simulation, its success depends directly on the involvement of subcontractors, suppliers and manufacturers [25]. Although there are certain advantages to be gained from 3D visualization of a model over time, if the schedule is not based on specific data from construction site workers, 4D simulation cannot be used at its full potential [25].

The limitations of the existing tools are also documented in the literature as an important challenge. First, the software currently available on the market contributes little or no to the development of the construction schedule, which means that users must make additional efforts after the creation of the schedule to perform 4D simulations [15]. Most of the software available assumes the existence of a schedule and a model, both completed. An important limitation of this approach would be the absence of a known method for preparing the 4D simulation in parallel with the creation of the construction schedule [15]. It has also been concluded in a recent study, that the benefits of 4D simulation come from improving understanding and communication between stakeholders, more than technical support for project schedule creation and control [22].

3 Research Approach

The research approach is essentially based on quantitative data, obtained through an online survey, supplemented by qualitative data from semi-structured interviews allowing to deepen and clarify the results of the online survey.

The questionnaire aims at collecting the opinion of industry professionals in Quebec, regarding the practices and issues associated with the BIM approach and, more particularly the 4D simulation. It is organized into four main sections. First, the respondents' situation is established through questions identifying their levels and areas of expertise as well as the characteristics of the companies for which they work.

Second, information has been gathered on current practices associated with the BIM approach in a section dealing with respondents' experience in this area, as well as the tools and uses made of BIM. Third, the current practices related to 4D simulation have been listed in order to paint a portrait of the use of this approach within the construction industry in Quebec. The last section of the questionnaire deals with issues related to the BIM approach and 4D simulation, to collect the opinion of professionals as to the factors hindering their adoption or use. Only the results of this fourth section of the questionnaire are presented in this paper. The survey was launched online in March 2019 via the LimeSurvey platform. The data collection lasted eight months and a total of 48 responses, including 34 complete and 14 partial responses, have been collected.

Some semi-structured interviews were conducted with various professionals working in the construction field in Quebec. The main objective of these interviews was to clarify certain subjects covered in the questionnaire distributed, to allow a better understanding. A total of three interviews were conducted over a period of three months.

4 Main Results

4.1 Profile of the Respondents

Among the types of companies for which they work, we note that 31% of respondents work in companies offering architectural services, 26% of them work in engineering firms, and 20% of them work for general contractors. In addition, there are also 8% of respondents working for specialized contractors, suppliers or manufacturers. According to the results obtained, 5% of respondents work for a client or owner, while the remaining 10% of the respondents work in other types of companies.

4.2 Importance of the Challenges According to the Practitioners

4.2.1 The Challenges Associated with the Staff

The temporary nature of a project team, the lack of qualified staff, as well as the expensive cost of training, were proposed to participants for evaluation as issues associated with 4D simulation in terms of staff training (Fig. 1).

First, 39% of respondents share the view that the temporary and unique nature of a project team is an important issue. Indeed, these characteristics generally imply having to train different stakeholders for different tasks from one project to another, in addition to the adaptation efforts required to work with different stakeholders on each of the projects. On the other hand, most of the participants thought that it was a minor issue (29%) or that they did not consider it to be an issue (18%). They would, therefore, believe that the knowledge acquired on a project is transferable to other projects and that standardization is possible. Second, about the lack of qualified personnel in Quebec, this is an issue classified as significant or critical by close to 75% of the respondents. According to a BIM director interviewed, "users are not always trained and competent in BIM or multidisciplinary activities". According to him, BIM coordinators and modelers would be given responsibilities requiring a certain level of experience, such as multidisciplinary coordination for example, without having

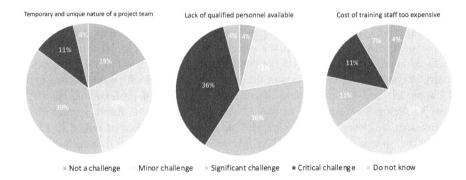

Fig. 1. The importance given to the challenges associated with the staff

adequate experience, because they would have an "ease with software for presentation and navigation, but not in terms of the relevance of the information contained in the models". Besides, several of the surveyed professionals affirmed that many companies proclaim themselves "BIM experts" as soon as they are certain to master the functionalities of a 3D modeling software and bid on BIM projects, without having the relevant qualifications or experience in the activities involved in the BIM approach. According to a modeling technician interviewed, there exists certain gaps within vocational and college level training, as well as in university level training. According to him, BIM software should be taught as part of professional studies and technical diplomas, and these concepts should be taught in a context of multidisciplinary coordination, and not be limited to teaching the software interface for modeling. Third, in terms of the cost of training BIM staff, a majority of respondents (54%) consider that this is not a big issue. This could be explained by the fact that university and college course programs are offered on the subject of BIM, the tuition fees in Quebec being well below the training costs offered by certain companies.

4.2.2 The Organization- and Contract-Related Challenges

Figure 2 presents the respondents' opinions on the challenges in terms of business organization (internal and external) and contracts. The difficult collaboration between 2D software users and BIM software users, on the same construction project, was proposed to participants as a challenge in organizational and contractual terms. Their responses suggest that this is a challenge considered major by almost 75% of the participants, with 46% of them thinking that it is a significant issue, and 25% of them considering it as a critical issue. This is a problem especially present when the use of the BIM approach is not a request from the client, and therefore does not form part of the contractual agreements. One respondent also specified that "the identification of needs and purposes for the use of BIM is not clear" and that this creates problems when applying/using the BIM approach. The poor definition of the roles and responsibilities of the various stakeholders (major issue according to more than 70% of respondents) could result from gaps in the BIM management plan because the roles and responsibilities of all stakeholders involved in the activities associated with the BIM approach are usually established there.

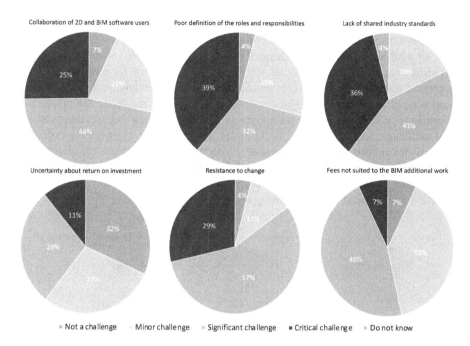

Fig. 2. The importance given to the organization- and contract-related challenges

The lack of shared standards for BIM practices in Quebec is considered an important issue by 43% of respondents, and critical by 36% of respondents. Uncertainty about the return on investment gives rise to mixed opinions among the professionals surveyed. In fact, 32% of respondents believe that this is not an issue, 29% of them believe that it is a minor issue, and the same percentage agree that this is an important issue. One respondent also mentioned that "significant benefits in terms of productivity gain" are not always felt, if one considers "the time spent on project implementation" which is sometimes limited on small projects. Resistance to change is perceived as a major issue by more than 85% of respondents, while 57% believe that it is an important issue and 29% agree that it is a critical issue. Finally, with regard to professional fees, the majority (65%) of participants believe that these are not suited to the additional efforts made to apply the BIM approach on construction projects. Indeed, 58% of them consider the inappropriate fees as an important or critical issue.

4.2.3   The Software-Related Challenges

Figure 3 shows the respondents' opinions regarding the challenges associated with 4D simulation in terms of IT infrastructures. Regarding the costs associated with the IT tools and infrastructure required, almost 40% of participants believe that this is an important or critical issue. According to a senior architect interviewed, it would no longer be possible to purchase licenses for BIM modeling software, as only annual license subscriptions would be available. This software would, therefore, be more "expensive in the long run" than 2D drawing software and this would create a "lack of affordable tools" pointed out by a respondent to the questionnaire. On the other hand, these costs associated with IT would constitute a minor issue for 43% of the participants, in addition to not being considered as an issue by 18% of the respondents. According to an experienced modeler, this would not be an issue for medium and large companies, since it is possible to obtain reducible prices depending on the quantities of leased servers and equipment. The respondents are divided regarding the insufficient performance of existing IT infrastructures as a challenge: half believe that this is a major challenge, and half are of the opposite opinion. Some respondents explained certain issues related to IT infrastructures, identifying in particular "the problem of updating when the same model is shared by several stakeholders" as well as the "multitude of platforms that change from one project to another" and which require adaptation and sometimes even training at each opportunity.

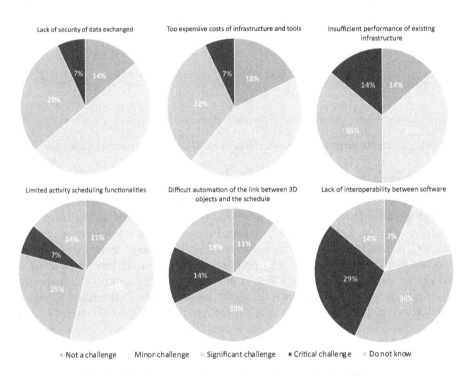

Fig. 3. The importance given to the software-related challenges

Other issues were highlighted by the participants, related to the limits of the software currently available on the market for 3D modeling and multidisciplinary coordination. They mention in particular "the difficulty of integration between different modeling and coordination environments (file formats, interoperability and integration problems, absence of a single tool that integrates the needs of all disciplines and the complete life cycle of a project, etc.)", as well as a lack of "maturity of available software". However, according to a BIM director interviewed, the problem with software comes down to the heaviness of the integrated models, caused in part by poor management of the information contained therein. The functionality (or limits) of the software would not constitute an issue in itself, but the constant improvements thereof would create sometimes superfluous needs for the users.

Regarding the limited activity sequencing functionalities, a majority of respondents believe that it is a minor (43%) or non-existent (11%) issue, while less than a third of participants consider this to be an important (25%) or critical (7%) issue. Less than 30% of the respondents found that the difficult automation of the link between 3D objects and schedule constitutes a minor or nonexistent issue, while more than half of the respondents are notice that this is significant or critical issue. Finally, the lack of interoperability between the software is a significant issue for 36% of the respondents, and critical for 29% of them. Only 21% of participants believe this is not a challenge.

5   Conclusion and Future Works

Based on an online survey and semi-directive interviews, this research explored the degrees of importance perceived by practitioners for different challenges associated with 4D simulation in terms of IT infrastructures and software, organization and contracts, and staff training. Regarding the challenges associated with the staff, the lack of qualified personnel available appear as the most important challenge while the cost of training seems to be a minor challenge. Regarding the organization and contract-related challenges, the difficult collaboration between 2D and BIM software users, the poor definition of roles and responsibilities, the lack of shared industry standards, and the resistance to change appear to be the most important challenges. Regarding the software-related challenges, the lack of interoperability and the difficult automation of the link between 3D objects and schedule activities are the main challenges identified.

The research focused on the particular context of the Quebec construction industry, but should be compared with other industrial contexts in order to proposed sustainable and global solutions to the identified challenges. Future work will focus on proposing avenues to address the main challenges, to ensure better adoption rates.

References

1. Boton, C., Forgues, D.: The need for a new systemic approach to study collaboration in the construction industry. Procedia Eng. **196**, 1043–1050 (2017)
2. Sacks, R., Eastman, C., Ghang, L., Teicholz, P.: BIM Handbook: A Guide to Building Information Modeling for Owners, Designers, Engineers, Contractors, and Facility Managers, 3rd edn. Wiley, Hoboken, New Jersey (2018)
3. Boton, C., Forgues, D.: Practices and processes in BIM projects: an exploratory case study. Adv. Civ. Eng. **2018**, 1–12 (2018)
4. Kreider, R., Messner, J., Dubler, C.: Determining the frequency and impact of applying BIM for different purposes on building projects. In: Proceedings 6th International Conference on Innovation in Architecture, Engineering and Construction (AEC), pp. 1–10 (2010)
5. Boton, C.: Supporting constructability analysis meetings with Immersive Virtual Reality-based collaborative BIM 4D simulation. Autom. Constr. **96**, 1–15 (2018)

6. Sampaio, A.Z.: The introduction of the BIM concept in civil engineering curriculum. Int. J. Eng. Educ. **31**, 302–315 (2015)
7. Kubicki, S., Boton, C.: 4D-based teaching of high-rise structural principles. In: Proceedings of the CIB W78-W102 2011 International Conference, Sophia Antipolis, (2011)
8. Shah, R.K., Dawood, N., Castro, S.: Automatic generation of progress profiles for earthwork operations using 4D visualisation model. Electron. J. Inf. Technology in Constr. **13**, 491–506 (2008)
9. Yabuki, N., Shitani, T.: A management system for cut and fill earthworks based on 4D CAD and EVMS. In: Proceedings of Computing in Civil Engineering conference. Cancun, Mexico, pp. 1–8 (2005)
10. Kubicki, S., Boton, C.: IT barometer survey in luxembourg: first results to understand IT innovation in construction sector. In: Computing in Civil and Building Engineering. American Society of Civil Engineers, Orlando, USA, pp. 179–186 (2014)
11. Vass, S., Gustavsson, T.K.: Challenges when implementing BIM for industry change. Constr. Manage. Econ. **35**, 597–610 (2017)
12. Kassem, M., Brogden, T., Dawood, N.: BIM and 4D planning: a holistic study of the barriers and drivers to widespread adoption. J. Constr. Eng. Proj. Manage. **2**, 1–10 (2012)
13. Brito, D.M., Ferreira, E.A.M.: Strategies for representation and analyses of 4D modeling applied to construction project management. Procedia Econ. Finance **21**, 374–382 (2015)
14. Koo, B., Fischer, M.: Feasibility study of 4D CAD in commercial construction. J. Constr. Eng. Manage. **126**, 251–260 (2000)
15. Tulke, J., Hanff, J.: 4D construction sequence planning: new process and data model. In: Proceedings of 24th CIB-W78 conference "Bringing ITC knowledge to work." Maribor, Slovenia, pp. 79–84 (2007)
16. Boton, C., Kubicki, S., Halin, G.: Designing adapted visualization for collaborative 4D applications. Autom. Constr. **36**, 152–167 (2013)
17. Boton, C., Kubicki, S., Halin, G.: The challenge of level of development in 4D/BIM simulation across AEC project lifecyle. A case study. Procedia Eng. **123**, 59–67 (2015)
18. Malleson, A., Kato, H., Pospíšilová, B., Watson, D., Friborg, G.: NBS International BIM Report 2016, p. 24 (2016)
19. Sediqi, M.: 4D BIM adoption: the incentives for and barriers to 4D BIM adoption within Swedish construction companies, pp. 1–63 (2018)
20. Mahalingam, A., Kashyap, R., Mahajan, C.: An evaluation of the applicability of 4D CAD on construction projects. Autom. Constr. **19**, 148–159 (2010)
21. McGraw-Hill Construction: SmartMarket Report: The Business Value of BIM in Europe - Getting Building Information Modeling to the Bottom Line in the United Kingdom, France and Germany, (2010)
22. Gledson, B.J., Greenwood, D.J.: Surveying the extent and use of 4D BIM in the UK. J. Inf. Technol. Constr. (ITcon). **21**, 57–71 (2016)
23. Davis, K.A., Songer, A.D.: Resistance to it change in the AEC industry: are the stereotypes true? J. Constr. Eng. Manage. **135**, 1324–1333 (2009)
24. Waterhouse, R., et al.: NBS International BIM Report 2017, p. 11 (2017)
25. Buchmann-Slorup, R., Andersson, N.: Bim-based scheduling of construction – a comparative analysis of prevailing and bim-based scheduling processes. In: 27th International Conference on Information Technology in Construction, pp. 113–123, (2010)

The Cooperative Management of Complex Knowledge in Planning: Building a Semantic-Based Model for Hydrological Issues

Mauro Patano$^{(\boxtimes)}$(iD), Domenico Camarda$^{(\boxtimes)}$(iD), and Vito Iacobellis(iD)

Politecnico di Bari, Via Amendola 126/b, 70126 Bari, Italy
domenico.camarda@poliba.it
https://www.poliba.it

Abstract. The management of issues related to water resources, a highly complex domain, has increasingly highlighted the critical role of knowledge towards shared, useful and effective planning decisions.

Hydrology is an applied science with a very large theoretical base, its corpus borders with many others science domains. The clarification of theoretical, methodological, data, language and meaning issues and differences is of central importance. Therefore, the development of a knowledge management system with semantic extensions can meet some of the needs described.

The main objective of this work is to investigate the potential for implementing a knowledge management system with semantic extensions, as well as to propose a functional architecture.

To achieve that, first a KMS with semantic exstensions has been implemented and then the same system has been populated with an experimental knowledge content.

Furthermore, a bottom-up extraction from the KMS of a simple ontology representing the data inserted in the KMS is considered, in order to show the KMS feature of clarifying and improving inter-domain communication, to enhance a common semantic understanding.

Keywords: Knowledge management · Regional planning · Ontology · Decision support system

1 Introduction

In recent decades, the use of water resources in settlement areas - either urban, rural or industrial - has led to increasing problems of consumption and competition towards a scarcely available resource.

Today, problems occur both at large and at small regional scale, in cities and villages, with even harshly different degrees of severity, so as to generate sometimes continuous and dramatic conflicts, as well known [37].

© Springer Nature Switzerland AG 2020
Y. Luo (Ed.): CDVE 2020, LNCS 12341, pp. 279–288, 2020.
https://doi.org/10.1007/978-3-030-60816-3_31

The management of these problems, as well as of the issues related to water resources in general, has increasingly highlighted the critical role of knowledge, towards shared, useful and effective decisions. The point under this circumstance is that the generation of aware and non-reductive knowledge represents a useful way to deal with the management of a highly complex domain.

For this reason, the need for cognitive support systems for water management policies has increasingly developed in recent times [22].

However, this need leads to operational reflections, which are not secondary but at least as complex as the complex world to which they aim to give decision support.

Water resource management involves interdisciplinary actions with ramifications in physical geography, earth sciences, engineering and planning [33]. In fact, the study of the movement, distribution and management of water encompasses and connects many different domains of natural sciences. The cooperation of scientists from various cross-sections of academia is needed for a more complete understanding of the systems involved [31].

Yet hydrology is an applied science. Many hydrologists work, among others, with policy experts, natural science experts, economists, engineers of different specializations, stakeholders belonging to both public and private organizations, ecologists, geoscience professionals, planners, doctors. So also the management of water-related problems in urban planning can benefit from better interdisciplinarity [25]. The clarification of theoretical and methodological differences and the resolution of disparities in data and languages both with other disciplines and within the extensive hydrological domain becomes of central importance [16,35].

The question of language and meanings is transversal to the needs of interdisciplinary collaboration and connection [17].

The development of a knowledge management system with semantic extensions can lead to the creation of a useful tool for solving some of the needs and demands identified. One of the advantages of such a system is that it allows to a large number of users, agents and decision-makers to easily create, verify, reuse, extend and store contents and meanings in a cooperative way.

The main objective of this work is to investigate the potential for implementing a new knowledge management system with semantic extensions. In this context, a functional architecture with processes strong interconnected and characterized by simple feedforward and feedback mechanisms is proposed.

2   Materials and Methods

2.1   The User-System Interaction Scheme

The continuous workflow of knowledge formation and evolution may be traced and supported by the system for the different, natural and artificial, kinds of agents. The collective elicitation of knowledge guarantees the reliability of information managed by the KMS and various kinds of fundamental interaction and

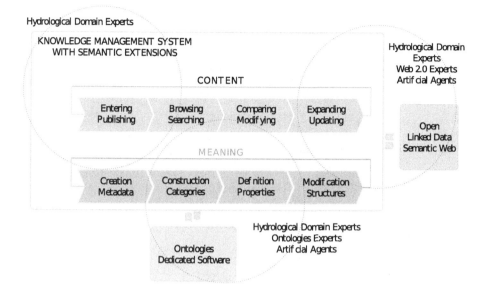

Fig. 1. The evolution of KMS with semantic extensions

knowledge flow have been examined. A graphical representation of the processes and agents involved in the system functioning is shown in Fig. 1.   In a first phase of the system-run, a major contribution by the hydrological domain experts is hypothesized since the core of the managed content is of hydrological theme. In the long-run also the cooperation of other agents has been expected: they are IT experts (for web 2.0 technologies and for ontology construction), other scientific domains experts as well as artificial agents.

2.2   The Implementation of the Knowledge Management System

The applicative prototype of the Knowledge Management System with Semantic Extensions has been developed with the implementation of a Semantic Medi-aWiki.

The system has been developed and implemented entirely with open-source software. A LAMP architecture has been deployed in a virtual environment. Some of the main software packages used are: Oracle VM Virtualbox [15], guest O.S. Ubuntu Server [14], PHP [12], Mysql Database [11], Mediawiki application server [10], Apache Web Server [1], Semantic MediaWiki extension [13], ICU International Components for Unicode [8], Lua Scripting Language [9], Page Forms [2], TemplateData [6], Scribunto [3], DataValues Validators [5], Parser-Hooks [4], WikiEditor [7]. In Fig. 2 a scheme of the architecture stack implemented is given. The web interface of the KMS has ben published on the intranet of our department and the system is now freely available for anyone to use.

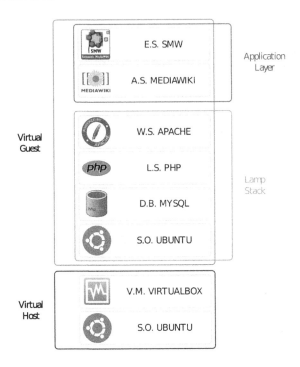

Fig. 2. The software stack of the KMS

2.3   The Knowledge Content

The system has ben populated with an initial knowledge base in the domain under consideration, characterized by concepts with different levels of generality and categorization. Therefore, the chosen content is a classification of hydrological models, as defined in scientific literature [38], ranging from general definition to some model-instances well known in literature [23]. The scheme of the more general taxonomy is reported in Fig. 3.

Then four istances of hydrological models have been selected from specific studies and added to the knowledge base managed by the system:

– DREAM [32]: a Distributed model for Runoff, Evapotranspiration, and Antecedent soil Moisture simulation.
– GEOTOP2 [24,36]: it simulates the combined energy and water balance at and below the land surface accounting for soil freezing, snow cover and terrain effects.
– THALES [26–28]: a physically based hydrologic model, which divides the watershed into irregular elements based on the streamlines and equipotential lines instead of representing them by regular rectangular grids. As many aspects of the hydrologic response depend on topography, this type of terrain-based model is an important development to accurately representing the surface and sub-surface runoff processes.

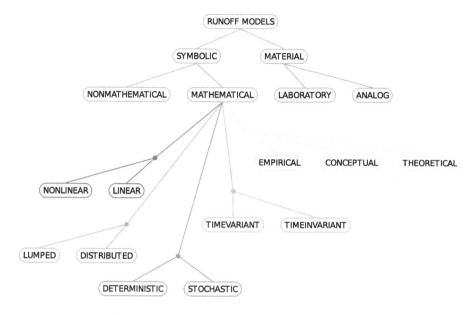

Fig. 3. General taxonomy of hydrological models

– TOPMODEL [18–21]: a physically based, distributed watershed model that
simulates hydrologic fluxes of water (infiltration-excess overland flow, saturation overland flow, infiltration, exfiltration, subsurface flow, evapotranspiration, and channel routing) through a watershed. The model simulates explicit
groundwater/surface water interactions by predicting the movement of the
water table, which determines where saturated land-surface areas develop
and have the potential to produce saturation overland flow.

The "meaning" in the KMS has been gradually extended by new tasks:

– definition of categories and sub-categories, see an example in Table 1.
– definition of properties and data-types, see an example in Table 2.
– implementation of categories and properties with semantic-markups
– implementation of templates and forms for both new annotations and special
queries
– export/linking of contents towards other CMSes or Data-repositories.

Table 1. Some of the higher categories and subcategories implemented in the system.

Category	Higher category	Semantic markup
Hydrology	-	`[[Category:Hydrology]]`
Hydrological model	Hydrology	`[[Category:Hydrological_Model]]`
Runoff model	Hydrological model	`[[Category:Runoff_Model]]`

Table 2. Some of the properties defined in the KMS with relative Markup and Data-Type.

Property	Semantic markup	Data-type
Starting properties		
Model name	[[HaNome:]]	Text
Author name	[[HaAutNom:]]	Page - List
Model distribution	[[HaDistribuzione:]]	Text
Modules number	[[HaNModuli:]]	Number
Time scale	[[HaScalaTemp:]]	Text - List
Basin dimensions	[[HaDimBacino:]]	Text - List
Zona applicazione	[[HaZona:]]	Text - List
Developement language	[[HaLinSvil:]]	Text - List
Last version	[[HaUlVer:]]	Number
Online availability	[[EOnLine:]]	Boolean
Download address	[[HaIndDown:]]	URL
License type	[[HaTipLic:]]	Text
Creation date	[[HaDataCreaz:]]	Date
Short description	[[HaDescBr:]]	Text
Long description	[[HaDescLn:]]	Text
Reference works	[[HaPubbl:]]	External identifier - List
Technical features		
Operativ system	[[HaSisOp:]]	Text
Source availability	[[HaSorg:]]	Boolean
Software dependencies	[[HaAltriSoft:]]	Text
Manuals availability	[[HaManu:]]	Boolean
Last version date	[[HaUlVerDat:]]	Date
Properties of data elaborated by models		
Genre of data input	[[HaDatIn:]]	Text
Genre of data output	[[HaDatOut:]]	Text
Calibration data	[[HaCalib:]]	Text
Properties for autors		
ORCID identification	[[HaORCID:]]	External identifier
Author affiliation	[[AutAffil:]]	Text - List
Author email address	[[AutEmail:]]	Email

3   Discussion and Conclusion

After looking for the system capability to support the creation and growth of
content enriched with semantic expression, a second objective has been to investi-

gate the possible interoperability of the system. Namely, the system's possibility to relate to other open data repositories and to act as a tool to process metadata has been checked [29].

Such goal has been explored in the final part of the work with the bottom-up construction of a simple ontology [30] for the experimented knowledge base, further showing the KMS feature of clarifying water-related disciplinary boundaries. The purpose of the ontology is to assist in improving communication within and beyond the hydrologic community, to ensure a common semantic understanding of concepts and to provide a tool for metadata processing.

The ontology proposed for the knowledge base, that describes concepts and relationships, has been extracted from the KMS using its own features and is expressed using the Web Ontology Language [39].

Figure 4 reports a graphical representation of a small part of final ontology in OntoGraph, a tool giving support for interactively navigating the relationships of OWL ontologies.

Figure 5 shows another part of the extracted ontology opened in the Class Hierarchy view of Protégé, a free, open-source ontology editor and framework for building intelligent systems [34].

Fig. 4. Part of the extracted ontology in OntoGraph

In the end by focusing research on the management of the complexity of hydrological knowledge, this paper aimed to investigate the construction of a cognitive management system for objectives of operational decisions in the water domain. By looking at a system capable of dealing with the complexity of hydrological knowledge, the research aims to support more aware and effective decisions and policies in the water domain at the different regional planning scales.

This field represents an interesting follow-up perspective and its development will be carried out by our group in the next future.

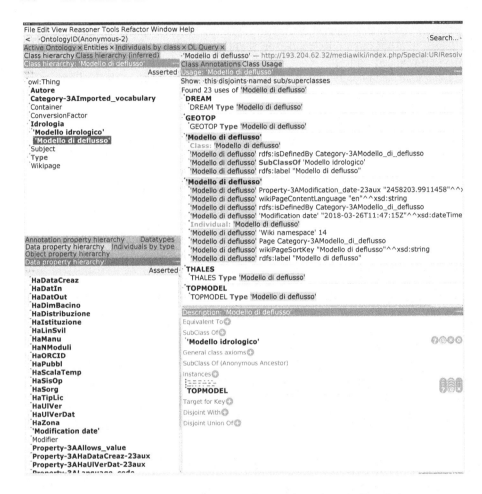

Fig. 5. Class Hierarchy View of part of ontology in Protégé

References

1. Apache. https://httpd.apache.org/
2. Extension: page_forms. https://www.mediawiki.org/wiki/Extension:Page_Forms
3. Extension: scribunto. https://www.mediawiki.org/wiki/Extension:Scribunto
4. Extensions: parserhooks. https://github.com/JeroenDeDauw/ParserHooks
5. Extensions: validators. https://github.com/DataValues/Validators
6. Extension: templatedata. https://www.mediawiki.org/wiki/Extension:Template Data
7. Extension: wikieditor. https://www.mediawiki.org/wiki/Extension:WikiEditor
8. Icu. http://site.icu-project.org/
9. Lua. http://www.lua.org/
10. Mediawiki. https://www.mediawiki.org/
11. Mysql. https://www.mysql.com/

12. Php. https://php.net/
13. Semantic-mediawiki. https://www.semantic-mediawiki.org/
14. Ubuntu. https://www.ubuntu.com/
15. Virtualbox. https://www.virtualbox.org/
16. Baldassarre, G.D., Brandimarte, L., Beven, K.: The seventh facet of uncertainty: wrong assumptions, unknowns and surprises in the dynamics of human–water systems. Hydrol. Sci. J. **61**(9), 1748–1758 (2016). https://doi.org/10.1080/02626667. 2015.1091460
17. Beven, K.: Facets of uncertainty: epistemic uncertainty, non-stationarity, likelihood, hypothesis testing, and communication. Hydrol. Sci. J. **61**(9), 1652–1665 (2016). https://doi.org/10.1080/02626667.2015.1031761
18. Beven, K., Freer, J.: A dynamic TOPMODEL. Hydrol. Process. **15**(10), 1993–2011 (2001). https://doi.org/10.1002/hyp.252
19. Beven, K., Kirkby, M.: A physically based, variable contributing area model of basin hydrology/un modèle à base physique de zone d'appel variable de l'hydrologie du bassin versant. Hydrol. Sci. Bull. **24**(1), 43–69 (1979). https://doi.org/10.1080/ 02626667909491834
20. Beven, K., Kirkby, M., Schofield, N., Tagg, A.: Testing a physically-based flood forecasting model (TOPMODEL) for three U.K. catchments. J. Hydrol. **69**(1–4), 119–143 (1984). https://doi.org/10.1016/0022-1694(84)90159-8
21. Beven, K., Lamb, R., Quinn, P., Romanowicz, R., Freer, J.: TOPMODEL, pp. 627–668. Water Resources Pubns (1995)
22. Borri, D., Camarda, D., Grassini, L.: Complex knowledge in the environmental domain: building intelligent architectures for water management. In: Ali, M., Esposito, F. (eds.) IEA/AIE 2005. LNCS (LNAI), vol. 3533, pp. 762–772. Springer, Heidelberg (2005). https://doi.org/10.1007/11504894_106
23. Devia, G.K., Ganasri, B., Dwarakish, G.: A review on hydrological models. Aquat. Procedia **4**, 1001–1007 (2015). https://doi.org/10.1016/j.aqpro.2015.02.126
24. Endrizzi, S., Gruber, S., Dall'Amico, M., Rigon, R.: GEOtop 2.0: simulating the combined energy and water balance at and below the land surface accounting for soil freezing, snow cover and terrain effects. Geosci. Model Dev. **7**(6), 2831–2857 (2014). https://doi.org/10.5194/gmd-7-2831-2014
25. Gong, W., Gupta, H.V., Yang, D., Sricharan, K., Hero, A.O.: Estimating epistemic and aleatory uncertainties during hydrologic modeling: an information theoretic approach. Water Resour. Res. **49**(4), 2253–2273 (2013). https://doi.org/10.1002/ wrcr.20161
26. Grayson, R.B., Blöschl, G., Moore, I.D.: Distributed parameter hydrologic modelling using vector elevation data: THALES and TAPES-C, Chap. 19, pp. 669–696. Water Resources Pubns (1995)
27. Grayson, R.B., Moore, I.D., McMahon, T.A.: Physically based hydrologic modeling: 1. a terrain-based model for investigative purposes. Water Resour. Res. **28**(10), 2639–2658 (1992). https://doi.org/10.1029/92wr01258
28. Grayson, R.B., Moore, I.D., McMahon, T.A.: Physically based hydrologic modeling: 2. is the concept realistic? Water Resour. Res. **28**(10), 2659–2666 (1992). https://doi.org/10.1029/92wr01259
29. Gruber, T.R.: Toward principles for the design of ontologies used for knowledge sharing? Int. J. Hum. Comput. Stud. **43**(5–6), 907–928 (1995). https://doi.org/10. 1006/ijhc.1995.1081
30. Guarino, N.: Formal ontology, conceptual analysis and knowledge representation. Int. J. Hum. Comput. Stud. **43**(5–6), 625–640 (1995). https://doi.org/10.1006/ ijhc.1995.1066

31. Krueger, T., Maynard, C., Carr, G., Bruns, A., Mueller, E.N., Lane, S.: A transdisciplinary account of water research. Wiley Interdisc. Rev. Water **3**(3), 369–389 (2016). https://doi.org/10.1002/wat2.1132
32. Manfreda, S., Fiorentino, M., Iacobellis, V.: DREAM: a distributed model for runoff, evapotranspiration, and antecedent soil moisture simulation. Adv. Geosci. **2**, 31–39 (2005). https://doi.org/10.5194/adgeo-2-31-2005
33. Montanari, A., et al.: "panta rhei—everything flows": change in hydrology and society—the IAHS scientific decade 2013–2022. Hydrol. Sci. J. **58**(6), 1256–1275 (2013). https://doi.org/10.1080/02626667.2013.809088
34. Musen, M.A.: The protégé project. AI Matters **1**(4), 4–12 (2015). https://doi.org/10.1145/2757001.2757003
35. Nearing, G.S., Tian, Y., Gupta, H.V., Clark, M.P., Harrison, K.W., Weijs, S.V.: A philosophical basis for hydrological uncertainty. Hydrol. Sci. J. **61**(9), 1666–1678 (2016). https://doi.org/10.1080/02626667.2016.1183009
36. Rigon, R., Bertoldi, G., Over, T.M.: GEOtop: a distributed hydrological model with coupled water and energy budgets. J. Hydrometeorol. **7**(3), 371–388 (2006). https://doi.org/10.1175/jhm497.1
37. Shiva, V.: Water Wars: Privatization, Pollution, and Profit. North Atlantic Books, Berkeley (2016)
38. Singh, V.: Hydrologic Systems, vol. 1. Prentice-Hall, New York (1988). https://books.google.it/books?id=MBVkjgEACAAJ
39. Yates, J.S., Harris, L.M., Wilson, N.J.: Multiple ontologies of water: politics, conflict and implications for governance. Environ. Plan. D Soc. Space **35**(5), 797–815 (2017). https://doi.org/10.1177/0263775817700395

A Collaborative Web Application Based on Incident Management Framework for Financial System

Chung Min Tae$^{(\boxtimes)}$ and Phan Duy Hung$^{(\boxtimes)}$

FPT University, Hanoi, Vietnam
mintae98@gmail.com, hungpd2@fe.edu.vn

Abstract. This study developed a system that utilizes incident management in the service operation area for systematic IT service management (ITSM). The implemented system utilizes Information Technology Infrastructure Library (ITIL) to enable efficient problem resolution through fast user error handling on the collaborative side and automatic identification as well as handling of the system. In addition, it is integrated with the system's dashboard to quickly solve problems based on a multi-tiered system through SSO-based authentication. This study is expected to provide a systematic and efficient IT service along with aspect of cooperative through the development and experimentation of ITIL incident management processes and programs, which based on the Service Level Agreement, the analyzed system as well as the management process defined in the real bank system.

Keywords: Data and information visualization · Data engineering tools and techniques · Integration and interoperability · Intelligent infrastructures and automated methods for integrating systems · ITSM · ITIL

1 Introduction

The financial IT industry is moving from infrastructure technology to service orientation. The financial system is a mission-critical system that plays an important role in the survival of a business or organization. Therefore, many financial companies are trying to improve their investment and efficiency in IT services. For these improvements, since the late 2000s, organizations have been working on developing Information Technology Infrastructure Library (ITIL) based on IT service management system to settle in organizational culture. It is closely related to the internalization of IT service operation, one component of ITIL, and its importance is growing. However, managing IT services through multiple systems and organizations in an IT center room are complex and time-consuming.

The financial system is a mission-critical system that provides and operates 24-h services. Mission-critical systems play a critical role in the survival of a business or organization [1]. Financial customers perform many financial transactions, such as depositing, with drawing and transferring deposits via branch or internet. In the past, most of the financial systems were traded through branch tellers, but now, transactions

© Springer Nature Switzerland AG 2020
Y. Luo (Ed.): CDVE 2020, LNCS 12341, pp. 289–301, 2020.
https://doi.org/10.1007/978-3-030-60816-3_32

are rapidly increasing online anytime, anywhere on mobile or PC. Customers can now easily open accounts such as term deposits and time deposits through digital banks.

This mission-critical financial system requires trust in transactions, which is very important. Therefore, it is necessary to build a system with high security and stability. The financial system in the technical aspect operates as multiple databases on multiple servers in order to process large volumes of transactions. Based on this, it consists of the Primary Center, Backup Center, and Disaster Recovery Center to consider the system availability, reliability, and stability. In addition, the software must be installed on multiple servers as well as operated and managed stably. In the organizational aspect, it is necessary to provide better financial services through systematic and integrated IT service management in the IT team, which is the integrated management of the entire system. Therefore, the important role of IT services in IT systems hardware and software is undeniable.

According to the research of Winniford, Conger, and EricksonHarris in 2009, less than half of the organization had fulfilled ITSM in any term [2]. The supporting divisions must handle a problematic challenge in terms of IT services managing when the demand for technology is very high and unstable. This problem should be solved by implementing a service framework (such as ITIL) that could meet the organization's objectives and needs [3]. With regard to financial services, it is difficult to systematically and integrally manage when developing and increasing technology. However, the management of IT services is interesting because it still needs to be analyzed, designed and improved.

Many finance customers demand 24×7 services and the company should be able to respond quickly and effectively on all customers IT infrastructure failures that may occur [4]. Based on these customer needs, expensive H/W and S/W are purchased to serve the management and operation of IT services in financial systems. However, investment is not the end, organizations, procedures, skills and human management must be run organically in order to properly operate many servers purchased. The finance business needs to set up appropriate IT processes and tools to automate IT processes, aim at increasing the quality of customer service and training employees the right attitude as well as skills in proactive response. Company realized that higher customer satisfaction could lead to a better reputation in a competitive market.

So far, internalization research had been focused for efficient IT service management and improvement. Information Technology Infrastructure Library (ITIL) has been developed since the late 2000s to settle in an organizational culture based on IT service management systems. However, ITIL's management process is complex and limited for IT staff to study, manage and perform on their own. In particular, the financial system can suffer more by operating large organizations and multiple systems to securely and quickly conduct large transactions. Therefore, it is necessary to develop integrated ITIL management procedures and systems that suitable for these environments.

This study focused on creating an IT service model to overcome these management limitations and maximize quality of service. To this end, we developed systems using incident management processes in the area of IT service operations. For the analysis and design of the process, the system development life cycle (SDLC) methodology and the UML diagram are partially drawn into the process flow [5]. The implemented system was able to solve and manage multiple systems through an integrated ITIL incident management process, rules-based and web application, by efficient and intelligent automation methods through collaboration. In addition, if the real financial system is applied to the banking sector, multiple systems can be accessed by single sign-on (SSO) login to easily solve, manage, and collaborate on problems.

2 Background

2.1 Information Technology Service Management

The IT service management system is a method for managing processes, resources, and technologies, in order to provide the agreed IT service level within a reasonable cost range. In a narrow sense, information system operations are designed with traditional technology-driven management and are a management-oriented and systematic approach by approaching the service perspective. In a broad sense, ITSM not only provides information system operation functions such as IT service delivery but also systematically manages everything related to IT, such as information system planning, organizational personnel management for information system management, project management, and quality management.

ITSM enables organizations to effectively reduce the cost and resources required to operate IT. As a result, ITSM is changing the way IT services are designed, delivered and managed, as well as the way organizations operating IT services are changing [6].

2.2 Information Technology Infrastructure Library (ITIL) Framework

ITIL is a progression-oriented framework that offerings the best practices which are perceived by industries. ITIL brings resolution for organizations in completing effective IT Service management. The best-known ITSM framework – ITIL initially developed by Telecommunication Agency (CCTA) and The British Central Computer. After that, ITIL framework second and third version was released in 2001 and 2007 by the Office of Government Commerce (OGC). ITIL V3 be made the five following IT service lifecycles [7]:

- Service strategy: Business operation needs and organizations' consistent service strategy outline.
- Service design: Better service management process by designing services and processes.
- Service transition: Services' live environment preparation.
- Service operation: Service level agreements obtain solution.
- Continual service improvement: Potential improvements in service management processes definition and analysis.

It is managed in a life cycle based on the areas of IT service operation and continuous service improvement.

2.3   Incident Management in ITIL

Implementing ITIL in a financial system requires a set of established processes that can improve IT services. In order to optimize the service, events that occur in daily work activities must be handled. Incidents are events that occur outside the standard operation of service, which can disrupt or degrade service quality. The goal of incident management is to bring services and processes back to normal service levels as soon as possible by mitigating the impact of IT service failures [8].

In the case of a financial IT Center, services such as servers, applications, networks, etc. can disrupt services and affect day-to-day work activities. In this regard, this study is based on the incident management framework of ITIL-Incident Management Framework. We will focus on developing web-based applications on the system. ITIL-accident management framework ensures the following key benefits:

- Save time by resolving failures (software, hardware or network) by referencing saved logs and restoring services to normal processes.
- Capacity of incident log storing and make it available as a solution for other incidents [9].
- Extract small incidents before it converts to critical incidents and causes bad effect to IT services quality [9].

The main goal of incident management is to maintain service level agreements by restoring operational activities to a normal state with minimal impact and minimal time through collaboration and a systematic system [10].

3   System Requirements

3.1   Architecture Overview

The Incident Management application developed in this study integrates ITIL Incident Management processes into a variety of technologies and architectures to integrate into the financial system. This is the result of the entire architecture, from data collection to visualization, by connecting each module to the operational financial system. The following are special considerations when integrating with the real bank system of this work:

- Big transactions (20,000,000 or more daily transactions).
- Distributed application server (10 or more application servers).
- Real-time transaction (300 TPS or more real-time transactions).
- Defined service level agreement (SLA) and generated events.

It is designed to make sure current system is not affected by considering related H/W, S/W, events and respective interfaces. We also considered distributed data collection and user login through SSO to integrate multi-level systems. Here is the overall system configuration (Fig. 1).

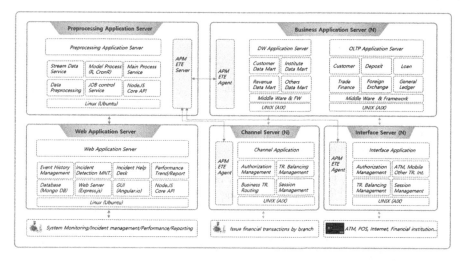

Fig. 1. Architecture of incident management system.

The ITIL Incident Management process of main components as below:

- Incident Identification: identify incidents that occurred in operational activities, the application should have a feature that can be used to accommodate the user's complaints and automatic identification.
- Incident Logging: access to open incidents record, the user should use the application to open the incidents log. Also, system can be automatic store the incidents log.
- Incident Categorization: determining and recording the category of incidents, the application should allow users to determine the category of incident.
- Incident Prioritization: prioritizing the incident based on the impact of operational activities, incidents log and category must be completed with the priority level to help users determine which incidents should be resolved first.
- Resolution and Discovery: applying the incident resolution and updating an incident record with the actions taken, any incident record in the application should solve the response field and status.
- Incident Closure: checking if the incidents are fully resolved and updating the incident status, the application should inform the stakeholder about the incident's status and actions are taken.

3.2   System Requirements

As described above, the six main activities of incident management serve as the basis for analyzing the requirements of this web application. The following table is an analysis of the requirements of this web application. The major functional requirements described in Table 1.

Table 1. Requirement analysis base on ITIL Incident Management Process

No	Incident process	Requirements	Application features
1	Identification	Determine the complaints from users and the system automatically recognizes	Client and Server-based from to entry facility problems/incidents
2	Logging	Record incident entries and allow system and user to access the records of data	Server-based web application with dashboard to access incident data history
3	Categorization	Determine the category of incidents and update the incident status	Problem/incident type on each incident record and can be updated by the user
4	Prioritization	Rank an incident based on its urgency and prioritization level	Menu to categorize incident based on the severity and impact
5	Resolution and Discovery	Update incident record and status with the action taken by the user	Interface to update incident status and action is taken
6	Closure	Check the incident status and notify the stakeholder about the resolution of any incident	Features to notify facility reporter about incident response

4   System Design and Implementation

4.1   Model Design

In this section, the research continues with a design of a model in-service process standard (Fig. 2). The process standard is designed by mapping to the standard ITIL-Incident Management process which including 6 main activities: Incident Identification, Incident Logging, Incident Categorization, Incident Prioritization, Resolution and Discovery, and Incident Closure. Those main activities are mapped to incident management system applications designed, which are used as standard software in the IT service operations of a system room. The asset and service desk data stored in the incident management system are captured, and then data is used for problem knowledge purposes to collaborate in the problem management system.

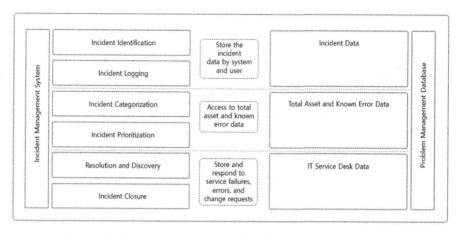

Fig. 2. Incident management model in target system.

4.2 Process Design

In this section, the standard activity diagram service process is described, collaborative aspect is also shown in Fig. 3 below.

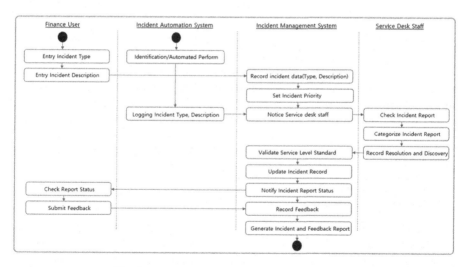

Fig. 3. Activity diagram service process standard.

In this incident management system standard, the process starts when the user enters a problem/incident report through the Web application. The application is accessible on every user computer by web browsers. First, the user can select the type of problem occurred, e.g. Hardware, Software, Network, etc. (Table 2). The user also has to input the elaboration from the problem in the Problem description item. After the problem is submitted, the system notifies the incident management staff (IT center) to take action about the incident record. The staff that has been notified to check incident record and priority level of the incident. The incident with higher priority will be examined and solved first then the lower priority will follow. After the corrective action is done by IT Center staffs, they update the problem report status in system with the resolution and discovery of the incident.

Specifically, events that occur in the system are automatically identified. The identified incident is recovered automatically by checking for known error data. When performing automatic recovery, the input channel is automatically registered as a system in the incident management system. Registered data is reported to the help desk and is recorded after confirming whether further actions have been taken.

Table 2. Service level agreement

No	Incident category	Incident level		Remark (Original Requirement)
		Minor	Major	
1	Software	30	5	Critical Error: Fixed shortly within 5 h (Can cause slow operation, system suspension or disabling some function on the system)
2	Hardware	30	5	
3	Network	30	5	
4	Others	24	48	Non-Critical Error: Fixed shortly within 48 h (Other error)

With resolution and discovery updates, an incident can be considered as the finish to manage. The system can then take advantage of collaboration through notification to the reporter of the incident (user) about report status. After users are notified and informed about resolution of their problem, they can submit feedback about the resolution. The system record feedbacks from the user and store the data for further report as well as visualization for management staff as an evaluation tool for the service process standard.

To this end, the current system was analyzed to obtain the following analysis results.

4.3 System Implementation

The development process for this web-based application uses "JavaScript" as a programming language along with a framework for developing "Node.js" and "Angular" applications. Database management uses Mongo database management system for database management of applications. Application development includes server side (backend) and client side (frontend). Platform for the development of Client-Side application. Following is the screenshot of backend view and function:

Backend Application

Fig. 4. Backend login page.

Fig. 5. Backend dashboard page.

Figures 4 and 5 show the first page that the IT Center staff access to application from backend. When an IT center employee enters a username and password to access the application, they logged through SSO, therefore, dashboard page is displayed, so he can view the report summary in the report data. This application also provides data visualization in bar charts, line graphs, and pie chart format. IT Center staff also can retrieve the formatted reports from the application by accessing the report menu on the dashboard page. Furthermore, the IT Center staff also can access the details of the problems reported in the application. The following figure shows the list of problems and menu to resolve the problems.

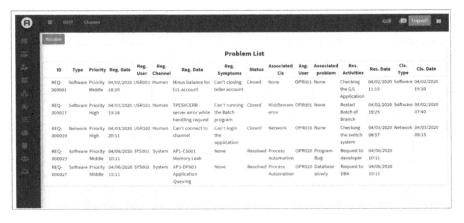

Fig. 6. Backend problem list page.

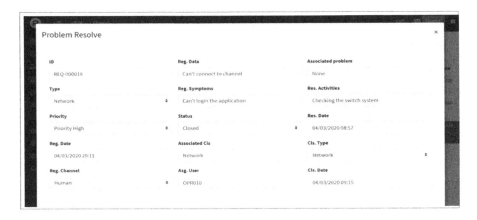

Fig. 7. Backend problem resolve page.

On the problem list and troubleshooting page (Fig. 6), IT center staff can view problem details and take actions to resolve them through collaboration. Problem examination and resolving also generated on this page, while IT Center staff fills problem action form as shown in Fig. 7.

The following section shows the frontend of the application user interface.

Frontend Application

Fig. 8. Backend login page.

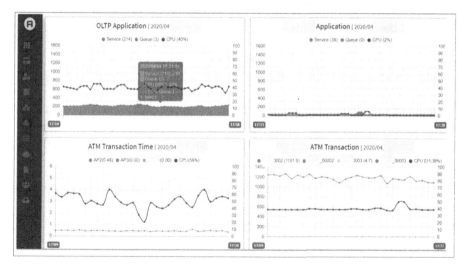

Fig. 9. Frontend system check and identification.

Figure 8 shows the login page of the frontend application. After login, there is a screen that shows the relationship between Application transactions and the system, which is finger 11, so that users access in the system can monitor and pre-identify the entire system. The user can report a problem by choosing "IT Service Report Problem" button and the form for inputting problem details will be shown as in Fig. 9. The problem submitted in this form will be inserted into the database and subsequently, the system will notify IT Center staff to resolve the problem.

The system also determines service level agreement maintenance and provides reports showing performance against SLA criteria as shown in Table 3.

Table 3. Result report of specific date

A. Incident Summary Report (Period: 03/06 ~ 03/22)					
Category	Type	Major	Minor	Sub Total	Remark
Software	GL-BIZ	0	2	2	General Ledger
	EI-BIZ	0	8	8	Interface Business
	CS-BIZ	0	6	6	Common Business
	RM-BIZ	0	5	5	Risk Business
	CD-BIZ	0	6	6	Card Business
	DP-BIZ	0	1	1	Deposit Business
Hardware		7	0	0	
Network		0	0	0	
Others		0	0	0	
Total		7	28	35	
B. Incident Summary Report (Period: 03/06 ~ 03/22)					
Type		Major	Minor	Sub Sum	
Unresolved		0	0		
Resolved		7	28	35	(S/W: 28, H.W: 7)
Total		7	28	35	

Table 3 shows the report created from the dashboard menu. Problem report data can be exported to excel and PDF format. The report shows various problem categories from the problem reported in the incident management application. From Table 3 we can see that the summary shows the total number of problems are 35. Also, the report shows the detail number of each problem category, e.g. Software, Hardware, Network, and Others. The Deadline section shows a number of problems reports that resolved below the service level agreement standard.

5   Conclusion and Perspectives

The incident management program is developed as the result of above study, which was applied to some operation servers and brought many positive results. By applying the ILIT-event management process, resolution time is reduced through systematic organization and collaboration procedures. Decision making when problem occurs was also shortened by integrating and visualizing the events of each system. Finally, it is possible to prevent incidents in automated system management by utilizing these events and rule base of error known DB.

The study also went through system design, development and implementation process. The system implemented in this study is already performing some functions as a solution integrated into production multiple servers. In the future, it is necessary to improve the automated identification system and automated recovery system by accumulating more Known Error DB. In addition, it can be used as decision-making information by adding a pre-prediction function through machine learning from system event and history data. This technology can use incident and problem management to benefit financial, public and retail industry users who need systematic and efficient collaborative system management.

References

1. Fowler, K.: Mission-critical and safety-critical development. Proc. IEEE Instrum. Meas. Mag. **7**(4), 52–59 (2004)
2. Winniford, M., Conger, S., Erickson-Harris, L.: Confusion in the ranks: IT service management practice and terminology. Inf. Syst. Manage. **26**(2), 153–163 (2009)
3. Hochstein, A., Zarnekow, R., Brenner, W.: ITIL as common practice reference model for IT service management: formal assessment and implications for practice. In: Proceedings of the IEEE International Conference on e-Technology, e-Commerce and e-Service, Hong Kong, pp. 704–710 (2005)
4. Spremic, M., Zmirak, Z., Kraljevic, K.: IT and business process performance management: case study of ITIL implementation in finance service industry. In: Proceedings of the 30th International Conference on Information Technology Interfaces, Dubrovnik, pp. 243–250 (2008)
5. Balaji, S., Murugaiyan, M.S.: Waterfall vs. V-Model vs. Agile: a comparative study on SDLC. Int. J. Inf. Technol. Bus. Manage. **2**(1), 26–30 (2012)
6. Marrone, M., Gacenga, F., Cater-Steel, A., Kolbe, L.: IT service management: a cross-national study of ITIL adoption. Commun. Assoc. Inf. Syst. **34**(1), 49 (2014). https://doi.org/10.17705/1CAIS.03449
7. Mahy, Y., Ouzzif, M., Bouragba, K.: Supporting ITIL processes implementation using business process management systems. In: Proceedings of the Third International Conference on Systems of Collaboration (SysCo), Casablanca, pp. 1–4 (2016)
8. Latrache, A., Nfaoui, E.H., Boumhidi, J.: Multi agent based incident management system according to ITIL. In: Proceedings of the Intelligent Systems and Computer Vision (ISCV), Fez, pp. 1–7 (2015)
9. Ghrab, I., Ketata, M., Loukil, Z., Gargouri, F.: Using constraint programming techniques to improve incident management process in ITIL. In: Proceedings of the Third International Conference on Artificial Intelligence and Pattern Recognition (AIPR), Lodz, pp. 1–6 (2016)
10. Ghosh, B.: Incident management & service level agreement: an optimistic approach. Int. J. Comput. Sci. Inf. Technol. **4**(3), 461–466 (2013)

Early Warning System for Shock Points on the Road Surface

Phan Duy Hung[(✉)]

FPT University, Hanoi, Vietnam
hungpd2@fe.edu.vn

Abstract. Transportation is one of the fields with many special applications of information technology. These include major applications such as self-driving cars, intelligent traffic control, etc. supportive solutions for drivers with digital maps, anti drowsiness devices, automatic parking, alert cameras for speed and traffic signs, etc. This paper presents an early warning system for shock points on the road surface, the road positions that when the vehicle runs at high speed across it, the vehicle will bounce. This will endanger the occupants and cause the vehicle to break down quickly. The causes may be potholes, elephant potholes or the points connecting the road with the bridge, unusually subsided road points, etc. Such warning systems are especially useful when the vehicle is running at high speed on long roads or highways. Early warning helps drivers proactively slow down when receiving an alert from the system via a mobile application. The system allows user contributions for more updated and reliable information. Managers can also use this information to plan repair or maintenance of routes.

Keywords: Road surface · Shock points · Early warning system · User contributions · Collaborative mobile systems

1 Introduction

In some countries, the number of deaths caused by traffic accidents is very high, partly due to the poor quality of roads, which have long-lasting effects on families and society. The construction of good quality road infrastructure and regular repairs are issues that many countries are very concerned about. However, most countries, especially developing and underdeveloped countries, do not have enough budget nor interest in this matter. The high population growth rate, the oversized and overloaded cars running on the road lead to high traffic volume and rapid deterioration of road infrastructure. Some statistics in Vietnam, a developing country are as follows:

- According to a report by the Vietnamese National Committee for Traffic Safety [1], for a year to November 15, 2018, a total of 18,736 traffic accidents occurred nationwide, killing 8,248 people and injuring 14,802 others. Road accidents account for a high proportion, with 18,490 cases in which 8,079 people were killed and 14,732 others injured.
- In the paper "Road, rail investment to push Vietnam infrastructure growth" [2], Fitch Group said, "Ongoing and upcoming road projects will be the primary drivers

© Springer Nature Switzerland AG 2020
Y. Luo (Ed.): CDVE 2020, LNCS 12341, pp. 302–311, 2020.
https://doi.org/10.1007/978-3-030-60816-3_33

of growth in Vietnam's transport infrastructure sector" and gave the number of billions of dollars. But huge amounts would be needed, and the plan would not be feasible without external financing, the Fitch report added.

The situation and the above figures require everyone to take action to contribute to reducing traffic accidents.

Achievements of the 4.0 industrial revolution have been widely applied in all areas of life. In the field of transportation, there have been many smart applications based on artificial intelligence, information and communication to improve traffic management capacity, provide support for people and vehicles in traffic.

Products include digital maps and voice directions [3]; anti-drowsiness devices [4]; speed warning cameras and traffic signs [5]; tire pressure warning [6].

Some study areas are still challenging, for example, the problems of controlling traffic lights; intelligent traffic planning, self-driving cars, etc.

Mohammad Faisal Naseer et al. proposed a scheme for smart road-lights and auto traffic-signal controller with emergency override, based on an Arduino microcontroller [7]. They estimate the extent of the existing vehicular concentration using ultrasonic sensors, providing different time slots to each road based on traffic density. The proposed system attempts to reduce the probability of traffic jams caused by unmanaged traffic lights. Another aim is to provide a hassle-free, pre-eminent clearance for emergency vehicles.

Jiaqi Shang et al. in [8] analysed the influence of Working Vehicles on Traffic Operation in Regional Road Networks Based on Microscopic Traffic Simulation. The research shows that the influence caused by work vehicle is related to the traffic volume on regional road network during the working time. Moreover, the influence on the aspects of the whole delay and links' safety is different when work vehicle implements the task with different working strategy. Higher speed on the first lane or lower speed on the second lane would produce a big influence on regional road network, which is especially obvious in early peak or latter peak.

In [9], Taylor Stone et al. propose that autonomous vehicles should be designed to reduce light pollution. Authors process design requirements in two scenarios: lighting infrastructure can be adapted for "driving in the dark"—parking lots and highways.

Studies related to the deterioration of road surface have also been considered.

M. Gavilán et al. present a vision-based road surface classification in the context of infrastructure inspection and maintenance, proposed as stage for improving the performance of a distress detection system [10]. A multi-class Support Vector Machine classification system using mainly Local Binary Pattern, Gray-Level Co-occurrence Matrix and Maximally Stable Extremal Regions derived features is implemented. Experiments with real application images show a significant improvement for the distress detection system performance by combining several feature extraction methods.

In [11], Michal Jankowski et al. resolve the problem of the road recognition with an entirely new picture preprocessing type. They give a new way of extracting data from pictures as "Growing Bubbles Algorithm". The algorithm was implemented as part of a real system to support the on-line driver decision. The system was tested in cars in real traffic with very promising results.

The above studies and solutions have solved many aspects for drivers and this paper introduces a new application for early warning of shock points on highways, national highways, there the vehicle travels at high speed. The shock points of interest are the contiguous sections between the bridge and the road, the unusual subsidence points, the rough junctions between the newly renovated sections and the old road sections, potholes on the road surface. When traveling at high speed through these points, the vehicle will bounce and endanger the occupants, and the vehicle may also malfunction. Users via mobile device-based application can enable automatic contribution of shock point detection information to the system. The application also has an important meaning for traffic management, managers can use the information to plan and allocate optimal time and budget for road maintenance.

The remainder of the paper is organized as follows: Sect. 2 describes the architecture and requirements of the system. In Sect. 3, the design and implementation section describes the system's automatic shock detection algorithm and the main screen designs of the system. Conclusions and perspectives are made in Sect. 4.

2   System Requirements

2.1   Architecture Overview

The system consists of three main parts: the server and the management website (Host), staff application, and user application (Fig. 1).

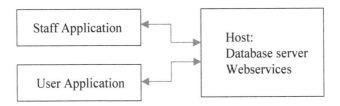

Fig. 1. Architecture overview.

Staff application. This application is for technicians who will go directly on the routes, manually or semi-automatically markup (add or disable) accurate information of shock points on the routes, then send data to the Host. The application is written for Android Phones with a built-in accelerometer sensor.

User application. The application is for users and has these main functions: find the address, indicate the route, display the list of warning points, produce early warnings in real-time when the vehicle is on the route. The application also has the function to collect locations of shock points on the routes users go through, manually or automatically send information to the Host. If the user-contributed warning point is not in the database yet, it will be checked. In the event that there is no condition to directly check at the location that has received the warning, if there are 5 or more alerts at that point, it will be verified as a checked warning point.

Host. The Host is a computer that stores a database of the system containing information such as users, staffs, managers. MongoDB is used as the database for the system. MongoDB is a cross-platform document-oriented database system. It has many advantages, with a dynamic schema and object-oriented structure, making it a great fit for real-time analytics and dashboarding along with e-commerce, mobile, archiving and more. In addition, webservices are used to communicate with mobile applications.

2.2   System Requirements

The system has three main types of users that are system users, staffs and administrators. The functional requirements of each user are described in Table 1.

Table 1. Functional requirements

Type	Content
Administrator	Create/Manage staff
	Manage user: Show, Lock, Unlock
	Manage map: Show, Update, Edit, Delete
	View reports: View, Export
Staff	Find/choose destination, Navigation
	Show/Hide shock point on the map
	Process data from accelerometer and send alarm point to Server
User	Create new account or login with Gmail
	Find/choose destination, Navigation
	Enable/Disable "Data Contribution"
	Show/Hide shock point on the route

3   System Design and Implementation

3.1   Discovering Characteristics of Signal

Staff application allows to manually mark all locations of shock points on the road. Data is collected with the following conditions:

- Collecting sample data with 5 different types of Android phones to ensure that signals are collected from a variety of built-in accelerometer sensors.
- Keeping car speed in the order of 60, 80, 100 and 120 km/h. This speed range limits the construction of a map of shock points in high-speed routes. For roads that allow only low speeds like inner city routes, the impact of shock points on people sitting on the vehicle is negligible.
- Collecting sample data with stuations of lane change, run on shock point, speed deceleration, speed acceleration.
- Taking 15 samples for each case, and the time for each sample is 10 s.

For each sample of data, the following calculations are performed:

- Calculate the **Total Sum** of Acceleration Vector (*STOT*) by the formula:

$$STOT = \sqrt{(Ax)^2 + (Ay)^2 + (Az)^2} \tag{1}$$

where Ax, Ay, Ax are three components in x-, y-, and z- axis of acceleration vector.

- Calculate the **Vehicle Acceleration Sensor Unit** (*VASU*) as the average value of *STOT* when the vehicle is running in a normal state (Fig. 2). The normal state is defined when the vehicle maintains a constant speed in the above speed ranges and runs on a good road surface.

$$VASU = \sum_{i=n_1}^{n_2} \frac{STOT_i}{(n_2 - n_1)} \tag{2}$$

where: n_1 to n_2 is the data range when the vehicle is running in a normal state.
Each vehicle, each speed range will have a unique *VASU* value.

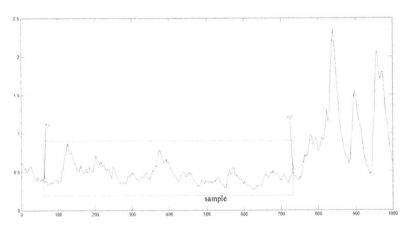

Fig. 2. *STOT* calculation.

- Calculate **Average Vehicle Value** (*AVV*) as the value of *STOT* divided by *VASU*.

$$AVV = \frac{STOT}{VASU} \tag{3}$$

AVV is a dimensionless value.

The x, y, z and *AVV* values are then filtered by a low-pass filter with a cut-off frequency of 5 Hz. Testing on all samples, we always have an *AVV* value in case the shock point exceeds 5.5 and is smaller than 5.5 in the remaining 3 cases. The sample signals x, y, z and *AVV* in situations of deceleration, acceleration, lane change and having shock points are described in the Figs. 3, 4, 5, 6 respectively.

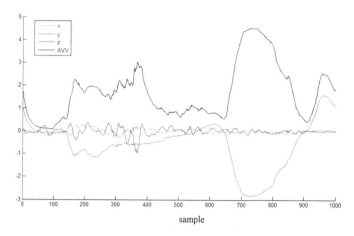

Fig. 3. Graphs of x, y, z and *AVV* in deceleration event (The car is running 80 km/h and braking slowly)

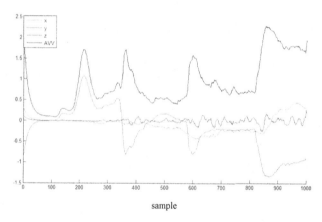

Fig. 4. Graphs of x, y, z and *AVV* in acceleration event (The car is running 60 km/h and accelerating)

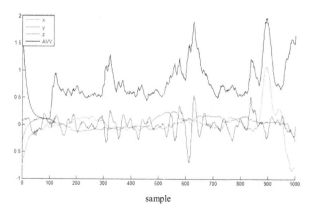

Fig. 5. Graphs of x, y, z and *AVV* in lane change event.

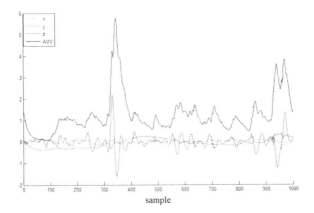

Fig. 6. Graphs of x, y, z and *AVV* in shock event.

3.2 Automatic Shock Point Detection Algorithm

In this problem, the information load regarding the shock points is very large and changes frequently, such as when new ones appearing on a surveyed road, or old ones that have been repaired. Therefore, manual marking will take a huge amount of effort and is not feasible and user's contribution is essential.

The automatic detection algorithm for shock points can help turn staffs' manual data marking into semi-automatic form. When moving on the road, if an application receives a warning about a new shock point, staff stops and checks the actual road surface condition and confirms whether the warning is correct or not.

The automatic shock detection algorithm also allows receiving a large amount of contribution information from the user's phone. The information with the user's permission will be checked at the server. When a sufficiently large number of user applications send an alert to the same location, the warning point is recorded as a shock point. The "same location" configuration is defined within the default 15-meter radius from the centroid point. This number can be changed to suit the actual road surface quality. A distance of 15 m ensures the significance of the statistics as well as requests for deceleration from a distance quite far from the problem area. The number of devices that send alarms to the same point to determine a shock point is configurable with a default number of 5.

The automatic shock point detection algorithm works with data collected from the accelerometer integrated with the phone. The algorithm requires high accuracy and it can distinguish shock points from situations such as acceleration, deceleration, lane change. In addition, the algorithm needs to respond quickly and does not depend on the position or orientation of the phone.

From the understanding of the signal characteristics in the previous section, the method used is to use a sliding window with a length of 10 s and a 2-s overlap length. The *AVV* value of 5.5 is used to simply detect the case of a shock point. This comparison does not depend on the type of phone, the location and orientation of the phone as well as the speed of the vehicle. Locations within 15 m will be considered as the same point and will not affect the purpose of the problem. The algorithm may need to correct some constant values in some cases, but with statistical data on large numbers, the proposed algorithm is sufficient to determine a real shock point.

3.3   Mobile Application Design

Some of the main screens of Mobile applications are listed below. Figure 7 shows the address and route search screen. For each route, the user can know the distance and the estimated travel time (Fig. 7). A list of all shock points on the selected route can be displayed (Fig. 8). Users can also choose to display real-time alerts when traveling. In that case, before the shock point, at a distance of 200 m, the application will alert both by image and voice so that the driver can reduce speed.

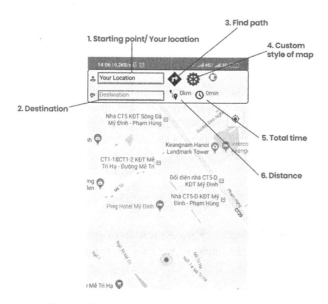

Fig. 7. Screen for searching address and routes.

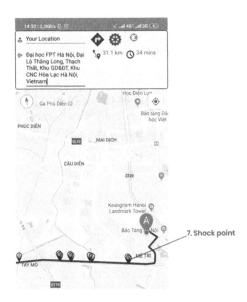

Fig. 8. A list of all shock points on the selected route.

4 Conclusion and Perspectives

The application of information and communication technology in the transport sector has brought great benefits to people who are participating in traffic and for traffic managers. This paper has developed an early warning system for shock points on the road surface so that road users can actively reduce speed and minimize traffic accidents. Users using Android phones with built-in accelerometer sensors can install the app for free. Users will know in advance the list of road surface shock points on their intended journey or turn on real-time alert, then each user is also a data contributor to the system. Statistical reports and shock points maps can be used for managers when planning road repairs and maintenance.

The system will continue to be enhanced with intelligent features such as automatic identification of potholes with images, warning of damaged road railings, flooded areas, etc.

References

1. https://vietnamnews.vn/society/485007/transport-minister-issues-measures-to-reduce-traffic-accidents.html. Accessed 22 Feb 2020
2. https://m-english.vov.vn/investment/road-rail-investment-to-push-vietnam-infrastructure-growth-380715.vov. Accessed 22 Feb 2020
3. https://play.google.com/store/apps/details?id=com.google.android.apps.maps. Accessed 22 Feb 2020

4. https://www.amazon.com/No-Nap-Anti-Drowsiness-Device/dp/B002KF2HAE. Accessed 22 Feb 2020
5. https://www.vietmap.vn/Product/OBU/VietMapS1. Accessed 22 Feb 2020
6. https://www.amazon.com/dp/B074WKVG6J/ref=dp_cerb_3. Accessed 22 Feb 2020
7. Naseer, M.F., Khan, K.B., Khaliq, M.S., Raheel, M.: Smart road-lights and auto traffic-signal controller with emergency override. In: Bajwa, I.S., Kamareddine, F., Costa, A. (eds.) INTAP 2018. CCIS, vol. 932, pp. 526–537. Springer, Singapore (2019). https://doi.org/10.1007/978-981-13-6052-7_45
8. Shang, J., Yan, X., Weng, J.: Influence of working vehicles on traffic operation in regional road networks based on microscopic traffic simulation. In: Wang, W., Bengler, K., Jiang, X. (eds.) GITSS 2016. LNEE, vol. 419, pp. 143–163. Springer, Singapore (2018). https://doi.org/10.1007/978-981-10-3551-7_11
9. Stone, T., Santoni de Sio, F., Vermaas, P.E.: Driving in the dark: designing autonomous vehicles for reducing light pollution. Sci. Eng. Ethics 26(1), 387–403 (2019). https://doi.org/10.1007/s11948-019-00101-7
10. Gavilán, M., et al.: Surface classification for road distress detection system enhancement. In: Moreno-Díaz, R., Pichler, F., Quesada-Arencibia, A. (eds.) EUROCAST 2011. LNCS, vol. 6927, pp. 600–607. Springer, Heidelberg (2012). https://doi.org/10.1007/978-3-642-27549-4_77
11. Jankowski, M., Mazurkiewicz, J.: Road surface recognition system based on its picture. In: Rutkowski, L., Korytkowski, M., Scherer, R., Tadeusiewicz, R., Zadeh, L.A., Zurada, J.M. (eds.) ICAISC 2013. LNCS (LNAI), vol. 7894, pp. 548–558. Springer, Heidelberg (2013). https://doi.org/10.1007/978-3-642-38658-9_50

Vehicle Motion Simulation Method in Urban Traffic Scene

Jinlian Du, Hao Zhou[✉], and Xueyun Jin

Beijing University of Technology, Beijing 110124, China
254541708@qq.com

Abstract. Vehicle motion simulation is an important part of traffic scene simulation, which is helpful for urban road planning and design, road capacity testing and other applications. Based on the characteristics of urban traffic scene, this paper studies the vehicle's movement behavior. On the basis of the intelligent car following model based on safe distance, an improved car following model is constructed by adding acceleration adjustment items which is suitable for real urban traffic scene. Besides, an improved vehicle lane change model is construct on the basis of two-lane change model based on acceleration analysis. Experiments show that the two vehicle motion models proposed in this paper are effective in simulating vehicle stop, start and lane change in urban traffic scene.

Keywords: Vehicle motion simulation · Traffic scene · Car following behavior · Lane changing behavior

1 Introduction

In recent years, with the rapid development of urban transportation, increasing traffic flow, traffic jams and vehicle accidents have become more and more serious. These problems have heavily hindered the development of urban economy and society, and decrease people's living standards and quality of life. At present, modern computer simulation technology is used to model and simulate the city's complex dynamic traffic system. In these technology, the simulation of vehicle movement has attracted attention because it can study how to plan urban traffic scientifically and rationally, reduce traffic accidents and congestion, and ensure the quality of travel.

Based on the intelligent car following model proposed by Treiber [1–3], this paper tries to solve the problem of slow start of car following, and study the two-lane change model based on acceleration analysis proposed by Kesting [4–6], trying to solve safety issues during vehicle lane change. The main contributions of this paper are:

(1) A new car following model is proposed based on analysis of vehicle speed, acceleration, and the distance between vehicles. This model can better simulate these characteristics of urban traffic scenes: small traffic safety distance, the acceleration of front vehicle has greater influence on the acceleration of rear vehicle when it starts.

(2) A new lane change model is established to ensure the security during the process of vehicle lane change by adding a parameter time point setting to the safe

© Springer Nature Switzerland AG 2020
Y. Luo (Ed.): CDVE 2020, LNCS 12341, pp. 312–321, 2020.
https://doi.org/10.1007/978-3-030-60816-3_34

distance calculation formula, and performing a safe assessment during the process of vehicle lane change.

2 Related Works

At present, most of the research on vehicle motion simulation is based on car following model. Car following model mainly studies the relationship between the speed of the front vehicle and the acceleration of the rear vehicle when two vehicles driving in the same lane and the rear vehicle does not change lane. Car following model was originally proposed by Gerlough [7]. It studies the characteristics of traffic flow under non-free driving conditions, and has great significance to the simulation and evaluation of modern traffic flow. Pipes [8] proposed a stimulus-response car-following model, which mainly studies the different behaviors of drivers under various stimuli in the actual driving environment. This model proposes that the driver will adjust speed by the speed difference between the front vehicle and the rear vehicle, and the following researches are all based on this hypotheses. Kometani [9] first proposed a car-following model based on the safe distance. The model believes that the driver should maintain a sufficient safe distance to avoid collisions when he cannot determine the movement of the front vehicle.

In recent years, researchers have been working on the lane-changing behavior of vehicles. Lane change model was proposed by Gipps [10]. This model takes into account driver's intention of change lanes. According to the influence of the nearby traffic environment changes on the driver, the behavior of the vehicle changing lanes is summarized as a decision tree to decide whether to change lane. However, the model does not take into account the procedure of lane changing, and thinks the lane-changing is completed instantaneously, so the effect of the simulation on vehicle lane change is limited. Two-lane transformation model proposed by Kesting [4–6] considers the effect of vehicle lane change on the acceleration of the rear vehicle on the target lane, and evaluates the safe distance of the vehicle after lane change to solve the safety problem. But the model does not take into account the safe distance of the vehicle during the lane change.

This paper improves the intelligent car following model proposed by Treiber. By adding acceleration adjustment items to the vehicle acceleration formula, it can simulate the characteristics of urban traffic scenes better, such as small safe distance, the acceleration of rear car is rapid when do car following. It also improve the applicability of the model. Besides, this paper also improve the two-lane change model based on acceleration analysis proposed by Kesting, carry out the safety evaluation of the vehicle during the lane change process, and lane change decision is made based on the safety evaluation result.

3 Construction of Vehicle Motion Behavior Model

In a real urban traffic scene, driver usually keeps pace with the front car, sometimes changes lane for reasons such as steering or partial overtaking. According to these characteristics, the behavior of vehicles on the road is divided into two types: car following behavior and lane changing behavior, so that the vehicle motion model is divided into car following model and lane changing model.

3.1 Car Following Model

Car following model proposed by Treiber is an intelligent car following model based on safe distance. The basic principle of the model is: when front vehicle L and rear vehicle M are driving in the same lane without lane change, the acceleration of M will be largely affected by the behavior of L. When the distance between them becomes larger, M accelerates; when the distance becomes smaller, M decelerates. The model can be described by the following formulas:

$$a(t) = a_{\max}\left[1 - (\frac{v(t)}{v_d})^\delta - (\frac{s^*(v(t), \Delta v(t))}{s(t)})^2\right]\tag{1}$$

$$s^*(v(t), \Delta v(t)) = s_{\min} + v(t)T + \frac{v(t)\Delta v(t)}{2\sqrt{a_{\max}b_{com}}}\tag{2}$$

$$\Delta v(t) = v(t) - v_L(t)\tag{3}$$

In formula (1), $a(t)$ is the acceleration of the rear vehicle M at time t, $a_{\max}$ is the maximum acceleration of M, $v(t)$ is the speed of M at time t, and v_d is the target speed M, δ ($\delta > 0$) is the acceleration index, $\Delta v(t)$ is the speed difference between M and L after time t, $s(t)$ is the distance between the two vehicles at time t, and $s^*(v(t), \Delta v(t))$ is the expectation distance value of the next vehicle M at time t desired distance; $s_{\min}$ in formula (2) is the minimum safe distance when the vehicle is in stationary situation; T is the reaction time of the rear vehicle M, $v(t)T$ is the reaction distance of a vehicle, b_{com} is the commonly used brake deceleration; In formula (3), $v_L(t)$ is the speed of the front vehicle L at time t.

When simulating vehicle movement by this model, if the vehicle is driving on a sparse highway lane, $s(t)$ is very large, $(\frac{s^*(v(t), \Delta v(t))}{s(t)})^2$ is tending to 0. After that, M will continue to accelerate until the speed is equal to the target speed. In addition, when $\Delta v(t) > 0$, it means that the rear vehicle is approaching the front car, and the desired distance of the rear vehicle M will become larger. When $\Delta v(t) < 0$, it means that the rear vehicle is moving away from the front vehicle, and the desired distance will become smaller.

Treiber model is proposed for the movement behavior of vehicles on the highway, without considering the complicated traffic conditions. When using this model to simulate vehicle movement, if two vehicles are driving in the same lane and no lane change behavior occurs, the front vehicle L travels to the signal area or when the vehicle is forced to stop in a congested area, the rear vehicle M will decelerate to a stop earlier. At this time, the distance between the two vehicles is generally the minimum safe distance s_{min} in stationary state. When the signal change or the road ahead becomes to clear, front vehicle L begin to accelerate. Since the distance between the two vehicles is the minimum safe distance s_{min} in stationary state, it is smaller than the desired distance $s^*(v(t), \Delta v(t))$ of M, so a(t) will be very small, or even a negative numbers. However, in a real traffic scene, even if the distance between two vehicles is small, the rear vehicle M will accelerate at an acceleration close to the front vehicle L instead of decelerating in order not to fall too far behind the front vehicle L. Therefore, when the rear car M restarts, it should first accelerate more to keep the distance from being pulled too far. In order to adapt to this situation, this paper improves the acceleration of the following car in the following model, and divides the acceleration into two parts: free acceleration and acceleration adjustment items, which are defined as shown in formula (4):

$$a(t) = a_{free} - a_{adjust} \tag{4}$$

Here a_{free} is the free acceleration item, used to represent the acceleration process of the vehicle running freely on the sparse road; a_{adjust} is the acceleration adjustment item;

The definition of a_{free} is shown in formula (5), which is the first half of formula (1) of the intelligent car following model:

$$a_{free} = a_{max} \left[1 - (\frac{v(t)}{v_d})^\delta \right] \tag{5}$$

The definition of a_{adjust} is shown in formula (6):

$$a_{adjust} = b_{com} \left(\frac{s^*(v(t), \Delta v(t))}{s(t)} \right)^2 (\varepsilon(\Delta v(t)) + \varepsilon(s_{min} + 0.2v(t)T - s(t))) \tag{6}$$

In formula (6), $b_{com} \left(\frac{s^*(v(t), \Delta v(t))}{s(t)} \right)^2$ indicates that the degree of adjustment of the vehicle is affected by the common deceleration b_{com} of the rear vehicle.

In this paper, limitation item $\Delta v(t)$ and $s_{min} + 0.2v(t)T - s(t))$ are used to solve the shortcomings of the basic intelligent car following model. $\varepsilon(x)$ is a step function, $\Delta v(t)$ and $s_{min} + 0.2v(t)T - s(t)$ are used to control whether the adjustment item works or not. Adjustment items will only work under the following two conditions:

(1) When the relative speed of the front vehicle and rear vehicle $\Delta v(t) > 0$, it means that the rear vehicle M is approaching the front vehicle L, then rear vehicle M needs to pay attention to the distance between two vehicles, and adjust the acceleration value to reach safe distance, then the rear vehicle will maintain the same speed as the front vehicle; when $\Delta v(t) < 0$, it means that the rear vehicle M is moving away from the front vehicle L, and the rear vehicle M will properly accelerate to follow the front vehicle L.

(2) When the distance s(t) between the two vehicles is less than defined value $s_{min} + 0.2v(t)T$, the rear vehicle M needs to increase the acceleration value to make the rear vehicle is not far from the front vehicle.

3.2 Lane Change Model

Kesting's two-lane change model is a widely used lane change model. This model considers the effect of vehicle lane change on the rear vehicle acceleration on the target lane, and evaluates the safe distance of the vehicle after changing lane. Therefore, it solves the safety problem after lane-changing. However, this model does not take into account the safe distance during the lane change procedure, and considers that changing lane is completed in an instant. This paper improves on the basis of the two-lane change model based on acceleration analysis proposed by Kesting, makes safety assessment during lane change procedure, and decide whether the lane change behavior can be performed according to the assessment result. These two lane change behavior models are explained below separately.

3.2.1 Free Lane Change Model

When a vehicle is in following state, if it want to change lane, it is necessary to compare the speed of the vehicle before and after lane-changing, and consider the impact on the front and rear vehicles of the target lane at the same time. The lane change of the vehicle is shown in Fig. 1.

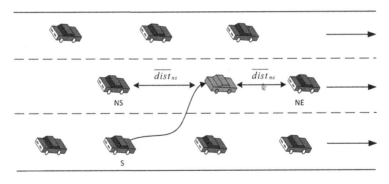

Fig. 1. Diagram of free lane change.

In Fig. 1, S is the vehicle which want to be changed lanes, NS and NE is the rear vehicle and front vehicle on the target lane after lane-changing. Kesting's restriction on lane change is:

$$
\begin{aligned}
&(a)\, \overline{a}_{ns} \geq -b_{com} \\
&(b)\, \overline{dist}_{ns} \geq \overline{dist}_{min}(ns,s) \\
&(c)\, \overline{dist}_{ne} \geq \overline{dist}_{min}(s,ne)
\end{aligned}
\tag{7}
$$

Here, the values with overbar are the values after the assumed lane change;

In condition (a), $\bar{a}_{ns}$ is the acceleration value of the rear vehicle NS after S enters the target lane. This acceleration value is estimated by the formula of the car following model by assuming S is the front car of NS after S changes lanes. If $\bar{a}_{ns} \geq 0$, it means NS will not slow down after S performs the lane change behavior, therefore, the lane-changing behavior of S is safe for NS; if $\bar{a}_{ns} < 0$, it means NS should perform deceleration after the lane change behavior of S. In order to ensure that the normal driving of NS, the brake deceleration of NS should not exceed common deceleration b_{com}.

Conditions (b) and (c) are to evaluate whether the distance between S and NS, S and NE after the lane change of S is greater than the safe distance between any two vehicles, $\overline{dist}_{ns}$ and $\overline{dist}_{ns}$ represent the distance between S and NS, S and NE respectively.

This model only considers the safety issue after lane change, does not consider the safe distance between vehicles during lane change. Therefore, this paper improves the model by evaluating safety situation of the lane change procedure as the basis to decide whether change lane or not. The conditions of the improved lane change model are:

$$(a)\ \bar{a}_{ns} \geq -b_{com}$$
$$(b)\ \overline{dist}_{ns} \geq \overline{dist}_{\min}(ns, s, T_c) \tag{8}$$
$$(c)\ \overline{dist}_{ne} \geq \overline{dist}_{\min}(s, ne, T_c)$$

$$\overline{dist}_{\min}(a, b, T_c) = s_{\min} + w_1(s^*(a) - (v(a) - v(b))T_c) \tag{9}$$

In formula (8), conditions (b) and (c) take into account the safety issues during the lane change procedure when calculating the desired distance between vehicles by adding parameter T_c. T_c is the time point during the lane change procedure. Because the speed of the vehicle does not change much during the lane change, the distance is checked on three time point: $T_c = 0.0$, $T_c = 0.5\,T_h$,and $T_c = T_h$ (T_h is the time required to change lanes).

Formula (9) is an evaluation formula for calculating the safe distance. In this formula, $s_{\min}$ is the minimum safe distance when the vehicle is at rest, w_1 is the weight, and $w_1(s^*(a) - (v(a) - v(b))T_c$ is the desired distance during the lane change of the vehicle S, which will change over time. The vehicle S can perform lane change behavior only when these three conditions are met simultaneously.

3.2.2   Assisted Lane Change Model

Sometimes vehicles need to change lanes due to traffic accidents and other reasons. In this case, vehicles often need the assistance of vehicles on the target lane to change lanes. Figure 2 is one of the scenarios that vehicle S is forced to change lanes. Since S has an intention to turn left ahead, S must change lanes to the left lane to make a turn.

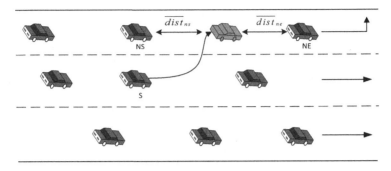

Fig. 2. Diagram of assisted lane change.

In the improved assisted lane change model, parameter time point T_c is added into the assisted lane change model conditions proposed by Kesting to evaluate the lane change process. The improved lane change model conditions are as follows:

$$
\begin{aligned}
&(a)\, t_{ns} = \frac{\Delta v_{ns}}{b_{com}} \leq \max\_time \\
&(b)\, \overline{dist}_{ns} \geq \overline{dist}_{\min}(ns, s, T_c) \\
&(c)\, \overline{dist}_{ne} \geq \overline{dist}_{\min}(s, ne, T_c)
\end{aligned}
\tag{10}
$$

Figure 2 shows the procedure of assisted lane change. In condition (a), t_{ns} is the lane change time taken by S, Δv_{ns} is the speed that NS can decelerate to cooperate with S, and b_{com} is commonly used brake deceleration, $\max\_time$ is the preset maximum lane change time. When the NS is willing to cooperate with S to decelerate, S can complete the lane change within maximum lane change time to satisfy condition (a).

In conditions (b) and (c), the calculation involved is similar to the calculation in the free lane change model. However, there are two differences. Firstly, in assisted lane change model, rear vehicle NS on the target lane usually cooperate with S with the common brake deceleration. Secondly, in the procedure of assisted lane change, the desired distance of the vehicle will be very small, so the value of the weight w_1 is reduced. Only when all three conditions are met, S can perform lane change behavior.

4   Results and Analysis of Experiments

To verify the effectiveness of the car following model and lane-changing model proposed in this paper, a vehicle motion simulation system was developed with OpenGL graphics library and Qt platform to simulate the behavior of vehicle motion.

In order to verify the effectiveness of the vehicle motion model constructed in this paper, an intersection with traffic lights is selected to record the speed change of the vehicles when they meet the traffic lights. During this period of time, the traffic light is red for 20 s, then turns into green. Vehicles gradually decelerates to a stop first, and accelerates to pass through the intersection. In the experiment, the improved method of this paper is compared with Treiber's intelligent car-following model, and the relationship between the speed and time of the two methods are shown in Fig. 3. The simulation effect of the car following behavior after passing the intersection is shown in Fig. 4.

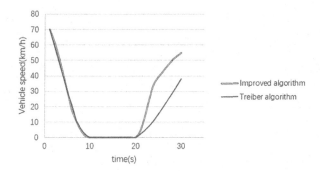

Fig. 3. The change of speed at the intersection

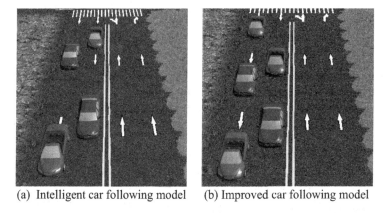

(a) Intelligent car following model   (b) Improved car following model

Fig. 4. Comparison of the simulation of the car following behavior after passing the traffic lights (Color figure online)

As shown in Fig. 3, when the traffic light is red, the difference between the change of speed and acceleration for improved car following model and intelligent car following model is not so big. However, when the signal light turns from red to green, vehicle's acceleration is faster, and the vehicle can reach a higher speed in a short time when the improved car following model is used to simulate the vehicle motion. As shown in Fig. 4, the distance between the vehicles is smaller after passing the signal lights for the improved car following model, which is more consistent with the movement of vehicles in the real traffic scene.

In the urban traffic scene, due to the better road conditions of the adjacent lane or the vehicle is willing to turn, the vehicle needs to change lanes. In this paper, safety assessment is performed during the lane change procedure, the test of the vehicle lane change model is shown in Fig. 5.

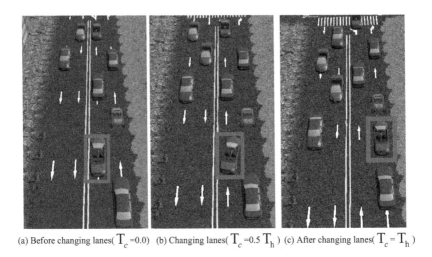

(a) Before changing lanes(T_c =0.0)   (b) Changing lanes(T_c =0.5 T_h) (c) After changing lanes(T_c = T_h)

Fig. 5. Simulation of vehicle lane changing behavior

When T_c = 0.0, the vehicle speed in the figure is 3.62 m/s, and the distance to the rear vehicle is 3.2 m. When T_c = 0.5 T_h, the vehicle speed is 3.71 m/s, and the distance to the rear vehicle is 3.8 m. When T_c = T_h, the speed is 3.76 m/s and the distance to the rear car is 4.5 m. During the lane change procedure, the distance between the vehicles before and during the lane change is generally smaller. Therefore, in the lane change behavior, the vehicle distance after the lane change should be checked, the vehicle distance during the lane change procedure should also be detected to ensure safety during vehicle changing lanes. The two-lane change model proposed by Kesting simplifies the vehicle lane change behavior to an instantaneous movement. The improved lane change model takes the vehicle safety issues during the lane change procedure into account, carry out safe distance during vehicle lane change to ensure the safety of vehicle lane changes.

5   Conclusion

In this paper, running model of vehicles is studied in combination with the characteristics of urban traffic scenarios, such as small distance between vehicles and complicated traffic rules, etc. Main works includes:

Firstly, the intelligent car follow model of Treiber is improved by adding adjustment items to the acceleration of the vehicle. A car following model suitable for urban traffic scenarios is constructed, so that it can better simulate urban traffic scenarios with characteristics of small safe distance of vehicles and greater impact of front vehicle acceleration on rear vehicle.

Secondly, lane change model proposed by Kesting's is improved by a safety assessment during lane change procedure. A vehicle lane change model suitable for urban scenes is constructed, which makes the vehicle safer when simulating lane change behavior.

Finally, this paper verifies the rationality of two models above by experiments.

References

1. Treiber, M., Hennecke, A., Helbing, D.: Congested traffic states in empirical observations and microscopic simulations. Phys. Rev. E Stat. Phys. Plasmas Fluids Relat. Interdiscip. Top. **62**(2), 1805–1824 (2000)
2. Treiber, M., Helbing, D.: Microsimulations of freeway traffic including control measures. Methoden und Anwendungen der Steuerungs-, Regelungs- und Informationstechnik **49**(11), 2001–2012 (2001)
3. Treiber, M., Helbing, D.: Memory effects in microscopic traffic models and wide scattering in flow-density data. Phys. Rev. E Stat. Nonlinear Soft Matter Phys. **68**(4), 119–128 (2003)
4. Kesting, A., Treiber, M.: Calibrating car-following models using trajectory data: methodological study. Transp. Res. Rec. **2088**(2088), 148–156 (2008)
5. Kesting, A., Treiber, M., Helbing, D.: Enhanced intelligent driver model to access the impact of driving strategies on traffic capacity. Philos. Trans. A Math. Phys. Eng. Sci. **2010**(368), 4585–4605 (1928)
6. Kesting, A., Treiber, M., Helbing, D.: General lane-changing model MOBIL for car-following models. Transp. Res. Rec. **1999**, 86–94 (2007)
7. Gerlough, D.L.: Simulation of freeway traffic by an electronic computer. In: Highway Research Board Proceedings, vol. 35 (1956)
8. Pipes, L.A.: An operational analysis of traffic dynamics. J. Appl. Phys. **24**(3), 274 (1953)
9. Kometani, E., Sasaki, T.: On the stability of traffic flow (report-I). J. Oper. Res. Soc. Jpn. **2**(1), 11–26 (1958)
10. Gipps, P.G.: A model for the structure of lane-changing decisions. Transp. Res. Part B **20**(5), 403–414 (1986)

Collaborative Application for Rapid Design of Paintings in Vector Format

Yalmar Ponce Atencio[1]([✉]) [iD], Manuel J. Ibarra[2]([✉]) [iD],
and Herwin Huillcen Baca[1]([✉]) [iD]

[1] Universidad Nacional José María Arguedas, Andahuaylas, Apurímac, Peru
{yalmar,hhuillcen}@unajma.edu.pe
[2] Universidad Nacional Micaela Bastidas de Apurímac, Abancay, Apurímac, Peru
manuelibarra@gmail.com

Abstract. Online cooperative or collaborative work have become common nowadays, because this helps to do any job without require meet together physically in one place. On the other hand, due to out current reality, inherent to many health conditions, traffic difficulties, and social insecurity; virtual or distance education is increasingly being promoted. In that sense, the main goal of this research work is develop a web based collaborative tool for rapid designing paints. This could be useful in many different areas, like as replacing the classical whiteboard, or express ideas to a workgroup, or even to design any realistic picture. This application allows to work together with a group of around ten connected users to collaborate virtually designing drawings in real time. The interaction experience depends on the internet bandwidth of all the users. For the implementation, many open source popular frameworks and programming utilities have been used. The presented results demonstrate the high scalability and versatility of our system being capable of managing hundreds of objects in real time.

Keywords: Cooperative Design (CD) · Collaborative application ·
Virtual education · Real time interaction · Cooperative painting ·
Programming patterns

1 Introduction

Web applications have become essential today, not only for their versatility but for their availability, leaving behind traditional desktop applications. In this sense, in recent years many applications have been re-implemented old well-known desktop applications, such is the case of the well-known application Microsoft Paint. This application, even in 2020, is still used, due to its simplicity and ease to use. However, nowadays there is a search for greater productivity and in general assignments are no longer done by one people. Currently, goals require to do a larger job, in which several people must be involved, and is no longer possible to work (for a long time) in the same place, so use applications

Y. Luo (Ed.): CDVE 2020, LNCS 12341, pp. 322–331, 2020.
https://doi.org/10.1007/978-3-030-60816-3_35

like the older Microsoft Paint is becoming less and less useful. Moreover, nowadays, there is an increasing demand by custom designs for digital games such as characters, avatars, landscape pieces, trees, plants, animals, vehicles, buildings and others, and do these designs could be better done by a collaborative work group [1,2]. As aforementioned, writing a document or essay, draw a paint or diagram could be a part of a larger job, and it must be share to other work group members and preferably interacting in real time. In that sense, it is necessary to create and use tools that allow working in a collaborative environment, so that any progress can be seen by the rest of the work team, with possibility that others may correct or edit, in order to finish the objective in a shortest time. Considering the aspects described above, this research work focuses the development of a drawing application that allows collaborative work under aspects that have been studied and that are considered important to perform much more productive work. Specifically have been considered the follow aspects:

1. It allows load and save predefined designs in catalogs or libraries.
2. It allows fast shape cloning with hotkeys.
3. Allows to edit shapes and figures using control points and handlers.
4. Allows geometric transformations like, scale, translation and rotation.
5. Allows import and export in vector format.
6. Allows, programmatically, the edition and creation of designs and shapes.

The proposed application, implements these aspects in a collaborative environment that allows documents to be shared in a work group with real-time interaction. The application is essentially aimed at users of school stage, where frequently is required to do homework, requested to a group of students. Likewise, also more advanced users can use our application since it can customize shapes and designs to save and load them in a future job. The designed system is able to create multiple documents (scenarios), where each document can be developed or edited by working on it simultaneously with a group of users who share the document. Therefore, several work groups can create their own documents, since the application is online and is accessible from any place using a web browser with internet connection.

We want to emphasize that our application is quick and simple to use compared to other existing applications. It is designed to create drawings or pictures quickly, as well as to support cooperative work in real time and with the ability to simultaneously edit documents.

The rest of the document is organized as follows: the related works are presented in the second section, the third section describes the implementation details of the application and its functionalities, the fourth section presents some experiments and results, finally, the fifth section presents the conclusions and future works.

2   Related Works

Since the 2000s, online applications have been developed massively, with the purpose for using them anywhere, anytime and mainly on any device. This was especially interesting because it allowed to change the way how the software development is done, passing from typical desktop applications to web applications. However, in many cases the implementation of a web application is more complicated compared to desktop applications, but in other cases occurs the opposite, since there are native mechanisms that are specifically for working on the web, such as concurrency, availability, ease to use, etc. There are a lot of researches approaching the implementation of web application, and more recently applications that allow collaborative work [3,4] like as text editors [5], coding [6], communication [3,7], health and medicine [8,9], games [10], drawing [11,12], sketching [13], graphics [14], e-learning [15], sharing [16], real time tracking [17], meeting [18], teaching [19–21], education [22], monitoring [23], and among others.

From these approaches, graphical applications are specially interesting, because involves a visual interaction and could helps to get better results [24,25]. However, implement graphical applications is complex and tedious, since that in a cooperative system, what a user changes or updates, it must be shown to the other users. In general, this kind of applications requires to transfer a lot of information, and the used devices must have better capabilities than for other types of applications considering that a lot of graphical elements will be added, making the interaction slower and complex for handling. Hence, efficient data structures and algorithms must be implemented. At this point, it is preferable, for example, to use vector formats instead of raster formats [26].

3   Implementation Details

For the implementation we use the XP agile methodology, since our main goal was develop a collaborative application with the aforementioned functionalities, for which, the programming languages JavaScript, CSS3 and HTML5 have been used. Additionally, for faster implementation, the Node.Js, Paper.js, jQuery, Socket.io, Spectrum and Filesaver frameworks were used.

In order to achieve the interaction, each client connects to the server through a socket connection (previously a socket_id is assigned to each connection created between a client and the server). A socket is a bidirectional connection, it means, each user is connected to the server, and the server is connected to each user in such a way it appears that each user is connected to all others in a room. The connection is maintained until the user disconnects from the application (closing the tab in the browser). Later, any changed piece (by any user) will be caught by the socket and, the server will emit this change to all the connected (to the server) users in the same room.

Furthermore, the implemented application has many useful features and functionalities to allow users to make really fast designs. Some of these characteristics are described below.

3.1   Layout Options

As in any tool or software for drawing, the typical options have been considered:

- **Freehand design.** It allows you to design or draw strokes, with the mouse or stylus, reducing the number of points for editing, but maintaining the best approximation to the original stroke.
- **Free-forms design.** It allows you to design or draw (closed) shapes based on strokes, with the mouse or stylus pen, reducing the number of points for editing, but maintaining the best approximation to the original shape.
- **Oval and rectangular shapes.** It allows to design circular or elliptical shapes and rectangular shapes with rounded or normal corners.
- **Polygons.** Allows to create arbitrary polygons, and its edges can be smooth or flat (see Figs. 1 and 2).

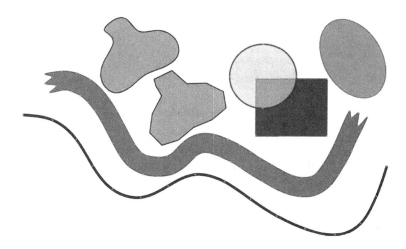

Fig. 1. Painting basic shapes.

3.2   Advanced Options and Functionalities

- **Selection and detail selection.** The first one is used to select objects or group of objects. The second one is used for selecting segment items, control points and handlers; and allows to manipulate them.

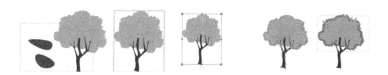

Fig. 2. Different selection possibilities.

- **Undo/Redo.** This operation uses a stack (array) which keeps track of the operations that have been performed. When the user performs an operation, you create an object that describes the operation and add it to the array. When the user hits undo, you can remove the last item from the array.
- **Pattern Repetitions.** Let's you draw designs with repetitive patterns. An example is design cloud shapes with configurable arc options for a greater realism (see Fig. 3).

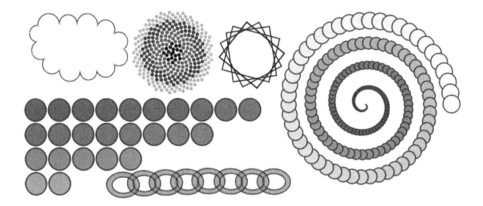

Fig. 3. Pattern Repetitions examples.

- **Predefined shapes.** The application is able to use predefined shapes from SVG files and organize them by themes, for example, landscapes, fruits, vegetables, clothes, geometric shapes, etc (see Fig. 4).

Fig. 4. Designs using predefined shapes, giraffe, zebra, trees and leaves.

- **Colors and lines width.** Allows you to change the body color or border color and the stroke thickness, of the selected object (see Fig. 6a).
- **Edit the shape of objects.** Allows you to edit the vertices or control points and the direction of curvature at each control point (see Fig. 6b).
- **Boolean operations.** It allows the operations of intersection, difference, union, and their combinations between two or more objects (see Fig. 6c).
- **Clone (Alt + mouse left button).** Usually it is necessary to make copies of a design that has already been made, it can also be considered the classic "copy/paste." The advantage of this option is that the copy is located in the same place from the original, giving the possibility that you can move the cloned object, with the mouse, wherever is needed, different from the copy and paste options of other well-known graphics editing applications (see Fig. 6d).
- **Zoom (Alt + Mouse Wheel).** For easier editing the zoom tool allows the editing of figure control points to be more precise (see Fig. 6e).
- **Import/Export SVG.** Paper.js allows to import and exports designs in SVG format. It is extremely helpful since we can import very interesting designs and use them in our documents, saving a lot of time. The application allows select the entire design or only parts and export them to SVG format or JSON.
- **Transformations (Scale and Rotation).** Lets you stretch and rotate a selection. The section can be composed of one or more objects.
- **JavaScript programming panel.** If you have programming knowledge and you want to make designs with patterns or for a fastest creation, this is a very helpful option (see the Fig. 5).

```
for(var i=0;i<5; i++) {
    for(var j=0; j<5; j++) {
        var oval = new Path.Circle(new Point(i*30, j*30), 14);
        oval.fillColor = "red";
        oval.strokeColor = "black";
    }
}
```

Fig. 5. Create a group shapes by programming.

Fig. 6. Application functionalities. Select colors and stroke thickness (a). Shape edition (b). Boolean operations (c). Cloning shapes (d). Zoom in/out (e). (Color figure online)

4   Results

The editor allows to design and edit quickly, since it is possible to load pre-designed drawings and use some or all of its elements. A first experiment shows how a predesigned vector drawing (in SVG format) was easily improved, achieving a more complete design (see Fig. 7).

In a second example, a drawing has been made from scratch, taking as reference a picture of a landscape taken from "google images". The elaboration of the painting took just over half an hour for an inexperienced user (see Fig. 8).

Fig. 7. Improving a predesigned drawing.

Fig. 8. On the top, a user has drawn a painting from scratch (on the left the original image and on the right the drawn image). On the bottom, two users interacting by using its browsers.

4.1 Equipment Used for Testing

Rapid tests were carried out with five users interacting simultaneously in a drawing. The main application was installer on a Server with Intel X2.5 GHz processor, 32 Gb RAM and Ubuntu 19.10 Operating System. The users have interacted with different devices like desktops, laptops, touchscreen laptops, tablets and cellphones. The tests were conducted using the browsers Firefox, Chrome and Chromium Edge, for the computers, and for tablets and cellphones the Firefox and Chrome browsers.

5 Conclusions and Future Work

As future work, the possibility of integrating to many LMS systems is considered, since nowadays there are an increasingly demand by using interactive whiteboard systems to e-learning platforms. Another important feature could be useful is incorporate suggestive patterns for auto complete in a similar way as in text editors. And finally, to use machine learning techniques in order to auto complete features by recognizing the thematic of paintings.

References

1. Shankar, A.R.: Physics engine basics. Pro HTML5 Games, pp. 47–72. Apress, Berkeley (2017). https://doi.org/10.1007/978-1-4842-2910-1_3
2. Tanaya, M., Chen, H., Pavleas, J., Sung, K.: Building a 2D Game Physics Engine: Using HTML5 and JavaScript (2017). https://doi.org/10.1007/978-1-4842-2583-7
3. Katayama, S., Goda, T., Shiramatsu, S., Ozono, T., Shintani, T.: A fast synchronization mechanism for collaborative web applications based on html5, pp. 663–668 (2013). https://doi.org/10.1109/SNPD.2013.13
4. Hammond, M.: Online collaboration and cooperation: the recurring importance of evidence, rationale and viability. Educ. Inf. Technol. **22**, 1005–1024 (2016). https://doi.org/10.1007/s10639-016-9469-x
5. Cho, B., Ng, A., Sun, C.: CoVim+CoEmacs: a heterogeneous co-editing system as a potential solution to editor war. In: Luo, Y. (ed.) CDVE 2018. LNCS, vol. 11151, pp. 64–68. Springer, Cham (2018). https://doi.org/10.1007/978-3-030-00560-3_9
6. Goldman, M., Little, G., Miller, R.: Real-time collaborative coding in a web IDE, pp. 155–164 (2011). https://doi.org/10.1145/2047196.2047215
7. Wenzel, M., Gericke, L., Gumienny, R., Meinel, C.: Towards cross-platform collaboration - transferring real-time groupware to the browser, pp. 49–54 (2013). https://doi.org/10.1109/CSCWD.2013.6580938
8. Andrikos, C., Rassias, G., Tsanakas, P., Maglogiannis, I.: Real-time medical collaboration services over the web, vol. 2015, pp. 1393–1396 (2015). https://doi.org/10.1109/EMBC.2015.7318629
9. Andrikos, C., Rassias, G., Tsanakas, P., Maglogiannis, I.: An enhanced device-transparent real-time teleconsultation environment for radiologists. IEEE J. Biomed. Health Inform. **23**, 374–386 (2018). https://doi.org/10.1109/JBHI.2018.2824312
10. Marin, C., Cloquell, J., Luo, Y., Estrany, B.: A multiplayer game with virtual interfaces. In: Luo, Y. (ed.) CDVE 2017. LNCS, vol. 10451, pp. 94–102. Springer, Cham (2017). https://doi.org/10.1007/978-3-319-66805-5_13
11. Yeom, J., Lee, G.: Designing a user interface for a painting application supporting real watercolor painting processes (2012). https://doi.org/10.1145/2350046.2350091

12. Jackson, W.: Interactive drawing: using paint and canvas classes interactively. Pro Android Graphics, pp. 479–513. Apress, Berkeley (2013). https://doi.org/10.1007/978-1-4302-5786-8_17

13. Sandnes, F.E., Lianguzov, Y., Rodrigues, O.V., Lieng, H., Medola, F.O., Pavel, N.: Supporting collaborative ideation through freehand sketching of 3D-shapes in 2D using colour. In: Luo, Y. (ed.) CDVE 2017. LNCS, vol. 10451, pp. 123–134. Springer, Cham (2017). https://doi.org/10.1007/978-3-319-66805-5_16

14. Coppens, A., Mens, T.: Towards collaborative immersive environments for parametric modelling. In: Luo, Y. (ed.) CDVE 2018. LNCS, vol. 11151, pp. 304–307. Springer, Cham (2018). https://doi.org/10.1007/978-3-030-00560-3_44

15. Ratajczak, J., Schimanski, C.P., Marcher, C., Riedl, M., Matt, D.T.: Mobile application for collaborative scheduling and monitoring of construction works according to lean construction methods. In: Luo, Y. (ed.) CDVE 2017. LNCS, vol. 10451, pp. 207–214. Springer, Cham (2017). https://doi.org/10.1007/978-3-319-66805-5_26

16. Ubik, S., Kubišta, J.: Scalable real-time sharing of 3D model visualizations for group collaboration. In: Luo, Y. (ed.) CDVE 2017. LNCS, vol. 10451, pp. 244–251. Springer, Cham (2017). https://doi.org/10.1007/978-3-319-66805-5_31

17. Qin, G., Li, Q., Li, S.: Vehicle route tracking system by cooperative license plate recognition on multi-peer monitor videos. In: Luo, Y. (ed.) CDVE 201. LNCS, vol. 9929, pp. 271–282. Springer, Heidelberg (2016). https://doi.org/10.1007/978-3-319-46771-9_35

18. Ibarra, M.J., Navarro, A.F., Ibañez, V., Soto, W., Ibarra, W.: mSIREMAP: cooperative design for monitoring teacher's classes in K-12 schools. In: Luo, Y. (ed.) CDVE 2017. LNCS, vol. 10451, pp. 114–122. Springer, Cham (2017). https://doi.org/10.1007/978-3-319-66805-5_15

19. Turkay, S.: The effects of whiteboard animations on retention and subjective experiences when learning advanced physics topics. Comput. Educ. **98**, 102–114 (2016). https://doi.org/10.1016/j.compedu.2016.03.004

20. Chen, J., Xu, J., Tang, T., Chen, R.: Webintera-classroom: an interaction-aware virtual learning environment for augmenting learning interactions. Interact. Learn. Environ. **25**, 1–16 (2016). https://doi.org/10.1080/10494820.2016.1188829

21. Sun, X.: Design and implementation of whiteboard in online classroom, p. 056 (2016). https://doi.org/10.22323/1.264.0056

22. Patel, C., Gadhavi, M., Patel, A.: A survey paper on e-learning based learning management systems (LMS). Int. J. Sci. Eng. Res. **4**, 171–176 (2013)

23. Liao, X., Huang, X., Huang, W.: Visualization of farm land use by classifying satellite images. In: Luo, Y. (ed.) CDVE 2018. LNCS, vol. 11151, pp. 287–290. Springer, Cham (2018). https://doi.org/10.1007/978-3-030-00560-3_40

24. Wibisono, A., Buchori, A.: Muhdi: whiteboard animation for android design using think talk write model to improve the post graduates students' concepts understanding. J. Adv. Res. Dyn. Control Syst. **11**, 535–543 (2019)

25. Mosina, Y.: An interactive whiteboard as a support tool to a teacher. English Am. Stud. **1**, 88–94 (2019). https://doi.org/10.15421/381911

26. Mukhyala, K., Masselot, A.: Visualization of protein sequence features using Javascript and SVG with pVIZ.js. Bioinformatics (Oxford, England) **30**, 3408–3409 (2014). https://doi.org/10.1093/bioinformatics/btu567

Implementation of Cooperative Sub-systems for Mobile Robot Navigation

Panus Nattharith$^{(\boxtimes)}$ (iD)

Department of Electrical and Computer Engineering, Faculty of Engineering,
Naresuan University, Phitsanulok, Thailand
panusn@nu.ac.th

Abstract. This work addresses the issue of mobile robot navigation system consisting of two cooperative sub-systems: a path planner sub-system and localizer sub-system. In the navigation system, the robot needs to localize itself and make its way to its desired location. Hence, the robot's behavioral ability in finding its position becomes a major issue, along with its ability to plan a path to its goal. In the proposed work, the localization and path planning techniques have been adopted, and a series of experiments have been conducted using ROS based mobile robot. The experimental results reveal that the implemented sub-systems can work cooperatively as the localizer can effectively guarantee the accuracy of the robot's current position and its orientation while the path planner can ensure that the robot maintains a safe distance from obstacles concurrent with finding an optimal path from its current position to the desired goal.

Keywords: Mobile robot navigation · Path planning · Localization · ROS

1 Background of Mobile Robot Navigation

Mobile robot navigation is one of the most challenging requirements for a mobile robot. It can be described as an algorithm that aims to lead the robot from an initial position to its goal without collisions. Navigation comprises two categories, namely global navigation and local navigation. The global navigation deals with navigation on a larger scale in which the robot cannot observe its goal from its initial position. In most cases, the robot uses a pre-defined map to plan its path as well as determining its position in the environment. One solution to the global navigation problem is to create a path that allows the robot to achieve its distant goal specified according to the global world model. Other approaches rely on techniques of localization, such as Monte Carlo localization [1], which require to work cooperatively with path planner. Local navigation, on the other hand, deals with navigation over short distances or from point to point, where the main focus is on obstacle avoidance [2, 3]. It allows the robot to move efficiently within its environment and to successfully attain its local goals. Successful navigation requires both global and local techniques with simultaneous execution of the localization and path planning sub-systems.

© Springer Nature Switzerland AG 2020
Y. Luo (Ed.): CDVE 2020, LNCS 12341, pp. 332–341, 2020.
https://doi.org/10.1007/978-3-030-60816-3_36

2   Mobile Robot Localization

Localization is the process of establishing where the robot is relative to a model of its working environment. As described in Sect. 1, the robot must be able to localize itself in a pre-defined map of its working environment. This section, therefore, introduces the localization technique adopted in this work.

One way to define the robot's position is to keep track of the robot's movements by simply using the odometry data. However, this method is unreliable due to the positional errors that are continuously accumulated as the robot moves around. For this reason, an approach in which the odometry data is supplemented by other sensory information is required to correct the robot's position. In this work, the Robot Operating System (ROS) [4] is adopted as part of a high level processing. The system utilizes a sub-system called AMCL node, derived from AMCL Player driver [5], for localization which makes use of odometry data and the laser range finder measurements along with a pre-defined map of the robot's working environment to estimate the robot's pose (x, y, θ). The processing of the data in AMCL is done using a Monte Carlo particle filter, which is a variant of the Bayes filter and employs a probabilistic method to estimate the robot's position [1]. The number of particles used by the filter can be dynamically adjusted to account for greater uncertainty and to match the computational capabilities of the system, i.e. when the robot's pose is highly uncertain, the number of particles is increased, on the other hand when the robot's pose is well determined, the number of particles is decreased. This results in a method known as Adaptive Monte Carlo Localization (AMCL) [6] in which the filter is able to make a trade-off between processing speed and localization accuracy. Two different outputs are available from the AMCL node. One is a representative sample of the pose hypotheses weighted by likelihood, while the other is the most-likely pose hypothesis.

The AMCL method is the most generally used method for mobile robot localization because of its simplicity of implementation and applicability [7]. Additionally, compared to other Bayesian filters, which can also be used for localization purpose, for example the Extended Kalman Filter (EKF) [8], the AMCL method has several advantages. Initially, it takes raw sensory data with any noise distribution as an input whereas the EKF method assumes Gaussian noise distribution [8, 9]. Secondly, in contrast to the EKF method, the AMCL method can be used for global localization where the robot is not informed of its initial position, and is robust to a so-called robot kidnapping problem where the robot is carried from its current position to an arbitrary position [7]. However, the AMCL method has one disadvantage which is the considerable amount of computation needed for the filter to work properly.

The overall implementation of the AMCL method is initialized by randomly distributing the initial number of samples (particles) over the entire map. At this point, all particles are assigned similar likelihood weight as the robot could be anywhere on the map. The robot then senses its environment using a representative sample of the laser readings. For each particle, the laser range data is compared to the ranges which would theoretically be correct if the robot's pose was equal to the pose of the particular particle. This comparison results in a likelihood weight being assigned to each particle. The theoretical ranges are computed using the map of the robot's working environment and a probabilistic model of the laser range finder. If the robot has not moved, the sense step is performed again. By letting the odometry data have higher priority than the laser range data, it is ensured that the pose estimate will correspond to the latest received odometry data. However, this may result in range data being queued up, especially when the number of particles is large, for example, in the initial phase of the filter's operation. The queued range data will be processed when the computational demand decreases as a result of the increasing pose estimate likelihood and the resulting decrease in the number of particles. If the robot has moved, the odometry data is used to update the filter. When updating the filter, a new set of particles is generated based on the likelihood weights of the prior set along with the motion model of the robot. The areas where the likelihood weights were high are assigned a larger number of particles than the areas where the likelihood weights were small. This cycle is continuously repeated during the AMCL filter operation.

3 Mobile Robot Path Planning

Path planning involves finding a path from the robot's current position to its goal. This obviously involves the robot knowing its current position and goal position. Both positions must be in the same frame of reference. The path planning will become a well understood problem when all of the above information is available to the robot. The key to achieve the goal is to use a pre-defined map to plan the path to the goal. In this section, the path planning algorithm employing the wavefront propagation [10] has been developed. The robot current position can be obtained by the localizer, previously described, while the robot goal position is given by the user. The output of this algorithm is a series of waypoints that the robot should visit to reach its goal.

Although ROS package includes a planner node utilizing Dijkstra's and A* techniques [4], the planning algorithm was developed in this study. This is because at the early stage in the development of the physical mobile robot, the laser range finder had not yet been installed on the robots, and thus the AMCL node for localization purposes could not be used. Consequently, the ROS planner could not be executed on the physical robot as it requires the position data given by the AMCL node. At that moment, the robot only used its odometry sub-system for localization which cannot be used as an input to the planner function in ROS.

The wavefront algorithm was chosen due to its advantages as it is simple, requires low computation, is able to find the shortest path, can deal with any shape obstacle, and the resolution of the map does not impede on the processing time required [10].

The wavefront algorithm involves a search technique, beginning at the starting point and propagating out until it reaches the goal point. A grid of cells is created from the pre-defined map using an appropriate size of cell. Each cell is initialized to a numerical value of 0. Cells known to contain a physical object or part of an object are assigned a numerical value of 1. The goal point is identified and allocated a value of 2. To create the wavefront values, any cells which surround the goal point are given a higher number depending on how close they are to the goal point. A value of 3 is assigned to the cells adjacent to the goal point, with the value of 4 assigned to the cells adjacent to those cells having a value of 3, and so on. Once the starting point is assigned a numerical value, the algorithm then proceeds to select the lowest value cell nearest to the starting point. It is marked as a waypoint. Then the algorithm moves to the selected cell and selects the nearest cell having the lowest value. It is also marked as the waypoint. The sequence is repeated until the goal point is reached. This creates the safe path, in terms of a series of waypoints, from the starting point to the goal point. However, some waypoints can be eliminated if the path from the previous waypoint to the next waypoint does not cross through the obstacle. Therefore, the algorithm can iteratively eliminate some waypoints and it is repeated until no other waypoint can be eliminated. Figure 1 displays an example of the wavefront values. The 1's represent the obstacles while the goal and the starting cells are 2 and 16, respectively. All other cells are marked according to their distance from the goal.

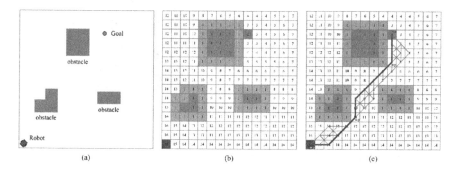

(a)   (b)   (c)

Fig. 1. Wavefront algorithm, (a) navigation scenario, (b) growing the obstacles in the map according to the robot's size and assigning a value for all cells, (d) a robot's path is created

One or more possible paths can be provided by the wavefront algorithm. However, the algorithm selects a preferred path by considering the path that has the lowest total cell value (distance cost). If any two or more paths have the same total cell value, the algorithm then selects the path that allows the robot to navigate a further distance away from the obstacles. By combining these two criteria, an optimal path is obtained in terms of both distance to goal and distance to the obstacles.

4 Mobile Robot Development

In this work, the physical mobile robot platform has been developed. It employs a differential drive system with two solid rubber tyre wheels. A caster wheel is also used to provide improved stability. The motors have been chosen as geared DC motors which have the optical encoders to get the rotation data from the motor shaft and transfer it to the robot system. Additional components were mounted on the robot including a RPLIDAR, serving as a laser range finder, a single board computer (Raspberry PI), a 32-bit microcontroller (Teensy), and an inertial measurement unit (IMU) which measures and reports the velocity, orientation and gravitational forces applied to the robot. Figure 2 a and b illustrate a 3D model of the robot and the physical robot, respectively.

As mentioned in previous sections, this work makes use of the Robot Operating System (ROS) as part of a high level processing. Therefore, most software development has been done using ROS environment. ROS is an open-source, meta-operating system for robot applications. It provides the services that expect from an operating system, including hardware abstraction, low-level device control, implementation of commonly-used functionality, message-passing between processes, and package management. It also provides tools and libraries for obtaining, building, writing, and running code across multiple computers. ROS is similar in some respects to robot frameworks, such as Player [5], CARMEN [11], and Orca [12].

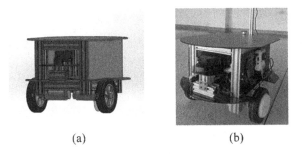

(a)   (b)

Fig. 2. (a) Concept design of the robot platform, (b) Constructed robot platform

The system overview of the robot system is shown in Fig. 3, in which the High-level computer, running ROS framework, and the Low-level microcontroller, designed to control peripheral sensors and actuators, are the main part of the robot system which work simultaneously and interdependently. They are connected to each other via a standard RS-232 serial communication. The Low-level microcontroller sends the sensor data and the other parameters of the robot to the High-level computer. Simultaneously, the High-level computer gets the sensor data and uses them to run the robot algorithms. Then the results of the algorithms are sent back to the Low-level microcontroller in order to execute the robot navigation tasks.

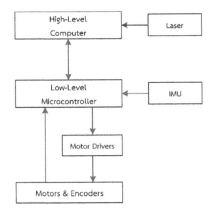

Fig. 3. System overview of the robot platform.

5   Experimental Implementation

In order to estimate the capability of the proposed work for expressing useful tasks, the developed sub-systems have been evaluated. The mobile robot was used initially to conduct several experiments. In keeping with the overall objectives of the cooperative sub-systems, the robot must be able to:

- Localize itself in its working environment.
- Wander around its working environment while keeping track of its own position
- Plan a safe path from its initial position to a desired destination.

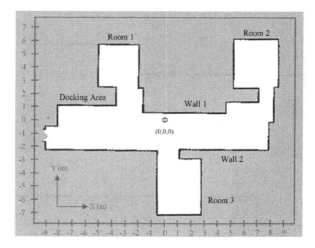

Fig. 4. Detail of the pre-define map which is constructed by the robot.

The pre-defined map is required for the robot to plan its path as well as determining its position in the environment. Therefore, before conducting the experiments, the robot need to wander around to gather knowledge of its entire working area, in order to use such data to build the map. Figure 4 displays the constructed map, given to the localization and planning sub-systems.

5.1   Experimental Results for Localization Sub-system

In this section, the mobile robot was used to conduct the experiments. During navigation, the robot must be able to localize itself in its working environment. Thus, this experiment aims to test the functionality of the localization sub-system of the robot and is carried out to verify its robustness.

In order to conduct the experiments, two navigation scenarios have been set up in which the robot actually starts at $(0, 0, 0)$, but the localizer is informed that it is initially located at $(2, -1, 0)$ and $(2, -1, \pi)$ for the test scenarios 1 and 2, respectively. The purpose of these test scenarios is to ensure that the robot is able to perform self-localization whenever the robot's perception of its surrounding disagrees with its stored map of the working environment. During testing, the robot is instructed to wander aimlessly around its working environment, it could discover that it is currently at the wrong location, and subsequently correct its position. The precision of the performed localization is monitored by logging the robot's true pose along with the estimated pose given by the localizer.

In the first test scenario, the actual initial pose of the robot is (0, 0, 0). However the robot's localizer is provided with the initial pose of (2, −1, 0). The actual path of the robot and the estimated positions of the localization sub-system are plotted in Fig. 5 in which the black arrows represent the initial heading directions of the robot and the localizer.

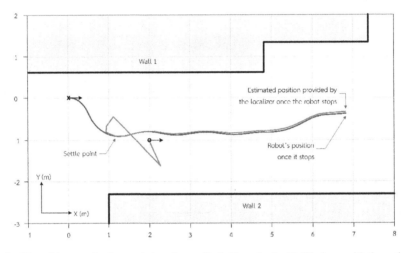

Fig. 5. Plot of the actual robot path (starting at (0, 0, 0) marked with **X**) along with the estimated position of the localization sub-system (initial pose of (2, −1, 0) marked with **O**)

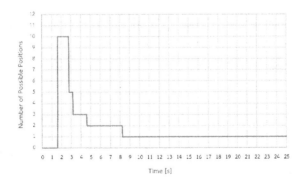

Fig. 6. Number of possible positions at each time step for test scenario 1

As mentioned in Sect. 2, the AMCL implementing the localization sub-system employs a set of range data available from the laser range finder; therefore, during navigation the environmental features must be detected in order for the localizer to estimate the robot's pose. Once the robot starts moving, the robot moves down the middle of the corridor to avoid hitting 'Wall 1' on its left side. At this point, the laser readings on the left side of the robot are affected by 'Wall 1', but the localizer's pose estimate should not detect anything on its left side at a small distance. Instead, it should be affected by 'Wall 2' on its right side. This results in a large number of possible robot's positions during this interval as shown in Fig. 6 because the robot's perception of its surrounding disagrees with the stored map of its environment. However, the number of possible positions decreases as the robot moves since the localizer is able to find a better pose estimate than the one currently provided to the robot. Consequently, the difference between the actual path and the estimated poses decreases and settles after about 8 s of moving.

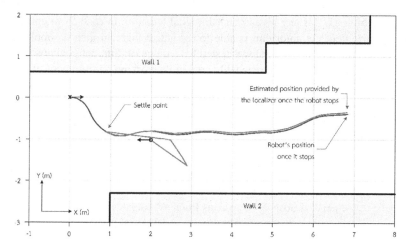

Fig. 7. Plot of the actual robot path (starting at $(0, 0, 0)$ marked with **X**) along with the estimated position of the localization sub-system (initial pose of $(2, -1, \pi)$ marked with **O**)

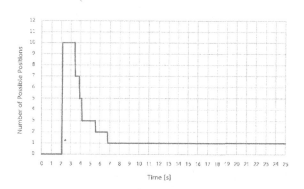

Fig. 8. Number of possible positions at each time step for test scenario 2

Figure 7 displays the result of the second test scenario in which the localizer is told that it is initially placed at $(2, -1, \pi)$ while the robot's actual initial pose is at $(0, 0, 0)$. This test scenario is more challenging than the first scenario as the localizer is informed the initial heading direction with 180 degrees different to the robot actual heading. The exact same explanation applies as for the first test scenario and the difference between the actual position and the estimated one settles after about 7 s of operation as shown in Fig. 8.

The test results indicate that the localization sub-system functions as intended as the difference between the actual path and the estimated poses decreases with time. The following section provides the test results for the planning sub-system.

5.2   Experimental Results for Path Planning Sub-system

The purpose of the experiments is to create the collision-free path from the robot's current position to its desired goal. The experimental results reveal that the path planning algorithm works for any given reachable goal location. In case of an unreachable goal being specified, the algorithm is able to recognize this and then it simply aborts. The developed planner sub-system was tested for a range of different goal positions and was able to plan the path to each reachable goal in its working environment. It was also tested and debugged using the wavefront driver provided by Player framework [5] as a benchmark. Each destination input was sent to the Player wavefront driver as well as the developed planner sub-system code. Utilizing the output of the Player driver, the code was debugged until its output matched the output of the Player driver.

Table 1. Comparison between the planning outputs from the Player driver and the developed planning sub-system from the different starting positions to the different goal positions

Start	Goal	Waypoints from Player driver	Waypoints from developed planner
Dock	Room 1	(−6.00, 0.00)	(−6.00, 0.00)
		(−2.63, 0.91)	(−2.58, 0.89)
		(−3.01, 4.01)	(−3.00, 4.00)
Room 1	Room 2	(−3.00, 4.00)	(−3.00, 4.00)
		(−1.69, −0.84)	(−1.72, −0.82)
		(7.53, 0.58)	(7.52, 0.55)
		(7.91, 1.37)	(7.89, 1.35)
		(7.96, 2.82)	(7.96, 2.80)
		(7.00, 5.00)	(7.00, 5.00)
Room 2	Room 3	(7.00, 5.00)	(7.00, 5.00)
		(7.96, 2.36)	(7.96, 2.36)
		(7.91, 1.85)	(7.93, 1.86)
		(7.76, 0.81)	(7.75, 0.78)
		(0.12, −2.16)	(0.12, −2.08)
		(1.00, −6.00)	(1.00, −6.00)
Room 3	Dock	(1.00, −6.00)	(1.00, −6.00)
		(−0.62, −1.25)	(−0.57, −1.25)
		(−6.01, 0.00)	(−6.00, 0.00)

The pre-defined map given to the planning sub-system is similar to the localizer tests (see Fig. 4) in which the x, y coordinates of the 'Docking area', 'Room 1', 'Room 2', and 'Room 3' are $(-6, 0)$, $(-3, 4)$, $(7, 5)$, and $(1, -6)$, respectively. Table 1 displays the outputs of the Player driver and the developed planner algorithm, in terms of a series of waypoints from the different starting positions to the different goal positions. The experimental results reveal that the planning sub-system successfully produces the collision-free paths for particular environment in terms of a series of waypoints that the robot should visit to complete its tasks.

6   Conclusions

The localizer and path planner were implemented and the test results demonstrate that they are able to work cooperatively. The localization sub-system enables the robot to perform self-localization whenever the robot's perception of its surroundings disagrees with its stored map of the working environment. In case of the planning sub-system, it works correctly for any given reachable goal positions. Regarding the performances of these sub-systems, they can be used for the robot to complete its navigation tasks robustly and effectively.

References

1. Dellaert, F., Fox, D., Burgard, W., Thrun, S.: Monte carlo localization for mobile robots. In: IEEE International Conference on Robotics and Automation (ICRA-99), (1999)
2. Nattharith, P.: Motor schema-based control of mobile robot navigation. Int. J. Robot. Autom. **31**(4), 310–320 (2016)
3. Nattharith, P., Guzel, M.S.: Machine vision and fuzzy logic-based navigation control of a goal-oriented mobile robot. Adapt. Behav. **24**(3), 168–180 (2016)
4. Marin-Plaza, P., Hussein, A., Martin, D., Excalera, A.D.L.: Global and local path planning study in a ROS-based research platform for autonomous vehicles. J. Adv. Transp., pp. 1–10 (2018)
5. Gerkey, B.P., Vaughan, R.T., Howard, A.: The player/stage project: tools for multi-robot and distributed sensor systems. In: Int. Conf. Adv. Robot. (ICAR 2003), (2003)
6. Fox, D., Burgard, W., Dellaert, F., Thrun, S.: Monte carlo localization: efficient position estimation for mobile robots. In: The sixteenth National Conference on Artificial Intelligence (AAAI'99), (1999)
7. Thrun, S., Burgard, W., Fox, D.: Probabilistic Robotics, MIT Press, (2005)
8. Koseoglu, M., Celik, O.M., Pektas, O.: Design of an autonomous mobile robot based on ROS. In: International Artificial Intelligence and Data Processing Symposium, (2017)
9. Xiaoyu, W., Caihong, L., Li, S., Ning, Z., Hao, F.: On adaptive monte carlo localization algorithm for the mobile robot based on ROS. In: The Chinese Control Conference, (2018)
10. Al-Jumaily, A., Leung, C.: Wavefront propagation and fuzzy based autonomous navigation. Int. J. Adv. Robot. Syst. **2**(2), 93–102 (2005)
11. Montemerlo, M., Roy, N., Thrun, S.: Perspectives on standardization in mobile robot programming: the carnegie mellon navigation (CARMEN) toolkit. In: IEEE/RSJ International Conference on Intelligent Robots and Systems (IROS 2003), (2003)
12. Kaupp, T.: ORCA: Component for Robotics. http://orca-robotics.sourceforge.net/. Accessed 2020

Searching for Extreme Portions in Distributions: A Comparison of Pie and Bar Charts

Frode Eika Sandnes[1,2(✉)] [iD], Aina Flønes[1], Wei-Ting Kao[1],
Patrick Harrington[1], and Meisa Issa[1]

[1] Oslo Metropolitan University, 0130 Oslo, Norway
{frodes,S305075,S334005,S333998}@oslomet.no,
phaa@gmail.com
[2] Kristiania University College, 0153 Oslo, Norway

Abstract. Aggregated data visualizations are often used by collaborative teams to gain a common understanding of a complex situations and issues. Pie and bar charts are both widely used for visualizing distributions. The study of pie versus bar charts has a long history and the results are seemingly inconclusive. Many report authors prefer pie charts while visualization theory often argues for bar graphs. Most of the studies that conclude in favor of pie charts have focused on how well they facilitate the identification of parts to the whole. This study set out to collect empirical evidence on which chart type that most rapidly and less erroneously facilitate the identification of extreme parts such as the minimum, or the maximum, when the distributions are similar, yet not identical. The results show that minimum values are identified in shorter time with bar charts compared to pie charts. Moreover, the extreme values are identified with fewer errors with bar charts compared to pie charts. One implication of this study is that bar charts are recommended in visualization situations where important decisions depend on rapidly identifying extreme values.

Keywords: Visualization · Distributions · Extreme values · Pie chart · Bar chart · Response time · Error · Perceived accuracy

1 Introduction

Visualizations of aggregated data are often used by collaborative teams, such as leaders of large organizations, to understand complex situations, issues, and relationships. Graphical visualizations can be effective in communicating certain characteristics or draw attention towards particular issues. Perhaps the most common visualization types include the line graph, scatterplot, bar graph and pie chart. Line graphs and scatter plots are used to visualize the relationship between two variables, while bar charts and pie charts are typically used to visualize the distribution or portions of various categories of a whole. In many situations pie charts and bar charts may be used with similar effectiveness. In such situations it is the personal preferences of the authors that determine what visualization method to use. This is especially the case if the purpose of a visualization is to show that something is uneven or unbalanced. Some argue that the

© Springer Nature Switzerland AG 2020
Y. Luo (Ed.): CDVE 2020, LNCS 12341, pp. 342–351, 2020.
https://doi.org/10.1007/978-3-030-60816-3_37

pie chart is more appealing, and research has also provided evidence that proportions are perceived in a shorter time with higher accuracy with pie charts compared to bar charts [1].

Visualizations can easily be generated with common tools such as Microsoft Excel, and consequently visualizations are often created by authors without any visualization training or expertise. In some situations, the choice of visualization technique is based on a belief that a particular visualization technique is superior to others. For instance, some argue that pie charts are more effective than bar charts because they can be used as a metaphor of dividing a cake, pie or pizza, while there are fewer obvious metaphors for bar charts. The renowned visualization expert Stephen Few writes "nothing that I teach is met with such fierce opposition as my low opinion of them. People cling to them aggressively" in his reading entitled "Our Irresistible Fascination with All Things Circular" [2]. Among visualization experts the strengths and weaknesses are well-understood, that is, that bar charts generally are more effective in situations where the portions are similar as it is easier to discriminate between different categories, while it is hard to distinguish between categories of similar but unequal size in pie charts [2]. This is because the human visual perception system has been shown to perform more accurately when determining length compared to determining area and angles.

Arguments in favor of pie charts include its ability to make part of a whole estimations easier than with bar charts. Pie charts also provide five easily recognizable anchors, namely 0%, 25%, 50%, 75% and 100% analogous to dial positions 0am, 3 am, 6 am and 9 am on a clock surface [3]. Pie charts are argued to be more attractive than bar charts. There are also situations where pie charts are not suitable such as visualizing small changes or how proportions change over time.

There is quite a long history of research into bar versus pie charts. Most of these studies have focused on assessing proportions of a whole and results have shown that pie charts are superior for this task [1]. However, in some situations the viewer may only be interested in determining the smallest or the largest portion. If important decisions are to be made on such information, it is crucial that the corresponding visualization results in the shortest possible response time with a low risk of erroneous assessments. This study therefore set out to explore how suited pie (see Fig. 1) and bar charts (see Fig. 2) are for supporting the identification of the extreme portions when the items are of similar, yet not identical, magnitude. Our hypotheses are that the bar chart leads to (a) more rapid identification of extreme portions and (b) fewer errors than pie charts.

The rest of this paper is organized as follows. Section 2 briefly review the related works on visualization. This is followed by a description of the methodology in Sect. 3, the results in Sect. 4 and discussion in Sect. 5. The paper closes with the conclusions in Sect. 6.

Fig. 1. Identifying the smallest item in a pie chart by locating the smallest angle, smallest area, smallest arc circle or a combination. Comparisons are difficult as items are not side-by-side.

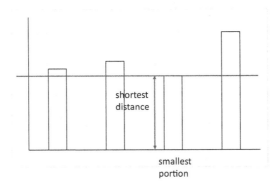

Fig. 2. Identifying the smallest item in a bar chart by locating the shortest distance (and/or smallest area). Comparison is easy as items are side-by-side.

2   Related Work

The pie chart has been around for more than 200 years and its introduction is often attributed to William Playfair [4]. The pie chart is often referred to as a circular chart. An informative survey of research into pie charts by Spence [4] illustrated that there has been much disagreement regarding the effectiveness of pie charts and bar charts. More recent studies show that the pie chart results in shorter response times and lower errors compared to bar charts for tasks involving the assessment of portions as a whole where participants have been asked to visually estimate a portion in charts as a numeric integer percentage [1].

Although the just noticeable difference in angle perception has been found to be related to the actual angle in general [5], it has also been found that it is actually not the angle that is the most influential characteristic of a pie segment, but rather its area and arc length [6, 7]. It has also been found that proportion judgements are affected by bias as small proportions sometimes are overestimated and large portions are underestimated [8].

Other studies are making less informed claims about the power of pie charts such as their power to communicate issues of climate changes [9]. A totally different take of the pie chart is a study that demonstrated how pie charts can be used in the sonification of data were the pie chart is visualized with audio when the person turns his or her head in different directions [10].

Despite the research results that supports the use of pie charts, visualization experts in general appears quite cautious about circular visualization tools [2, 11]. The literature has mostly focused on more exotic circular diagrams such as radar diagram [12], petal charts [13] and polar plots [14]. There has also been research on bar charts addressing issues on how to represent large scales [15] or using diverging stacked bars for illustrating Likert responses [16]. Embellishments to strengthen visualizations is yet another technique that has received some attention [17].

3   Method

3.1   Experimental Design

A controlled within-groups experimental design was selected with chart type as independent variable and task completion time, error rate and preference as dependent variables. The independent variable chart type had two levels, namely bar chart and pie chart.

3.2   Participants

A total of 20 participants was recruited for the experiment of which 10 were female and 10 males. Their ages ranged from 20 to 56 years of age with a mean age of 33 years. None of the participants reported having any visual impairment. All the participants had completed secondary education and nine participants had completed higher education. Two of the participants reported a diagnosis of dyscalculia.

3.3   Materials

A total of 10 datasets were created and used to create 20 charts, that is 10 pie charts with 10 corresponding bar charts that were shuffled into random order. Each dataset comprised a set of different but similar numbers. These numbers were organized into a random order such that the corresponding chart had the bars and pie-slices in a non-decreasing or increasing order. Unnecessary visual elements were removed from the charts, such as text percentages and titles, to prevent diverting attention away from the task of assessing the portions. Each item was numbered for naming purposes.

The 10 datasets comprised of 3 to 14 data points ($M = 7.6$, $SD = 2.8$). The data points were randomly generated in different absolute ranges, although this was not intended to have any effect on the visual perception. The relative ranges were limited to making the portions appear close-to-similar. The mean normalized ranges in percentages of the datasets were ($M = 38.5\%$, $SD = 30.1\%$). The mean difference between the smallest item and the second smallest item was ($M = 5.0\%$, $SD = 6.1\%$). This measure can be considered an indicator of task difficulty.

All the charts were created with Microsoft Excel using shades of grey rather than color as different colors are believed to affect the perception of area [18]. Different levels of grey are also likely to affect the perception of area, but to a lesser degree. The differentiation with color is not needed with bar charts but may help with the differentiation of items. Each item had a unique shade of grey with a clear black outline. All bars had the same color. Each item was labelled. Figure 3 shows an example of a pie and a corresponding bar chart used in the experiments. An additional five charts were generated as a control with a reversed order of the items.

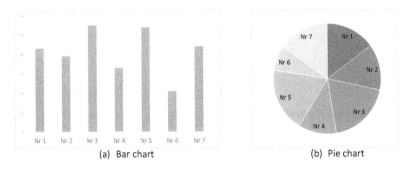

(a) Bar chart   (b) Pie chart

Fig. 3. A dataset with 7 items visualized as a bar chart and a pie chart. The task is to identify the smallest item, namely item 6.

3.4 Task

For each chart presented the participant had to identify and verbally report the number and/or point at the smallest item.

3.5 Procedure

The participants were tested individually in an isolated setting indoors. The total of 25 charts were shown using a PowerPoint presentation. Each participant viewed the charts in the same order, but the presentation order of the charts was randomized. The time to complete each task, that is, the time from when the chart was displayed until the oral response was given, was measured manually using a stopwatch as well as the correctness of the answer. At the end of the session the participants were asked to rate their perceived accuracy of both the pie and the bar charts using a scale from 1 to 10 where 10 represent most accurate and 1 least accurate.

No personal information was collected from the participants. The General Data Protection Regulations (GDPR) was adhered to and no data collection permits and approvals had to be solicited because the experiment was anonymous and did not involve any sensitive information. Participants had the opportunity to withdraw from the experiment at any time.

3.6   Analysis

For each person, the median time to interpret the pie and bar charts were determined for each participant, respectively. The data were analyzed using the open source statistical analysis software package JASP version 0.11.0.0 [19].

4   Results

4.1   Task Completion Time

A Shapiro Wilks test revealed that the median task completion times were not normally distributed ($W = 0.861$, $p = .008$). Therefore, the non-parametric Wilcoxon signed rank test was used to compare the task completion times of the two chart types. The test revealed that there was highly significant effect of chart type on task completion time ($W = 0.0$, $p < .001$). Figure 4 shows that the mean completion time with the bar chart ($M = 2.24$, $SD = 0.48$) was nearly half that of the completion time with the pie charts ($M = 5.26$, $SD = 1.99$).

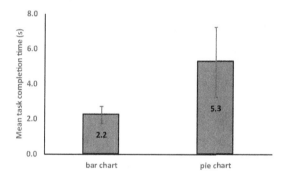

Fig. 4. The observed time to identify the smallest item in pie charts and bar charts. Error bars show standard deviation.

4.2   Error Rate

Figure 5 shows the error rates observed for the two visualization methods. A Wilcoxon signed rank test revealed that the error rates were significantly lower with bar chart compared to the pie charts ($W = 0.0$, $p < .001$). The mean error rate was only 1% ($M = 1.05$, $SD = 4.59$) with the bar chart, while it was a massive 51.1% with the pie chart ($M = 51.05$, $SD = 14.10$).

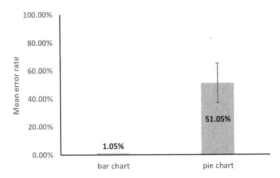

Fig. 5. The error rates observed with pie charts and bar charts. Error bars show standard deviation.

4.3   Perceived Accuracy

Figure 6 shows the perceived accuracies of the two visualization methods. A Wilcoxon signed rank test ($W = 190$, $p < .001$) revealed that the perceived accuracies were significantly higher with the bar chart ($M = 9.1$, $SD = 1.1$) than with the pie chart ($M = 5.3$, $SD = 1.3$).

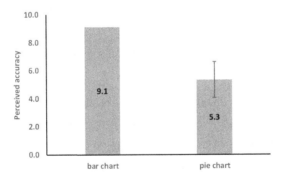

Fig. 6. The perceived accuracy of pie chart and bar charts. Error bars show standard deviation.

5   Discussion

The results support the hypothesis and the advice given in the visualization literature. It takes less time to locate the smallest item with the bar chart compared to the pie chart. Although not tested, one may expect that we would have gotten similar results if the task involved finding the largest number as well. Clearly, identifying the shortest bar is faster and easier than locating the pie slice with the smallest area and smallest angle. Bar chart comparisons are performed along one dimension, in this case the vertical dimension, while the pie chart comparisons need to be performed along two dimensions simultaneously.

The results show that the bar chart also resulted in nearly no errors, while errors are easily made with the pie chart suggesting that it is actually very hard to make accurate visual comparisons between pie chart items of similar magnitude.

The actual accuracy also matches the perceived accuracy as the participants subjective scoring of the two chart types as the bar chart obtained a nearly perfect score, while the pie chart was rated much lower in terms of accuracy.

The experiment was conducted under indirect time pressure. The participants were not instructed to conduct the task as quickly as possible but were informed that the task was timed. Consequently, most participants performed the task quickly. We argue that it is appropriate to test such visualization methods under time pressure to somewhat mimic real situations where decisions must be made quickly based on a rapid glance at a chart. It is therefore crucial that such the perceived impression is as correct as possible.

5.1 Limitations

The participants in this study represent a limited cohort in that all had completed secondary education. It would have been interesting to repeat the experiment also including a cohort of participants without secondary education and then assumedly less practice in interpreting charts.

The measurements were obtained manually, and small measurement inaccuracies may therefore have been introduced. More precise measurements would be possible if the experimental setup was implemented with automatic measurements, for instance based on registering when and if the participants pressed the right item on a touch display.

Usually pie charts make extensive use of colors, although effective use of colors becomes increasingly difficult with many items. The lack of color in the experiment may have made it less comparable to pie charts usually found in mainstream publications. Shades of grey was used to distinguish different pie chart items. These grayscales may have somehow affected the perception of the items for the pie chart. One alternative would be to use the same color for all the pie items, for example a white background, hence utilizing only the sector outline to indicate size.

Another potential shortcoming of the experiment was the inclusion of gridlines with the bar charts, while the pie charts did not have any support lines of any kind. However, it is uncertain if the gridlines are beneficial or not in identifying the smallest item. Moreover, it must be noted that only very weak gridlines were included, that is, the default gridlines included by Excel when making bar charts.

The participants were probed about how effective they found the two chart types after the experiments. In addition, it would also have been interesting to also probe the participants' preferences before the experimental task to test the assumption that many individuals believe pie to be better than bars. However, the actual presence of pie charts in various contexts is indeed evidence that pie charts are considered useful.

6 Conclusions

An experiment was conducted to assess how well bar and pie charts supports the search for extreme portions when these portions have similar size. The results quite clearly confirm the superiority of the bar chart in fast and correct identification of extreme portions compared to pie charts. The participants perceived accuracies are also consistent with the observed accuracies. Implications of these result is that bar charts should always be used if the task involves identifying extreme items and these items are of similar size. A generalization of this is that also any visualization with unknown data, i.e., automatically generated data should employ bar charts and not pie charts. However, it is important to select the visualization method according to purpose. For instance, if the goal is to illustrate imbalance or unequal quantities the pie chart may be used as well as a bar chart and if the goal is to determine parts of the whole a pie chart may be a more effective option.

References

1. Hollands, J.G., Spence, I.: Judging proportion with charts: the summation model. Appl. Cogn. Psychol. Official J. Soc. Appl. Res. Mem. Cogn. **12**(2), 173–190 (1998)
2. Few, S.: Our irresistible fascination with all things circular. Perceptual Edge Visual Business Intelligence Newsletter, pp. 1–9 (2010)
3. Skogstrøm, N.A.B., Igeltjørn, A., Knudsen, K.M., Diallo, A.D., Krivonos, D., Sandnes, F.E.: A comparison of two smartphone time-picking interfaces: convention versus efficiency. In: Proceedings of the 10th Nordic Conference on Human-Computer Interaction, pp. 874–879. ACM (2018)
4. Spence, I.: No humble pie: the origins and usage of a statistical chart. J. Educ. Behav. Stat. **30**(4), 353–368 (2005)
5. Xu, Z.X., Chen, Y., Kuai, S.G.: The human visual system estimates angle features in an internal reference frame: a computational and psychophysical study. J. Vision **18**(13), 10–10 (2018)
6. Bertini, E., Elmqvist, N., Wischgoll, T.: Judgment error in pie chart variations. In: Proceedings of the Eurographics/IEEE VGTC conference on visualization, pp. 91–95. IEEE (2016)
7. Skau, D., Kosara, R.: Arcs, angles, or areas: individual data encodings in pie and donut charts. Comput. Graph. Forum **35**(3), 121–130 (2016)
8. Hollands, J.G., Dyre, B.P.: Bias in proportion judgments: the cyclical power model. Psychol. Rev. **107**(3), 500–524 (2000)
9. van der Linden, S.L., Leiserowitz, A.A., Feinberg, G.D., Maibach, E.W.: How to communicate the scientific consensus on climate change: plain facts, pie charts or metaphors? Clim. Change **126**(1), 255–262 (2014). https://doi.org/10.1007/s10584-014-1190-4
10. Franklin, K.M., Roberts, J. C.: Pie chart sonification. In: Proceedings on Seventh International Conference on Information Visualization, pp. 4–9. IEEE (2003)
11. Macdonald-Ross, M.: How numbers are shown. AV Commun. Rev. **25**(4), 359–409 (1977)
12. Burch, M., Weiskopf, D.: On the benefits and drawbacks of radial diagrams. In: Huang, W. (ed.) Handbook of Human Centric Visualization, pp. 429–451. Springer, New York (2014). https://doi.org/10.1007/978-1-4614-7485-2_17

13. Sandnes, F.E.: On the truthfulness of petal graphs for visualisation of data. In: Proceedings of NIK 2012 The Norwegian Informatics Conference, Tapir Academic Publishers, pp. 225–235 (2012)
14. Redford, G.I., Clegg, R.M.: Polar plot representation for frequency-domain analysis of fluorescence lifetimes. J. Fluoresc. **15**, 805 (2005)
15. Hlawatsch, M., Sadlo, F., Burch, M., Weiskopf, D.: Scale-Stack bar charts. In: Computer Graphics Forum, Oxford, UK: Blackwell Publishing Ltd. **32**(3), 181–190 (2013)
16. Heiberger, R.M., Robbins, N.B.: Design of diverging stacked bar charts for Likert scales and other applications. J. Stat. Softw. **57**(5), 1–32 (2014)
17. Sandnes, F.E., Dyrgrav, K.: Effects of graph embellishments on the perception of system states in mobile monitoring tasks. In: Luo, Y. (ed.) CDVE 2014. LNCS, vol. 8683, pp. 9–18. Springer, Cham (2014). https://doi.org/10.1007/978-3-319-10831-5_2
18. Sandnes, F.E.: Universell Utforming av IKT-systemer, 2nd edn. Universitetsforlaget, Oslo (2018)
19. JASP Team: JASP (Version 0.9) [Computer software] (2018)

Visualizing Features on Classified Fauna Images Using Class Activation Maps

Yoanne Didry[✉], Xavier Mestdagh[✉], and Thomas Tamisier[✉]

Luxembourg Institute of Science and Technology (LIST),
41, rue du Brill, 4422 Belvaux, Luxembourg
{yoanne.didry,xavier.mestdagh,thomas.tamisier}@list.lu

Abstract. This article highlights first the power of deep learning in a collaborative context for the automatic extraction of information from images and complementarily the benefit of Class Activation Maps (CAM) for identifying in a visual way the features taken into account for extracting this information. Experimental results illustrate the approach as a whole on a significant challenge of classifying newt images.

Keywords: Amphibian · Underwater camera trap · Transfer learning · Class Activation Maps · Collaborative survey

1 Introduction

Amphibians, in particular newts, draw attention of researchers and regulatory bodies over the world as pertinent bio-indicators to assess wetland conservation status [1]. In order to improve on standard capturing methods we developed an apparatus, called Newtrap, especially designed for in-situ observation of newts. Newtrap is an innovative framework for amphibians survey made of an improved underwater camera trap and a visual interface for managing and processing captured images. The main advance of Newtrap is to combine on the one hand an original physical design of the trap to place the newt in a standardized position with the belly fully visible, and on the other hand a powerful hardware to automate the photography of the newt. A camera looks into the tunnel and is triggered by the motion of individuals. Newtrap is then able to automate the production of ventral images without any newt handling [2]. In this article, the main goal is to focus on the task of building a model to determine the sex of the adult great crested newt (one particular species of newt). For this, we will use transfer learning, a common technique to solve one classification problem by using the result of a different but related problem [3]. After building the model, we will then visualize the features used to build this model, using CAM.

2 Transfer Learning

As a first classification trial we focused on the identification of the sex, on a dataset consisting of 2449 images depicting males newt and 1241 images of

© Springer Nature Switzerland AG 2020
Y. Luo (Ed.): CDVE 2020, LNCS 12341, pp. 352–356, 2020.
https://doi.org/10.1007/978-3-030-60816-3_38

females, with resized resolution of 224 × 224. This dataset has been collected in the field, and annotated with a collaborative website called Newtrap Manager [2]. Compared with the last training set used in [2], which contains only cropped pictures of the body of 1162 males and 796 females, the dataset contains the full pictures from the trap. Also, we achieved a significantly higher classification accuracy of 99% vs 85%. Furthermore, we have use Class Activation Maps analysis [6] (CAM) analysis, which helps to explain the built model. The dataset is split into 80% training and 20% test sets. The main advantage of convolutional neural networks (CNN) is to rely on models pre-trained on large data sets, and use transfer learning to customize the models to the final goal. For this task we have used Inception V3 [5] pre-trained models deployed by Google with a huge dataset of 1000 classes of web images. We customized the pre-trained model using fine-tuning, that is unfreeze a few of the top layers of a frozen model base and jointly train both the newly-added classifier layers and the last layers of the base model. This allows us to fine-tune the higher-order feature representations in the base model in order to make them more relevant for the specific task[1]. Visually, we can observe the difference between a male and female great crested newt near the cloaca area (red circle), as we can see in Fig. 1. The male cloaca is swollen and dark while the female cloaca is reddish[2].

Fig. 1. Left: a female great crested newt, right: a male great crested newt (Color figure online)

We use Tensorflow for the implementation of CNN, a common choice for deep learning classification tasks [4]. First of all, we have used the data augmentation technique[3] to increase the size training dataset. The base model used is an InceptionV3 model. With the include_top = False argument, we load a network that doesn't include the classification layers at the top, which is ideal for feature extraction. Once the base model is created, our sequential model uses it, along with a GLobalAveragePooling2D layer, and a Dense layer, as output. The top 100 layers of the previously described model is trained with 50 epochs, with a train generator that flow images in batches of 32, is fine-tuned with 50 more epochs.

---

[1] https://www.tensorflow.org/tutorials/images/transfer_learning.
[2] https://amphibiaweb.org/species/4295.
[3] https://keras.io/api/preprocessing/image/.

Indeed we were only training a few layers on top of an Inception V3 base model. The weights of the pre-trained network were not updated during training. One way to increase performance even further is to fine-tune the weights of the top layers of the pre-trained model alongside the training of the classifier previously added. We can see in Fig. 2 the training and validation accuracy before and after fine tuning. As we can see the training accuracy reaches 99% after fine-tuning, and 92% in the validation set. The sample source code for the training part can be found on Github[4].

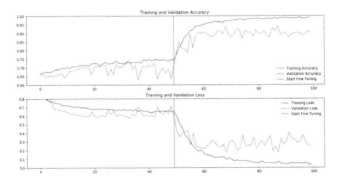

Fig. 2. Training and validation accuracy/loss, before and after fine-tuning

3   CAM: Class Activations Maps

In the computer vision community, it is often useful to verify that a model is working properly, indeed it is often said that a deep neural network is a black box, and it is very difficult to understand how the model makes predictions. Interpretability of models is very important to trusting them, and therefore we must be able to understand how the model predicts. CAM uses the class-specific gradient information flowing into the final convolutional layer of a CNN to produce a coarse localization map of the important regions in the image. We perform global average pooling on the convolutional feature maps and use those features within a fully-connected layer that produces the desired output. More specifically, we can identify the importance of the image regions by projecting back the weights of the output layer onto the convolutional feature maps. The CAM technique produces generic localizable deep features that can aid users understanding the mechanism of discrimination within the model. The sample source code for generating the CAM on newt pictures can be found on Github[5]. A sample output produced can be see in Fig. 3.

A significant result is that all the different CAM generated in the test set validates, after inspection by a domain expert, what we know about the cloaca

---

[4] https://github.com/dyoann/CDVE2020/blob/master/train.py.
[5] https://github.com/dyoann/CDVE2020/blob/master/cam.py.

color difference between male or female great crested newt. Indeed, this explains how the gender model with 92% validation accuracy makes sense as the discrimination is based mostly on the correct local area of the picture, around the cloaca, which is in red in the heatmap overlay in Fig. 3.

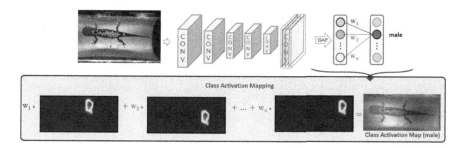

Fig. 3. Class activation mapping: the predicted class score is mapped back to the previous convolutional layer to generate the CAM [6] (Color figure online)

4   Conclusion

We described in this paper how data annotated in a collaborative visualisation tool, called Newtrap Manager, were used to build a gender model of adult great crested newt. Thanks to the use of CAM, we validate the rationale of the model. This enables users of Newtrap to visualise what features are important. In the future, we plan to integrate transfer learning and CAM features within Newtrap Manager, and also extend it to various animals. The prototype will also be made ready for industrial use.

Acknowledgements. Thanks to Remy Haas and Lionel L'Hoste for retrieving the pictures on the field and annotating them in Newtrap Manager. We would like to thank the NVIDIA AI Technology Center Luxembourg for the fruitful discussions and technical advice. This work has been financed by the Luxembourg FNR through the POC17 NEWTRAP.

References

1. Dornelas, M., et al.: Quantifying temporal change in biodiversity: challenges and opportunities. Proc. Roy. Soc. B Biol. Sci. **280**(1750) (2012)
2. Didry, Y., Mestdagh, X., Tamisier, T.: Newtrap: improving biodiversity surveys by enhanced handling of visual observations. In: Luo, Y. (ed.) CDVE 2019. LNCS, vol. 11792, pp. 277–281. Springer, Cham (2019). https://doi.org/10.1007/978-3-030-30949-7_32
3. Pan, S.J., Yang, Q.: A survey on transfer learning. IEEE Trans. Knowl. Data Eng. **22**(10), 1345–1359 (2009)

4. Ertam, F., Aydin, G.: Data classification with deep learning using TensorFlow. In: 2017 International Conference on Computer Science and Engineering (UBMK). IEEE (2017)
5. Tang: Intelligent Mobile Projects with TensorFlow. Packt Publishing, May 2018. Chapter 2. ISBN 9781788834544
6. Zhou, B., et al.: Learning deep features for discriminative localization. In: Proceedings of the IEEE Conference on Computer Vision and Pattern Recognition (2016)

Social Media Analytics in Comments of Multiple Vehicle Brands on Social Networking Sites in Thailand

Sanya Khruahong[(⊠)], Anirut Asawasakulson,
and Woradech Na Krom

Faculty of Business, Economics and Communications, Naresuan University,
Phitsanulok, Thailand
{sanyak61,aniruta,woradechn}@nu.ac.th

Abstract. This paper proposes data analytics in comments of multiple vehicle brands by using Social Media Analytics (SMA), which collects data from social networking sites. Generally, it can intensively evaluate the information to make business decisions and find trends or some significance. However, Google research has shown that vehicle companies should study consumer behaviors from the Internet when people decide to buy a new car. Therefore, SMA can lead to creating motivation or a strategy for the business model. This research investigates the use of comments on social networking sites to analyze the relationship model of car purchase decisions of consumers in Thailand that relate to public relations, marketing, awareness, and the company's brand value. We use the principles of the online social data analysis process, which are 1) Capture 2) Understanding 3) Presenting and is called the CUP framework, by collecting 76,331 comments on ten vehicle brands. Finally, the results show that the positive sentiment has a suitable average to be more than 69.85%, and the average negative sentiment should not exceed 30.15%. This result may help the automobile business entrepreneurs to determine the guidelines for marketing activities in the vehicle industry in Thailand.

Keywords: Social Media Analytics · Social networking · Data analytics · Sentiment analysis

1 Introduction

Nowadays, cars are high-priced products, so consumers need to study and consider various factors before purchasing a vehicle to ensure that purchasing their vehicle is worthwhile. Some factors may affect the consideration, such as the after-sales service, the company's reputation, and the discount price. While consumers want to buy a new car, they will always search for product information, whether from television, the Internet, public relations documents, experts, or people who know it. These include car design, engine type, and materials used in car assembly, or technology. In addition to asking the salesperson at the car service center, most consumers choose to search for information on the Internet. These can be either the website or social media, in which consumers tend to ask questions or maybe like, share, post on various social media; this

© Springer Nature Switzerland AG 2020
Y. Luo (Ed.): CDVE 2020, LNCS 12341, pp. 357–367, 2020.
https://doi.org/10.1007/978-3-030-60816-3_39

information expands endlessly. So, car companies need to apply this data to develop their companies.

Therefore, data analytics is a methodology for analysis with enormous amounts of information to find the facts and summarize the issues that are relevant in the data. Data is vast and complicated; no traditional data management tools can store it or process it efficiently [1, 2]. The effective Big Data research methodology improves some common planning objections for business, notably aligning investment advantages with strategy. It was applied to many kinds of research. Big Data was developed on repeatability and similarity of freeway traffic flow for long-term prediction [3]. This paper used real traffic flow big data from Shenzhen of China for a demonstration of prediction algorithms. However, data from city traffic networks should be used to cover the entire area to increase forecasting accuracy. Moreover, Big Data has developed applications in Smart Farming [4], and healthcare organizations [5] which use Big Data analytics may have differentiated follow-by-the-different situations so they may use Big Data technologies to differentiate.

Currently, Social media data becomes accessible communication on the Internet, in which media and text on social media are extensive. Analysis of social media data using advanced computational techniques has become a new research field. Social Media Analytics (SMA) [6, 7] is data collection and analysis from social networking sites such as Facebook, Instagram, LinkedIn, Twitter, and YouTube. SMA has contributed to natural disaster management [8], and SMA has been developed with Twitter messages for urban smart tourism ecosystems in San Francisco [9]. Both articles used text from social media by using the method of Social Media Analytics. Furthermore, *CUP framework* [10] is one of the excellent standards for Social Media Analytics include a three-stage process: capture, understanding, and presenting. This framework can also apply to study substantial factors of opinion on social networking sites that the product evaluation may examine from the result of the sentiment analysis.

In this paper, we use CUP framework for the analysis of multiple vehicle brands from comments on Social Media in Thailand. Moreover, sentiment analysis is applied to the analysis of online customer comments. We sincerely hope that the results of this research may be useful to the car-related entrepreneurs in setting guidelines for marketing activities or applying to other businesses for public relations.

In Sect. 2, we describe the purpose of this paper and reviews the works related to this research. Section 3 details the research methodology and investigates the analysis of vehicle data. Finally, we discuss the results, conclusions, show the most significant potential advantage to the company, and suggest future work.

2   Related Works

This research will focus on data analytics; therefore, Social media websites are text-based data; preparing and analyzing the data is the challenge to be met in this paper. Some unique situations occur when analyzing text data from social networking sites, which will be discussed in this paper. This section will review the related work of data analytics and social media analytics, including Social Media Analytics, Social Networking Site, Big Data Analytics, and AI for Thai.

2.1 Social Media Analytics

Social Media Analytics (SMA) is involved with producing and assessing informatics tools and frameworks to collect, monitor, analyze, summarize, and visualize social media data, a target application that would have specific requirements before beginning development [10, 11]. Social Media Analytics proffers great potential with crucial possible relevance as a vibrant, new area of inquiry, potentially drawing on methods. In particular, the primary interest of corporate social media activities is how to use them as an additional channel for marketing effectively. Organizations can use social media analytics to recognize new potential customers [12]. Moreover, SMA was applied to sets of dance styles on YouTube to show that it is possible to identify plausible patterns of subtopic difference, gender, and sentiment [13]. Furthermore, the warning system framework was deployed for detecting people and vehicles in danger both in flood and fire images [14], from which this paper used the image from social media for analysis. However, these techniques need to obtain more pictures to develop for improving accuracy.

Social media analytics encompasses a variety of modeling and analytical techniques from different fields [10]. Social Media Analytics involves a three-stage process: capture, understanding, and presenting, is called the *CUP framework*.

Firstly, the 'Capture' stage helps identify conversations on social media platforms related to its activities and interests. Vast numbers of relevant data across hundreds or thousands of social networking sites using data feeds and APIs for managing. The capture uses online platforms of social networking sites such as Facebook, Twitter, and YouTube. This stage is a preparation of a dataset for the 'Understanding stage'. Several preprocessing steps may be operated, including data modeling, data, and record linking from different sources, stemming, part-of-speech tagging, feature extraction, and other syntactic and semantic operations that can assist analysis. Therefore, the balance of the necessity must get information to assist in a more refined understanding of the capture stage.

Secondly, the 'Understanding stage' is the heart of the social media analytics process. It assesses meaning from the cleaned data, which can involve methods of statistics and other techniques received from text and data mining, natural language processing, machine translation, and network analysis. The understanding stage contributes information about user sentiment, how customers feel about a business and its products, and their behavior, including the likelihood of, say, purchasing in response to an ad campaign. This stage gets many useful metrics, and trends about users which can be produced, covering their backgrounds, interests, concerns, and networks of relationships. Sentiment analysis [15] is used to interpret and classify emotions (positive and negative) in text data using text analysis techniques.

Lastly, in the 'Presenting stage', the aim is to design the results from different analytics, including summarizing, evaluation, for presentation to users in an easy-to-understand format. Visualization techniques are useful for performance, such as the visual dashboard, representing information from multiple sources. Furthermore, modern visual analytics are used for the simple display of information. Each presentation may support customized views for different users and make sense of vast numbers of data.

To sum up, the research methodology in this paper follows this Social Media Analytics process with *CUP framework*. Topic modeling has primary application in all stages. Then, sentiment analysis is the core approach behind many social media monitoring systems, primarily supporting the 'Understanding stage'. For the visual analytics is primary in the 'Understanding' and the 'Presenting stage'.

2.2 Sentiment Analysis

Sentiment analysis [16, 17] is text analysis techniques for the interpretation and analysis of emotions (positive, negative) within text data, which can help businesses process vast amounts of data in an efficient. Sentiment analysis uses various Natural Language Processing (NLP) [18] algorithm that is useful in social media monitoring, which approaches to extract sentiments associated with polarities of positive or negative for particular points from a text. The field of sentiment analysis is well-suited to many types of intelligence applications. Indeed, business intelligence appears to be one of the main factors behind the corporate interest in the area. In this paper, Using *S-Sense* [19] is the Sentiment Analysis for the Thai language, which is applied to the analysis process. *S-Sense* classifies each text into four classes: announcement, request, question, and sentiment. It is well applied to this research.

2.3 Social Networking Site

Social networking site is the online platform to connect to friends, often through social networking sites such as Facebook, Twitter, and YouTube [20, 21]. It has grown extremely fast in the past decade. Almost all users use social networking for clicking likes, commenting, and sharing, which lets people share some interesting and informative content. These behaviors can be very influential on society in both positive and negative ways. Moreover, social networking sites were applied to knowledge sharing and learning among tertiary students [22]. This study aimed to investigate the impact of social networking site use, based on the findings of the literature review and the involved cognitive theory. In summary, data on social networking sites should be used for analyzing to find something, and it would provide some insight into those things, which the *CUP framework* can apply to these data.

2.4 Big Data Analytics

Big Data Analytics (BDA) is an advanced analytic method performed on big data sets [23, 24]. Big data and analytics have collaborated to create one of the most profound trends in the analysis. Accordingly, Big Data Analytics is applied to many concepts for solving a problem. For example, it was deployed in supply chain management between 2010 and 2016 and provided insights into industries [25, 26]. This paper used survey methods for getting data, which may not be enough for analysis. Furthermore, Big data was developed for intelligent transportation systems (ITS) [27], which had several applications. It has consisted of asset maintenance, prediction of traffic flow on the road, analysis of traffic accidents on the road, planning for using the public transportation service, planning of a personal travel route, and rail transportation management. The approach points out that BDA can apply to everything if it has enough data for analysis. However, the *CUP framework* is one of the data analytics, which can analyze data on a set of car information.

2.5   AI for Thai

Thai AI Service Platform is called *AI for Thai* (www.aiforthai.in.th); it developed by the National Electronics and Computer Technology Center (NECTEC) Thailand, which provides a service for the software developer in the Thai language. It is an essential technological foundation for businesses, developers, and researchers in modern information technology. It can be extended to benefit Thailand in every field. There are many APIs services to implement: Word segmentation, Text cleansing, Sentiment analysis is called "S-Sense" [19] and Machine translation, which they support in Python coding.

After the literature review, we found that Big data on a social networking site can contribute to obtaining some opinions on business analysis. We will follow the research methodology of the Social Media Analytics process [10]. The *CUP framework* is followed as the SMA process; uses the *S-Sense* algorithm in *AI for Thai service* for the sentiment analysis.

3   Research Methodology

This section describes how to implement for analyzing by using Social Media Analytics algorithm followed by capture, understanding, presenting for analyzing.

3.1   Capture Stage

This paper collected real Thai user's comments on Facebook and YouTube, which were related to cars made by the ten famous brands in the market. All the data are in the form of text sets only. The information collection has focused on posts that recommendations for the car or review of a new car model and are elated to public relations, marketing, informational awareness, and the brand value of the company. Then we choose only those posts with a high number of views and which were posted in the period from July 1st, 2019 to March 30th, 2020. We used the *ExportComments.com* web service to Microsoft Excel files, which get comments from the link that we specified to them, as shown in Fig. 1.

	Name (click to view profile)	Profile ID	Date	Likes	Comment		(view source)
1	Korawit Matc	ID: 1000023 #############		0	สามารถติดกับ	ได้ไหมครับ	view comment
1-1	Mercedes-Be	ID: 1340078 #############		0	สวัสดีครับ คุณ Ko	ในส่วนนี้ทางเราขออนุญาตส่งข้อความส่วนตัวครับ เพื่อให้ทา	view comment
2	Pako Kaewth	ID: 1457422 #############		2	ราคา ☺		view comment
2-1	Mercedes-Be	ID: 1340078 #############		1	สวัสดีครับ คุณ Pa	สำหรับ DashCam รองรับทั้งระบบ iOs และ An	view comment
3	Praewploy N	ID: 7593345 #############		0	Petch Nu		view comment
4	Thanapat Cha	ID: 1768014 #############		0	อยากดูรีวิวการใช้งานครับ		view comment
5	Mercedes-Be	ID: 1340078 #############		6	รุ่นรถยนต์ที่รองรับ (เป็นเพียงข้อมูลเบื้องต้นเท่านั้น กรุณาตรวจสอบฟังก์ชันรถยนต์	view comment
6	Kanlaya Tanti	ID: 1000008 #############		1	dynamic ติดได้ไหมคะ		view comment
6-1	Bee Zheng	ID: 6832036 #############		1	Kanlaya Tanti		view comment

Fig. 1. Raw data of the comments from Social Networking Sites

The number of all comments in this paper is 76,331 comments of ten car brands, consisting of six Asian brands (A) and four Western brands (W), as shown in Table 1. Data analytics needs to understand the meaning of the text; therefore, Thai word segmentation is an essential issue for processing the Thai language because the language structure is complicated. We developed on JupyterLab with Python to segment all sentences of comments set to being Thai words. We created two-word segmentation techniques, which include, firstly, segmentation by LextoPlus approach with Thai words in the Thai dictionary and secondly, segmentation by using the keywords in which the word meaning can describe something which would be useful to analyze, as shown in Table 2.

Table 1. Number of comments from the collection

Car	Number of Comments
A1	19,609
A2	11,354
A3	4,262
A4	8,229
A5	2,392
A6	10,480
W1	2,870
W2	6,121
W3	8,950
W4	2,064

Table 2 presents the number of words after a word segmentation. It shows the most frequent word that is found in each brand by LextoPlus is "ครับ" (Khrab). This word shows that Thai men had a higher interest interested in cars than women because *Khrab* is the ending word of sentence for men. Moreover, the maximum frequency of words that are word segmentation with the keyword segmentation is "รถ" (Car). Therefore, almost all users comment and reply to the posts on Facebook and YouTube; they gave opinions about the car mainly. When this process was finished, then our focus was directed to sentiment analysis on the 'Understanding stage'.

Table 2. The result of Thai word segmentation by LextoPlus and Keywords

Brands	Thai word segmentation by LextoPlus			Thai word segmentation by Keywords		
	Words	Max freq.	Min freq.	Words	Max freq.	Min freq.
A1	13,881	11,328	1	10,920	3,719	1
A2	10,494	6,614	1	7,964	2,756	1
A3	8,648	4,308	1	6,576	1,003	1
A4	10,053	3,863	1	7,619	1,400	1
A5	5,649	1,538	1	4,123	495	1
A6	10,040	5,781	1	7,627	2,335	1
W1	5,943	1,467	1	4,515	556	1
W2	10,064	1,750	1	8,648	633	1
W3	12,230	5,029	1	9,343	2,548	1
W4	5,273	1,432	1	3,956	483	1

3.2 Understanding Stage

This section presents a significant effect on the information of sentiment analysis involving statistical methods on the AI for Thai. In Fig. 2 detail, the example of the result of sentiment analysis, include a comment, core, intent 1-4, positive word, negative word, and keyword.

Fig. 2. Example of the result of sentiment analysis

From that process, scores from 1 to 100 will set the Positive sentiment, but if the status is in the minus range, the state will be set to Negative sentiment. Both use positive and negative words as consideration. The results are shown in Table 3.

Table 3. Shows the result of sentiment analysis of all vehicle brands

Brands	Sentiment		Total
	Positive	Negative	
A1	10,201 (75.18%)	3,367 (24.82%)	13,568
A2	4,970 (65.34%)	2,636 (34.66%)	7,606
A3	1,560 (69.55%)	683 (30.45%)	2,243
A4	3,581 (70.40%)	1,506 (29.60%)	5,087
A5	1,127 (72.43%)	429 (27.57%)	1,556
A6	4,024 (64.43%)	2,222 (35.57%)	6,246
W1	1,068 (69.67%)	465 (30.33%)	1,533
W2	829 (73.43%)	300 (26.57%)	1,129
W3	3,731 (66.92%)	1,844 (33.08%)	5,575
W4	937 (71.20%)	379 (28.80%)	1,316

The analysis finds some words on the rule for measurement of the score and evaluates the comments. The bar charts illustrate the type of comments, as shown in Fig. 3 (a–d), including Question, Sentiment (Positive and Negative), Announcement, and Request. Brand A1 had posted to announce their car, or Brand A1, A2, A6, and W3, had many questions (a) on comments that meant the customer was interacting with these car products. The brand A1 has high sentiment (b) because there was a grand opening of the new model in this period of our data collection, which has been widely discussed with interest in design, model, and price. Brand W1 scores 6 in the announcement chart (c) because this brand is a high-end brand, so it may not be possible to promote the car often. The request (d) is a comment in general topics in which brand A1 and A4 are high, 1,057, and 1,073, respectively.

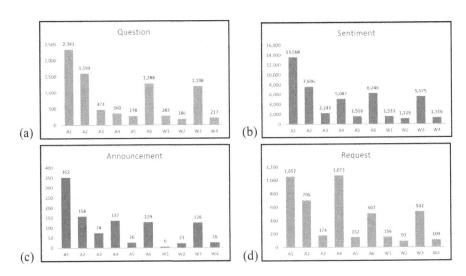

Fig. 3. Classification of the comments according to their types

3.3   Presenting Stage

However, these results need to be compared with real sales in the same period for monitoring and the direction of public relations, marketing activities, and car design.

In Fig. 4, the line chart illustrates the percentages of sentiment analysis, which has used data from ten brands; the positive linear is 69.85%; interestingly, though, if the positive sentiment is more than 69.85%, it is good. Furthermore, the negative linear is 30.15%, which means that negative sentiment should be less than 30.15%. The high positive sentiment of the brand is more than 69.85% including A1 (75.18%), A4 (70.40%), A5 (72.43%), W2 (73.43%), and W4 (71.20%). We believe that these brands would gain significant benefit by presenting their information on social networking sites. It leads to a reply by the user's positive opinion on various posts and may create a good image and efficiently promote sales. However, we found that five brands have a high negative sentiment, which is higher than 30.15%, including A2 (34.66%), A3 (30.45%), A6 (35.57%), W1 (30.33%), and W3 (33.08%). These brands may lack efficiency in presenting effective car information.

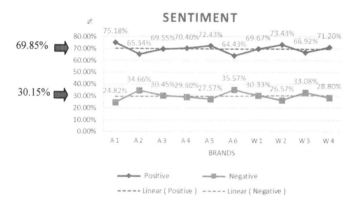

Fig. 4.   Sentiment analysis of all vehicle brands

4   Conclusion and Future Work

This paper investigates the analysis of comments on social networking sites. In this paper, we apply the principles of the Social Media Analytics for sentiment analysis, including 1) Capture 2) Understanding 3) Presenting, which is called the *CUP framework*. Facebook and YouTube data were collected the 76,331 comments of selected posts about ten vehicle brands in Thailand between July 1st, 2019, to March 30th, 2020. The results of this research show that men are more interested in researching cars on social networks than women. Therefore, public relations or a presentation style of ten brands should focus on male customers. Furthermore, sentiment analysis results show that the positive sentiment has a suitable average to be more than 69.85%, and the average negative sentiment should not exceed 30.15%. As can be seen, brand A1, A4, A5, W2, and W4 are car companies that can make functional market activities and achieve a positive attitude from the customer. Finally, these results may support the automobile business entrepreneurs applying to determine the guidelines for marketing activities of the Thailand vehicle industry.

Nevertheless, the results may not guarantee accuracy because we have some constraint information. In the future, we should collect much data to improved precision in the analytics. Furthermore, both interior and exterior car functions should be analyzed because they may be factors for a customer determining to buy the car.

References

1. Jain, P., Gyanchandani, M., Khare, N.: Big data privacy: a technological perspective and review. J. Big Data **3**(1), 1–25 (2016). https://doi.org/10.1186/s40537-016-0059-y
2. Oussous, A., et al.: Big data technologies: a survey. J. King Saud Univ. Comput. Inf. Sci. **30**(4), 431–448 (2018)
3. Hou, Z., Li, X.: Repeatability and similarity of freeway traffic flow and long-term prediction under big data. IEEE Trans. Intell. Transp. Syst. **17**(6), 1786–1796 (2016)
4. Wolfert, S., et al., Big data in smart farming–a review. Agric. Syst. 153, 69–80 (2017)
5. Wang, Y., et al.: Big data analytics: understanding its capabilities and potential benefits for healthcare organizations. Technol. Forecast Soc. Change **126**, 3–13 (2018)
6. Lee, I.: Social media analytics for enterprises: typology, methods, and processes. Bus. Horiz. **61**(2), 199–210 (2018)
7. Brooker, P., et al.: Doing social media analytics. Big Data Soc. **3**(2), 2053951716658060 (2016)
8. Wang, Z., Ye, X.: Social media analytics for natural disaster management. Int. J. Geogr. Inf. Sci. **32**(1), 49–72 (2018)
9. Brandt, T., et al.: Social media analytics and value creation in urban smart tourism ecosystems. Inf. Manage. **54**(6), 703–713 (2017)
10. Fan, W., Gordon, M.D.: The power of social media analytics. Commun. ACM. **57**(6), 74–81 (2014)
11. Zeng, D., et al.: Social media analytics and intelligence. IEEE Intell. Syst. **25**(6), 13–16 (2010)
12. Stieglitz, S., et al.: Social media analytics. **6**(2), 89–96 (2014)
13. Thelwall, M.: Social media analytics for YouTube comments: potential and limitations. Int. J. Soc. Res. Methodol. **21**(3), 303–316 (2018)
14. Giannakeris, P., et al.: People and vehicles in danger-A fire and flood detection system in social media. In: 2018 IEEE 13th Image, Video, and Multidimensional Signal Processing Workshop (IVMSP), IEEE (2018)
15. Cambria, E.: Affective computing and sentiment analysis. IEEE Intell. Syst. **31**(2), 102–107 (2016)
16. Bakshi, R.K., et al.: Opinion mining and sentiment analysis. In: 2016 3rd International Conference on Computing for Sustainable Global Development (INDIACom). IEEE (2016)
17. Liu, B.: Sentiment analysis and opinion mining. Synth. Lect. Hum. Lang. Technol. **5**(1), 1–167 (2012)
18. Medhat, W., Hassan, A., Korashy, H.: Sentiment analysis algorithms and applications: a survey. Ain Shams Eng. J. **5**(4), 1093–1113 (2014)
19. Haruechaiyasak, C., et al.: S-sense: a sentiment analysis framework for social media sensing. In: Proceedings of the IJCNLP 2013 Workshop on Natural Language Processing for Social Media (SocialNLP) (2013)

20. Hampton, K.N., et al.: Social Networking Sites and our Lives, vol. 1. Pew Internet & American Life Project Washington, DC (2011)
21. Phua, J., Jin, S.V., Kim, J.J.: Uses and gratifications of social networking sites for bridging and bonding social capital: a comparison of Facebook, Twitter, Instagram, and Snapchat. Comput. Hum. Behav. **72**, 115–122 (2017)
22. Eid, M.I., Al-Jabri, I.M.: Social networking, knowledge sharing, and student learning: The case of university students. Comput. Educ. **99**, 14–27 (2016)
23. Russom, P.: Big data analytics. Fourth Quarter. 19(4), 1–34 (2011)
24. Kambatla, K., et al.: Trends in big data analytics. J. Parallel Distrib. Comput. **74**(7), 2561–2573 (2014)
25. Tiwari, S., et al.: Big data analytics in supply chain management between 2010 and 2016: insights to industries. Comput. Ind. Eng. **115**, 319–330 (2018)
26. Kache, F., Seuring, S.: Challenges and opportunities of digital information at the intersection of Big Data Analytics and supply chain management. International Journal of Operations & Production Management (2017)
27. Zhu, L., et al.: Big data analytics in intelligent transportation systems: a survey. IEEE Trans. Intell. Transp. Syst. **20**(1), 383–398 (2018)

Static and Dynamic Parameter Settings of Accelerated Particle Swarm Optimisation for Solving Course Scheduling Problem

Thatchai Thepphakorn[1], Saisumpan Sooncharoen[2],
and Pupong Pongcharoen[2(✉)]

[1] Faculty of Industrial Technology, Pibulsongkram Rajabhat University,
Phitsanulok, Thailand
[2] Centre of Operations Research and Industrial Applications (CORIA),
Department of Industrial Engineering, Faculty of Engineering, Naresuan
University, Phitsanulok 65000, Thailand
pupongp@nu.ac.th

Abstract. The university course timetabling problem (UCTP) is one of the most challenging scheduling problems and also classified to be a Non-deterministic Polynomial (NP)-hard problem. An Accelerated Particle Swarm Optimisation based Timetabling (APSOT) program was developed to generate the best-so-far timetables with the minimal total operating costs. Two new variants of Accelerated Particle Swarm Optimisation (APSO) including Static and Dynamic (S-APSO and D-APSO) were proposed and embedded into the APSOT tool. The analysis of variance on the experimental results indicated that the main effects and interactions of D-APSO were statistically significant with a 95% confidence interval. The S-APSO and Maurice Clerc PSO (MCPSO) outperformed the other variants of PSO for most datasets whereas the execute times required by all variants of PSO were slightly different.

Keywords: Cooperative applications · Timetabling · Metaheuristics · Particle swarm · Parameter setting · Experimental design

1 Introduction

Course timetabling operations face by academic institutions must be periodically accomplished before the beginning of a semester [1]. For some universities, a lot of introductory courses providing for all degree programs students may be initially scheduled by responsible central officers [2]. The initial timetables are then sent to departmental officers to fill in the remaining courses offered by departments/colleges [2]. This sequential scheduling process is not only time consuming task, but also requires significant work from skilled staffs. Moreover, all users' preferences and educational resources' utilisation (e.g., laboratory, auditorium, lecture hall) sharing across departments may not be optimised. Therefore, the development of an automated timetabling program that embedded swarm intelligence (SI) can be an efficient alternative. In addition, collaboration of technologies and intelligence methods for a large education entity can be classified as a one of cooperative applications.

© Springer Nature Switzerland AG 2020
Y. Luo (Ed.): CDVE 2020, LNCS 12341, pp. 368–380, 2020.
https://doi.org/10.1007/978-3-030-60816-3_40

SI has received great attention in the communities of optimisation, computer science, computational intelligence, bio-inspired algorithms, and SI-based algorithms [3]. Bio-inspired algorithms, e.g., Ant Colony Optimisation [4], Firefly Algorithms [5], Shuffled Frog Leaping [6], Artificial Immune System [7], have become very popular to solve the NP-hard problems within a reasonably practical time. However, they do not guarantee to get optimum solutions [8]. Particle Swarm Optimisation (PSO) has been applied to almost all areas of optimisation problems [3] due to very few parameters to adjust, little memory requirement to compute, and easy to understand and implement [9].

According to a comprehensive literature survey on Scopus database covering the period from the past to the present, several variants of PSO have been applied to solve the university course timetabling problem (UCTP) including: (i) conventional PSO (called PSO) [10, 11]; (ii) standard PSO (called SPSO) [11–13]; and (iii) Maurice Clerc PSO (called MCPSO) [11, 14–16]. However, the application of Accelerated PSO or APSO (both S-APSO and D-APSO) to deal with the UCTP has not been found. In term of comparative study, there is no report related with the performance comparison among those variants of PSO to solve this problem. Moreover, the best parameter settings of both S-APSO and D-APSO to solve the UCTP have not been investigated.

The aims of this paper were to: (i) develop an Accelerated Particle Swarm Optimisation based Timetabling (APSOT) program to solve the real-world UCTP; (ii) investigate the appropriate parameter settings for static and dynamic APSO (S-APSO and D-APSO) via statistical experimental design and analysis; and (iii) explore the performances of APSO in terms of the quality of solution and execution time before comparing with PSO, SPSO, and MCPSO. The next section briefly describes the basic concepts of APSO and conducts the literature surveys. Section 3 explains the UCTP and its constraints followed by the steps of the proposed APSOT program in Sect. 4. Section 5 presents the experimental results and analysis followed by conclusions.

2 Accelerated Particle Swarm Optimisation

Conventional Particle Swarm Optimisation (PSO) was developed by Kennedy and Eberhart in 1995 [17]. It was inspired by swarm behaviour in nature, e.g., fish and bird schooling [18]. PSO has become one of the most popular methods based on swarm intelligent because of its flexibility and simplicity [18]. It has also been applied to solve almost every area in optimisation, computational intelligence, and design applications [18]. New variants of PSO have been therefore introduced by modifying or adapting a conventional PSO, e.g., standard PSO (SPSO) [13], Maurice Clerc PSO (MCPSO) [15], Accelerated PSO (APSO) [18].

The basic processes of conventional PSO and APSO can be described as follows. For initialisation process, the essential parameters of both methods must be specified. Particle or solution x_i is randomly created before determining its fitness value (solution quality) using the objective function $f(x_i)$. Where, i is the index of particles ($i = 1, 2, 3, ..., P$) whilst P is population size. Then, the iteration best particle (x_{best}^t) and the global best particle (g_{best}^*) are identified by the following Eq. (1) [19]. Where, t is the index of iterations (or generation) whilst I_{now} is the current iteration.

$$x_{best}^t = \min\{f(x_i^t)\}, \quad i \in (1, 2, 3, \ldots, P),$$

$$g_{best}^* = \min\{f(x_i^t)\}, \quad i \in (1, 2, 3, \ldots, P), \quad t \in (1, 2, 3, \ldots, I_{now}) \tag{1}$$

For conventional PSO, a new particle i or solution (x_i^{t+1}) is produced by using velocity and position vectors according to Eq. (2) and Eq. (6) [18], respectively. Where v_i is the velocity for a particle i; α and β denote the acceleration constants; ε_1 and ε_2 are two random vectors distributed within a range from 0 to 1 [18].

$$v_i^{t+1} = v_i^t + \alpha \varepsilon_1 \left(g_{best}^* - x_i^t\right) + \beta \varepsilon_2 \left(x_{best}^t - x_i^t\right) \tag{2}$$

$$v_i^{t+1} = v_i^t + \beta \left(g_{best}^* - x_i^t\right) + \alpha \varepsilon_t \tag{3}$$

$$\alpha = \alpha_0 \gamma^t, \quad (0 < \gamma < 1) \tag{4}$$

$$x_i^{t+1} = (1 - \beta)x_i^t + \beta \left(g_{best}^*\right) + \alpha \varepsilon_t \tag{5}$$

$$x_i^{t+1} = x_i^t + v_i^{t+1} \tag{6}$$

In case of static APSO (S-APSO), generating a new solution x_i^{t+1} can be achieved by using velocity and position vectors according to Eq. (3) and Eq. (6). Where ε_t is drawn from $N(0, 1)$ [18]. For dynamic APSO (D-APSO), new velocity and position for a solution x_i^{t+1} can be updated by using Eq. (3)–(4), and Eq. (6) [18]. Where, α_0 is the initial value of the randomness parameter, a range from 0.5 to 1 was suggested by Yang [18]. Where, γ is a control parameter which Yang [18] recommended that should be set $\gamma = 0.9$–0.97. However, updating velocity and position vectors for both two variants of APSO can be replaced by using only Eq. (5) [18].

After movement process of APSO variants, the fitness value for a new solution x_i^{t+1} is evaluated by using the objective function. The x_{best}^t will be replaced by a new solution x_i^{t+1} if its fitness value is better than that obtained from the x_{best}^t. Moreover, if the fitness value obtained from the x_i^{t+1} is better than that obtained from the g_{best}^* solution, the g_{best}^* will be also replaced by a new solution x_i^{t+1}. These processes are repeated until getting to the maximum iteration (I) or the given stop criterion.

The performance of metaheuristics usually bases on the parameters used [20]. The best values for the parameters also depend on the problem domain and the instance. Identifying appropriate values for the parameters is very important to obtain the best solutions [20]. There are many parameters to be assigned for both S-APSO and D-APSO before solving any problem including: (i) number of population (or particle) sizes (P); (ii) acceleration constants (α and β); and (iii) control parameter (γ). A literature survey on Scopus database covering the period from the past to April 2020 using "accelerated particle swarm*" OR "accelerated PSO" AND "course timetabl*" as keywords, there are no any research work to apply both S-APSO and D-APSO to solve course timetabling problems. Moreover, the appropriate parameter settings of both S-APSO and D-APSO for course timetabling have not been investigated and reported. In order to fulfil this research gaps, the range of APSO parameters used in scheduling problems have been surveyed again by using "accelerated particle swarm*" OR "accelerated PSO" AND "schedul*" as keywords as shown in Table 1.

Table 1. Literature review of APSO parameter settings to solve scheduling problems

Authors	Applications	Parameter investigation	APSO's parameter settings					
			Static	Dynamic	P	α	β	γ
Fakhar et al. [21]	Hydro-thermal scheduling		✓		200	0.2	0.5	
Adhikari and Srirama [22]	Container-based scheduling	✓	✓		60	1.0	0.55	
Hussain et al. [23]	Hydro-thermal scheduling	✓	✓		200	0.2	0.5	
Fakhar et al. [24]	Hydro-thermal scheduling	✓	✓		100–200	0.2	0.5	
Adhikari and Amgoth [25]	Workflow scheduling	✓	✓		20	1.0	0.55	
Hropko et al. [26]	Optimal dispatch scheduling	✓	✓		100	0.7	1.0	
Yang et al. [27]	Project scheduling			✓	10–50	0.1-0.5	0.1-0.7	0.7
Range					10–200	0.1–1.0	0.1–1.0	0.7

3 University Course Timetabling Problem (UCTP)

Timetabling is an important and active area of research with applications in several fields, e.g., transportation, sport, hospital, employees, high school, university [28]. The aim of the UCTP is to find a method to allocate all course or events into the given timeslots and classrooms whilst all constraints required by the problem must be satisfied [1]. Generally, constraints found in the UCTP can be divided into two categories including hard constraints (HC) and soft constraints (SC) [8]. HCs are the most important constraints, in which all candidate timetables must be satisfied to be the feasible timetables [20]. SCs are more relaxed, in which the total number of SC violations are acceptable but it should be minimised [4]. The details of HCs and SCs considering for this research can be described as follows.

HCs considered were [11]: (i) all lectures/laboratories required for each course must be scheduled and assigned to distinct periods (HC_1); (ii) students and lecturers can only attend one lecture at a time (HC_2); (iii) only one lecture can take place in a room at a given time (HC_3); (iv) lecturers and students must be available for a lecture to be scheduled (HC_4); (v) all courses must be assigned into proper rooms according to their given requirements, including building location, room facilities, and room types (HC_5); and (vi) all lectures within a course requiring consecutive periods must be obeyed (HC_6).

In term of SCs considered were [11]: (i) all courses should be scheduled in the appropriate types of room in order to avoid unnecessary operating or renting costs (currency unit per period) (SC$_1$); (ii) the courses taught by the given lecturer(s) should be assigned on their available or preferred day and periods in order to save the lecturing or hiring costs (currency unit per period) (SC$_2$), and (iii) the classrooms should be scheduled in consecutive working periods of a day in order to reduce the number of times to clean or setup after using the rooms (per time) (SC$_3$).

For this research, the quality of the feasible candidate timetables can be evaluated by using the objective function or $f(x_i)$, in which it was represented by considering SC$_1$–SC$_3$. The aim of the $f(x_i)$ is to minimise the total operating costs considered from the candidate timetables as shown in Eq. (7) [11];

$$\text{Minimise } f(x_i) = W_1 SC_1 + W_2 SC_2 + W_3 SC_3 \qquad (7)$$

Where, W_1–W_3 are weightings for SCs, each of which are not restricted and depend upon the user preferences for each institution. For this work, W_1–W_3 were set to be 50 (currency units per hour), 300 (currency units per hour), and 2.5 (currency units per times), respectively.

4   Accelerated PSO Based Timetabling (APSOT) Program

The proposed APSOT tool for solving the real world UCTP has been developed by using a general programming language called TCL/TK with C extension. Two variants of an accelerated Particle Swarm Optimisation (APSO) were embedded in the APSOT tool including static APSO (S-APSO) and dynamic APSO (D-APSO). All procedures for the APSOT tool can be described to five steps and shown in Fig. 1.

```
Begin
   Input data and set initial parameters for S-APSO and D-APSO
   Sort a list of courses using constructive heuristics          Step 1
   Create initial population, xi (i = 1,2,3,…,P)
   Set random keys for each xi
While t < Max_Generation(G) do
   For (i=1, i<= Max_Pop(P), i++) do
      If S-APSO do Update velocity xi using Eq.(3)              Step 2
      If D-APSO do Update velocity xi using Eq.(3)and(4)
      Update particle's position xi using Eq.(6)
      If xi = an infeasible timetable do                        Step 3
         Repair xi to be a feasible timetable
      Evaluate objective functions f(xi) using Eq. (7)
      If f(xi) < f(x'best) do Replace x'best by new solution xi  Step 4
      If f(xi) < f(g'best) do Replace g'best by new solution xi
Output results and visualisation of g'best                      Step 5
End
```

Fig. 1. Pseudo code of the APSOT program

Step 1: this is an initialisation process of APSO. The first procedure is to upload all course timetable data and assign essential parameters for both S-APSO and D-APSO. After determining the total number of events (n) from total teaching periods required for all courses, an event list containing a set of n events is created. In order to increase the probability of getting feasible timetables in an initialisation process, the sequence of all events in the list is sorted by using a constructive heuristic, called the largest unpermitted period degree [29].

Next procedure is to generate an empty timetable (or solution). The length of an empty solution/timetable (or dimensions) is considered from the numbers of timeslots/day, working day/week, and available rooms. After that, all events from a sorted event list are sequentially assigned into the empty timetable for producing an initial population x_i. Then, a random key technique [5] is conducted for movement updating. A new list having the same dimension size with the timetable is generated, in which each dimension keeps a uniformly distributed random numbers $r \in (0, 1)$. Processes of solution initialisation x_i ($i = 1, 2, 3,..., P$) will be repeated until reach the maximum population (P).

Step 2: the movement process of S-APSO and D-APSO is performed. Each particle x_i is chosen for velocity updating according to their variants. The velocity of particle x_i for S-APSO is updated by using Eq. (3) whilst the x_i velocity for D-APSO is produced by using Eq. (3) and Eq. (4). Then, the position of particle x_i is updated by using Eq. (6) for both APSO variants. Step 3: a new solution x_i may be either feasible or infeasible timetable after velocity and position updating. Consequently, the repair process was design and integrated in the proposed APSOT tool for rectifying infeasible timetables to be feasible timetables. Step 4: fitness function for each timetable x_i will be determined by using Eq. (7). A solution x_{best}^t can be replaced by a new solution x_i, if the fitness value of x_i is better than that obtained from x_{best}^t. Moreover, a solution g_{best}^* will be replaced by the x_i, if the fitness value of x_i is better. Step 5: The procedures from step 2 to step 4 will be repeated until reach the maximum generations (G) before decoding the best timetables for all lecturers, students, and rooms.

5 Experimental Results and Analysis

The objective of the APSOT program is to construct course timetables with the lowest total operating costs. The aims of the computational experiments were to: (i) investigate which main factors and their interactions were statistically significant for S-APSO and D-APSO before summary their appropriated parameter settings; and (ii) explore the performances of both proposed methods and compare their performances with the other PSO variants obtained from the previous research [11] including conventional PSO, standard PSO (called SPSO), and Maurice Clerc PSO (called MCPSO). Personal computer with Core i7 3.20 GHz CPU and 8 GB RAM was used to determine the computational time required to execute experimental runs. Eleven real-world university course timetabling datasets for this computational experiments were adopted from the previous research [30].

5.1   Parameter Investigation for S-APSO and D-APSO

The experiment was aimed to investigate which factors and their interactions for S-APSO and D-APSO are statistically significant before identifying the best parameter settings for both methods. The main factors for S-APSO and D-APSO included (i) the combination of population (particle) sizes and the number of generation (PG), which determines the total number of solutions generated (or amount of search) and the execution time, the value was fixed at 24,000 for this experiments; (ii) the acceleration coefficients (α and β); and (iii) the control parameter (γ) for D-APSO only. The range of possible factor values for both proposed methods were considered from comprehensive literature reviews according to Table 1. Full factorial experimental designs for S-APSO and D-APSO considered for this experiment are shown in Table 2.

Table 2. Experimental factors and their levels for S-APSO and D-APSO

Factors	Levels	Factor values for D-APSO			Factor values for S-APSO		
		−1	0	+1	−1	0	+1
PG	3	10 * 2400	50 * 480	200 * 120	10 * 2400	50 * 480	200 * 120
α	3	0.1	0.5	1.0	0.1	0.5	1.0
β	3	0.5	0.7	1.0	0.5	0.7	1.0
γ	3	0.5	0.7	0.9	–	–	–

The total number of computational runs required for S-APSO would be $3^3 = 27$ runs per replication whereas the total number of runs for D-APSO would be $3^4 = 81$ runs per replication. This work, the first problem instance was considered and replicated ten times by using different random seeds for both methods. The computational results obtained from D-APSO ($3^4 * 10 = 810$ runs) and S-APSO ($3^3 * 10 = 270$ runs) were analysed by using the analysis of variance (ANOVA). The results of ANOVA for S-APSO and D-APSO including source of variation (*Source*), degrees of freedom (*DF*), sum squares (*SS*), mean squares (*MS*), F and P-values are shown in Table 3.

According to Table 3, PG and $PG*\gamma$ for D-APSO were statistically significant with a 95% confidence interval in terms of main effect and first level interactions. Moreover, the most influential factor in this experiment was PG because it had the highest F-value. The best parameter settings for each method were determined by using the lowest mean obtained from main effect plots. The appropriate settings for D-APSO parameters shown in Fig. 2 are: $PG = 50 * 480$; $\alpha = 0.1–1.0$; $\beta = 0.5–1.0$; and $\gamma = 0.5–0.9$. The appropriate settings for S-APSO parameters are: $PG = 10 * 2,400–200 * 120$; $\alpha = 0.1–1.0$; and $\beta = 0.5–1.0$ as shown in Fig. 3.

5.2   Performance of S-APSO and D-APSO

The aims for this experiment are: (i) to explore the performance of the S-APSO and D-APSO to find the best practical timetables with the lowest total operating costs; and

Table 3. Results of ANOVA for D-APSO and S-APSO

Source	D-APSO					S-APSO				
	DF	SS	MS	F	P-value	DF	SS	MS	F	P-value
PG	2	94,349	47,175	6.490	**0.002**	2	6,486	3,243	0.120	0.890
α	2	1,061	531	0.070	0.930	2	152,556	76,278	2.730	0.067
β	2	30,351	15,176	2.090	0.125	2	53,662	26,831	0.960	0.384
γ	2	23,154	11,577	1.590	0.204	2	209,953	23,328	0.840	0.584
Seeds	9	393,832	43,759	6.020	**0.000**	9	22,128	5,532	0.200	0.939
PG*α	4	2,122	531	0.070	0.990	4	106,685	26,671	0.960	0.433
PG*β	4	47,497	11,874	1.630	0.164	4	245,453	61,363	2.200	0.070
α*β	4	543	136	0.020	0.999	4	6,486	3,243	0.120	0.890
PG*γ	4	165,585	41,396	5.700	**0.000**	–	–	–	–	–
α*γ	4	561	140	0.020	0.999	–	–	–	–	–
β*γ	4	26,009	6,502	0.890	0.467	–	–	–	–	–
Error	768	5,581,965	7,268			242	6,754,043	27,909		
Total	809	6,367,028				269	7,550,967			

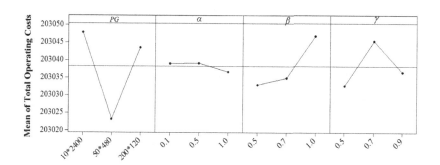

Fig. 2. Example of D-APSO main effect plots of *PG*, α, β and γ factors

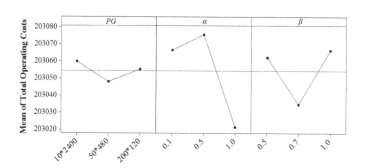

Fig. 3. Example of S-APSO main effect plots of *PG*, α, and β factors

Table 4. Performance comparisons among five variants of PSO

Problem instances	Aanalysis	PSO	SPSO	MCPSO	S-APSO	D-APSO	ANOVA P-value
1	Minimum	201,818.00	203,016.50	202,668.50	**201,433.00**	202,968.00	0.664
	Maximum	203,171.00	203,157.50	203,135.50	203,113.50	**203,075.00**	
	Average	202,944.90	203,098.75	203,030.80	**202,910.20**	203,018.10	
	Std. Deviation	410.98	41.28	134.34	519.43	39.32	
	Time (min.)	4.11	4.67	4.69	4.66	4.27	
2	Minimum	382,642.25	382,308.50	382,239.00	**381,677.25**	382,365.50	**0.003**
	Maximum	383,226.75	383,587.50	383,409.50	**383,002.00**	383,322.25	
	Average	382,918.73	382,899.98	382,744.20	**382,360.90**	382,920.25	
	Std. Deviation	218.27	364.81	391.59	398.42	333.15	
	Time (min.)	13.31	15.68	19.94	16.69	16.37	
3	Minimum	306,607.00	306,226.50	**304,349.25**	306,014.00	306,476.75	**0.000**
	Maximum	307,060.75	306,968.50	**306,025.75**	307,173.75	307,323.25	
	Average	306,854.75	306,721.83	**305,400.33**	306,533.45	306,920.50	
	Std. Deviation	163.04	213.26	596.58	330.04	247.64	
	Time (min.)	27.28	27.43	30.23	27.24	28.47	
4	Minimum	309,080.50	309,487.50	**307,855.75**	309,898.75	309,431.50	**0.000**
	Maximum	310,454.25	310,572.75	**309,819.75**	310,747.50	311,011.75	
	Average	310,000.63	310,214.98	**308,821.35**	310,287.13	310,459.18	
	Std. Deviation	464.64	382.26	597.81	314.05	500.13	
	Time (min.)	17.10	18.71	20.47	19.93	19.99	
5	Minimum	492,730.25	492,272.25	492,248.50	**491,550.50**	491,897.50	0.230
	Maximum	493,295.75	493,584.00	493,737.00	**493,245.75**	493,285.00	
	Average	492,910.05	492,891.90	493,002.15	**492,576.60**	492,909.05	
	Std. Deviation	197.49	409.66	500.36	549.29	388.98	
	Time (min.)	28.27	30.09	36.48	32.87	30.32	
6	Minimum	410,454.25	410,641.00	**409,361.50**	410,756.00	410,656.75	**0.000**
	Maximum	411,378.75	411,411.25	**410,730.00**	411,466.25	411,247.00	
	Average	410,920.58	410,996.38	**410,328.68**	411,080.38	411,026.00	
	Std. Deviation	313.63	292.61	409.93	236.99	245.38	
	Time (min.)	39.80	44.79	41.47	47.33	45.74	
7	Minimum	419,401.25	419,593.75	**418,731.50**	419,776.00	419,389.75	**0.002**
	Maximum	**420,700.00**	421,531.75	420,752.00	421,270.25	421,242.50	
	Average	420,140.45	420,682.20	**419,722.18**	420,625.60	420,618.43	
	Std. Deviation	423.41	638.07	688.56	446.98	637.50	
	Time (min.)	41.05	40.96	35.03	33.76	33.12	
8	Minimum	588,397.75	588,163.25	587,955.00	588,381.75	**587,789.00**	0.671
	Maximum	589,833.50	**589,722.75**	589,903.75	589,761.25	589,753.50	
	Average	589,052.68	589,157.05	589,177.85	589,052.98	**588,764.55**	
	Std. Deviation	437.18	486.07	623.7	453.36	713.33	
	Time (min.)	78.69	74.13	86.97	73.24	70.67	
9	Minimum	617,025.50	**614,460.50**	616,349.00	616,035.50	616,599.00	0.182
	Maximum	618,316.50	618,367.50	**618,259.00**	618,300.25	618,685.50	
	Average	617,520.33	**616,870.45**	617,236.60	617,404.75	617,679.13	
	Std. Deviation	359.96	1,232.41	612.54	661.70	683.26	
	Time (min.)	46.80	46.16	59.02	48.78	47.92	

(continued)

Table 4. (*continued*)

Problem instances	Aanalysis	PSO	SPSO	MCPSO	S-APSO	D-APSO	ANOVA P-value
10	Minimum	567,010.00	**565,280.25**	566,033.25	567,209.75	566,888.50	**0.024**
	Maximum	568,678.50	**568,462.25**	568,658.00	568,901.00	570,131.25	
	Average	568,015.40	**567,074.58**	567,615.93	567,900.95	568,480.93	
	Std. Deviation	582.57	1,115.39	1,051.13	512.23	1,181.96	
	Time (min.)	75.17	72.94	80.95	78.07	72.97	
11	Minimum	956,835.50	956,906.75	956,528.50	**954,465.50**	955,751.50	0.466
	Maximum	**959,939.00**	960,907.25	961,157.00	960,920.50	960,740.75	
	Average	958,331.60	958,783.73	958,843.10	**957,755.43**	958,909.38	
	Std. Deviation	898.69	1,279.39	1,734.03	2,314.70	1,470.02	
	Time (min.)	142.03	155.73	186.13	163.18	158.72	

(ii) to compare their performances with other PSO variants obtained from a previous research including PSO [11], SPSO [11], and MCPSO [11]. The best parameter settings for S-APSO and D-APSO were adopted from previous experiment. Eleven real-world course timetabling instances were adopted from literature [30] in order to explore and compare the performance of these algorithms. Each instance for each proposed method was repeated ten times by using different random seeds. The computational results shown in Table 4 were analysed in terms of Minimum, Maximum, Average (currency unit), Standard (Std.) Deviation, Time (Minute unit), and ANOVA.

According to Table 4, it can be summarised that the average values of the best so far timetables created by both S-APSO and MCPSO were better that those values generated by SPSO, D-APSO and PSO for most instances (four out of eleven instances). S-APSO also had the best performance for the largest problem size. For instance numbers 9 and 10 related with medium-large problem sizes, SPSO outperformed the other approaches whereas D-APSO also outperformed the remaining methods for an instance number 8. Moreover, the results of ANOVA indicated that the performance differences produced by all PSO variants were statistically significant with a 95% confidence interval (P-value $\leq$ 0.05) up to six problem instances.

In term of the lowest Minimum values of the best so far solutions, both MCPSO and S-APSO outperformed the remaining methods (four out of eleven instances). In case of the lowest Maximum values, MCPSO also outperformed the other algorithms for instance numbers 3, 4, 6, and 9. The values of Standard Deviation obtained from all variants of PSO were moderately different for all problem instances. However, the computational time required by all methods were slightly different.

6   Conclusions

An Accelerated Particle Swarm Optimisation based Timetabling (APSOT) program has been designed and developed for solving the university course timetabling problem. Static and dynamic Accelerated Particle Swarm Optimisation (called S-APSO and D-

APSO) were embedded in the APSOT program to generate lecture, student, and classroom timetables with the lowest total operating costs.

Advance statistical tools (e.g., experimental designs, analysis of variances) were adopted to explore the statistically influential factors before identifying the best parameters settings for both S-APSO and D-APSO. The statistical analysis on the computational results suggested that *PG* and *PG*γ* for D-APSO were statistically significant with a 95% confidence interval in terms of main effect and first level interactions excepted for S-APSO. Both S-APSO and Maurice Clerc PSO (MCPSO) outperformed the other methods for most instances whereas SPSO and D-APSO out-performed the other PSO variants for medium-large problem sizes. However, the computational times required by all variants of PSO were slightly difference.

Acknowledgements. The second author would like to acknowledge Naresuan University Graduate School for granting Ph.D. scholarship. This work was also part of research project supported by the Thailand Science Research and Innovation (TSRI) and Office of the Higher Education Commission (OHEC) under grant number MRG6080066.

References

1. Babaei, H., Karimpour, J., Hadidi, A.: A survey of approaches for university course timetabling problem. Comput. Ind. Eng. **86**, 43–59 (2015)
2. Murray, K., Müller, T., Rudová, H.: Modeling and solution of a complex university course timetabling problem. In: Burke, E.K., Rudová, H. (eds.) PATAT 2006. LNCS, vol. 3867, pp. 189–209. Springer, Heidelberg (2007). https://doi.org/10.1007/978-3-540-77345-0_13
3. Yang, X.-S.: Swarm intelligence based algorithms: a critical analysis. Evol. Intell. **7**, 17–28 (2014). https://doi.org/10.1007/s12065-013-0102-2
4. Thepphakorn, T., Pongcharoen, P., Hicks, C.: An ant colony based timetabling tool. Int. J. Prod. Econ. **149**, 131–144 (2014)
5. Khadwilard, A., Chansombat, S., Thepphakorn, T., Thapatsuwan, P., Chainate, W., Pongcharoen, P.: Application of firefly algorithm and its parameter setting for job shop scheduling. J. Ind. Technol. **8**, 49–58 (2012)
6. Dapa, K., Loreungthup, P., Vitayasak, S., Pongcharoen, P.: Bat algorithm, genetic algorithm and shuffled frog leaping algorithm for designing machine layout. In: Ramanna, S., Lingras, P., Sombattheera, C., Krishna, A. (eds.) MIWAI 2013. LNCS (LNAI), vol. 8271, pp. 59–68. Springer, Heidelberg (2013). https://doi.org/10.1007/978-3-642-44949-9_6
7. Pongcharoen, P., Chainate, W., Pongcharoen, S.: Improving artificial immune system performance: inductive bias and alternative mutations. In: Bentley, P.J., Lee, D., Jung, S. (eds.) ICARIS 2008. LNCS, vol. 5132, pp. 220–231. Springer, Heidelberg (2008). https://doi.org/10.1007/978-3-540-85072-4_20
8. Lewis, R.: A survey of metaheuristic-based techniques for University Timetabling problems. OR Spectr. **30**, 167–190 (2008). https://doi.org/10.1007/s00291-007-0097-0
9. Rana, S., Jasola, S., Kumar, R.: A review on particle swarm optimization algorithms and their applications to data clustering. Artif. Intell. Rev. **35**, 211–222 (2011). https://doi.org/10.1007/s10462-010-9191-9
10. Chen, R.M., Shih, H.F.: Solving university course timetabling problems using constriction particle swarm optimization with local search. Algorithms **6**, 227–244 (2013)

11. Thepphakorn, T., Pongcharoen, P.: Variants and parameters investigations of particle swarm optimisation for solving course timetabling problems. In: Tan, Y., Shi, Y., Niu, B. (eds.) ICSI 2019. LNCS, vol. 11655, pp. 177–187. Springer, Cham (2019). https://doi.org/10. 1007/978-3-030-26369-0_17

12. Kanoh, H., Chen, S.: Particle swarm optimization with transition probability for timetabling problems. In: Tomassini, M., Antonioni, A., Daolio, F., Buesser, P. (eds.) ICANNGA 2013. LNCS, vol. 7824, pp. 256–265. Springer, Heidelberg (2013). https://doi.org/10.1007/978-3-642-37213-1_27

13. Ahandani, M.A., Vakil Baghmisheh, M.T.: Hybridizing genetic algorithms and particle swarm optimization transplanted into a hyper-heuristic system for solving university course timetabling problem. WSEAS Trans. Comput. **12**, 128–143 (2013)

14. Oswald, C., Anand Deva Durai, C.: Novel hybrid PSO algorithms with search optimization strategies for a university course timetabling problem. In: Proceedings of the 5th International Conference on Advanced Computing, ICoAC 2013, pp. 77–85 (2014)

15. Ho, I.S.F., Safaai, D., Zaiton, M.H.S.: A combination of PSO and local search in university course timetabling problem. In: Proceedings of the International Conference on Computer Engineering and Technology, pp. 492–495 (2009)

16. Ho, S.F.I., Safaai, D., Zaiton, M.H.S.: A study on PSO-based university course timetabling problem. In: Proceedings of the International Conference on Advanced Computer Control, pp. 648–651 (2009)

17. Kennedy, J., Eberhart, R.: Particle swarm optimization. In: IEEE International Conference on Neural Networks, pp. 1942–1948 (1995)

18. Yang, X.-S.: Nature-Inspired Optimization Algorithms. Elsevier, London (2014)

19. Zhang, Y., Wang, S., Ji, G.: A comprehensive survey on particle swarm optimization algorithm and its applications. Math. Prob. Eng. **2015**, 38 (2015)

20. Thepphakorn, T., Pongcharoen, P., Hicks, C.: Modifying regeneration mutation and hybridising clonal selection for evolutionary algorithms based timetabling tool. Math. Prob. Eng. **2015**, 16 (2015)

21. Fakhar, M.S., Kashif, S.A.R., Ain, N.U., Hussain, H.Z., Rasool, A., Sajjad, I.A.: Statistical performances evaluation of APSO and improved APSO for short term hydrothermal scheduling problem. Appl. Sci. **9**, 2440 (2019)

22. Adhikari, M., Srirama, S.N.: Multi-objective accelerated particle swarm optimization with a container-based scheduling for Internet-of-Things in cloud environment. J. Netw. Comput. Appl. **137**, 35–61 (2019)

23. Hussain, H.Z., Haider, A., Fakhar, M.S., Ahmad, J., Butt, M.A., Khokhar, K.S.: Short-term scheduling of non-cascaded hydro-thermal system with transmission losses using accelerated particle swarm optimization algorithm. Pak. J. Eng. Appl. Sci. **22**, 20–29 (2018)

24. Fakhar, M.S., Kashif, S.A.R., Saqib, M.A., Mehmood, F., Hussain, H.Z.: Non-cascaded short-term pumped-storage hydro-thermal scheduling using accelerated particle swarm optimization. In: 2018 International Conference on Electrical Engineering (2018)

25. Adhikari, M., Amgoth, T.: Multi-objective accelerated particle swarm optimization technique for scientific workflows in IaaS cloud. In: 2018 International Conference on Advances in Computing, Communications and Informatics, pp. 1448–1454 (2018)

26. Hropko, D., Ivanecký, J., Turček, J.: Optimal dispatch of renewable energy sources included in virtual power plant using accelerated particle swarm optimization. In: 2012 ELEKTRO, Rajeck Teplice, pp. 196–200 (2012)

27. Yang, X.-S., Deb, S., Fong, S.: Accelerated particle swarm optimization and support vector machine for business optimization and applications. In: Fong, S. (ed.) NDT 2011. CCIS, vol. 136, pp. 53–66. Springer, Heidelberg (2011). https://doi.org/10.1007/978-3-642-22185-9_6

28. Bettinelli, A., Cacchiani, V., Roberti, R., Toth, P.: An overview of curriculum-based course timetabling. TOP **23**(2), 313–349 (2015). https://doi.org/10.1007/s11750-015-0366-z
29. Thepphakorn, T., Pongcharoen, P.: Heuristic ordering for ant colony based timetabling tool. J. Appl. Oper. Res. **5**, 113–123 (2013)
30. Thepphakorn, T., Pongcharoen, P., Vitayasak, S.: A new multiple objective cuckoo search for university course timetabling problem. In: Sombattheera, C., Stolzenburg, F., Lin, F., Nayak, A. (eds.) MIWAI 2016. LNCS (LNAI), vol. 10053, pp. 196–207. Springer, Cham (2016). https://doi.org/10.1007/978-3-319-49397-8_17

Author Index

Printed in the United States
By Bookmasters